D1710505

REMEMBER ME?

Volume 1

A collection of recipes from my personal files
and Cook's Corner columns

by Alice S. Colombo

Cover designed by Warren Lynch

Printed by Publishers Printing Company
Shepherdsville, KY 40165

www.remembermecookbook.com

First Printing: 1,000 copies   October 2011
Second Printing: 1,000 copies   November 2011
Third Printing: 1,000 copies   December 2011
Fourth Printing: 10,000 copies   February 2012

ISBN: 978-0-615-60272-1

For additional copies or information, go to my website:

www.remembermecookbook.com

This cookbook has been too long in coming. When I was working as Assistant Food Editor for *The Courier-Journal* and writing Cook's Corner, I was often asked to write a cookbook – I always said I would when I retired. That was ten years ago so, before all of you forget me, I think it's time to keep my promise and write the book.

I want to thank all of you who read the column, clipped the recipes, tried them, called about them and still occasionally call me about a recipe – without you and the many restaurateurs who shared their recipes, there would have been no column – thank you.

The recipes marked with © appeared in *The Courier-Journal* and are copyrighted. The others are a collection from my Mother, my husband's Mother, my sisters, relatives, friends, old clippings from magazines I no longer have and recipes developed by me. I hope you will use this book often and that you will enjoy trying the recipes as much as I have enjoyed sharing them with you.

I want to thank my husband, John, my sons Chris, Alan (deceased) and Greg for being my connoisseurs – they were the judges as to whether a recipe was worth keeping.

I want to give special thanks to David Hawpe who hired me to fill in for his secretary during her pregnancy leave. A four-month job for David turned into a seventeen-year job as Assistant Food Editor – he found me a job that changed my life. I had the opportunity of working with some of the finest in the field of journalism – many came to The C-J kitchen to taste-test and share their thoughts of the day.

Last, but by no means least, I thank my friend, Mary Pat Martin, who spent hours helping me with this book. It would not be had she not insisted we get started and follow a timetable – we did it and we are happy we did. Thanks to all – you are loved.

iv

Foreword

It's the classic American newsroom story line - young person with no journalism training or credentials shows up, talks his or her way into an assignment, learns on the job and, over time, becomes a star. Of course in Alice Colombo's case, she was 47 when she showed up one year to fill in for my secretary, who was off becoming a mother. However, she is indeed a self-made culinary institution.

It can be done. Keith Runyon started as a slick-cheeked obituary clerk and became editor of the newspaper's editorial page. Jody Demling began as a sports clerk and now is one of the C-J's most valuable assets - a walking encyclopedia of Kentuckiana high school sports and an expert on the recruitment of prep athletic stars. But this path to a top job in journalism is difficult to travel, at best.

Alice did it. After her four months as a fill-in secretary, it was obvious to us that she had energy, determination, skill and charm to spare. We moved her to the kitchen, where she ultimately wrote 17 years' worth of Cook's Corner columns and turned herself into an expert in food styling. She worked her way into the procession of the great newspaper food editors, such as Cissy Gregg and Camille Glenn. She did it with a combination of innate culinary know-how and impeccable taste, as well as a deep and broad familiarity with Louisville's food culture.

She brought so much to her job, including a sunny disposition, a kind heart and a mature sensibility. That last quality was particularly important when she was serving as assistant to an exuberantly talented, entirely lovable young food editor who needed a steadying influence in the C-J kitchen.

Alice rounded out an extraordinary food photography team that included artist Steve Sebree and renowned shooters Gary Chapman and Pam Spaulding.

In those years she remade herself. With no previous background, she became an expert at everything from choosing the right backdrops for Sunday Magazine food photography to solving the endless challenges presented by food photo shoots. Examples: Preventing an ooze of chocolate icing under the hot studio lights, or making fake ice cream look like the real Ehrler's product in an ad layout. As her work became more widely known, she took on many clients such as Papa John's, Long John Silver's, Purnell's. Heaven Hill, Kentucky Fried Chicken, Bon Apétit, to name a few. She designed and fabricated a tuxedo, jockey silk, Derby Festival and Red jacket for the Maker's Mark bottle. She continues that commercial work today, "because I love it."

She loved the newspaper environment from day one, back in 1983. "The whole place buzzed," she remembers. There is the occasional less-than-happy memory, such as the party to which she wasn't invited celebrating a $5,000 award for an ad layout she designed and created. She and the C-J were meant for each other, as her many friends at Sixth and Broadway will attest.

Having grown up in Louisville, Alice knows the city's food culture intimately, from the church picnics and fish fries of her childhood to the dramatic growth of fine dining in recent decades. Like me, she can remember when Lentinis on Bardstown Road was a big night out. It's all reflected in her book, along with her family's German and Irish culinary traditions and the great Italian food heritage into which she married, as well as contributions from friends throughout this Ohio River region. She offers recipes she collected from eateries great and small, famous and obscure. The selections are comprehensive, which makes her cookbook volume a superb choice for a new bride.

Alice has an artist's sensibility. Indeed, she has made herself into a skillful painter, one who is not even daunted by the travails of watercolor. , Now in her 70s, she is a work in progress. So is her cookbook, which she calls a Volume 1. I look forward to Volume 2.

David V. Hawpe
Former Editor and Editorial Director
The Courier-Journal

Table of Contents

Appetizers and Beverages

There are many versions of Kentucky mint juleps but my favorite has always been the one served at the Derby breakfast of my friend, Federal Judge George Long of Glenmary. They are NEVER prepared in advance so you wait in line to get the one made just for you – it's worth the wait and while you are waiting, you can catch up on the latest with whoever is in front or behind you. If you get there early enough, your mint julep is served in a antique sterling silver mint julep cup with a sterling straw. George ALSO serves the very best eggnog at his Christmas party and, again, if you get there early enough, your nog is served in a antique sterling eggnog cup.

Glenmary Farm's mint juleps

3 or 4   mint sprigs
½ to 1   teaspoon superfine sugar
(see note)
Shaved ice
Bourbon
Napkin

Makes 1 julep.
Place 4 to 5 mint leaves in the bottom of a mint julep cup or glass. Crush the mint with a spoon to extract the juice from the leaves. Add sugar (the amount depends on how sweet you like your mint julep). Mull the sugar with the mint leaves until you have a paste. Fill cup with shaved ice. Add bourbon until you can see it. Top with a mound of shaved ice. Add a couple of sprigs of mint and a straw. Wrap cup with a napkin and serve. Simple but wonderful.
  Note: If you can't find superfine sugar place your granulated sugar in a food processor or blender. Blend until powdery. After you turn it off, let the powder settle for a minute before you open the food processor otherwise you'll be snorting sugar dust.

Glenmary Farm's holiday eggnog

12   eggs, separated
1   cup sugar, or to taste

Makes 20 servings.
In the large bowl of an electric mixer beat the yolks to combine. While beating, slowly

1	quart whole milk	add 1 cup sugar. Remove bowl from mixer.
4	cups bourbon	Add milk and stir to thoroughly combine.
½	cup rum	Slowly, slowly add bourbon and stir.
1	cup whipping cream	Refrigerate.
¼	cup additional sugar	Just before serving, add the rum. Whip the
	Nutmeg	cream until soft peaks form (you can

add 1 cup sugar. Remove bowl from mixer. Add milk and stir to thoroughly combine. Slowly, slowly add bourbon and stir. Refrigerate. Just before serving, add the rum. Whip the cream until soft peaks form (you can sweeten the whipped cream to taste if desired). Beat the egg whites until frothy. While beating, slowly add ¼ cup sugar. Beat until stiff but not dry. Place chilled eggnog into serving bowl. Add whipped cream. Stir slightly. Top bowl with beaten egg whites and a grating of fresh nutmeg.

Churchill Downs has the mint julep as the signature drink of the Derby. I called Pimlico and Belmont Park to see if they had a drink for the Preakness and the Belmont. Following is what they shared with me.

Preakness black-eyed Susan©

Makes 1 serving.

1	ounce vodka
1	ounce rum
¾	ounce triple sec
	Lime wedge
	Pineapple juice
	Orange juice

Fill a 12-ounce glass with ice. Add vodka, rum and triple sec. Add lime wedge and equal parts of pineapple juice and orange juice. Shake well and serve.

Belmont Breeze©

Makes 1 serving.

1½	ounces Seagram's 7
¾	ounce Harvey's Bristol Cream sherry
½	ounce fresh lemon juice
1	ounce simple syrup (recipe follows)
1½	ounces fresh orange juice
1½	ounces cranberry juice

Combine Seagram's 7, sherry, lemon juice, simple syrup, orange juice and cranberry juice. Shake with ice. Top with 7-Up and club soda. Garnish with mint sprig and lemon wedge.

Simple syrup: Combine 2 cups sugar with 2 cups water. Bring to a boil. Boil 5 minutes without stirring. Chill until ready to use.

1   ounce 7-Up
1   ounce club soda
    Mint sprig
    Lemon wedge

Regina Leitner's freezer hot buttered rum

1   quart vanilla ice cream,
    softened
1   cup brown sugar
1   cup (2 sticks) butter,
    softened
2   teaspoons fresh grated
    nutmeg (1 whole nutmeg)
    Rum
    Whipped cream

Cream together brown sugar and softened butter. Grate nutmeg and add to butter mixture. Add this to softened ice cream. Mix thoroughly. Place in a container and return to freezer. When ready to serve, place some of the ice cream mixture in a coffee mug. Fill mug with hot water. Add one jigger of rum. Top with whipped cream and serve.

Hasenour's Tom-and-Jerry hot cocktail©

1   egg, separated
    Superfine granulated sugar
    Pinch baking soda
1   ounce rum
    Hot milk
1½ ounces Maker's Mark
    whiskey
    Brandy
    Nutmeg

Batter makes 12 to 14 drinks.
First, prepare batter using yoke and white of 1 egg. Separate the egg, beating the white until frothy. Beat the yolk thoroughly. Combine white and yolk. Add enough superfine sugar to stiffen (I used about ¾ cup). Add to this a pinch of baking soda and ½ ounce of the rum to preserve batter. Add a little more sugar to stiffen (I used an additional ¼ cup).
To serve, warm a Tom-and-Jerry mug (a regular coffee mug). In the mug dissolve 1 tablespoon of the batter in 3 tablespoons hot milk. Add Maker's Mark, then fill mug with hot milk to within ¼ inch of the top. Stir. Top with a touch of brandy, a sprinkle of nutmeg and a little more rum. The secret to a good Tom and Jerry is a very stiff batter and a warm mug.
   Note: If you can't find superfine sugar place your granulated sugar in a food

4

processor or blender. Blend until powdery. After you turn it off, let the powder settle for a minute before you open the food processor otherwise you'll be snorting sugar dust

Tropical slush©

9 cups water
3 cups sugar
2 tea bags
1 12-ounce can frozen lemonade, thawed
1 12-ounce can frozen orange juice, thawed
1 15-ounce package frozen sliced strawberries, thawed
1 20-ounce can pineapple tidbits or crushed pineapple
2 bananas, sliced thin
2 cups rum, vodka or bourbon (see note)
7-Up, ginger ale or Sprite (optional, see note)

Makes about 30 servings.
In a medium saucepan heat 7 cups water and the sugar. Bring to boil and cook until sugar is dissolved. Cool.
Bring remaining 2 cups water to a boil. Drop in tea bags. Set aside to cool.
In a large bowl combine the sugar mixture, tea mixture, lemonade, orange juice, strawberries, pineapple, sliced bananas and liquor. Pour into freezer containers and freeze. When ready to serve, scrape slush into glass and, if desired, fill glass with 7-Up, ginger ale or Sprite. Return unused slush to freezer.
Makes about 30 servings.
   Note: Slush does not freeze as solid when liquor is added. Also, after scraping the slush into a glass, I fill the glass with 7-Up, ginger ale or Sprite. Some of my friends serve it plain with a spoon so you can eat it. You be the judge.

Lynn's Paradise Café smoothie©

2 cups ice cubes
1 ripe banana, broken in quarters
1 cup fruit juice (pineapple, orange or apple)
½ cup just-overripe fresh fruit

Makes 2 smoothies.
Put all ingredients in blender. Blend until smooth.
   Note: Any just over ripe fruit can be used such as peaches, bananas, strawberries and blueberries.

Huber's strawberry daiquiri©

1   12-ounce can frozen limeade
2   tablespoons confectioners' sugar
2   cups strawberries (or more if desired)
    Ice cubes

Makes 12 servings.
Place limeade, sugar and strawberries in blender. Swirl till blended. Fill blender with ice cubes. Blend until smooth and frothy.
   Note: You may substitute peaches, blackberries or raspberries for the strawberries.

Peach melba soda©

1   large very ripe peach
¼   cup fresh raspberries
4   scoops vanilla ice cream
    7-Up or ginger ale

Makes 2 servings.
Peel and seed peach. Cut into fourths. Place in blender along with raspberries and 2 scoops vanilla ice cream. Blend on low speed. Add a small amount of 7-Up or ginger ale.
Pour into soda glasses. Fill with 7-Up or ginger ale to within 2 inches of rim. Place a scoop of ice cream on edge of each glass, balanced so its bottom touches surface of soda. Serve with a long-handled spoon and a straw.

Instant hot chocolate mix

1   25.6 ounce package non-fat dry milk
1   22-ounce jar powdered coffee creamer
1   pound confectioners' sugar
1   39-ounce can powdered, sweetened chocolate flavoring for milk
1 to 1¼   cups Hershey cocoa

Makes about 88 servings using ¼ cup mix.
Blend non-fat dry milk powder in blender until powder is very fine. Mix remaining ingredients with dry milk and store in air-tight container. Use ¼ to ⅓ cup of mixture per coffee-mug serving. Fill with boiling water and stir.
   Note: If you want the mix sweeter, add more confectioners' sugar. If you want more chocolate flavor, add more cocoa.

Pineapple party punch©

1	46-ounce can pineapple juice, chilled
1	quart cranberry juice, chilled
6	ounces frozen lemonade concentrate, thawed
¾	cup sugar
	Red food coloring, if desired
2	2 liter bottles ginger ale, chilled

Makes 36 servings.

In a large punch bowl, combine pineapple juice, cranberry juice, lemonade concentrate, sugar and food coloring. Just before serving, pour in ginger ale. Garnish with ice ring or serve over ice.

Note: To make decorative ice ring or mold, pour about ½-inch water, juice or punch into mold of appropriate size for punch bowl. Arrange fruit slices or pieces as desired; freeze. Add liquid to cover pieces; freeze again.

Bennigan's pina colada©

¼	cup Coco Lopez cream of coconut
½	cup pineapple juice
2	cups ice milk

Makes 2 to 3 servings.

Place all ingredients in container of blender. Blend until smooth. Serve immediately.

Elegant Cappuccino©

3	tablespoons brandy
3	tablespoons gin
3	tablespoons rum
2	cinnamon sticks
3	tablespoons dark crème de cacao
3	tablespoons light crème de cacao
2	tablespoons Galliano
5	whole cloves
3	cups melted vanilla ice cream
3	cups freshly brewed espresso or strong black coffee
	Unsweetened whipped cream
	Grated semisweet chocolate

Makes 8 servings.

In a jar with a tight-fitting lid combine brandy, gin, rum, cinnamon sticks, dark crème de cacao, light crème de cacao, Galliano and cloves. Cover and let stand at least 5 hours (24 hours is better).

In a saucepan melt ice cream. Bring to a simmer. To serve, strain liquor mixture evenly into 8 heated 8-ounce mugs. Add 6 tablespoons espresso, then 6 tablespoons simmering ice cream to each mug. Top with whipped cream and grated semisweet chocolate. Serve immediately.

If you are trying to think of a gift for the person who has everything, think no more. Why not make a special liqueur. It's easy to do and can be done well in advance of the giving.

Simple syrup for liqueurs©

Makes 1½ to 2 cups.

2   cups sugar
1   cup water

Place sugar and water in a saucepan. Bring to a boil and cook 5 minutes. Cool.

Chocolate liqueur©

Makes 2 cups.

2   teaspoons pure chocolate extract used for baking
½   teaspoon pure vanilla extract
1½ cups vodka
½   cup simple syrup (see recipe)

Place all ingredients in a sterilized, glass quart jar. Let mature several days.

Crème-de-framboise©

Makes about 1 quart.

1½ cups raspberries
Grated zest of ½ lemon
3   cups brandy
2   cups simple syrup (see recipe)

Lightly crush berries. Add lemon zest. Place in large, sterilized glass jar with brandy. Steep 2 to 4 weeks. Strain and filter, squeezing all the berries through a fine cloth. Add the simple syrup and mature 4 to 6 weeks.

Tia Maria©

Makes 4 cups.

2   cups water
2   cups white sugar
½   cup powdered instant coffee
½   chopped vanilla bean
1½ cups rum

Boil water and sugar until dissolved. Remove from heat. Slowly add coffee and stir. In a large, sterilized glass jar, add the vanilla bean and the rum. Add the cooled sugar, water and coffee solution. Cover tightly and shake vigorously each day for 3 weeks.
Strain, run through a filter, then bottle.

8

Berry liqueur©

Makes 2 cups.

1	16-ounce package sweetened berries (any kind)
1½	cups vodka or 1 cup vodka and ½ cup brandy
⅓	cup simple syrup (see recipe)

Add juice and berries to alcohol that has been placed in a sterilized glass jar. Stir and steep one week. Crush berries through strainer and filter. Add simple syrup. Taste. Add additional simple syrup, if needed.

Appetizers

I am starting the appetizer section with my favorite appetizer – egg rolls. The original recipe was given to me by a dear friend from the Philippines, Marietta Garcia. The rolls are best when made using Lumpia wrappers, a very, very thin wrapper made from wheat flour. If you cannot find Lumpia, you can use won ton wrappers. They are much thicker and the egg roll isn't as crisp but, in a pinch, they will do. This recipe looks long and complicated but it isn't – I am giving you directions that are easy to follow.

The egg rolls can also be used as an entrée. Serve with fried rice and spinach patties.

Egg Rolls

Makes about 35 rolls

1	3-pound Boston butt (or 2½ pounds ground pork)
1 to 1½	teaspoons Accent or MSG
1 to 2	tablespoons vegetable oil
2	cloves garlic, pressed
¾	cup diced onion
	Black pepper, fresh ground
2 to 3	tablespoons soy sauce
¼ to ½	cup bread crumbs
1	medium-size carrot, peeled and diced small
1	8-ounce can water chestnuts, diced
1	8-ounce can bamboo shoots, diced (optional)
2 to 3	eggs, beaten
	Salt, to taste

If not using ground pork, cut meat from bone of butt and run through a meat grinder. Sprinkle meat with Accent or MSG and set aside. (We like to grind our own pork). Sauté pressed garlic in hot vegetable oil for about a minute, stirring constantly (don't let the garlic burn – it makes the oil bitter). Add onion and cook until transparent. Add ground pork – season with 2 to 3 turns of fresh ground black pepper, soy sauce and bread crumbs (not too many – you want the mixture to be a bit juicy). When no more pink remains in the meat, remove from heat. Add diced carrots, water chestnuts and, if using, bamboo shoots. Stir for a few minutes. Add beaten eggs. Season to taste with salt. Stir until mixture is cool.

8

1   21-ounce package Lumpia or
    spring roll wrappers
    Oil for frying
    Sweet and sour sauce
    Hot mustard sauce

Like any other wrapper, Lumpia dries out quickly. After opening, dampen the edges and cover with a lightly dampened cloth. Gently lift 1 wrapper at a time and place on a dinner plate or flat surface. Place 2 to 3 tablespoons of mixture in a line about a third down from the top of the wrapper. Fold over from the top and roll once. Fold in the ends and continue to roll. Moisten edge with water to seal. Place in a container, flap side down, and cover with plastic wrap or wax paper. If you have more than 1 layer of rolls in the container, separate with 2 sheets of wax paper. Rolls can be fried and served immediately or frozen for later use.

To cook, place a small amount of vegetable oil in a skillet. When oil is hot, place egg rolls in skillet, flap side down, and fry until golden. Turn and fry other side. Serve with sweet and sour sauce and/or hot mustard.

Mushroom Turnovers

Pastry:
1   8-ounce package cream
    cheese, room temperature
⅔   cup butter, room temperature
2   cups all-purpose flour
¾   teaspoon salt
Filling:
3   tablespoons butter
1   large onion, finely chopped
½   pound fresh mushrooms,
    chopped
¼   teaspoon dried thyme
½   teaspoon salt
¼   teaspoon pepper
2   tablespoons all-purpose flour

Makes 36.

To make pastry: Mix cream cheese and butter thoroughly. Add flour and salt and work until smooth. Place in a bowl or roll in plastic wrap and chill at least 30 minutes.

To make filling: While dough is chilling, heat butter in a skillet. Add onion and brown. Add mushrooms and cook, stirring often, about 3 minutes. Add dried thyme, salt and pepper. Stir to combine. Sprinkle with flour. Stir in sour cream and cook gently until thickened.

On a lightly floured surface, roll dough to ⅛-inch thickness. Cut into rounds with a 3-inch biscuit cutter. Place 1 to 2 teaspoons filling on each round. Fold dough over. Press

¼ **cup sour cream**
1 **egg**
1 **teaspoon milk**

edges together with a fork. Place on a lightly greased baking sheet. Beat egg with milk. Brush tops with egg mixture. Bake in a preheated 425-degree oven for 10 to 15 minutes or until lightly browned.
Note: May be frozen before baking.

Baltimore barbecued chicken wings©

This recipe is from the files of Camille Glenn and is another one of my favorites. Until you have had these, you cannot appreciate the delicacy of chicken wings. No matter how many I make, I never have enough. The recipe calls for butter and unsalted butter. I use whatever I have – in these, I don't notice that much difference.

4 **shallots or scallions (green onions; white bulb only), finely chopped (shallots are best)**
⅓ **cup water**
1 **teaspoon dry mustard**
2 **tablespoons tarragon white wine vinegar**
2 **tablespoons good-quality ketchup**
2 **tablespoons lemon juice**
8 **tablespoons (1 stick) butter, cut into pieces and chilled**
½ **teaspoon Tabasco sauce, or to taste**
  Cayenne pepper, to taste
  Salt, to taste
1½ to 2 **pounds chicken wings**
6 **tablespoons (¾ stick) unsalted butter, at room temperature**

Makes 4 servings.
Combine the shallots or scallions with the water in a small stainless steel or enamel saucepan. Simmer until the shallots are soft, 1½ to 2 minutes. Don't allow them to sizzle or boil dry. Add mustard, vinegar, ketchup and lemon juice to the shallots and cook over low heat 5 to 6 minutes. Remove from the heat and allow the flavors to ripen about 30 minutes.
Heat oven to 450 degrees.
Reheat the sauce over low heat until just warm, no hotter. Beat in the chilled butter 1 piece at a time. Add the Tabasco, cayenne and salt. Set aside.
Rinse the chicken wings and dry them well with paper towels. Lay them bone-side down in a large roasting pan. Season with salt, then brush with 3 tablespoons of unsalted butter and place in the oven. Cook wings, basting several times with the pan drippings and remaining butter, for 30 to 40 minutes. Allow the wings to become golden and crisp. Continue to cook, brushing with the sauce several times for about 20 minutes. Be careful not to let the sauce burn.

Pesto cheesecake©

Pesto:

- 3 cups (packed) fresh basil leaves, washed and patted dry
- 6 cloves garlic, peeled and chopped
- 1 cup pine nuts or English walnuts
- 1 cup extra virgin olive oil
- 1 cup freshly grated Parmesan cheese

Pesto cheesecake:

- 1 cup bread crumbs (preferably made from toast – about 6 slices)
- ½ cup grated Parmesan cheese
- ½ cup butter, melted
- 2 pounds cream cheese
- 4 eggs
- ¼ cup whipping cream
- 2 cups pesto
  Sun-dried tomatoes packed in oil

Makes a lot – see note.

To make pesto: Combine basil, garlic and nuts in the bowl of a food processor, or half of each in a blender container. Chop roughly, in two batches if using a blender. With motor running, add olive oil in a steady stream. Add cheese and continue to blend into a smooth paste. Store in refrigerator or, if keeping for several months, freeze.

To make cheesecake: Heat oven to 325 degrees.

Combine bread crumbs, Parmesan and butter. Stir to blend. Press into bottom and part way up the sides of a 9-inch springform pan. Bake 5 to 10 minutes.

Beat cream cheese until smooth. Add eggs one at a time, beating after each addition. Add whipping cream and pesto. Blend thoroughly. Pour batter into prepared pan. Bake about an hour or until center is set (it will puff up then fall again as it bakes). When cool, place in refrigerator until ready to serve. Before serving, run a knife around sides to loosen. Remove sides of pan. Set cheesecake on serving plate. Drain sun-dried tomatoes and chop coarsely. Top cheesecake with bits of sun-dried tomato. Serve with crackers or thin slices of French bread.

Note: Serves a lot – you may want to half the recipe and bake in a smaller pan. Can be frozen.

Bristol Bar and Grill's green chili won tons©

Makes 5 to 6 servings.

Filling:
- 2½ pounds Monterey Jack cheese, grated
- 12 ounces diced green chilies
- 6 ounces canned chopped jalapenos
- 1 pound won ton skins
- Oil for frying

Guacamole:
- 2 ripe avocados
- 1 green onion, finely chopped
- 2 tablespoons lemon juice
- ½ cup sour cream
- ½ teaspoon ground coriander
- ½ teaspoon chili powder
- Salt and pepper to taste

To make filling: Combine cheese, chilies and jalapenos. Mix well.

Use about 1 ounce of filling in each won ton skin. Fold in the sides, then roll up skin to enclose filling in a miniature egg-roll shape. Seal the skin with water to be sure the won tons stay closed during frying.

Heat oil for deep-frying to 320-degrees. Deep-fry won tons until brown. Drain briefly and serve hot with guacamole

To make the guacamole: Mash avocados. Mix in onion, lemon juice, sour cream, coriander, chili powder and salt and pepper to taste. Blend to make a smooth mixture.

Bristol Bar & Grill's artichoke fritters with rémoulade sauce©

Makes about 2 dozen, depending on size.

Fritters:
- 2 14-ounce cans artichoke hearts, in water
- 3 eggs
- 1 cup all-purpose flour
- ½ cup Dijon mustard
- 1 teaspoon vinegar
- Salt and pepper, to taste
- Oil for deep frying
- Remoulade sauce (recipe follows)

Remoulade sauce:
- 1 small onion, coarsely chopped
- 4 ribs celery, coarsely chopped

To make fritters: Drain and mash artichoke hearts. Mix in eggs, flour, mustard, vinegar and salt and pepper, blending well.

Portion and shape fritters by rolling batter in a large spoon. Carefully drop into 5 to 6 inches of oil heated to 375 degrees.

Keep fritters separated to prevent raw spots. Fry until golden brown. Fritters need no turning.

To make remoulade sauce: In a food processor or blender, puree the chopped onion, celery, parsley, mustard, oil and lemon juice. Texture will be somewhat grainy. Add basil, cayenne and paprika during machine's final pulses.

1 bunch parsley, leaves only,
   coarsely chopped
¼ cup Dijon mustard
½ cup olive oil
1 teaspoon lemon juice
1 tablespoon dried basil
   Dash cayenne
2 tablespoons paprika

Makes 2 cups.

Parmesan or Cheddar cheese leaves

1 cup all-purpose flour
½ cup butter
1 cup grated Parmesan cheese
   or grated Cheddar cheese
¼ teaspoon salt
   Dash white pepper
   Dash cayenne pepper
2 tablespoons cold water
1 egg, slightly beaten – brush
   on leaves before baking
   Paprika – sprinkle on leaves
   before baking

Makes about 2 dozen, depending on size.
Using a pastry blender or 2 knives, combine flour and butter. Stir in cheese, salt, white pepper and cayenne pepper. Stir with a fork to combine. Sprinkle evenly with 2 tablespoons cold water. Toss with a fork. Using your hands, form into a ball. Between sheets of wax paper, on a slightly damp surface, roll out to ¼-inch thickness. Cut as desired (I use little leaf shaped cutters – you can use anything). Place in a plastic freezer container with wax paper between layers. Cover and freeze until ready to bake.
To bake, place frozen leaves on ungreased baking sheet about 1-inch apart. Brush tops lightly with beaten egg. Sprinkle with paprika. Bake in a preheated 400 degree oven about 10 minutes or until golden. Serve warm or cold.

Schnitzelbank's sauerkraut balls©

¾ pound ground beef
¼ pound ground pork
1 to 1½ cups well-drained sauerkraut
1 teaspoon caraway seed
⅛ teaspoon cayenne pepper, or
   to taste

Makes 30 to 35 balls.
In a pan or skillet, brown beef and pork. Drain and press out as much grease as possible. Using a spoon, break meat into fine pieces.
Drain sauerkraut. Press between sheets of paper toweling to remove all liquid.

½ teaspoon garlic powder
1 teaspoon seasoned salt
1 8-ounce package cream cheese
1 egg, beaten
1 cup bread crumbs
  Oil for frying

Place meat, sauerkraut, caraway seed, cayenne, garlic powder, salt and cream cheese in the bowl of an electric mixer. Mix thoroughly. Cover and refrigerate for 24 hours.

Use a melon ball scoop to form balls or shape and roll into balls, using hands. Dip each ball in beaten egg and roll in bread crumbs.

Place oil in a deep fryer or pot. Bring to 350 degrees. Drop sauerkraut balls in and fry a few at a time until golden.

Note: Sauerkraut balls can be frozen. Thaw before frying.

Spanakopita

(Spinach and cheese triangles)

2 10-ounce packages frozen chopped spinach
½ cup finely chopped onion
1 clove garlic, minced
1 tablespoon butter
1½ cups ricotta cheese
4 ounces feta cheese, crumbled
2 eggs
½ cup fresh, chopped dill or 1 tablespoon dried
1 teaspoon dried oregano
  Freshly grated nutmeg, about ⅛ teaspoon
  Freshly ground pepper
2 pounds fillo or phyllo dough
1 cup melted butter or margarine (or more, if needed)

Makes 30 triangles.

Thaw and drain spinach by pressing it firmly in a sieve or ricer. Sauté onion and garlic in butter just until translucent – do NOT burn. Combine spinach mixture with cheeses, eggs, dill, oregano and nutmeg. Season with a little pepper. Feta is very salty so no additional salt may be needed.

Brush a sheet of fillo with a little melted butter. Fold in thirds lengthwise. Brush again with butter. The dough should be long and skinny.

Place about a tablespoon of filling on one end of the strip and fold a corner over to enclose it. Continue folding into triangles, as you would fold an American flag, until you get to the end. Tuck the ends under. Brush tops with butter and bake in a preheated 350-degree oven for 20 minutes.

To freeze: Place in sturdy containers, separating layers with wax paper or freeze on baking sheet and, after frozen, place in a sturdy container. Before baking, brush unthawed triangles with a little melted butter and bake at 350 degrees for 35 to 40 minutes.

Spinach balls

This recipe is from my friend, Madelyn Grattan. It's easy and very good.

Makes 30 to 36, depending on size of balls.

½ cup Stove Top Stuffing, chicken or turkey flavored
½ cup grated Parmesan cheese
1 10-ounce package chopped spinach, thawed and drained well
6 tablespoons butter

Place all ingredients in a bowl. Mix thoroughly. Chill until mixture can be rolled into small balls. Form into balls and place on a baking sheet. Chill. Bake in a preheated 350-degree oven 10 to 12 minutes.

To freeze, place balls on a baking sheet. Place in freezer until balls are frozen. Remove balls from baking sheet and place in a freezer-friendly container until ready to serve. Bake as above for 12 to 15 minutes.

Taco dip

Makes 10 to 12 servings.

2 pounds Velveeta cheese
1 pound ground beef
1 pound breakfast sausage
1 medium onion, chopped
1 10¾-ounce can cream of mushroom soup
1 10-ounce can chopped tomatoes and green chilies, drained
Jalapeno peppers, chopped (to taste)

Cut Velveeta into chunks and place in crock pot set on high.

In a large skillet, brown ground beef and sausage. Sauté the onion in some of the grease from the beef until translucent. Drain well. Add beef, sausage and onion to cheese. Stir. Add cream of mushroom soup, tomato wedges and green chilies and jalapeno peppers. Stir to combine. Cook on high until cheese melts. Turn to low while serving with corn chips, scoop chips or tortilla chips.

Benedictine cheese

Makes ½ pound.

1	8-ounce package cream cheese, room temperature
2 to 3	tablespoons grated cucumber (about half a cucumber)
1	teaspoon grated onion
1	tablespoon mayonnaise
1	drop green food coloring

Place cream cheese in the bowl of a food processor. Peel, seed and finely grate cucumber onto several layers of paper toweling (too much liquid from the cucumber will result in runny Benedictine). Add the grated cucumber, onion, mayonnaise and food coloring to the cheese. Process to thoroughly combine. Place in airtight container and refrigerate.

Pimento cheese

I make this cheese several different ways –some in my family don't like jalapeno and others don't like olives so, I make a batch using the Cheddar, pimento and mayonnaise. To some of that I add the jalapeno juice and jalapenos and to some other, I add chopped olives – everyone is happy and you have three different spreads. You can do as I do or you can add all the ingredients for a super pimento cheese.

Makes 1¼ pounds.

16	ounces sharp Cheddar cheese, room temperature
1	4-ounce jar chopped pimento
2 to 4	tablespoons mayonnaise
1	teaspoon jalapeno juice (optional)
3 to 4	slices pickled jalapeno, finely chopped (optional)
4 to 5	olives, chopped (optional)

Cut Cheddar into small pieces. Place in the bowl of a food processor. Drain juice from pimento and add to cheese along with mayonnaise. Process until well blended. Add the pimentos. Process just to blend pimento with cheese.

For jalapeno flavored cheese, add the jalapeno juice when you add the pimento juice. Blend well. Chop the sliced jalapeno and add to the cheese mixture. Process until well blended. Add pimento and process just to blend pimento with cheese.

For olive flavored cheese, add chopped olives when you add the pimento. Process just until blended. Place in an airtight container and refrigerate.

Boursin cheese spread©

Makes 2½ cups.

1 clove garlic, minced
2 8-ounce packages cream cheese, room temperature
1 cup butter, room temperature
½ teaspoon dried oregano
½ teaspoon dried basil
½ teaspoon dried dill weed
½ teaspoon dried marjoram
½ teaspoon dried thyme
½ teaspoon pepper
Freshly cracked black pepper
Fresh vegetables and crackers

Place all ingredients except fresh cracked black pepper and vegetables and crackers in bowl of food processor. Process until smooth, stopping once to scrape down sides. Line a 2½-cup container with plastic wrap or aluminum foil. Press cheese mixture into container. Cover and refrigerate 2 to 3 hours before serving.

A half-hour before serving, remove from refrigerator. Just before serving, remove wrapper from cheese. Roll edge of cheese in freshly cracked pepper. Serve surrounded with fresh vegetables and crackers.

Note: This is my version of Boursin cheese – feel free to use your choice of dried herbs.

Cranberry-orange cheese ball

Makes one 8-ounce ball.

1 8-ounce package cream cheese, room temperature
½ cup finely chopped dried cranberries
¼ cup finely chopped pecans
Zest of half orange
2 tablespoons orange juice
Wheat thins or bagel chips

Combine cream cheese, 3 tablespoons chopped dried cranberries, chopped pecans, orange zest and orange juice. Mix to blend thoroughly. Form mixture into a ball. Roll in remaining chopped cranberries. Refrigerate until ready to serve with wheat thins, bagel chips or crackers of your choice.

Cheese torte©

Makes a 2½ pound torte.

1 12-ounce package grated sharp Cheddar cheese, softened
1 cup chopped pecans
1 medium onion, finely chopped

Start by thawing spinach. When you are ready for it, it will be ready for you.

In a bowl, combine softened Cheddar cheese with pecans, onion and enough mayonnaise to hold mixture together. Line a 1-quart soufflé dish or deep dish with a flat bottom

2 to 3 tablespoons mayonnaise
2 8-ounce packages cream cheese, softened
⅓ cup chutney
⅓ cup frozen chopped spinach
¼ teaspoon garlic salt
⅛ teaspoon dried oregano
1 tablespoon beef granules
⅛ teaspoon dried basil
Dash each of pepper, ground celery seed, cumin and nutmeg

and straight sides with plastic wrap. Spread half this mixture over bottom of dish.

In another bowl, combine 8 ounces cream cheese with chutney. Blend thoroughly. Spread over Cheddar cheese mixture. Thaw spinach. Drain completely, squeezing all water from spinach. Put in a bowl with remaining 8 ounces of cream cheese, garlic salt, oregano, beef granules, basil, pepper, ground celery seed, cumin and nutmeg. Blend until beef granules have dissolved. Spread over chutney mixture. Top with remaining Cheddar cheese mixture. Cover with plastic wrap overhang. Refrigerate or freeze until ready to use. If frozen, thaw overnight in refrigerator. Serve with crackers, toast rounds or thin slices of French baguettes.

Note: You can cut the recipe in half or you can make 2 tortes – use one and freeze the other.

Cheese wafers

Makes about 50, depending on size of balls.

Preheat oven to 350 degrees.
Combine all ingredients in a bowl. Mix well. Shape into small balls. Place on an ungreased baking sheet and press each down with tines of a fork. Bake in preheated oven 10 minutes. Serve warm or cold. Store in an airtight container. Can be frozen.

2 cups (8 ounces) shredded sharp Cheddar cheese, room temperature
2 cups all-purpose flour
1 cup butter or margarine, room temperature
2 cups crispy rice cereal or nuts
¼ teaspoon cayenne pepper or more, depending on how hot you like it
½ teaspoon paprika

Salmon ball©

1 14.75-ounce can red salmon
1 8-ounce package cream cheese, softened
1 tablespoon lemon juice
1 teaspoon celery seed
¼ teaspoon salt
2 teaspoons grated onion
1 teaspoon prepared horseradish
   Coarsely ground black pepper, to taste
   Pecans, walnuts or fresh parsley

Drain salmon. Remove skin and bones. With a fork, flake salmon then set aside. Combine cream cheese, lemon juice, celery seed, salt, onion, horseradish and black pepper. Mix thoroughly. Gently stir in salmon. Place mixture in a well-oiled 3-cup mold. Chill several hours or overnight. See note. When ready to serve, unmold onto serving platter. Cover with pecans, walnuts or parsley. Serve with assorted crackers.

   Note: If you have a fish-shaped mold, use it. After unmolding, place slivered almonds to look like scales on a fish. Use a slice of olive for the eye. Place some parsley sprigs around base of "fish".

Asiago/Parmesan cheese dip

1 cup sour cream
1 cup mayonnaise
½ cup minced green onion
½ cup diced button mushrooms
¼ cup diced sun-dried tomatoes
½ cup finely grated Asiago cheese
½ cup finely grated Parmesan cheese
   Salt and white pepper, to taste (see note)

Makes about 3 cups.
Thoroughly combine all ingredients. Refrigerate.
Serve with chips, bagel chips, tortillas or French bread.

   Note: Before adding salt, check the flavor. Asiago and Parmesan can be salty.

Rosemary cashews

1 pound cashews, see note
2 tablespoons minced fresh rosemary
½ teaspoon cayenne pepper
2 teaspoons light brown sugar

Preheat oven to 350 degrees. Roast nuts for five minutes.
Combine rosemary, cayenne pepper, brown sugar and salt with the melted butter. Pour over cashews and stir to combine.

1 tablespoon kosher salt
1 tablespoon unsalted butter, melted

Note: If using salted nuts and salted butter, eliminate kosher salt. Check the taste - if not salty enough, sprinkle with some kosher salt.

Granola mix©

Makes about 10 cups.

5 cups rolled oats, old-fashioned or quick-cooking
¾ cup wheat germ
1 cup shredded coconut
¾ cup shelled raw or toasted sunflower seeds
2 cups chopped mixed nuts
½ cup packed dark brown sugar
¾ cup water
¾ cup vegetable oil
¼ cup honey
¼ cup molasses
¾ teaspoon salt
1 teaspoon ground cinnamon
2 teaspoons vanilla extract
2 cups raisins, chopped dates or other dried fruit

Preheat oven to 300 degrees. In a large bowl, combine oats, wheat germ, coconut, sunflower seeds and nuts. Stir until evenly distributed.

In a medium saucepan, combine brown sugar, water, oil, honey, molasses, salt, cinnamon and vanilla. Heat and stir until sugar is dissolved. Do not boil. Pour syrup over oats mixture. Stir with a wooden spoon until syrup coats other ingredients.

Spread mixture in two 9-by-13-by-2-inch baking pans. Bake in preheated oven 20 to 30 minutes, stirring occasionally. Cool. Stir in raisins, chopped dates or other dried fruit. Store in a container with a tight-fitting lid in a cool dry place. Use within six months.

Swedish nuts

Makes about 1 pound.

3 egg whites
¼ teaspoon salt
½ teaspoon cinnamon
1 cup sugar
1 pound pecans
½ cup butter, melted

Beat egg whites until stiff. Add salt and cinnamon. While beating, slowly fold in sugar, beating until stiff. Fold in pecans until they are well coated.

Melt butter in a large shallow baking pan (jellyroll pan is perfect). Spread the nuts in the meringue with the melted butter. Mix together but don't worry about mixing too much.

Place in a preheated 300-degree oven. Stir

about every 10 to 15 minutes or until nuts become coated in the sweet covering, about 45 minutes (the butter will bake into the nuts – this may take a bit longer than 45 minutes). Store in airtight container.

Soups, Chili and Stews

Oxtail soup for eight

3 to 4	whole oxtails (about 5 pounds)
¾	cup all-purpose flour
3	tablespoons shortening
2½	quarts water
4	teaspoons salt
¾	teaspoon pepper
2	tablespoons parsley
2 to 3	bay leaves
2	medium onions, sliced
1	1 pound, 6-ounce can tomatoes
3	tablespoons Worcestershire sauce
4	teaspoons sugar
1	cup chopped celery
¼	teaspoon powdered cloves
½	pound carrots, sliced thin
1	14.5-ounce can green beans, drained
4	large potatoes, peeled and diced
½	cup pearl barley

Makes 8 servings.
Dredge pieces of oxtail in flour. In a large kettle or Dutch oven melt shortening. When hot, brown oxtail. Add water, salt, pepper, parsley and bay leaves. Cover and simmer for 2 hours. Add remaining ingredients and simmer an additional 1 to 1½ hours. Taste and correct seasonings. Serve hot in heated pottery bowls.

Cream soup mix©

Makes 4 to 6 servings, depending on what you add.

¼	teaspoon black pepper
½	teaspoon dried thyme
½	teaspoon dried basil
1	tablespoon dried onion flakes
2	tablespoons cornstarch
2	tablespoons chicken bouillon granules
1	cup nonfat dried milk powder

Mix ingredients. If you don't use mixture right away, store in an airtight container or zip bag. To make soup, put the mixture in a large saucepan and add 2 cups of cold water. Cook on medium heat. Stir constantly until the mixture thickens. Next, add other ingredients (mushrooms, corn, cooked chicken, cooked potatoes, etc.). Let the soup cook a few minutes longer. Serve while hot.

Bobby J's spinach-blue cheese soup©

Makes 12 cups.

1½	cups chopped onion
¼	cup butter
¾	cup brandy
1	tablespoon thyme
3	cups chopped tomatoes with juice
2	cups chopped spinach
1½	cups blue cheese crumbles
8	cups chicken broth

In a large kettle, sauté chopped onion in butter until tender. Add brandy and cook until alcohol evaporates. Add thyme and tomatoes. Bring to a boil. Add spinach, blue cheese and chicken broth. Heat until cheese melts.

Brennan's New Orleans turtle soup©

Makes 10 to 12 servings.

3	pounds turtle meat
2	bay leaves
2	tablespoons plus 1 teaspoon salt
4	quarts cold water
½	cup (1 stick) butter

In a stockpot, combine the turtle meat, bay leaves and 2 tablespoons of salt. Add 4 quarts of cold water and bring the mixture to a boil over high heat. Reduce the heat to medium and cook until the turtle meat is tender, about 2 hours; add additional water, if

½ cup onion, finely chopped
½ cup celery, finely chopped
½ cup green bell pepper, finely chopped
½ teaspoon garlic, minced
1 cup fresh parsley, finely chopped
4 ounces (½ cup) tomato paste
1 teaspoon caramel coloring (optional)
¼ cup Worcestershire sauce
1 teaspoon black pepper
1 teaspoon paprika
1 cup all-purpose flour
3 large hard-boiled eggs, finely chopped
1 cup sherry and 1 tablespoon rum
1 lemon, thinly sliced

necessary, to maintain about 3 quarts of liquid during cooking. Strain the turtle meat, reserving the stock. Dice the turtle meat and set aside.

In a large pot, melt the butter and add the onion, celery, bell pepper, garlic, parsley, tomato paste, caramel coloring (if using), Worcestershire, pepper, paprika and remaining teaspoon of salt. Cook the mixture over low heat until the vegetables are very tender. Stir in the flour.

Increase the heat to medium and cook until the flour absorbs all of the butter. Pour the turtle stock into the pot and bring the stock to a boil. Add the turtle meat and simmer for 30 to 40 minutes. Just before serving, remove the bay leaves and add the chopped eggs, sherry, rum and lemon.

Dagwood's Portuguese kale soup©

Makes 8 to 10 servings.

3 quarts beef broth
1 tablespoon bruised fennel seed
½ teaspoon ground allspice
1 10-ounce package fresh kale
¾ pound chopped potatoes
¾ pound chopped cabbage
1 15.5-ounce can dark red kidney beans, rinsed
½ pound hot breakfast sausage
½ pound chorizo sausage (or Italian)
2 cloves garlic, minced
1 medium onion
½ cup Burgundy wine

In a large pot, bring beef broth to a boil. Add bruised fennel seed (to bruise fennel seed, place in a mortar, press the pestle against the mortar and rotate, grinding the seed between them) and allspice.

Meanwhile wash, stem and tear kale. Stir into stock. Wash, peel and coarsely chop potatoes. Hold in cold water. Peel, core and coarsely chop cabbage. When kale is tender, add cabbage, potatoes and dark red kidney beans.

In a separate pan, brown and coarsely crumble breakfast sausage. Strain off all oil. Add sausage to soup. Chop chorizo (or Italian) sausage into bite-size pieces (¾-inch). Brown in pan. Meanwhile peel and mince garlic. Peel onion and slice from top to bottom into long ¼-inch strips. With slotted spoon, remove sausage from frying pan and add to beef broth. Drain half the oil from pan. Sauté onion and garlic in remaining oil until slightly golden. Add to beef broth. Return pan to heat and deglaze with wine. Add to broth. Reduce heat and cook until potatoes and cabbage are just tender. Don't overcook. It is better to turn the soup off and let the flavors meld. Adjust the seasonings. Serve with crusty French bread and a glass of Burgundy wine.

The Grove Park Inn Resort's sweet red pepper soup©

Makes 10 servings.

¼	cup bacon drippings
3½	red bell peppers, diced
1	onion, diced
1	tablespoon chopped garlic
⅛	teaspoon paprika
¼	cup tomato paste
¼	teaspoon Tabasco
⅛	teaspoon cayenne pepper
1½	cups cooking sherry
6	tablespoons butter
6	tablespoons all-purpose flour
3	14.5-ounce cans chicken stock
1	pint whipping cream
	Salt, to taste

Put bacon drippings in skillet; heat. Add peppers. Cook until peppers soften. Add onion and garlic, stirring to cook evenly. When onion becomes translucent and peppers are soft, add paprika and tomato paste. Stir. Add Tabasco and cayenne pepper. Cook until mixture starts to stick. Add sherry and cook out alcohol, about 5 minutes.

Pour mixture into a blender or food processor and mix until smooth.

Melt butter in a large pan. Add flour. Stir and cook 3 to 4 minutes. Slowly add chicken stock. Cook until slightly thickened. Add cream. Heat to just below boiling. Add red pepper mixture. Heat to very low simmer. Salt to taste.

Porcini's asparagus soup with smoked Gouda cheese©

Makes 2 quarts.

Asparagus soup:
| 2 | quarts water |

Bring water to a boil. Cut carrot, onion and celery into bite-size pieces. Add to boiling

½ carrot, peeled
½ small yellow onion, peeled
1½ ribs celery
1 pound thin asparagus, chopped
Dash salt
½ teaspoon ground black pepper
¼ teaspoon ground thyme
¼ teaspoon ground marjoram
1 tablespoon chopped fresh parsley
4 ounces unsalted butter, melted
1 cup all-purpose flour, sifted

Smoked Gouda croutons:
3 to 4 slices Italian or French bread, ¼ inch thick
3 tablespoons garlic butter, melted
2 ounces grated smoked Gouda cheese

water along with asparagus. Bring back to a boil. Reduce heat and simmer 35 to 40 minutes.

Strain vegetables reserving broth.. Put reserved broth back in pot. Puree the cooked vegetables for 3 to 4 minutes in food processor, then add back to pot of broth along with salt, pepper, thyme, marjoram and parsley. Continue to simmer over low flame. In a skillet over medium-low heat, combine the melted butter and sifted flour. Cook until the mixture is thick and has a nutty aroma, about 8 to 12 minutes, stirring constantly. Whisk this mixture into broth mixture and bring back to a boil. Mixture must be brought back up to a boil to properly thicken. Reduce to a simmer.

To make croutons: Brush bread slices on both sides with garlic butter (butter that has been seasoned to taste with garlic) and place on sheet pan in a hot, 375-degree oven. Bake 8 to 10 minutes or until crisp and golden (this step may be done a day in advance, if desired). Top the croutons with grated cheese and return to oven just long enough to melt cheese. Dice up croutons and sprinkle over top of soup.

The Soup Line Restaurant's minestrone soup©

1 large carrot, chopped
1 medium onion, chopped
2 cups chopped celery
½ to 1 clove garlic, chopped
¼ cup olive oil
2 quarts beef broth or chicken broth
4 cups diced canned tomatoes

Makes 10 to 12 servings.
In a heavy soup kettle sauté carrot, onion, celery and garlic in olive oil for 10 minutes. Add broth, tomatoes and macaroni. Cook until macaroni is tender. Add beans, spinach, salt, pepper and parsley. Simmer for 1 hour.

½ to 1   cup elbow macaroni or rice
  2   cups red beans (not kidney)
  1   10-ounce box frozen chopped
    spinach or 2 cups chopped
    cabbage
1½   teaspoons salt
1½   teaspoons black pepper
  2   tablespoons chopped parsley

Timothy's white chili©

  1   pound large white beans
  6   cups chicken broth
  2   cloves garlic, minced
  2   medium onions, chopped
  1   tablespoon oil
  2   4-ounce cans mild green
    chilies, chopped
  2   teaspoons ground cumin
1½   teaspoons oregano
 ¼   teaspoon ground cloves
 ¼   teaspoon cayenne pepper
  4   cups diced cooked chicken
    breast
  3   cups grated Monterey Jack
    cheese
    Salsa (recipe follows)
    Sour cream

Salsa:
  2   peeled tomatoes, chopped
  1   4-ounce can chopped green
    chilies
  1   onion, chopped
  2   cloves garlic, minced
 ¼   cup fresh cilantro, chopped

Makes 8 to 10 servings.

To make chili: Combine beans, broth, garlic and half the onions in a large soup pot. Bring to a boil. Reduce heat and simmer until beans are soft (2 hours or more), adding more broth or water as necessary.

In a skillet, sauté remaining onions in oil until tender. Add chilies and seasonings and mix thoroughly. Add to bean mixture. Add chicken and simmer 1 hour.

Serve topped with grated cheese, salsa and sour cream.

To make salsa: You can use store-bought chunky Mexican tomato salsa or make your own.

To make your own, combine chopped tomatoes, green chilies, onion, garlic and cilantro. Stir to combine.

J. P. Karouz Restaurant and Catering's chili©

Makes 10 to 12 servings.

2½ pounds ground chuck
2 large yellow onions, diced
4 ounces (8 tablespoons) chili powder
1½ teaspoons garlic powder
1½ teaspoons ground cumin
¾ teaspoon oregano
4 tablespoons sugar
2 14.5-ounce cans tomatoes
3 10.75-ounce cans tomato puree, plus 2 cans of water
2 15.5-ounce cans light red kidney beans

In a large skillet, brown ground chuck and onions. Add chili powder, garlic powder, cumin, oregano and sugar. Cook on low heat for 10 minutes.
In a 1-gallon pot, combine the meat mixture with the remaining ingredients. Cook over low heat for 2 hours.

Afro-German Tea Room's chili©

Makes 8 to 10 servings.

2 pounds ground chuck
4 14.5-ounce cans diced tomatoes
2 15.5-ounce cans red beans
3 4-ounce cans green chilies
2 tablespoons Mexene chili powder
A shake of red pepper flakes
A shake of cumin
1 teaspoon oregano
1 small white onion, diced
2 teaspoons minced garlic

In a large pan, cook meat. Drain off grease. Add remaining ingredients. Cook slowly for at least 30 minutes.

Hoppin John soup©

Makes 6 to 8 servings.

¼ pound bulk pork sausage, preferably spicy hot

Brown sausage in large pot or Dutch oven over medium-high heat. Pour sausage into

½	cup chopped onion
1	pound (about 3) turnips, peeled and diced
2	carrots, peeled and diced
3½	cups chicken stock
3 to 4	cups water
½	teaspoon salt, or to taste
½	cup uncooked brown rice
1	12-ounce package frozen black-eyed peas
8	ounces fresh mustard greens, rinsed well, drained and shredded; or one 10-ounce package frozen chopped mustard or turnip greens, defrosted
½	teaspoon red pepper flakes

colander to drain off fat. Wipe out pot and return sausage to pot.

Add onion, turnips and carrots. Cook for 5 minutes, stirring often, until onion is soft. Add chicken stock and water. Bring to a boil and add salt and rice. Lower heat to simmer. After 20 minutes, add black-eyed peas and greens. Cook 20 minutes longer until rice and vegetables are tender. Add red pepper flakes and adjust seasoning to taste.

Split pea soup©

½	pound bacon, diced
1	pound split peas
1	small onion, diced
1	small carrot, diced
	Parsley, to taste
2 to 3	quarts water
	Salt and pepper to taste

Makes 6 to 8 servings.
In a heavy saucepan, sauté bacon until crisp. Add split peas, onion, carrot and parsley. Cover with water. As peas cook, add additional water as needed until peas are tender and soup is thick. Peas should be tender after about 2 hours of cooking. Season to taste with salt and pepper.

The Soup Line Restaurant's Great Northern bean soup©

1 to 2	pounds Great Northern beans
1	medium onion, diced (optional)
½ to 1	cup chopped ham (optional)
	Salt and black pepper, to taste
1	tablespoon ketchup (optional)

Makes 4 quarts.
Check beans for stones and bad beans. Rinse. Place in a soup kettle. Cover with water to soak overnight. (Use 2 pounds beans if you like a thick soup.)
Drain off water. Cover beans with 3 to 4 quarts cold water. Add onion, ham and salt and pepper. When beans are almost done, add ketchup, if desired. If the soup becomes

too thick during cooking, add hot water to thin to desired consistency. Taste for seasoning. Add salt and pepper, if needed.

Note: Onion is not used in this soup. Ketchup is used for color. If you don't like ham, you can season with bacon grease and bacon bits. This is a basic recipe that can get you started on your own signature soup.

Rainbow Blossom's white bean soup©

1¼ cups navy beans
1 quart water
2 tablespoons olive oil
1 medium onion, diced
2 cloves garlic, crushed
1 rib celery, diced
1 carrot, diced
¼ pound mushrooms, sliced
1 medium potato, diced
¼ to ½ teaspoon summer savory
1 teaspoon oregano
1 teaspoon sage
1 teaspoon salt
½ teaspoon black pepper
Pinch cayenne pepper
1¼ quarts vegetable stock (see note)
½ medium to large summer squash, diced

Makes 2 to 2½ quarts.
Place beans and water in a large kettle. Cook 1 hour. While beans are cooking, prepare vegetables.

In a large skillet heat olive oil. Add onion, garlic, celery, carrot, mushrooms and potato. Sauté lightly. Add to the beans along with the herbs, salt and peppers. Go light on the herbs at first – you can always add more. Add vegetable stock.

Bring soup to a boil, then reduce the heat and simmer 1 to 1½ hours or until beans are tender. Add the squash in the last 20 minutes of cooking. Adjust the seasonings and serve.

Note: To make vegetable stock, I cooked a carrot, onion, potato, rib of celery and a few sprigs of parsley in 1¼ quarts water. When the vegetables were tender, I pureed them in the blender and added all to the beans. The soup was delicious.

The Terrace's black bean soup©

4 cups cleaned black beans
4 quarts water
2 cups chicken stock
10 ounces Italian sausage (hot

Makes 8 to 10 servings.
To make soup: Check through beans. Toss any undesirables and pieces of gravel. Rinse beans. Place in a large kettle. Cover with water. Soak overnight. Next day drain

or mild)
- 2 medium carrots, chopped
- 1 medium onion, chopped
- 3 ribs celery, chopped
- 1 bay leaf
- 1 teaspoon thyme
- ¼ teaspoon sage
- 1 teaspoon onion powder
- 1 teaspoon chopped fresh garlic
- 1 teaspoon cumin
- ½ teaspoon black pepper
- 2 tablespoons chopped fresh parsley
- 2 tablespoons chopped green chilies
- 1 medium red onion, chopped

Cumin sauce:
- 1 cup sour cream
- 2 teaspoons chopped fresh garlic
- ½ teaspoon salt
- ½ teaspoon onion powder
- ¼ teaspoon cumin
- ½ teaspoon Tabasco
- 1 teaspoon Worcestershire sauce

beans. Rinse.

Return to kettle along with water and chicken stock. Begin cooking over medium-high heat.

While beans are cooking, sauté Italian sausage. Drain off fat. Chop fine and add to beans. Add chopped carrots, onion, celery, bay leaf, thyme, sage, onion powder, garlic, cumin, black pepper, parsley and green chilies.

Bring to a boil. Reduce heat to a simmer and cook 1½ to 2 hours, adding more water if needed. This is a thick soup so don't go overboard adding water.

Top each serving with chopped red onion and a dollop of cumin sauce.

To make sauce: Combine all ingredients and chill for 1 hour. Use about 1 tablespoon per serving of soup.

This is a very versatile recipe and all ingredients may be adjusted to taste.

 Note: This soup will become thick if allowed to cook until beans are very tender and liquid has evaporated. You can cut the amount of water to half. If more is needed, add as you cook. Make sure the soup has started to boil before you begin timing. I like to run the soup through the blender – makes it thick and smooth – delicious.

Joe Huber Family Restaurant's beef noodle soup©

Makes 8 to 10 servings.

Noodles:
- 2 cups all-purpose flour
- 1½ teaspoons salt
- 4 eggs
- 2 tablespoons water

Soup:

To make noodles: Place flour and salt in a mixing bowl. Beat eggs with water to combine. Stir or work with your hands, folding the flour over the eggs until the dough can be rolled into a ball.

Place on a floured surface and knead until

1 pound beef ribs
1 quart tomato juice
6 quarts water
1 small onion, diced
4 ribs celery, diced
3 carrots, diced
1 teaspoon parsley
4 fresh Italian tomatoes, peeled and diced (optional)
  Salt and pepper, to taste

mixture feels smooth (about 10 minutes). Roll out to about 1/16-inch thickness. Cut with a pizza cutter into strips about ½-inch wide and 2 inches long. Let set to dry 2 to 3 hours.

To make soup: Using an 8-quart soup pot, combine ribs, tomato juice, water, onion, celery, carrots, parsley, Italian tomatoes (if available), salt and pepper. Bring to boil and then reduce to simmer. Simmer 3 hours or longer. Remove ribs to a platter.

When cool enough to handle, remove meat from bone and return meat to pot. Bring back to boil. Add noodles and cook 20 to 25 minutes (or until noodles are tender).

Romano's Macaroni Grill lentil bean soup©

2 tablespoons olive oil
½ cup diced carrots
½ cup diced celery
½ cup diced onion
2 tablespoons chopped garlic
½ cup cooked pancetta (Italian bacon), ground and well-rendered
1 small bay leaf
6 cups chicken stock
6 cups beef stock
1 pound lentil beans
1½ teaspoons ground black pepper
¼ pound angel hair pasta
  Parmesan cheese

Makes 8 to 10 servings.

Heat olive oil in a large pot and sauté carrots, celery, onion and garlic until al dente.

Grind pancetta. Fry until most of grease is rendered. Drain. Add to carrot mixture along with bay leaf, stocks, lentil beans and black pepper. Bring soup to a boil, stirring often. Reduce heat and simmer until lentils are tender, about 2 hours.

Ten minutes before serving add dry angel-hair pasta. Cook until pasta is tender. Serve garnished with freshly grated Parmesan cheese.

Hart County Kentucky burgoo©

2	pounds pork shank
2	pounds veal shank
2	pounds beef shank
2	pounds breast of lamb
1	4-pound hen
8	quarts cold water
1½	pounds potatoes, peeled and diced
1½	pounds onions, peeled and diced
1	bunch carrots, diced
2	green peppers, diced
2	cups chopped cabbage
2	cups corn, fresh or canned
2	pods red pepper
2	cups diced okra
2	cups lima beans
1	cup diced celery
1	quart tomato puree
	Salt and cayenne to taste
	Tabasco to taste
	A-1 sauce to taste
	Worcestershire sauce to taste
	Chopped parsley

Makes 3 gallons.

Put all the meat into the cold water and bring slowly to a boil. Simmer until the meat is tender enough to fall from the bones. Lift the meat out of the stock. Cool and chop up the meat, discarding the bones.

Prepare vegetables and add to stock along with the chopped meat. Allow to simmer until thick. Burgoo should be very thick but still soupy.

Add seasonings to taste, continuing until the burgoo is almost done. Add chopped parsley just before serving.

Note: Stir frequently with a long-handled spoon or paddle during the first part of the cooking and almost constantly after it gets thick. Use at least a 4-gallon kettle and cook about 10 hours.

Steve Clements Catering Derby Café's burgoo©

2	pounds boneless chicken breast
1	pound beef stew meat
1	pound pork, cubed
2 to 3	quarts water
1½	teaspoons coarsely ground pepper

Makes 1 gallon.

In a large kettle, simmer chicken, beef and pork in water with coarsely ground pepper and cayenne pepper until tender, about 40 minutes.

Add tomato puree, potatoes, onions, tomatoes, corn, carrots and seasonings.

Cook slowly over low heat for several hours

½ teaspoon cayenne pepper
2 10.5-ounce cans tomato
    puree
12 medium potatoes, diced
4 large onions, chopped
6 to 8 medium tomatoes, peeled
    and diced
1 15.25-ounce bag frozen corn
1 pound fresh carrots, peeled
    and sliced
1 tablespoon salt, or to taste
1 teaspoon pepper
1 teaspoon garlic powder, or to
    taste
1 bay leaf

or until meat and vegetables are done and stew is thick but still soupy. Keep a close watch so burgoo doesn't scorch.

Windward Inn's cabbage soup©

¾ cup chopped onion
⅔ cup diced celery
8 tablespoons butter, divided
1½ pounds cabbage, shredded
2 teaspoons chopped parsley
2 ounces mushrooms, diced
    small
½ pound frozen peas, cooked
3 quarts hot chicken stock
¾ cup all-purpose flour
½ pound frankfurters, sliced
¼ teaspoon salt
    Dash pepper

Makes 8 to 10 servings.
In a large kettle over medium heat sauté onion and celery in 6 tablespoons of the butter until nearly tender. Add cabbage and chopped parsley. Turn heat to low. Cover kettle and cook for 5 minutes.
Sauté mushrooms in remaining 2 tablespoons butter. Set aside. Cook peas until defrosted. Drain and set aside. Heat chicken stock.
Remove cover from kettle and add flour, blending well. Cook 2 to 3 minutes. Add chicken stock gradually. Mix until smooth. Simmer 30 minutes. Add sautéed mushrooms, cooked peas, sliced frankfurters and salt and pepper. Bring to a boil. Reduce heat and simmer 5 minutes. Serve while hot.

Terrace Restaurant's cream of cauliflower soup©

Makes 8 to 10 servings.

6	tablespoons butter, divided
½	cup diced white onion
½	cup diced celery
⅛	teaspoon garlic in oil
1	cup cream
1	quart milk
1	quart water
1½	tablespoons chicken base or 2 bouillon cubes
½	tablespoon beef base or ½ bouillon cube
½	teaspoon dry mustard
⅛	teaspoon white pepper
1	medium head cauliflower
4	tablespoons all-purpose flour
1	cup half-and-half
1	teaspoon salt

In a large kettle melt 2 tablespoons of the butter. Add onion, celery and garlic. Sauté until onion is soft, but do not allow to brown at all. Add cream, milk, water, chicken and beef bases, dry mustard, white pepper and cauliflower.

Bring to a boil. Reduce heat and simmer until cauliflower is soft.

Combine remaining 4 tablespoons butter with 4 tablespoons flour, forming a roux. Add to soup mixture. Simmer to thicken. Add half-and-half. Bring almost to a boil, stirring continuously. (This soup will scorch quickly, so watch carefully.) Reduce heat to simmer until ready to serve. Taste before adding the salt. The bases will add a lot of flavor, sometime making it unnecessary to add salt.

Anchorage Country Store Cheddar cheese soup©

Makes 4 to 6 servings.

4	cups chicken broth
2	cups potatoes, cubed
1	cup green beans cut into 1-inch lengths
1	cup carrots, thinly sliced
1	cup cauliflower florets
1	cup corn
½	cup all-purpose flour
½	cup cold water
1½	teaspoons cumin
2	cups Cheddar cheese, shredded

In a large stock pot bring chicken broth to a boil. Add potatoes, green beans and carrots. Bring back to boil and simmer 15 minutes. Add cauliflower and corn and cook 5 minutes.

Combine flour, water and cumin. Stir until blended. Add to vegetable mixture. Cook until thickened, stirring constantly. Simmer 2 minutes. Add cheese and serve.

Derby Café's creamy roast chicken and almond soup©

½ pound margarine
6 boneless, skinless chicken
  breast halves
  Salt and white pepper, to taste
1½ to 2 cups sliced, blanched
  almonds
½ gallon milk
1 pint heavy cream
1 pint strong chicken stock
½ bunch celery, diced
½ white onion, diced
1½ cups all-purpose flour
  Tabasco sauce
  Worcestershire sauce
  Dry mustard

Makes 12 servings.

Melt margarine in a large skillet. Remove from heat.

Place chicken breasts in a shallow pan. Brush with melted margarine. Sprinkle with salt and white pepper. Roast in 425-degree oven until golden brown. When cool enough to handle, dice into bite-size pieces.

Place almonds on a cookie sheet. Toast in a 350-degree oven until golden brown.

In a large kettle over low flame, heat milk, heavy cream and chicken stock. Watch closely while heating because mixture will scorch easily. Reheat melted margarine and slowly sauté diced celery and onion for 5 to 7 minutes. Make a roux by adding flour to sautéed vegetables. Cook, stirring constantly, for 3 to 4 minutes.

Slowly add vegetable roux to hot milk mixture a spoonful at a time, stirring until completely dissolved after each addition. Season to taste using Tabasco, Worcestershire, white pepper and dry mustard. Stir in diced chicken breasts and almonds.

Phil Dunn's chicken vegetable soup©

3 pounds chicken breasts
1 yellow onion, peeled and
  diced
1 red onion, peeled and diced
4 ribs celery, diced
1 red pepper, cored and diced
1 yellow pepper, cored and
  diced
2 carrots, peeled and diced
7 ounces butter

Makes 2½ gallons.

Place 1 gallon water in a large kettle. Add chicken breasts. Bring to a boil and cook until tender, about 30 minutes. While the chicken is cooking, skim the broth to remove any scum that forms on top. Remove chicken to a platter.

While the chicken is cooking, prepare the vegetables. Sauté onions, celery, peppers and carrots in 6 ounces of butter over medium heat until vegetables are soft.

1 cup flour
1 tablespoon cumin
1 yellow squash, diced
1 zucchini, diced
1 quart tomatoes, diced
  Salt and pepper, to taste

Add flour and cumin to make a roux. Cook slowly for 2 to 3 minutes, stirring constantly. While stirring, slowly add some chicken broth to the vegetable mixture. As it loosens, add vegetable mixture to the remaining broth. Stir.
Sauté yellow squash and zucchini separately in remaining butter. Add to broth along with the tomatoes and salt and pepper to taste. Cook slowly for 20 minutes. Dice the chicken into bite-size pieces. Add to soup.

Molly Malone's creamy Cajun chicken soup©

1 small yellow onion, julienned
1 green pepper, medium dice
1 cup thin-sliced mushrooms
2 tablespoons chopped garlic
2 tablespoons olive oil
½ cup all-purpose flour
2 cups chicken stock
1 quart whipping cream
8 ounces chicken breast
  Cajun spice
2 cups Parmesan cheese
  Salt and pepper, to taste

Makes 8 to 10 servings.
In a large pot, sauté onion, pepper, mushrooms and garlic in oil until tender. Add flour and cook until mixture is thick and starts to stick to the pan. Add chicken stock and whipping cream, mixing well with a wire whisk until clumps are dispersed. Add grilled, diced chicken and let simmer. When soup begins to thicken, add Cajun spice (I used about a teaspoon but you may prefer it spicier), grated Parmesan cheese and salt and pepper. Stir well, simmer for a few minutes. Serve while hot.

O'Charley's chicken harvest soup©

¼ pound butter
¾ cup all-purpose flour
2½ to 3 quarts water
2 tablespoons chicken base
2 quarts chicken stock (see chicken tenders recipe)
1 pound fresh carrots, diced
6 to 7 ribs celery, diced
1 medium onion, diced

Makes 8 to 10 servings.
To make soup: In a large kettle, melt butter. Add flour and cook 3 to 4 minutes. Slowly add the 2½ to 3 quarts of water, stirring constantly. (The amount of water used depends on how thick you want the soup.) Simmer 20 minutes. Add chicken base and chicken stock.
While chicken stock mixture is cooking, bring 2 quarts of water to a boil in a separate

¾ teaspoon white pepper
¾ teaspoon garlic powder
Cooked chicken tenders
(see recipe)
10 ounces egg noodles (see directions for cooking)

Chicken tenders:
2 quarts water
2 tablespoons chicken base
1 small onion, cut in quarters
½ rib celery, cut in 2-inch segments
2½ pounds chicken tenders, thawed (or chicken breasts cut into 3-inch pieces)

kettle. Add carrots, celery and onion. Cook 6 minutes. Drain. Add to chicken stock mixture along with pepper and garlic powder. Simmer 10 minutes. Add diced cooked chicken. Cook noodles according to following directions. Add to soup.

To cook noodles: In a large kettle, bring 1 gallon of water to a boil. Add 1 to 2 teaspoons salt. Drop noodles into boiling water. Cook 3 to 4 minutes. Drain and rinse with cold water. Add to soup. Noodles will continue to cook in the hot soup. Also, the soup will thicken some after the noodles are added.

To make chicken tenders: In a large kettle, bring water, chicken base, onion and celery to simmer. Add chicken. Gently simmer until done, about 5 to 6 minutes. Do not overcook. Drain chicken and reserve stock. (This can be used for the stock in this soup.) Place chicken in freezer to stop the cooking process. When cool, dice into ½-inch cubes using a sharp knife. Add to soup.

O'Charley's chicken tortilla soup©

1 cup diced onion
¾ cup diced celery
1½ tablespoons diced jalapeno peppers
⅓ cup vegetable oil
1½ teaspoons chopped garlic
½ teaspoon lemon pepper seasoning
1½ teaspoons ground cumin
1½ teaspoons hot sauce
½ teaspoon Worcestershire sauce

Makes 6 to 8 servings.
Sauté onion, celery and jalapeno peppers in oil until onion is translucent. Add garlic, lemon pepper seasoning, cumin, hot sauce, Worcestershire sauce and chicken base. Mix well. While stirring, slowly add flour. Cook 5 minutes over low heat.
Slowly add hot water and mix well with wire whisk to smooth out lumps.
Add tomatoes and bring to a simmer.
Simmer 40 minutes, stirring frequently.
Dice grilled chicken and add to soup.
Garnish soup with fried tortilla slivers or

4 teaspoons chicken base
½ cup seasoned flour
4¾ cups hot water
9 ounces diced tomatoes
½ pound grilled chicken
  Tortilla slivers or chips
  Chives, avocado, Monterey
  Jack and Cheddar cheeses
  (for optional garnish)

chips. If desired, top with fresh chives, diced avocado, Monterey Jack and Cheddar cheeses.

Rick's cream of chicken with mushrooms soup©

Makes 6 to 8 servings.

6 cups water
3 tablespoons Worcestershire sauce
1 teaspoon garlic powder
½ teaspoon white pepper
1 tablespoon chicken base
2 cups celery, chopped
2 carrots, chopped
1 medium onion, chopped
1 pound mushrooms, chopped
4 cups milk
3 tablespoons butter, room temperature
3 tablespoons all-purpose flour

In a large stockpot, combine water, Worcestershire, garlic powder, white pepper, chicken base, celery, carrots, onion and mushrooms. Simmer until hot. Add milk. Heat to just below boiling.

Make a roux by combining softened butter and flour. Mix in soup, taking care to avoid lumps. As it's heated, the soup will thicken.

The Fish House's fish chowder©

Makes 6 to 7 cups base.

1½ pounds cubed potatoes
½ cup butter
1 medium onion, chopped
4 6.5-ounce cans minced clams with juice
14 ounces cod, cut into bite-size pieces
¾ teaspoon dill weed
¾ teaspoon basil

Peel and pare potatoes. Cut into bite-size pieces. Cook in salted water until tender. Drain thoroughly.

While potatoes are cooking, melt butter in a large heavy kettle. Add onion and cook until translucent. Add clams, cod, dill weed, basil, salt and pepper. Simmer until fish is tender. Add shrimp and cooked potatoes. Cook just until shrimp have turned in color.

1   **teaspoon salt**
1¾ **teaspoons white pepper**
¼   **pound peeled and deveined shrimp**
    Heavy whipping cream

This is the base for the chowder. When ready to serve, heat equal parts of base and heavy whipping cream just to serving temperature. This chowder is thin – not a dish thickened with cornstarch or arrowroot.

    Note: The base can be frozen. When ready to serve, thaw base, add equal amount of heavy whipping cream and heat to serving temperature.

Legal Sea Foods New England clam chowder©

Makes 8 servings.

4   **quarts littleneck clams (about 1⅔ cups cooked and chopped) (see note)**
1   **clove garlic, chopped**
1   **cup water**
2   **ounces salt pork, finely chopped**
2   **cups chopped onions**
3   **tablespoons all-purpose flour**
4½ **cups clam broth (see note)**
3   **cups fish stock**
1½ **pounds potatoes, peeled and diced into ½-inch cubes**
2   **cups light cream**
    Oysters crackers (optional)

Clean the clams and place them in a large pot along with the garlic and water. Steam the clams just until opened, about 6 to 10 minutes, depending on their size. Discard any clams that do not open. Drain and shell the opened clams, reserving the broth. Mince the clam flesh, and set aside. Filter the clam broth either through coffee filters or cheesecloth and set aside.

In a large, heavy pot, slowly render the salt pork. Remove the cracklings and set them aside. Slowly cook the onions in the fat for about 6 minutes, stirring frequently, or until cooked through but not browned. Stir in the flour and cook, stirring, for 3 minutes. Add the reserved clam broth and fish stock, and whisk to remove any flour lumps. Bring the liquid to a boil, add the potatoes, lower the heat, and simmer until the potatoes are cooked through, about 15 minutes.

Stir in the reserved clams, salt-pork cracklings and light cream. Heat the chowder until it is the temperature you prefer. Serve in large soup bowls with oyster crackers on the side.

    Note: When I tested the recipe, I used a

pint of fresh clam strips. For the clam broth, I used bottled clam juice. If you like the flavor of garlic, mince a clove or two and cook with the onions.

Also, because I was using fresh clam strips, I changed the cooking procedure a bit: After adding the potatoes to the broth, I cooked the mixture about 15 minutes, then added the clams. Cook 10 to 12 minutes, add salt-pork cracklings and light cream. Heat to the temperature you prefer. The chowder was delicious, and I didn't have the mess of shucking clams.

Turner's Hall of Fame Clam Chowder©

Makes 10 servings.

6	quahogs (East Coast large hard shell clams)
10	cherrystones (medium-sized clams)
1	cup water
4	ounces clarified butter
1	clove garlic, minced
1	medium onion, chopped
1	rib celery, chopped
½	teaspoon white pepper
1	small bay leaf
¼	teaspoon thyme
1	cup all-purpose flour
4 to 5	cups bottled clam juice
1	large potato, peeled and diced, then blanched for about 5 minutes
1	pint heavy cream

Wash clams thoroughly. Place quahogs in pot with ½ cup of the water. Cover tightly and steam until clams open. Remove and reserve clams and liquid. Repeat this process with cherrystones. (If you are using topneck clams, you will probably also need to make 2 batches so only 1 layer of clams is steamed at a time.)

Remove clams from shell, chop coarsely and set aside. Strain and reserve cooking liquid and juices from clams in a separate container.

Add clarified butter and garlic to the cooking pot. Sauté 2 to 3 minutes. Add onion, celery, white pepper, bay leaf and thyme. Sauté until onion is translucent. Add flour to make a roux. Stirring constantly, cook over low heat for 5 minutes, taking care not to brown.

Still stirring, slowly add clam juice, first using your cooking liquid and adding bottled juice to total about 5 cups. Stir constantly to avoid

lumps. Simmer for 10 minutes.
The soup will be very thick at this point so be careful it does not burn. Add potatoe and cook until tender. Add cream and clams and bring back to a boil. Season to taste.
Remove bay leaf and serve immediately.

Apple pie soup©

This thick soup is good hot or cold and is reminiscent of the filling in apple pie. Use tart apples, such as Granny Smith. The flavor will be enhanced by using freshly grated whole nutmeg.

Makes 8 to 10 servings.

6	large tart apples, peeled, cored and sliced
2	tablespoons fresh lemon juice
¼	cup sugar
¾	cup raisins
4	cups water
¼	cup honey or brown sugar
¼	teaspoon ground cloves
1	teaspoon freshly grated nutmeg
½	teaspoon cinnamon
¼	teaspoon ground allspice
2	tablespoons applejack (apple brandy), optional
1	cup cream, sour cream, yogurt or buttermilk

Peel, core and slice apples. Toss in lemon juice as you peel them. Place in a large pot with the sugar, raisins and water. Heat slowly to a boil. Cover, reduce heat to low and simmer 45 minutes to an hour, stirring now and then to prevent sticking. Apples should be soft.

Cool apples slightly, then puree in batches in a blender or food processor, or run through a food mill (for a chunkier soup) with the honey or brown sugar. Pour mixture into a large bowl. Stir in spices and remaining ingredients, adding choice of dairy product. Depending on the sweetness or tartness of your apples, your soup may need additional sweetening or lemon juice. An extra dash of nutmeg will draw out the flavors.

Serve garnished with an extra dollop of sour cream, whipped cream or yogurt and a dusting of nutmeg.

Gazpacho Allo Spiedo©

Makes 5 quarts.

1	medium cucumber, chopped
1	medium yellow squash,

Place cucumber, yellow squash, onion, carrot, peppers, zucchini and basil in bowl of

chopped
1 red onion, peeled and chopped
1 carrot, peeled and chopped
1 red bell pepper, chopped
1 yellow bell pepper, chopped
10 pepperoncini peppers, chopped
1 medium zucchini, chopped
20 fresh basil leaves
4 1-pound-6-ounce cans whole, peeled tomatoes in juice
1 tablespoon minced fresh garlic
4 tablespoons balsamic vinegar
Tabasco, to taste
1 tablespoon salt
1 tablespoon black pepper
1 tablespoon red wine

food processor (do in 2 or 3 batches) and mince. Place in a large container.
Place tomatoes in bowl of processor. Puree. Add to minced vegetables along with garlic, vinegar, Tabasco, salt, pepper and red wine. Refrigerate overnight for best flavor. Recipe can be divided in half or multiplied.

Jack Fry's white gazpacho©

6 cups chicken stock
2 cups dry white wine
½ cup white wine vinegar
1 white onion, finely chopped
4 green onions, sliced
3 cucumbers, peeled, seeded and diced
2 green bell peppers, diced
2 ribs celery, diced
3 heads Belgian endive, trimmed, quartered and thinly sliced (see note)
¼ cup olive oil
5 tablespoons chopped fresh dill

Makes 3 quarts.
In a saucepan combine chicken stock, wine and vinegar. Bring to a boil and simmer 10 minutes. Remove from heat, cool completely and refrigerate.
In a large bowl combine remaining ingredients. Add chilled chicken stock mixture. Stir until well-blended. Serve very cold.

Note: Belgian Endive is a small (about 6-inch-long) cigar-shaped head of cream-colored, tightly packed, slightly bitter leaves.

2   cloves garlic, minced
¼   teaspoon white pepper
    Salt to taste

The Feed Bag's chicken gumbo©

Makes 8 to 10 servings.

4 to 6   chicken breast halves
1   cup chopped celery
1   cup chopped green pepper
1   cup chopped onion
1   cup fresh or frozen okra
1   cup fresh, frozen or canned corn
1   tablespoon thyme
1   tablespoon oregano
1   teaspoon garlic powder
1   tablespoon Cajun Seasoning
    Dash of red hot sauce
1   tablespoon gumbo filé (mixed with water until gooey)
3   14.5-ounce cans diced tomatoes
2   cups uncooked rice

Place chicken breasts in a kettle with enough water to cover. Cook until done, about 20 minutes. Remove chicken to a platter. Strain chicken broth. Return broth to kettle. Add celery, green pepper, onion, okra, corn, thyme, oregano, garlic powder, Cajun Seasoning, hot sauce and gumbo filé paste. Bring to a rolling boil.
Chop chicken into bite-size pieces and return to kettle. Add tomatoes. Bring back to boil. If soup is too thick, add chicken broth.
Cook rice according to package directions.
To serve, place desired amount of rice in serving bowl. Add gumbo. Serve immediately.

Joe's O.K. Bayou gumbo©

Makes 10 to 12 servings.

½   cup butter or margarine
1   12-ounce package frozen okra
⅔   cup vegetable oil
¾   cup all-purpose flour
1   12-ounce package frozen chopped onion
5   ounces frozen chopped bell pepper

In a large, heavy pot melt the butter. Add okra and cook over medium heat until no longer stringy, about 15 to 20 minutes, stirring often.
In another large iron pot or skillet heat and stir oil and flour together to make a dark roux. When the mixture reaches a mahogany color, slowly stir in a cup of hot water. Stir until smooth. Add slightly thawed

3 quarts water
1 1 pound-6-ounce can tomatoes, chopped
1 teaspoon chopped garlic
2 teaspoons salt
½ teaspoon ground bay leaves
½ teaspoon black pepper
1 teaspoon Tabasco
¼ teaspoon crushed red pepper flakes
2 pounds chicken breasts, cut into chunks
2 pounds kielbasa sausage cut into ¼-inch slices

onion and bell pepper. Stir. Combine this and the okra mixture in the larger pot. Add water, tomatoes, garlic, salt, ground bay leaves, black pepper, Tabasco and red pepper flakes. Bring to a boil. Add chicken and kielbasa. Bring back to a boil. Lower heat and simmer 30 minutes. Serve over fluffy rice.

Casa Grisanti's minestrone©

1 cup diced carrot
1 cup diced zucchini
1 cup diced yellow squash
1 cup diced mushrooms
1 cup diced prosciutto ham
4 cups rich chicken broth
1 cup fusilli pasta
2 tablespoons basil pesto
2 tablespoons fresh Parmesan cheese
Sprinkling of fresh oregano
Sprinkling of fresh Italian parsley
Cracked pepper to taste
1 whole tomato (peeled, seeded and diced)

Makes 4 to 6 servings.
Combine carrot, zucchini, yellow squash, mushrooms, prosciutto and chicken broth. Bring to a boil. Simmer 15 minutes. Add pasta, pesto, cheese, oregano, parsley, cracked pepper and tomato. Remove from heat. Serve piping hot.

Equus mushroom fume©

1½ pounds onions
1½ pounds mushrooms

Makes about 2 quarts, or 4 to 6 servings.
Puree onions and mushrooms in food processor. In a large 1-gallon pot, heat oil.

2 tablespoons soy oil

1½ cups cabernet or Burgundy wine

2½ quarts beef stock

2 tablespoons thickening agent (arrowroot, roux or cornstarch)

2 cups heavy cream
Salt and pepper, to taste

Add pureed mixture of onions and mushrooms and sauté over medium heat until they are translucent, about 20 minutes. Add wine and reduce by half.

Add beef stock and reduce entire mixture by a third. Thicken soup to desired consistency (arrowroot, a roux or cornstarch are all acceptable thickening agents) and adjust seasoning. Strain out mushrooms and onions. Stir in the 2 cups cream, heat and serve.

Note: Arrowroot and cornstarch should be mixed with cold water before adding to hot soup. Arrowroot's thickening power is about twice that of wheat flour. Cornstarch has a better thickening power than wheat flour but will thin if cooked too long or stirred too vigorously.

When I prepare any of these thickeners, I start with 2 tablespoons thickening agent with 2 to 3 tablespoons cold water and add a little at a time, allowing some cooking time between each addition. For a roux, I use 2 tablespoons soft butter and 2 tablespoons flour blended into a paste. It is stirred into the hot mixture, small amounts at a time.

Kunz's Fourth and Market French onion soup©

Makes 4 servings.

1 large Spanish onion (peeled and sliced julienne style)

2 tablespoons butter

½ cup dry sherry

3 cups beef bouillon

½ teaspoon oregano

½ teaspoon sweet basil

1 bay leaf
Pinch of salt and white

In a 2-quart saucepan, sauté sliced onion in butter until onion has almost caramelized. Add dry sherry and let reduce by half. Add beef bouillon, oregano, sweet basil, bay leaf, salt, pepper and garlic. Simmer 30 to 45 minutes. When ready to serve, place soup in 4 oven-ready bowls. To each bowl add a garlic crouton and top with 1 slice provolone cheese. Sprinkle each with Parmesan. Put

pepper, to taste
Pinch of garlic

Topping:

4 slices provolone cheese
4 ounces Parmesan cheese
4 garlic croutons (see note)

bowls under broiler until cheese has melted over the sides and the top has browned. Serve immediately.

Note: No recipe was given for garlic croutons. I used 4 slices of day-old French bread. Spread lightly with butter and sprinkle with garlic seasoning. Place under broiler until golden.

Ursula's Bavarian Inn cream of onion soup©

¼ pound butter
3 large onions, chopped
½ cup all-purpose flour
1½ quarts veal stock (or beef), preferably homemade
2 egg yolks
½ cup sweet cream
White pepper
Nutmeg

Makes 8 servings.

In a large soup pot melt butter. Add onions. Sauté very slowly until deep golden but not brown. Sprinkle in flour. Blend and cook until flour is a deep golden color. Meanwhile, heat stock. Add hot stock to onions, stirring well to blend the flour. Simmer slowly 30 minutes.

Puree soup through sieve or in a blender. Reheat thoroughly and remove from heat. Beat egg yolks into cream. Add a few spoonsful of hot onion soup to cream mixture, then stir egg-cream mixture into soup pot. Keep warm but do not boil. Season to taste with white pepper and fresh grated nutmeg.

O'Charley's Restaurant's loaded potato soup©

1 gallon water
2½ pounds Idaho potatoes
1 tablespoon chicken base
2 to 3 teaspoons white pepper
2 teaspoon salt
2 to 3 teaspoons black pepper
2 10¾-ounce cans Cheddar cheese soup/sauce
1 pound margarine

Makes 1½ to 2 gallons.

In a large kettle, bring the water to a boil. Peel potatoes and cut into ½-inch cubes. Add to water, along with chicken base, white pepper, salt and black pepper. Cook about 12 minutes or until potatoes are about half-cooked.

Add the Cheddar cheese sauce. Simmer for 10 minutes.

In a saucepan, melt the margarine. Add the

1½ cups all-purpose flour
2 cups half-and-half
  Chives, bacon bits and
  parsley for garnish

flour to form a roux. Cook 3 to 4 minutes, stirring constantly. Stir into potato mixture. Simmer an additional 3 to 4 minutes.
Add half-and-half. Heat just to serving temperature – do not boil.
Pour into serving bowls and garnish with chives, bacon bits and parsley.

Garrett's German potato soup©

Makes 12 1-cup servings.

½ pound bacon, diced
1 cup thinly sliced green onions
½ cup all-purpose flour
2 quarts hot water
4 tablespoons ham base
1 tablespoon chicken base
3 tablespoons sugar
1 pound peeled potatoes, medium diced
¼ cup white vinegar
1 cup half-and-half
  Salt and white pepper to taste
  Chopped onions, diced hard-cooked eggs and bacon crumbles for garnish

In a heavy saucepan over medium heat cook bacon until lightly browned. Do not drain fat. Add green onions and sauté for 2 minutes. Next mix in flour, stirring until well-blended and evenly cooked, about 2 to 3 minutes.
Remove from heat. Add water, ham base, chicken base and sugar, mixing well. Stir in potatoes. Return to heat and bring to a boil. Reduce heat and simmer about 15 minutes or until potatoes are tender. Add vinegar and let simmer 2 minutes. Blend in half-and-half. Heat to simmering, stirring frequently. Season to taste with salt and white pepper.
Serve hot topped with any or all of the garnishes.

The Inn on Spring's sweet potato bisque©

Makes 6 to 8 servings.

1 pound peeled sweet potatoes
2 cups chicken broth
5 ounces canned pears in juice
½ cup mirepoix (⅓ carrot, ⅓ onion, ⅓ celery, chopped)
1 tablespoon butter
1 teaspoon dry thyme
2 cups heavy cream

In a large saucepan, combine sweet potatoes and broth. Bring to a boil. Reduce heat. Simmer 25 minutes or until potatoes are almost tender. Add pears, including juice, and cook until mushy.
Sauté mirepoix in butter until onion is translucent. Add mirepoix, thyme and half the cream to the sweet potato mixture. Pour

½ teaspoon chili paste	into the container of a blender or food processor. Puree.
	Return to saucepan and heat. Add remainder of cream and chili paste. Stir until well-blended. Heat and serve.

The Irish Rover's leek and potato soup©

Makes 5 quarts.

5 pounds potatoes, peeled and cubed	In a large pot, combine potatoes, leek, carrots, bay leaf, thyme, salt and white
1 leek, including green part, roughly chopped	pepper. Add chicken broth and enough water to cover vegetables. Bring to a boil.
1½ pounds carrots, peeled and cubed	Turn heat to simmer and cook until vegetables are soft.
1 bay leaf	In a separate pan, heat milk. When
4 teaspoons thyme	vegetables are soft, add milk to vegetable
1 tablespoon salt	mixture.
1 tablespoon white pepper	Make a roux, or paste, by combining the
2 14.5-ounce cans chicken broth	softened butter and flour. Stir into hot soup, a tablespoon at a time, allowing several
4 cups water, approximate	minutes of cooking between each addition
5 cups milk	until soup reaches desired thickness.
3 tablespoons butter, room temperature	
4 tablespoons all-purpose flour	

Kunz's seafood chowder©

Makes 2 quarts or 8 to 10 servings.

3 tablespoons butter, divided	In a large saucepan, heat 2 tablespoons of
⅓ medium onion, finely chopped	butter until melted. Add onion, carrot, celery, thyme and parsley. Cook until the onion is
⅓ cup grated carrot	transparent. Add seafood. Sauté lightly.
1½ ribs celery, finely chopped	Deglaze pan with wine or sherry.
Pinch of thyme	Add fish stock and bring to a rolling boil. Let
1 bunch parsley, chopped	simmer 15 minutes. Add hot cream. Season
1 pound seafood (4 ounces	with salt and white pepper. Simmer 10 to 15

each clams, white fish,
salmon and scallops or fish
of choice)

6	ounces white wine or sherry
6	cups shrimp stock, fish stock or clam juice
1 to 1½	cups heavy cream, heated
	Salt and white pepper, to taste

minutes. Before serving, add remaining 1 tablespoon butter that has been cut into small pieces.
Serve immediately.

Uptown Café's oyster-artichoke soup with Havarti cheese

Makes 12 servings.

2	tablespoons olive oil
2	shallots, finely chopped
¼	medium yellow onion, finely chopped
5	cloves garlic, finely chopped
1	cup dry white wine
3	cups clam juice
1½	chicken bouillon cubes
8	ounces artichoke hearts, quartered
6	cups whipping cream
¼	pound butter
1 to 1½	cups all-purpose flour
¾	pound Havarti cheese, grated
¼	cup Parmesan cheese, finely grated
1½	pounds select oysters, in juice
	White pepper to taste
	Freshly grated black pepper to taste
	Tabasco sauce to taste

Heat oil and sauté shallots, onion and garlic until translucent. Add white wine and flame off alcohol with match or let boil for a minute in order to allow alcohol to evaporate. Add clam juice and chicken bouillon.
In food processor, puree artichoke hearts. Add to clam juice mixture. Bring to medium boil. Add half the whipping cream and turn heat down to medium low.
Make a roux with the butter and flour. Let cook over low heat 3 to 4 minutes. Slowly add to clam juice mixture. Cook at low temperature 3 to 4 minutes.
Add Parmesan and Havarti cheeses to clam-juice mixture, stirring constantly.
Puree half the oysters in their juice. Rough chop remaining oysters. Turn soup off and add remaining cream. Allow to cool. Add oysters. Season with white and black pepper and Tabasco to taste.

The Café at the Louisville Antique Mall tomato dill soup©

Makes 10 to 12 servings.

¼ cup vegetable or olive oil
½ yellow onion, diced
2 ribs celery, chopped
1 to 2 cloves garlic, crushed
1 to 2 tablespoons dill weed, or to taste
2 8-ounce cans diced tomatoes
1 8-ounce can crushed tomatoes
1 46-ounce can V-8 juice
1 tablespoon soy sauce
1 tablespoon Worcestershire sauce
2 tablespoons sugar
1 tablespoon salt
1 tablespoon chicken base
1 quart water
2 cups heavy whipping cream

Heat oil in a large stockpot. Add onion, celery, garlic and dill weed. Sauté until onion is tender.
Place diced tomatoes in food processor. Add onion mixture. Process to puree. Return mixture to stockpot. Add crushed tomatoes, V-8 juice, soy sauce, Worcestershire sauce, sugar, salt, chicken base and water. Bring to a simmer. Cook 30 minutes.
Whisk cream into soup just before serving.

Clements Catering tomato-artichoke soup©

Makes 2 quarts.

4 tablespoons plus 1 stick unsalted butter, divided
2 small onions, finely diced
3 cups canned artichoke hearts, drained, rinsed and chopped
4 medium tomatoes, peeled and diced
3 tablespoons dried basil
1 bay leaf, broken
3 cups chicken broth
4 tablespoons tomato paste
2 cups heavy cream
½ cup all-purpose flour

Melt 4 tablespoons of the unsalted butter in a medium stockpot. Add diced onions. Sauté until translucent. Quickly add coarsely chopped artichoke hearts, diced tomatoes, basil and bay leaf. Adjust heat to medium and add chicken broth. Bring to a gentle simmer, stirring occasionally.
Add tomato paste and heavy cream. Return to a gentle simmer.
In a heavy saucepan melt remaining stick of butter. Add the flour and cook, stirring constantly, over low heat until the mixture just starts to brown. Let this roux cool and whisk it into the hot soup to thicken.

Remington's tortilla soup©

½ cup diced onion
½ cup diced celery
½ teaspoon minced garlic
2 tablespoons olive oil
6 ounces cooked lean chicken breast, diced
2 teaspoons jalapenos, seeds removed
2 teaspoons chopped cilantro
1 teaspoon cumin
1 teaspoon chili powder
½ teaspoon paprika
1 tablespoon tomato paste or 2 fresh tomatoes
6 cups chicken broth
4 to 6 small uncooked corn tortillas, torn into small pieces
Sour cream
Additional diced chicken
Avocado, diced
Tortilla chips, broken
Monterey Jack cheese

Makes about 6 servings.
Sauté diced onion, celery and garlic in olive oil. Add diced cooked chicken. Lower heat, cover pan and let mixture sweat. Slowly add jalapenos, cilantro, cumin, chili powder and paprika. Blend in tomato paste. Cook on medium heat for about 2 minutes. Add chicken broth.

Bring mixture to a boil. Add tortillas (the tortillas will dissolve as they cook). Stir occasionally. When soup has reached desired thickness, remove from heat; let cool. Puree in food processor. Strain.

To serve, reheat and serve hot topped with a tablespoon of sour cream, additional diced chicken, diced avocado, broken tortilla chips and Monterey Jack cheese.

Cunningham's vegetable soup©

1 8-ounce can sliced carrots, drained
1 8-ounce can green beans, drained
1 8-ounce can whole kernel corn, drained
1 8-ounce can peas, drained
1 8-ounce can whole tomatoes
1 8-ounce can tomato puree

Makes 4 to 5 quarts.
In a large stockpot, combine carrots, green beans, corn, peas, crushed tomatoes, tomato puree, celery, onion, chicken base, water and potatoes. Bring to a boil. Reduce heat and simmer until done, about 30 minutes after bringing to a boil.

1½ cups diced celery
1 medium onion, diced
4 tablespoons powdered
chicken base
1 gallon water
4 medium potatoes, peeled and
diced

Hasenour's beef barley soup©

Makes 6 to 10 servings.

2 cups uncooked beef cut into
½-inch cubes
3 cups peeled tomatoes
1 cup diced onion
1 cup diced celery
8 cups water
6 to 8 beef bouillon cubes
1 cup uncooked barley
¼ teaspoon black pepper
Salt, to taste

Place beef cubes and peeled tomatoes in a
large saucepan. Cook 45 minutes over low
heat. Add onion and celery. Stir. Add
water, bouillon cubes, barley, pepper and
salt to taste. Cook 1 hour.
Let soup rest for 25 minutes to thicken and
bring the flavors together. Warm soup
before serving.
   Note: If soup should become too thick,
use water and/or tomato juice to thin.

O'Charley's steakhouse vegetable soup©

Makes 8 to 10 servings.

2½ quarts water
1 package (¾-ounce) au jus
sauce mix
2 tablespoons beef base
3 cups canned diced tomatoes
1¼ pounds beef, cubed (or
leftover medium to rare prime
rib, trimmed of fat and gristle)
1 small yellow onion, diced
1 pound carrots, diced
6 to 7 ribs celery, diced
1¼ pounds fresh new potatoes,
skin on, diced

Place water, au jus and beef base in a large
kettle. Bring to a rolling boil. Reduce heat
and simmer for 10 minutes. Add diced
tomatoes.
While this is cooking, brown beef (if not using
leftovers) in a small amount of oil. Drain and
add to soup mixture.
In a kettle, bring about 1 quart of water to a
boil. Add onion, carrots and celery. Cook 6
minutes. Drain. Add to soup. Do the same
with the washed and diced potatoes – only
cook for 10 minutes. Add to soup. Add
pepper, Worcestershire sauce and Tabasco.

¾ teaspoon white pepper
2 tablespoons Worcestershire sauce
1 to 2 teaspoons Tabasco

Simmer until potatoes and meat are done.

Beef stew in red wine©

2 pounds beef (rump or eye of round), cut into 1½-inch pieces
Flour for dusting beef
Salt
1 tablespoon vegetable oil
1 medium onion, chopped coarsely
1 to 2 carrots, peeled and coarsely chopped
1 rib celery, coarsely chopped
2 tablespoons olive oil
3 to 4 tablespoons butter
2 tablespoons water
1 imported bay leaf
1 teaspoon crushed dried rosemary
½ to 1 teaspoon tomato paste
1 cup dry red wine
1 cup homemade beef or veal stock
1 pint box tiny pearl onions, peeled and sautéed in butter until they take on a little color
12 to 15 mushroom caps that have been sautéed in butter

Makes 6 to 8 servings.
Dust the meat with flour. Sprinkle with salt. Heat the vegetable oil in a large, heavy skillet. Sear the meat in the oil until it has browned on all sides.

In a heavy Dutch oven (not aluminum), sauté the onion, carrots and celery in the olive oil, 1 tablespoon of the butter and 2 tablespoons water. Cook over medium heat until the water evaporates and the vegetables are well coated with oil.

Add the browned meat to the pan with the seasoning vegetables. Add bay leaf, rosemary and tomato paste. Add red wine and broth to not quite cover the top of the meat. Cover the pan and place in preheated 325-degree oven for approximately 1½ hours or until the meat is tender. (The timing will depend upon the cut of meat.) Add the tiny onions 20 minutes before the stew is done.

Garnish the stew with the mushrooms, or fold the mushrooms into the stew 10 minutes before serving.

Camille Glenn's Old Piney beef stew©

I had to include this recipe - it's the best beef stew I've ever eaten. My good friend, Camille, died last year at the ripe old age of 100. She would be delighted to know that her beef stew recipe was being shared with all of you.

Makes 4 to 6 servings.

4 to 5	tablespoons rendered beef suet or vegetable oil
3 to 4	pounds well-marbled beef (short ribs, rump, brisket or chuck), cut into 2-inch pieces
	Salt and pepper as needed
1	onion
2	imported bay leaves
2	ribs celery
1	teaspoon thyme
3	sprigs parsley
2 to 2½	cups beef stock or water
2	tablespoons soft butter creamed with 2 tablespoons all-purpose flour

Vegetables:

6	small fresh carrots (peeled and cut in 2-inch lengths)
12	tiny onions (peeled)
3	ribs celery (cut in 2-inch lengths)
3	Idaho potatoes (peeled and cut in halves or quarters)
	Salt and freshly ground black pepper
	Chopped parsley

Heat 4 tablespoons fat in a heavy skillet. Add a few pieces of meat at a time, allowing them to brown all over. (If too many pieces of meat are added at a time, the beef will stew instead of brown.) Season the meat with salt and pepper as it browns and toss it into a Dutch oven that is not too large.

Allow just enough room for the vegetables. Add onion, bay leaves, celery, thyme and parsley sprigs. Cover with 1½ cups of the beef stock or water. Bring the liquid to a boil on top of the stove. Cover and place in a preheated 325-degree oven for 1½ to 1¾ hours in all, depending upon the tenderness of the meat.

When the fat rises to the top, skim it off and baste the meat several times with the pan juices.

From time to time check the broth or liquid, adding more if it is needed or reducing it on top of the stove if it needs to thicken. The liquid should not cover the meat at any time. Continue to skim and baste to keep the top of the meat moist.

Blend the butter and flour for thickening. After about 1¼ hours, when the meat cubes have begun to get tender, add the butter and flour in one corner of the pan, whisking it into the liquid so it will not lump. Discard seasoning vegetables (onion and celery), bay leaves and parsley sprigs.

Add the other vegetables, placing them in between the meat and under the broth. The broth should be a good brown color by this time. Allow the vegetables to cook until tender but not mushy, about 25 to 30 minutes. Keep basting the vegetables so they will absorb the flavors of the stock.

Again, never stir the stew. Allow the vegetables to stand out separately and not be mushy looking.

Taste for salt. Give the stew a final seasoning of pepper. Sprinkle with chopped parsley.

Baptist Hospital East beef stew©

Makes 6 to 8 servings.

2 to 3	tablespoons vegetable oil
3	pounds raw beef tips, not stew meat
1	14.5-ounce can crushed tomatoes
¾	cup diced onion
½	teaspoon pepper
2	teaspoons Worcestershire sauce
3½	cups hot water
2	tablespoons beef base
¼	teaspoon crushed rosemary
¼	teaspoon garlic powder
1	bay leaf (discard before serving)
1	10-ounce package frozen carrot slices
1	10-ounce package frozen peas
½	cup diced celery
1	cup cold water
2	tablespoons all-purpose flour
1	15-ounce can potatoes, diced

Heat oil in a Dutch oven. Add beef. Cook over high heat, stirring frequently until beef is well-browned. Add tomatoes, onion, pepper, Worcestershire sauce, hot water, beef base, rosemary, garlic powder and bay leaf. Simmer, covered, until meat is tender, about one hour. Add carrots, peas and celery. Simmer until vegetables are tender.

Mix together the cold water and flour. Stir to form lump-free mixture. Add to meat and vegetables, stirring constantly. Cook 5 minutes or until mixture has thickened. Add diced potatoes. Heat thoroughly. Remove bay leaf.

Salads and Salad Dressings

Rooftop's four-lettuce salad©

Makes 6 to 8 servings.

1	head chicory lettuce
1	head romaine lettuce
1	head escarole lettuce
1	head iceberg lettuce
1	pound mushrooms
1	medium zucchini squash
6	hard-boiled eggs
12	cherry tomatoes
1 to 2	11-ounce cans mandarin orange sections
1	pound baby shrimp

Rooftop house dressing:

½	cup white vinegar
⅔	cup mayonnaise
2	tablespoons French mustard
2	tablespoons granulated sugar
2	teaspoons finely chopped onion
2	teaspoons monosodium glutamate (MSG)
1	teaspoon salt
2	cups soybean or vegetable salad oil
2	teaspoons chopped parsley
3	tablespoons orange-blossom honey

Clean and wash lettuces. Pat dry or spin dry in salad spinner.
Clean and slice mushrooms. Wash and dice zucchini; it does not have to be peeled.
Cook eggs. When cool, peel and slice.
Wash and slice tomatoes in half. Drain orange sections.
Cook shrimp, if necessary. Peel and refrigerate till ready to use.
When ready to serve combine a mixture of lettuces on each salad plate. Add several slices of mushroom, squash, egg, tomato, orange and shrimp.
Top with house dressing or pass for each person to use as desired.
To make dressing: In a food processor or blender combine vinegar, mayonnaise and mustard. Blend till smooth. Add sugar, onion, MSG and salt.
With blender running, very slowly add salad oil until well-blended. Using a long-handle spoon, stir in parsley and honey.
Refrigerate till ready to use.
Makes 4 cups.

Back Home's corn bread salad©

Makes 6 servings.

12	corn muffins
2	cups mayonnaise
1	large green pepper, chopped

In a large bowl, break up corn muffins. Add mayonnaise, green pepper, onion and celery.
Fold in tomatoes and salt and pepper to

1   medium onion, chopped
½   cup chopped celery
2   tomatoes, diced
    Salt and pepper to taste
¼   pound bacon, optional

Azalea's pecan salad©

2   poached apples (recipe follows)
1½   pounds mesclun greens (mixture of baby greens)
1¼   cups champagne basil vinaigrette (recipe follows)
12   ounces candied pecans (recipe follows)
9   ounces Stilton bleu cheese

Poached apples:
2   Granny Smith apples
2   cups apple juice
2   cups water
⅓   cup brown sugar
2   whole cloves

Champagne basil vinaigrette:
3   tablespoons minced shallots
2   tablespoons lemon juice
2   egg yolks
2   tablespoons sugar
¼   cup champagne vinegar
¼   cup olive oil
½   cup vegetable oil
2   teaspoons chopped fresh basil
¼   teaspoon chopped fresh oregano
    Salt and pepper, to taste

Candied pecans:

taste. Cut bacon into small pieces. Fry until crisp. Drain. Sprinkle over top of salad.

Makes 6 servings.
To make salad: When ready to serve, divide apple slices among six plates, fanning them on the side of the plate. Mix the greens with the vinaigrette. Divide it among the plates, crunching it together to form a mound with some height. Top with pecans and Stilton bleu cheese, allowing some to fall onto the plate.
To poach apples: Peel and core the apples. Slice into wedges. In a saucepan combine remaining ingredients. Add apples. Bring mixture to 170 degrees (warm, but not boiling). Poach until apples are fork tender. Strain the apples from the liquid and shock in ice water. (Poaching liquid can be reserved for another time.)
Makes 2 cups.
To make vinaigrette: Place shallots and lemon juice in food processor and puree. Add egg yolks, sugar and vinegar. With processor running, very slowly add oils so they emulsify. Stir in basil and oregano. Season to taste with salt and pepper. Makes 1¼ cups.
To make pecans: Heat oven to 350 degrees. Place pecans in a shallow pan. Place in oven just to heat, about 5 minutes. When warm, remove from oven and toss them in the egg white. Return to oven and

1 cup pecans
1 egg white
¼ cup granulated sugar

bake 5 minutes. Remove from oven and toss in sugar. Return to oven until sugar coats pecans but does not burn. Immediately upon removing pecans from oven, sprinkle with additional sugar. Makes 1 cup.

The Upper Crust cornucopia salad with poppy seed dressing©

Wash, drain and tear lettuce into bite-size pieces. Head lettuce, leaf, Romaine and red leaf are just a few types of lettuce that may be used. The amount depends on the number of people you are serving.

Cut into bite-size pieces cantaloupe, pineapple and strawberries. Wash and stem red seedless grapes. Allow 2 to 3 pieces of each fruit per person.

Toss lettuce in bowl. Sprinkle fruit on top.

At this point you can add shredded Cheddar cheese, raisins and pecans if you desire. Leave the cheese off if your main dish includes lots of cheese. Omit any other items after evaluating your menu.

The salad is truly a cornucopia of fruits and vegetables because you can also add slivers of carrot, chunks of cucumber, red cabbage, sweet peas, bean sprouts or any other fresh vegetable. It's the following dressing that makes the salad.

The Upper Crust poppy seed dressing©

Makes 1⅓ cups.

⅓ cup honey
¼ cup red wine vinegar
1 teaspoon minced onion
1 teaspoon dry mustard
¾ cup vegetable oil
2 tablespoons poppy seed

Combine honey, red wine vinegar, onion and mustard in container of electric blender. Process on low and gradually add oil. After thoroughly blended, add poppy seeds and blend until mixed through. Chill. Stir well before serving.

Kunz's asparagus vinaigrette©

Makes 4 servings.

Vinaigrette dressing:
1 cup white vinegar
¼ cup fresh lemon juice
1 clove fresh garlic, finely chopped
½ pimento, finely diced

To make vinaigrette: Combine vinegar, lemon juice, garlic, pimento, basil, salt, white pepper and onions. Beat with a whisk, slowly adding olive oil. Blend thoroughly after each addition of oil. Makes 1½ to 2 cups.

⅛ cup fresh basil, finely diced
Salt and white pepper, to
taste
4 green onions, finely diced
2 cups olive oil
Salad:
24 fresh asparagus spears
4 romaine leaves
4 radicchio leaves
1 head iceberg lettuce
½ pint alfalfa sprouts
4 cherry tomatoes

To make salad: Four to 6 hours before serving, clean asparagus. Blanch in boiling, salted water until half-cooked. Immediately drop into ice water to stop cooking. Drain and add asparagus to vinaigrette. Marinate 4 to 6 hours.

To serve salad, arrange romaine and radicchio at the top of a salad plate. Slice iceberg lettuce into ¼-inch slabs. Arrange at the bottom of the plate. Place 6 asparagus spears on each plate on top of iceberg lettuce, fanning them out. Place alfalfa sprouts on each side. Slice cherry tomato in half and place on top of sprouts. Ladle vinaigrette over the top.

Derby Dinner Playhouse's broccoli-cauliflower salad©

½ pound bacon, fried, drained
and crumbled
1 red onion, chopped
1 head broccoli, cut up
½ head cauliflower
¼ cup sunflower seeds
¼ cup raisins, optional
1 cup Hellmann's mayonnaise
2 tablespoons vinegar
½ cup sugar

Makes 6 to 8 servings.

Fry the bacon, drain on paper towels and break into bits. Chop the onion. Wash and divide the broccoli and cauliflower into florets. Combine in a large bowl with the sunflower seeds and raisins. Toss to combine. Set aside.

In a separate bowl combine the mayonnaise, vinegar and sugar. Stir to blend. Pour over broccoli-cauliflower mixture. Toss to combine thoroughly.

O'Callaghan's broccoli salad©

Dressing:
2 large garlic cloves, minced
1 2-ounce can anchovy fillets,
drained and patted dry
6 tablespoons olive oil
2 tablespoons red wine vinegar
1⅓ cups homemade mayonnaise

Makes 8 to 10 servings.

To make dressing: Puree garlic and anchovies. Slowly add oil and vinegar. Blend until smooth. Add mayonnaise and bleu cheese. Add salt and pepper to taste. Blend well. Fold in capers. Refrigerate. Makes about 2½ cups.

To make salad: Steam broccoli in boiling

(or Hellman's)
6 tablespoons (about 3 ounces) Danish bleu cheese
Salt and freshly ground pepper
2 tablespoons small capers, drained

Salad:
3 pounds broccoli, washed and trimmed to 2½-inch spears
1 medium red onion, thinly sliced
2 hard-boiled eggs, peeled and chopped fine
24 small black olives
1 small red sweet pepper cut into ⅛ inch strips

water for 5 to 8 minutes. Remove and rinse with cold water. Drain and let cool.

To serve, arrange broccoli on tray. Arrange sliced red onion on top of broccoli. Pour chilled dressing over top. Sprinkle with chopped eggs, black olives and arrange red pepper strips over all. Refrigerate till ready to serve.

Fresh broccoli-mandarin salad

1 egg plus 1 egg yolk, lightly beaten
¼ cup granulated sugar
1½ teaspoons cornstarch
1 teaspoon dry mustard
¼ cup water
¼ cup tarragon wine vinegar
3 tablespoons softened margarine
½ cup mayonnaise
4 cups fresh broccoli florets
6 slices bacon, cooked and crumbled
2 cups fresh sliced mushrooms
½ cup slivered almonds, toasted
1 11-ounce can mandarin

Makes 10 to 12 servings.
In top of double boiler, whisk together egg, egg yolk, sugar, cornstarch and mustard. Combine water and vinegar. Slowly pour into egg mixture, whisking constantly. Place over hot water and cook, stirring constantly, until the mixture thickens. Remove from heat. Stir in margarine and mayonnaise. Chill. Toss dressing with remaining ingredients in serving bowl.
   Note: Dressing may be prepared a day or 2 in advance.

oranges, drained
½ cup raisins
½ large red onion, sliced

Vincenzo's Caesar salad©

2 anchovy fillets, minced
1 teaspoon garlic, minced
2 dashes Tabasco
Pinch of pepper
Juice of 1 lemon
1 tablespoon red wine vinegar
4 to 5 tablespoons olive oil
Romaine lettuce
Croutons, for garnish
Reggiano Parmigiano cheese,
for garnish

Makes 2 salads.
Make a paste of anchovies, garlic, Tabasco, pepper and lemon juice. Whisk in vinegar and oil to make a dressing. Toss with romaine lettuce. Plate the salads. Garnish with croutons and grated cheese.

Jack Fry's chicken Caesar salad©

1 head romaine lettuce, washed and broken into bite-size pieces
2 whole roasted red peppers, julienned
2 tablespoons toasted pine nuts
1½ cups garlic croutons
8 slices bacon, chopped and cooked
1 to 1¼ cups Caesar dressing (recipe follows)
2 whole grilled chicken breasts, cut into ½-inch strips
½ white onion sliced into thin rings, dredged in flour and

Makes 4 servings.
Toss lettuce with roasted peppers, toasted pine nuts, croutons, bacon and Caesar dressing to coat. Place lettuce mixture on individual plates. Arrange grilled chicken strips on top. Garnish the center of each salad with a mound of deep-fried onion rings.
  Note: To toast pine nuts, place nuts in a pie pan. Heat oven to 350 degrees. Bake nuts until golden. Watch carefully because they burn easily.
To roast peppers, place under broiler. When peppers have blistered on all sides remove from broiler. Let cool. Remove skins.
To make dressing: In a large bowl, combine vinegar, garlic, anchovy paste, Worcestershire sauce, Tabasco and black

deep-fried
Caesar dressing:
- ½ cup red wine vinegar
- 1½ teaspoons chopped garlic
- 1 tablespoon anchovy paste
- 2 tablespoons Worcestershire sauce
- 1 dash Tabasco
- Cracked black pepper to taste
- 2 cups salad oil

pepper. Slowly whisk in oil. Store in refrigerator.
Makes 2½ cups.

Jack Fry's warm Brie salad©

Makes 4 servings.

Dressing:
- ¾ teaspoon minced garlic
- ¾ teaspoon dried basil
- 2 tablespoons red wine vinegar
- 1 tablespoon Dijon mustard
- ¾ teaspoon grain mustard
- ½ cup olive oil
- ¼ cup salad oil

Salad:
- Kentucky Bibb lettuce
- 8 ounces Brie (2 ounces per salad)
- ½ cup toasted sliced almonds (see note)

To make dressing: Whisk together garlic, basil, vinegar and mustards. While whisking, slowly add olive oil and salad oil.

To make salad: Toss lettuce with 2 tablespoons dressing (you will have dressing left over). Arrange lettuce on a serving dish. Microwave Brie just to soften, about 45 seconds.

Place Brie in center of lettuce. Sprinkle with toasted almonds. Serve immediately.

Note: To toast almonds, spread them in a shallow pan. Bake in a hot, 350-degree oven until golden, about 10 minutes. Watch carefully; nuts burn quickly.

The Hillside Inn's fried chicken salad©

This is a great salad to use as an entrée.

Makes 8 servings.

- 2 cups all-purpose flour
- 1 teaspoon salt
- 1 teaspoon pepper
- 1 teaspoon paprika
- ½ teaspoon cayenne pepper

To make salad: Combine flour, salt, pepper, paprika and cayenne pepper. Mix well. Pound each chicken breast flat. Dip in buttermilk and then roll in flour mixture. Deep fry until done. Set aside.

4 whole boneless chicken
   breasts
1 cup buttermilk
   Jalapeno honey dressing
   (recipe follows)
   Lettuce, shredded
   Mushrooms, sliced
   Green pepper, diced
   Green onions, diced
   Tomato wedges

Jalapeno honey dressing:
2 cups mayonnaise
6 tablespoons honey
1 tablespoon finely diced
   jalapeno pepper, or to taste
   Salt and pepper, to taste

When ready to serve, prepare a bed of shredded lettuce. Cut fried chicken breasts into a few slices. Arrange on lettuce. Sprinkle with sliced mushrooms, diced green pepper and green onions. Garnish with tomato wedges. Pour the honey dressing over the salad or serve separately in a small container.

To make dressing: Combine ingredients, stirring until well-blended. Let stand for at least 1 hour before serving.

Curried chicken salad©

2 cups cooked chicken, diced
1 8-ounce can water chestnuts,
   drained and chopped
½ pound seedless grapes
½ cup chopped celery
½ cup (2-ounce package)
   slivered almonds
¾ cup low-calorie mayonnaise
1 teaspoon curry powder
1½ teaspoons soy sauce
2 teaspoons lemon juice
1 11-ounce can mandarin
   oranges, drained

Makes 4 servings.

Mix together chicken, water chestnuts, grapes, celery and almonds. Combine mayonnaise, curry powder, soy sauce and lemon juice. Stir until well-blended. Add mandarin oranges and mayonnaise mixture to the chicken. Chill until ready to serve.

Bristol Bar and Grille's grilled chicken and spinach salad©

Makes 6 salads.

6	5-ounce boneless chicken breasts cut into strips
4 to 6	tablespoons butter
¾	pound mushrooms, sliced
1	pound spinach leaves
1	8-ounce can sliced water chestnuts
1	large red bell pepper, sliced
1	large red onion, sliced

Soy-bacon dressing:

1	cup bacon grease
½	cup soy sauce
¾	cup rice vinegar
½	cup mirin rice wine
4	tablespoons brown sugar
2 to 3	tablespoons cornstarch

To make salad: In a skillet, sauté cut-up chicken breasts in butter. Remove breasts from pan and set aside.

Add mushrooms to skillet. Sauté till golden. Set aside.

To serve, divide cleaned spinach leaves among 6 platters. Place water chestnuts, bell pepper and chicken on top of leaves. Place sautéed mushrooms around edge of platters. Place red onion on top, and top each platter with 2 ounces of dressing.

To make dressing: Combine bacon grease, soy sauce, rice vinegar and rice wine. Bring to simmer. Combine brown sugar and cornstarch. Add to bacon grease mixture. Cook just until dressing starts to thicken. Serve hot over spinach salad.

The Café at the Louisville Antique Mall's chicken salad©

Makes 10 to 12 servings.

2	teaspoons salt
½	teaspoon ground black pepper
½	teaspoon ground white pepper
½	teaspoon thyme
½	teaspoon basil
½	teaspoon parsley
½	cup vegetable oil
3	pounds boneless, skinless chicken breasts
1	cup chopped celery, small dice
2	Gala apples, medium size, chopped
⅓	cup chopped pecans

Mix salt, black pepper, white pepper, thyme, basil and parsley with vegetable oil. Coat chicken breasts with seasoned oil mix and bake in a 350-degree oven until done. Chill. When ready to mix salad, cut chicken breasts in ½-inch dice. In a large bowl, mix chicken, celery, apples and pecans. In a separate bowl, combine mayonnaise, white pepper, sugar, salt and cider vinegar. Stir to blend thoroughly. Add to chicken mixture. Chill for 2 hours before serving.

1⅓ cups mayonnaise
¼ teaspoon white pepper
1 teaspoon sugar
1 teaspoon salt
2 teaspoons cider vinegar

Crescent House hot chicken salad©

This was the most popular entrée at the Crescent House Tea Room. It is easy to prepare and freezes extremely well.

3 cups cooked chicken, cubed
1½ cups celery, chopped
¾ cup slivered almonds
1 8-ounce can sliced water chestnuts
½ teaspoon salt
2 teaspoons grated onion
3 tablespoons lemon juice
1½ cups mayonnaise
1 10¾-ounce can condensed cream of chicken soup
¾ cup grated sharp Cheddar cheese
1½ cups crushed potato chips (about 4 ounces)

Makes 8 servings.
Combine everything but the cheese and potato chips in a greased 9-by-13-by-2-inch casserole dish. Combine cheese and crushed potato chips and sprinkle on top. Bake in a preheated 325-degree oven for 45 minutes, or until lightly browned.

Grapevine Pantry's Oriental salad©

6 to 8 boneless chicken breasts
1 cup teriyaki marinade and sauce
3 tablespoons butter, margarine or vegetable oil
1 large head iceberg lettuce, torn into bite-size pieces
1 pound fresh spinach, chopped
1 small head red cabbage,

Makes 6 to 8 servings.
To make salad: Cut chicken into ½-inch strips and marinate in teriyaki sauce for at least 30 minutes. When ready to cook, heat butter in large skillet. Add chicken strips and cook until done, 12 to 15 minutes. Set aside. While chicken is cooking, clean and prepare lettuce, spinach, red cabbage, mushrooms, red onion and red pepper. Layer in a large salad bowl or distribute among serving plates. Top with mandarin orange segments,

shredded
½   pound mushrooms, sliced
1   small red onion, sliced into
    rings
1   red pepper, sliced into rings
1   11-ounce can mandarin
    orange segments
1   cup toasted slivered almonds
1 or 2   3-ounce cans chow mein
    noodles

Poppy seed dressing:
½   cup vinegar
1   cup sugar
1½ teaspoons Dijon mustard
2   cups vegetable oil
2   tablespoons poppy seeds

almonds, chow mein noodles and cooked chicken. Serve with poppy seed dressing.

To make dressing: Combine vinegar, sugar and mustard in blender. Process on low while gradually adding oil. After thoroughly blending, add poppy seeds and stir until mixed through. Chill.

Uptown Café's wilted spinach salad with grilled chicken breasts©

Chicken:
8   8-ounce chicken breasts
2   cups olive oil
½   cup soy sauce
¼   teaspoon ground ginger or 1
    teaspoon fresh ginger,
    minced
¼   cup sherry

Dressing:
1   cup olive oil
⅓   cup soy sauce
¼   cup lemon juice, fresh
1   teaspoon chopped fresh
    garlic
¼   teaspoon black pepper,
    freshly ground

Salad Ingredients:
1   pound fresh spinach, washed
    and stemmed

Makes 8 servings.

To prepare chicken: Remove skin and bone from chicken breasts. Place in a large bowl. Combine olive oil, soy sauce, ginger and sherry. Pour over chicken. Marinate overnight.

Remove chicken from marinade; grill 3 to 4 minutes on each side. Slice and set aside..

To make dressing: In a skillet, combine olive oil, soy sauce, lemon juice, garlic and black pepper. Heat.

To assemble salad: Divide spinach among 8 serving plates. Top with sliced chicken. Sprinkle each salad with water chestnuts and bacon. Place 2 to 4 quarters of egg on each plate. Top with hot dressing.

1   8-ounce can water chestnuts, sliced
8   strips bacon, fried crisp and crumbled
4 to 8   hard boiled eggs, quartered

Turkey salad for a crowd©

1	8-pound turkey breast
2	tablespoons salt
	Half a small onion
1	handful celery leaves
2	bay leaves
7 to 8	peppercorns
⅓	lemon
6	cups coarsely chopped celery
2½	cups coarsely chopped pecans
4 to 5	cups Hellman's mayonnaise
1	tablespoon finely chopped onion
¼	teaspoon cayenne pepper
3	tablespoons yellow mustard
	Juice of half lemon
	Salt to taste

Makes 24 servings.

To prepare turkey: Thaw and wash turkey breast. Place in a large kettle and cover with cold water. Add salt, onion, celery leaves, bay leaves, peppercorns and the piece of lemon. Simmer until very tender, 2½ to 3 hours. Cool for an hour in the cooking water. Drain.

To prepare salad: When turkey is cool enough to handle, chop meat coarsely and place in a huge bowl or container large enough to mix all the ingredients of the salad. Add celery and pecans.

In a separate bowl, combine the mayonnaise, onion, cayenne, mustard and lemon juice. Blend well and add to the turkey. A pair of clean hands is probably the best way to accomplish the mixing, which should be thorough. Taste and add salt as needed. Select a bowl large enough to hold all the salad. Oil the bowl and line it with plastic wrap, completely covering inside of bowl. Pack turkey salad into bowl, cover with plastic wrap or foil. Refrigerate overnight.

To serve: Select a platter large enough to accommodate the salad mold plus the garnish. Remove cover from top of salad, center the platter on top of it, then turn the whole thing over carefully. The salad will drop right out. Pull off plastic wrap and garnish as desired

Afro-German Tea Room's coleslaw©

1 medium head cabbage, shredded
1 medium red onion, thinly sliced
2 carrots, grated on the large hole side of grater
1 tablespoon sugar
1 teaspoon salt, or to taste
  Pepper to taste
2 teaspoons dill weed
1 tablespoon red wine vinegar
1½ cups mayonnaise
¾ cup sour cream

Makes 8 to 10 servings.
Prepare vegetables and toss in a large bowl. Combine remaining ingredients and pour over vegetables. Stir until well-blended. Cover and refrigerate until ready to use.

Huber's German slaw©

1 medium cabbage (3 to 3½ pounds) chopped
2 ribs celery, chopped
½ carrot, chopped
1 small onion, chopped
5 strips bacon, fried crisp
2 tablespoons oil
1 cup vinegar
1 cup sugar
2 tablespoons water
1 teaspoon salt
¼ teaspoon black pepper
¼ teaspoon celery seeds

Makes 8 to 10 servings.
Wash and chop cabbage, celery, carrot and onion. Set aside in a large bowl.
Fry bacon until crisp. Drain and crumble.
Add bacon and oil to chopped vegetables. In a saucepan, heat vinegar, sugar, water, salt, pepper and celery seeds until sugar dissolves. When cool, add to chopped vegetables.

Luby's Cafeteria German bacon slaw©

1½ pounds shredded cabbage
½ cup diced celery
½ cup diced bell pepper
½ cup crisply cooked and

Makes 8 to 10 servings.
In a large bowl combine all ingredients. Refrigerate until ready to serve.

broken up bacon
½ cup sliced green onions
1 cup mayonnaise
Salt, pepper and garlic
powder to taste

Cobb salad©

½ head iceberg lettuce
½ bunch watercress
1 small bunch curly endive
½ head romaine
2 tablespoons minced chives
2 medium tomatoes, peeled, seeded and diced
1 whole chicken breast, cooked, boned, skinned and diced
6 slices bacon, cooked and diced
1 avocado, peeled and diced
3 hard-boiled eggs, diced
½ cup Roquefort, crumbled

Special French dressing:
¼ cup water
¼ cup red wine vinegar
¼ teaspoon sugar
1½ teaspoons lemon juice
½ teaspoon salt
½ teaspoon black pepper
½ teaspoon Worcestershire sauce
¾ teaspoon dry mustard
½ clove garlic, minced
¼ cup olive oil
¾ cup vegetable oil

To make salad: Chop lettuce, watercress, endive and romaine in very fine pieces using knife or food processor. Mix together in one large wide bowl or individual wide shallow bowls. Add chives.

Arrange tomatoes, chicken, bacon, avocado and eggs in narrow strips or wedges across top of greens. Sprinkle with cheese. Chill. At serving time, pass the dressing.

To make dressing: Combine ingredients. Mix thoroughly and chill. Shake well before using.

Makes about 1½ cups.

Jack Fry's cucumber tomato salad with dill vinaigrette

Cucumber tomato salad:
- 2 cucumbers, sliced thin
- Sugar
- 1 red onion, sliced
- Salt
- 1 tomato, diced
- 1 cup mayonnaise

Dill vinaigrette:
- 2 tablespoons chopped dill
- 2 tablespoons sugar
- 2 tablespoons Dijon mustard
- 2 tablespoons red wine vinegar
- 1 cup olive oil
- Salt and pepper, to taste

Makes 2 to 4 servings.

To make salad: After slicing cucumbers, drizzle with sugar and allow to drain for 15 minutes. Sprinkle sliced onion with salt and allow to drain 15 minutes. After draining, combine cucumbers, onion and tomato. Coat with mayonnaise. Chill until ready to serve.

To make vinaigrette: Combine dill, sugar, mustard and vinegar. While whisking, slowly add oil. Season to taste with salt and pepper. Place cucumber-tomato salad on plate. Drizzle with dill vinaigrette. Makes about 1¼ cups.

   Note: This is excellent topped with medium-rare grilled salmon.

Porcini apple salad with hot apple dressing©

Salad:
- 2 ounces baby lettuce blend
- 4 ounces saga blue cheese
- 4 ounces toasted walnuts
- 1 apple, cored and chopped

Hot apple dressing:
- 1¼ cups apple cider or apple juice
- 2 tablespoons malt vinegar
- 2 tablespoons sugar
- ⅛ teaspoon nutmeg
- ⅛ teaspoon allspice
- ½ teaspoon cinnamon
- ½ teaspoon ginger
- Pinch ground cloves
- 2 teaspoons cornstarch

Makes 4 servings.

To make salad: In a large stainless steel bowl gently toss baby lettuce, saga blue cheese, toasted walnuts and chopped apples. Divide among 4 plates.

To make dressing: In a saucepan combine 1 cup apple cider, malt vinegar, sugar, nutmeg, allspice, cinnamon, ginger and cloves. Bring to a boil.

Combine cornstarch with remaining ¼ cup apple cider or juice to make a slurry. Add to boiling mixture. Return to boil and cook 2 minutes. Remove from heat and let sit about 5 minutes until slightly cooled.

Just before serving, top each salad with about 6 tablespoons of hot apple dressing. Makes about 1½ cups dressing.

Blue Dog Bakery and Café's wheat-berry salad©

Makes 10 to 12 servings.

3 cups wheat berries (see note)
2 cups (10 ounces) frozen lima beans
¼ cup walnut oil
¾ cup canola oil
⅛ to ¼ cup sherry vinegar
1 cup dried cranberries or currants
1 cup walnuts, chopped
2 cups diced celery
1 cup chopped scallions
Salt and pepper, to taste

In a large saucepan cover berries with water. Cook al dente. Drain. Cook lima beans al dente. Drain. Combine walnut oil, canola oil and vinegar. Add to warm berries and lima beans. Toss. Soften dried fruit by soaking in water, if needed. When bean mixture has cooled, add dried fruit, walnuts, celery and scallions. Toss. Season to taste with salt and pepper.

Note: Wheat berry is another name for the whole wheat kernel.

Ethel's overnight vegetable salad

Makes 8 to 10 servings.

1 15-ounce can Lesueur tiny green peas, drained
1 15.25-ounce can white shoe peg corn, drained
1 14.5-ounce can French-style green beans, drained
1 medium onion, diced
¾ cup diced celery
1 2-ounce jar diced pimento, drained
½ cup vegetable oil
½ cup white vinegar
¾ cup sugar
½ teaspoon salt
½ teaspoon pepper

In a large bowl, combine peas, corn, green beans, onion, celery and pimento. Set aside. In a saucepan combine oil, vinegar, sugar, salt and pepper. Heat just until sugar dissolves. Pour over vegetables. Stir. Cover and refrigerate 6 to 8 hours or overnight before serving.

Norma Wessling's German potato salad

Makes 8 to 10 servings.

4	pounds potatoes
1	pound bacon
1	onion, chopped
	All-purpose flour
¼	cup water
¾	cup white vinegar
½ to 1	cup sugar, or to taste
	Salt and pepper, to taste

Place potatoes in a pan with water to cover. Bring to a boil. Cook until potatoes are tender. Drain. When cool enough to handle, peel and slice.

While potatoes are cooking, dice bacon into ¼-inch pieces. Fry until crisp. Remove bacon from drippings and set aside. Cook onion in the drippings until translucent. Add enough flour to partially absorb drippings. Add water, vinegar and sugar to taste. Cook until thick. Season with salt and pepper. Stir. Pour over potatoes. Stir to combine. Sprinkle bacon bits over top. Serve warm – excellent.

Evelyn Kleinhelter's German potato salad©

Makes 10 to 12 servings.

6	pounds potatoes
1	large onion, chopped
3	ribs celery, diced
¼	cup chopped pimento, drained
1	pound bacon, diced
	Bacon drippings (from fried, diced bacon)
1⅔	cups white vinegar
1½	cups water
4	eggs
½	cup all-purpose flour
1½	cups sugar
	Salt and pepper, to taste

Place potatoes in a large pan. Cover with water. Bring to a boil and cook until potatoes are tender. When cool enough to handle, peel and cut potatoes into thin slices. Place in a large serving bowl along with chopped onion, celery and pimento.

In a skillet, fry diced bacon until crisp. Remove bacon from skillet and drain on paper towels. Add to potato mixture.

To the bacon drippings, add vinegar and 1 cup water. Beat eggs and add remaining ½ cup water and flour to make a thickening. Add to vinegar mixture and cook over medium-high heat until thickened. Add sugar and stir until dissolved. Season to taste with salt and pepper. Pour over hot potatoes; mix thoroughly. Serve warm.

Alice Colombo's version of Stewart's potato salad©

5 large Idaho potatoes
1 small onion, chopped
½ cup chopped celery
1 small green pepper, chopped
1 2-ounce jar chopped pimento
3 hard-boiled eggs, chopped
⅓ to ½ cup pickle relish
1 cup Hellmann's mayonnaise
   Salt and pepper, to taste

Makes 10 servings.
Boil potatoes until tender. Cool. Peel and dice into cubes. Place in a large mixing bowl along with remaining ingredients. Stir until well-blended.

  Note: There is no real recipe for Stewart's potato salad – only what was in it. The mayonnaise was homemade – made with uncooked eggs. The U.S. Food and Drug Administration warns that eating anything made with raw egg yolks risks salmonella poisoning. However, if you still want to make homemade mayonnaise, most basic cookbooks will have a recipe – this book will not.

Kentucky Derby Museum's potato salad©

3½ pounds red skinned potatoes, quartered
1 cup celery, diced
1½ ounces pimento, diced
1 medium onion, minced
3 eggs, hard boiled and chopped
2 tablespoons fresh parsley
¼ cup bacon grease
¼ cup sweet pickle relish
1¾ cups mayonnaise
¼ cup cider vinegar
1½ teaspoons sugar
   Salt and pepper, to taste

Makes 12 generous servings.
Boil potatoes until fork tender. Cool. Combine celery, pimento, onion, eggs, parsley, bacon grease, relish, mayonnaise, vinegar, sugar, salt and pepper. Stir until blended. Pour over potatoes.
Toss gently so potatoes don't break up. Adjust seasonings to taste.

Kunz's seafood salad©

Makes 4 servings.

2	tablespoons sour cream
2	tablespoons mayonnaise
½	teaspoon lemon pepper
	Dash Tabasco
	Dash Worcestershire sauce
	Garlic powder to taste
	Salt and white pepper to taste
1	pound shredded imitation crab meat
2	ribs celery, diced fine
1	green onion, diced fine

Combine sour cream, mayonnaise, lemon pepper, Tabasco, Worcestershire sauce, garlic powder and salt and pepper. Add crab meat, celery and onion. Toss.

My friend, Nancy Royce, proprietor of Bloom's shared this recipe with me.

Bloom's Café's spinach salad©

Makes 4 salads.

For the salad:

1	pound baby spinach leaves
1	small red onion, peeled and sliced thin
1	red pepper, seeds removed and sliced into julienne strips
½	cup sliced mushrooms
½	cup grape tomatoes, halved
2	slices hickory-smoked bacon, fried crisp and crumbled
½	cup toasted walnuts
¼	cup shaved Parmesan cheese

Onion-mustard salad dressing:

1	small onion, peeled and diced
1	teaspoon prepared mustard
1	teaspoon salt
1	teaspoon celery seed

To make salad: Wash and clean spinach. Divide spinach among 4 plates. Top with rings of red onion and red pepper strips, sliced mushrooms and halved tomatoes. Sprinkle with crumbled bacon, nuts and Parmesan cheese. Dress to taste with onion-mustard dressing.

To make dressing: In a bowl, whisk all ingredients well. Use to dress spinach salad. Makes about 1½ cups.

2 teaspoons soy sauce
2 teaspoons lemon juice
¼ teaspoon garlic powder
1 teaspoon dry mustard
¼ teaspoon curry powder
1 cup Mazola oil
¼ cup balsamic vinegar
⅔ cup sugar

Café Metro's spinach salad©

Salad:
1 10-ounce package fresh spinach
4 tablespoons julienned carrot
4 tablespoons raisins
4 tablespoons rough-chopped pecans
6 tablespoons apple cubes
3 tablespoons scallions, white part only, cut thinly on the bias

Dressing:
½ teaspoon minced garlic
½ teaspoon peeled and minced fresh ginger
½ teaspoon minced onion
3 tablespoons apple cider
1 tablespoon plus ¾ teaspoon vinegar
2 tablespoons peanut butter
1½ teaspoons curry powder
¾ teaspoon ground coriander seed
¼ teaspoon black pepper
2 tablespoons sour cream

Makes 4 servings.
To make salad: Remove stems from spinach. Wash, dry and tear into bite-size pieces. Place all ingredients in a large bowl.
To make dressing: Place all ingredients in a mixing bowl and whisk well.
Toss the salad ingredients with the dressing and divide among 4 bowls.

The Silver Dart Lodge's maritime Waldorf salad©

3	Granny Smith apples
3	red delicious apples
	Juice of 1 lemon
4 to 5	ribs celery
3	cups seedless red grapes
1	cup raisins
¾	cup coconut
1	tablespoon cinnamon
½	cup mayonnaise
¼	cup whipping cream

Makes 14 to 16 cups.
Wash and core apples. Cut into bite-size pieces. Drop into lemon juice and enough water to cover. Let soak 5 minutes. Drain Wash celery and grapes. Dice celery fine. Combine grapes and celery with apples, raisins, coconut and cinnamon. Toss. Add mayonnaise and whipping cream. Mix thoroughly. Chill for 30 minutes before serving.

Hasenour's wilted lettuce©

	Leaf lettuce
½	pound bacon, diced
¾	cup chopped onion
½	cup salad oil
1	cup vinegar
¼	cup brown sugar
1	teaspoon salt
	Pinch black pepper
	Hard-boiled egg for garnish

Makes enough dressing for 6 to 8 salads.
Dice bacon into ½-inch pieces. Fry in skillet until lightly brown and crisp. Remove bacon from drippings. Drain and set aside. Add chopped onion to bacon drippings. Cook until golden brown. Add salad oil, vinegar, brown sugar, salt and pepper. Simmer 10 minutes. Just before serving, add crisp bacon pieces.
Makes about 2 cups dressing.
Dress leaf lettuce according to taste.
Garnish with sliced, hard-boiled egg.

Mandarin orange salad©

10	cups mixed salad greens
1	11-ounce can Mandarin orange segments, drained
3	green onions, sliced (optional)
	Orange vinaigrette (recipe follows

Makes 8 servings.
To make salad: Wash salad greens and drain thoroughly. Tear into pieces. Combine with orange segments and sliced green onions, if using. Drizzle with orange vinaigrette and toss gently. Sprinkle with glazed almonds or chopped pecans.
To make vinaigrette: Combine all

Glazed almonds or pecans
(recipe follows)

Orange vinaigrette:
- ⅓ cup salad oil
- 1 tablespoon white wine vinegar
- ⅓ cup balsamic vinegar
- 2 teaspoons fresh grated orange zest (orange part of rind only)
- ½ cup fresh orange juice
- 2 tablespoons sugar
- ½ teaspoon poppy seeds
- ½ teaspoon salt, or to taste
- ⅛ teaspoon pepper

Glazed almonds or pecans:
- 1 egg white
- ¼ cup sugar
- 1 cup sliced almonds or coarsely chopped pecans
- 2 tablespoons butter, melted

ingredients in a jar. Cover tightly and shake vigorously. Chill.

Makes 1½ cups.

To make glazed nuts: Beat egg white at high speed with an electric mixer until foamy. Gradually add sugar, beating until stiff peaks form. Fold in nuts.

Melt butter in a shallow pan. Add nut mixture. Stir to coat. Bake in a preheated 325-degree oven for 30 minutes or until nuts dry and no longer stick together. During baking, stir mixture every 5 minutes. Cool.

Makes 1 cup.

Colombo's church picnic summer salad©

- 1 cup water
- ½ cup vinegar
- ½ cup sugar
- 2 to 3 cucumbers, sliced thin
- 1 medium onion, sliced thin
- 1 green pepper cut into bite-size pieces (optional)
- 1 tomato cut into bite-size pieces

Makes about 6 to 8 servings.

In a saucepan combine water, vinegar and sugar. Heat until sugar dissolves. Cool. Peel and slice cucumbers and onion. Core and cut up green pepper (if using). Place in a bowl. Pour cooled vinegar mixture over sliced vegetables. Add tomatoes just before serving.

Mrs. Nancy Woodmansee's summer cucumbers

- ½ cup white vinegar
- ½ cup sugar

Makes 6 to 8 servings.

In a saucepan combine vinegar, sugar, salt and water. Bring to a rolling boil. Cook until

1 teaspoon salt
1 cup water
1 teaspoon celery seed
3 to 4 cucumbers, sliced

mixture starts to thicken. Set aside to cool. Slice cucumbers. Sprinkle with celery seed. When sugar mixture cools, pour over cucumbers. Cover and chill at least 2 hours before serving. Will keep refrigerated 2 to 3 weeks.

Beaumont Inn blue cheese dressing©

Makes 1 quart.

1 small garlic clove
1 teaspoon water
¼ pound blue cheese, crumbled
1 quart real mayonnaise

Peel the garlic and chop very fine, then crush and mash it in a small saucer with the water. Place blue cheese and mayonnaise in a large bowl. Add the garlic mixture. Mix thoroughly. Cover tightly. Refrigerate at least one hour before serving. Can be kept for a couple of weeks in refrigerator.

Rough River State Resort Park's blue-cheese dressing©

Makes 5 to 6 cups.

1 quart mayonnaise
Dash Tabasco sauce
6 to 8 ounces crumbled blue cheese
Salt and pepper, to taste
1 cup water
1 tablespoon Worcestershire sauce

Combine all ingredients. Mix well. Refrigerate.
   Note: You can add as much or as little Tabasco and Worcestershire sauces as you like.

The Golden Lamb's celeryseed dressing©

Makes about 2 cups.

½ cup sugar
1 teaspoon dry mustard
1 teaspoon salt
1 teaspoon celery seeds
¼ teaspoon grated onion
1 cup salad oil
⅓ cup vinegar

Combine sugar, dry mustard, salt and celery seeds. Add onion. Add small amount of oil; mix well. Add vinegar and oil alternately, mixing after each addition, ending with oil.

Blue Boar cottage-cheese dressing for head lettuce salad©

1 pound small-curd creamed
   cottage cheese
1 cup mayonnaise
⅓ teaspoon white pepper
1½ teaspoons onion juice
½ teaspoon salt
   Head iceberg lettuce
   Paprika

Makes 9 servings.
Thoroughly mix cottage cheese, mayonnaise, white pepper, onion juice and salt together. Chill 2 hours to allow flavors to blend. When ready to serve line salad plates with lettuce leaves. Cut ½-inch slices from head lettuce and place on lined plates. Top with about ⅓ cup dressing, spreading it out to cover the slice of lettuce. Sprinkle lightly with paprika.

Overlook Restaurant's French dressing©

1 10¾-ounce can tomato soup
¼ cup sugar, or to taste
2 tablespoons Worcestershire
   sauce
1½ teaspoons onion powder
1½ teaspoons ground mustard
1½ teaspoons paprika
1½ teaspoons celery seed
¾ teaspoon garlic salt
½ cup vegetable oil
⅓ cup vinegar

Makes 2 cups.
Place all ingredients in bowl of electric mixer. Beat at low speed until well blended.

The Old Stone Inn's fruit-salad dressing©

1 cup sour cream
¼ cup confectioners' sugar, or
   to taste
3 tablespoons half-and-half
¼ teaspoon vanilla

Makes about 1½ cups.
Place sour cream, confectioners' sugar and half-and-half in blender and blend thoroughly. Remove mixture and add vanilla. Stir to blend.

Liberty Street's honey-mustard dressing©

1 cup mayonnaise
¼ cup honey
6 tablespoons Dijon mustard
½ teaspoon poppy seeds

Makes 1½ cups.
Place all ingredients in a large bowl. Mix until well-blended.

Merrick Inn honey dressing©

1⅓ cups sugar
2 teaspoons paprika
½ teaspoon salt
10 tablespoons cider vinegar
2 tablespoons mild onion juice
2 teaspoons celery seed
2 teaspoons dry mustard
⅔ cup honey
2 tablespoons fresh lemon juice
2 cups salad oil

Makes 3½ cups.
Place all ingredients in a bowl, or blender, and beat until well-blended. Store at room temperature. The honey will thicken if the dressing is refrigerated.

Grapevine Pantry's house dressing©

1½ cups sugar
1 teaspoon dry mustard
to 1½ teaspoons paprika
1 to 2 tablespoons minced onion, or to taste
2 cups vegetable oil
1 cup vinegar
1 teaspoon celery seed

Makes 4 cups.
Using a blender or electric mixer, combine sugar, mustard, paprika and minced onion. Beating constantly, gradually add the oil and vinegar. Constant beating is a must. Add celery seed and stir.

Joe Huber Family Farm Orchard & Restaurant's house dressing©

2 cups sour cream
1½ tablespoons dark Heinz apple cider vinegar

Makes 3½ to 4 cups.
Combine all ingredients in a jar. Shake to mix thoroughly. Refrigerate until ready to use.

1   cup mayonnaise
2¼ teaspoons tarragon vinegar
1½ teaspoons Hidden Valley
     Ranch Dressing Mix
¼   cup milk
¼   cup sugar
½   teaspoon black pepper
½   teaspoon celery seed
1½ teaspoons parsley flakes
½   teaspoon garlic powder
½   teaspoon garlic salt
¾   teaspoon onion flakes
     Few drops green food
     coloring

Stafford's One Water Street Restaurant orange salad dressing©

Makes 1½ cups.

1   11-ounce can mandarin
    oranges (well-drained –
    makes about ⅔ cup of
    orange sections
¾   cup salad oil
2   tablespoons orange juice
2   tablespoons sugar
2   tablespoons white wine
    vinegar
½   cup plus 1 tablespoon
    whipping cream
    Bibb lettuce
    Dried cherries, for garnish

Using a mixer with a whipping attachment, add first 6 ingredients in order, 1 at a time into the mixing bowl and mix for about 4 minutes. Serve chilled over Bibb lettuce or the lettuce of your choice. Garnish with dried cherries.

Hasenour's Parmesan and cracked peppercorn dressing©

Makes 8 servings.

2   cups mayonnaise
1   cup sour cream
1   cup freshly grated Parmesan
    cheese
2   tablespoons freshly ground

Combine mayonnaise and sour cream. Add cheese and pepper. Mix. Add vinegar and minced shallots. Stir to thoroughly blend. Add salt to taste. Chill and serve cold.

black pepper
¼ cup red wine vinegar
2 shallots, minced
Salt, to taste

Stafford's raspberry vinaigrette dressing©

½ cup sugar
½ cup raspberry vinegar
1 cup heavy cream
1½ cups salad oil
½ cup pureed raspberries

Makes 1 quart.
Whip sugar and vinegar until sugar dissolves. Add cream and whip until mixture starts to thicken. As you whip, drizzle the oil slowly until fully incorporated. Then add fruit puree.
Variations: Substitute dark sweet cherries, blueberries, cranberries, etc. in season. If using canned fruits, drain.

Ramsi's Café on the World's raspberry salad dressing©

12 ounces frozen raspberries
9 tablespoons rice vinegar
3 tablespoons balsamic vinegar
3 tablespoons honey, or to taste
2 limes
1 tablespoon plus 1½ teaspoons concentrated pomegranate juice
1½ cups salad oil

Makes about 3½ cups.
Strain thawed raspberries to remove seeds. Combine raspberries, vinegars, honey, juice of limes and pomegranate juice in a food processor. Pour mixture into a large bowl. While whipping with a wire whisk, slowly add salad oil. Store in refrigerator for up to 2 months.

Lilly's lemon-Parmesan salad dressing©

½ cup lemon juice
⅔ cup grated Parmesan cheese
2 teaspoons salt

Makes about 3 cups.
Combine lemon juice, cheese, salt, pepper and eggs in the container of a blender. Blend on low speed. Slowly add peanut oil

1 teaspoon pepper
4 eggs
1 cup peanut oil

(it is important that the oil be added slowly) while the blender is running. Blend until thick. Refrigerate until ready to serve.

Note: Because of salmonella, the Food and Drug Administration does not advise using raw eggs in uncooked food.

Garrett's smoked tomato dressing©

Makes 3 cups.

1 large (8-ounce) fresh tomato, peeled
2½ tablespoons olive oil
¾ teaspoon Liquid Smoke
2 tablespoons sugar
¼ teaspoon salt
⅛ teaspoon fresh garlic, finely diced
1 teaspoon capers, finely diced and drained
1⅔ cups mayonnaise
2 to 3 tablespoons fresh parsley, finely diced

Cut tomato in half horizontally. Squeeze out all juice and discard. Chop tomato into bite-size pieces.

In a bowl, combine olive oil, Liquid Smoke, sugar, salt and garlic. Add chopped tomato. Marinate 45 minutes.

After marinating, place tomato mixture into container of blender and blend 1 to 2 minutes. Add capers, mayonnaise and parsley. Blend an additional 3 to 5 minutes. Refrigerate.

Thousand Island dressing©

Makes 1¾ cups.

1 cup Hellman's Mayonnaise
½ cup chili sauce
1 tablespoon Worcestershire sauce
1½ teaspoons fresh lemon juice
1 hard-boiled egg, chopped
1½ to 2 tablespoons chopped green pepper
1½ to 2 tablespoons chopped pimento

In a bowl combine mayonnaise, chili sauce, Worcestershire sauce and lemon juice. Stir to blend. Add chopped egg, green pepper and pimento. Mix to combine. Refrigerate until ready to use.

Porcini's balsamic salad dressing©

1   cup balsamic vinegar
1   teaspoon lemon juice
⅓   cup brown sugar
1   tablespoon minced shallots
1   teaspoon total chopped fresh herbs (basil, rosemary, parsley and thyme, any one or any mixture)
¾   teaspoon Italian seasoning
1   teaspoon minced garlic
1   teaspoon salt
    Fresh ground black pepper, to taste
3   cups good quality olive oil

Makes 4 to 4½ cups.

Place balsamic vinegar, lemon juice, brown sugar, shallots, herbs, Italian seasoning, garlic, salt and black pepper in the container of a food processor. Process 4 to 5 minutes. With processor running, slowly drizzle olive oil into other ingredients until all of the oil has been added. Refrigerate until ready to use.

Breads, Rolls, Muffins and Sweet Rolls

Baking powder biscuits©

2   cups flour
1   tablespoon baking powder
½   teaspoon salt
½   cup (1 stick) butter, cut into pieces
⅔   cup milk

Makes 12 to 15 biscuits.

In a large bowl, combine flour, baking powder and salt. With a pastry blender, cut butter into the flour mixture as you would do when making pie crust. Add milk and stir to blend. Turn dough out on a lightly floured surface and knead 8 to 10 times.
Roll or pat to ½-inch thickness. Cut with a biscuit cutter and place on a lightly greased baking sheet. Bake in a preheated 450-degree oven for 10 minutes or until lightly browned.

Bolton's Landing angel biscuits©

5 cups soft winter wheat self-rising flour (White Lily, if available)
¼ cup granulated white sugar
1 ¼-ounce package dry yeast
1 cup white refined lard
2 cups buttermilk

Makes 18 biscuits.

In a large bowl, combine flour, sugar and yeast. Cut in lard, using a pastry blender or 2 knives, until there are no pieces larger than a pea. Add buttermilk. Stir until well-blended. Cover mixture with plastic wrap. Let the dough rest in the refrigerator for 1 to 2 hours.

Before baking, knead on moderately floured surface until mass forms smooth, consistent dough. Do not over knead. Roll dough out to ½-inch thickness. Cut with a 3-inch biscuit cutter. Fold each biscuit in half and place on a paper-lined baking sheet. Cover pan with plastic wrap and refrigerate until needed. Before baking, brush each biscuit with melted butter. Bake in a preheated 350-degree convection oven for 8 to 10-minutes or until golden. In a conventional oven, bake at 375-degrees for 10 to 12 minutes.

Beaten Biscuits©

2 pounds all-purpose flour
½ teaspoon salt
2 tablespoons sugar
1 teaspoon baking powder
½ pound lard
¾ cup milk
¾ cup water

Makes about 8 dozen.

Sift together flour, salt, sugar and baking powder 3 times. Work in the lard until mixture is mealy. Pour in liquids and mix with a wooden spoon until you can gather the dough with your hands into a ball. Place the dough on a cutting board or counter top and beat with a rolling pin or knead until dough blisters and pops good and loud.

Pat out ½-inch thick and cut with a 1½-inch biscuit cutter.

Puncture biscuits with fork 3 times all the way through. Place on an ungreased baking sheet and bake in a 325-degree oven for about 30 minutes.

86

Nashville House fried biscuits©

2 cups warm milk
2 tablespoons sugar
1 tablespoon plus 1 teaspoon dry yeast
¼ cup lard or shortening, melted
1 tablespoon salt
4 cups flour
2 to 3 cups vegetable oil or shortening for frying

Makes 3 to 3½ dozen.
Dissolve yeast and sugar in warm milk. Add shortening, salt and flour. Stir until mixture pulls away from sides of bowl and forms a ball. Cover with a tea towel and set dough in a warm place to rise, about 1 hour. When dough has about doubled in size, punch down and work into biscuits. Drop into hot fat (should be about 3 inches deep), slightly hotter than 350 degrees. (If fat is too hot, the biscuits will be soggy in the center.) Cook till golden on all sides.

Cheesy biscuits©

2 cups buttermilk baking mix
⅔ cup milk
½ cup shredded Cheddar cheese
¼ cup butter or margarine, melted
½ teaspoon garlic powder, or to taste

Makes 10 to 12 biscuits.
Heat oven to 450 degrees.
In a mixing bowl, combine baking mix, milk and shredded cheese with a wooden spoon until a soft dough forms. Beat vigorously 30 seconds. Roll dough to about ½ inch thickness, then cut into biscuits. Place onto an ungreased cookie sheet and bake 8 to 10 minutes or until golden brown.
In a separate bowl, combine melted butter or margarine and garlic powder. Brush over warm biscuits before removing from cookie sheet. Serve warm.

Grapevine Pantry's potato rolls©

1 cup scalded milk
⅔ cup oil
½ cup sugar
1 teaspoon salt
1 cup mashed potatoes
1 ¼-ounce package dry yeast

Makes 2 to 3 dozen.
Combine hot milk, oil, sugar and salt. Add potatoes and let cool. Dissolve yeast in warm water. Add to cooled potato mixture. Add well-beaten eggs and approximately 5 cups flour. Mix well with your hands. Place dough on a floured surface and knead

¼ cup warm water
2 eggs, well-beaten
5 cups all-purpose flour, approximate

8 to 10 times. Return to bowl that has been lightly oiled. Turn dough to oil all sides. Refrigerate overnight.
Three hours before baking remove from refrigerator. Place on floured surface. Knead several times. Roll out to about ½-inch thickness. Cut with a biscuit cutter, glass or can. Place on greased baking sheet. Let rise until double in bulk.
Bake in a 400-degree oven for 10 to 20 minutes. Serve immediately.

Pesto-pine nutbread

1¾ cups warm water (110 degrees)
2¼ teaspoons Rapid Rise yeast
1 teaspoon sugar
¼ cup olive oil
2 cloves garlic, minced
2½ teaspoons salt
4½ cups bread flour
¾ cup finely chopped fresh basil
¾ cup freshly grated Parmesan cheese
1 cup pine nuts, toasted
½ teaspoon black pepper

Makes 2 loaves.
Heat water to 110 degrees. Add sugar and yeast. Stir. Let stand until foamy, about 10 minutes. Mix in oil, minced garlic and salt. Stir. Add 2½ cups flour. Mix in basil, cheese, pine nuts and pepper. Mix in enough additional flour to form soft dough. Turn out onto floured surface and knead until smooth and elastic, adding more flour if sticky, about 5 minutes.
Oil a large bowl. Place dough in bowl and turn over to coat all sides. Cover with plastic wrap. Let dough rise in warm area until double in bulk, about 1 hour.
Punch dough down. Divide in half. Shape each half into an 8-inch long oval. Place loaves on a large baking sheet. Using a knife, cut 4 slits in top of each loaf, spacing evenly. Cover with towel; let rise at room temperature until almost double in volume, about 30 minutes.
Preheat oven to 375 degrees. Bake until golden brown and, when bread is tapped on

bottom, sounds hollow, about 35 minutes. Transfer to a rack to cool.

   Note: Bread can be made a day in advance. Wrap in foil and let stand at room temperature.

The Depot's flowerpot bread©

Makes 4 pots.

2	tablespoons yeast
½	cup hot (110 degrees) water
1	tablespoon sugar
1	teaspoon salt
1½	teaspoons shortening
1	cup warm milk
3 to 5	cups bread flour

The garden-center variety of clay pot was not made to be used for cooking. If using this type of pot, wash thoroughly with hot, soapy water. Rinse and dry. Line pot with aluminum foil. An easy way to do this is to wrap the foil around the outside of the pot. Pull foil down from the pot, and slide the formed foil into the pot. Press to shape. Grease foil with vegetable shortening or a non-stick spray. Combine yeast and warm water (110 degrees). Set aside.

In the large bowl of an electric mixer combine sugar, salt and shortening. Heat milk to warm. Add to bowl. Turn mixer on low speed and run to dissolve shortening; then slowly add 1½ cups bread flour. Continue mixing until smooth. Add yeast mixture. Continue mixing until smooth. Slowly add flour until dough pulls away from side of bowl and is smooth and easy to handle. You may need 3½ to 5 cups flour in all.

Place dough in a greased bowl. Set in a warm place to rise until double in size. After dough has doubled in size, knead down. Divide into 9-ounce balls. Drop a ball of dough into prepared flowerpot.

Set in a warm place to rise again until about 1 inch above top of pot. Bake in a preheated 350-degree oven for 30 minutes. Butter top and enjoy.

Porcini Tuscan bread©

4	¼-ounce packages active dry or compressed yeast
2½	cups warm water (115 to 120 degrees)
1	tablespoon salt (see note)
6 to 7	cups bread flour
	Cornmeal

Makes 2 loaves.

In a large bowl, dissolve yeast in warm water (if using compressed yeast, crumble into water). Add salt and enough flour to form a soft dough. Turn out on a lightly floured surface and knead by hand for 10 minutes (if using an electric mixer with a dough hook, mix 4 minutes on low speed). Oil the inside of a large clean bowl. Place the prepared dough into the bowl. Turn to coat all sides. Cover tightly with plastic wrap. Let rise until double in bulk (in a warm place, about 2 hours).

When dough has finished rising, punch down, turn out onto a floured surface and flatten into an oblong shape, about 8 inches wide, 10 inches long and ¾-inch thick (there is enough dough for 2 shapes). Dough will be very soft but try to use a minimum of additional flour in handling. Roll dough tight, in jellyroll fashion. Flatten this to about 1 inch and roll again (this activates the web of gluten that will keep the loaf from flattening out in the oven). Roll the dough under your hands in a fat cigar shape, to about 10 inches in length.

Dust a sheet pan lightly with cornmeal. Place shaped dough on pans. Bake in a preheated 400-degree oven with steam for 15 minutes. (When I tested the recipe, I sprayed water on the bread – this should be done three times during the first 8 minutes of baking.) Reduce heat to 375 degrees and continue to bake another 20 to 30 minutes. Cool on a rack.

90

Afro-German Tea Room's Irish soda bread©

4 cups unbleached flour
1½ teaspoons salt
1 teaspoon baking soda
1 teaspoon baking powder
1¾ to 2 cups buttermilk

Makes 1 loaf.

Thoroughly combine flour, salt, baking soda and baking powder. Add buttermilk to form soft dough, as in biscuit dough. Place on a lightly floured surface and knead until smooth.

Form into large round loaf. Cut an X across the top with a sharp knife or razor blade. Place on a greased baking sheet. Bake in a preheated 375-degree oven for 50 to 60 minutes.

Romano's Macaroni Grill focaccia bread©

2¾ cups milk
2 ¼-ounce packages dry yeast
1 clove garlic, crushed
2 cups semolina flour
6 cups all-purpose flour
2 teaspoons salt
1 teaspoon dill
1 teaspoon basil
1 teaspoon oregano
1 teaspoon black pepper
½ cup grated Romano cheese
3 tablespoons olive oil

Makes 10 to 12 servings.

Heat milk to 90 degrees. Add yeast and crushed garlic. Set aside.

In large bowl of electric mixer, combine semolina, all-purpose flour, salt, dill, basil, oregano and black pepper. Stir until blended. Add milk mixture, grated cheese and olive oil. Beat until dough pulls away from side of bowl.

On a lightly floured surface roll dough to ½-inch thickness. Brush top with additional olive oil. Flip over onto baking pan and brush with olive oil. Sprinkle with additional salt.

Cover with a clean cloth and let rise until doubled in thickness, about 1 to 1½ hours.

Bake in a preheated 400-degree oven until done, about 20 minutes.

Serve with olive oil sprinkled with fresh cracked pepper.

Note: You must use semolina flour in this recipe. It is available in most grocery and specialty stores.

Mary Ward's homemade tortillas

3 cups self-rising flour
½ cup shortening
1 cup hot water

Makes about a dozen.
Using a pastry blender, combine flour and shortening. Heat water to boiling. Make a depression in center of flour mixture. While stirring, slowly add water. Stir to combine. Knead about 10 minutes, as you would bread, until it feels smooth. Return to bowl, cover with a towel and allow to rest for 10 minutes.

When ready to fry, break off a small amount (about 2.5 ounces) and form into a ball. On a lightly floured surface, roll into a circle about 10-inches in diameter (the tortilla will be very thin). Place on a hot griddle just until starting to brown - about 5 to 10 seconds - turn and fry about 2 to 3 seconds. Remove to a tortilla warmer or place on a clean tea towel. Keep tortillas covered. Use as you would any other flour tortilla.

Makes about one dozen. Can be frozen.

Tips: It is important to form the dough into a nice flat round circle. This helps when rolling into a circle.

Preheat the griddle – this takes some practice to get the temperature right.

Cool tortillas completely before storing. They can be placed in plastic bags and refrigerated for a week or they can be frozen for about 3 months.

If you don't have self-rising flour, try my recipe using all-purpose flour.

Flour tortillas

3 cups all-purpose flour
1 tablespoon baking powder
¾ teaspoon baking soda

Makes about a dozen.
Using a pastry blender, combine flour, baking powder, baking soda, salt and shortening. Heat water to boiling. Make a

1½	teaspoons salt
½	cup shortening
1	cup hot water

depression in center of flour mixture. While stirring, slowly add water. Stir to combine. Knead about 10 minutes, as you would bread, until it feels smooth. Return to bowl, cover with a towel and allow to rest for 10 minutes.

When ready to fry, break off a small amount (about 2.5 ounces) and form into a ball. On a lightly floured surface, roll into a circle about 10-inches in diameter (the tortilla will be very thin). Place on a hot griddle just until starting to brown - about 5 to 10 seconds - turn and fry about 2 to 3 seconds. Remove to a warmer or place on a clean tea towel. Keep tortillas covered. Use as you would any other flour tortilla. Can be frozen about 3 months.

Homemade croutons©

½	teaspoon salt
¼	teaspoon pepper
½	teaspoon thyme
½	teaspoon garlic powder
½	teaspoon onion powder
½	teaspoon celery seed
1½	teaspoons dried parsley
1	pound butter or margarine, melted
2½	pounds of different breads (rye, whole wheat and white) cut into ½–inch cubes

Makes 2½ to 3 pounds.
Preheat oven to 275 degrees.
Combine salt, pepper, thyme, garlic and onion powders, celery seed and dried parsley.
In a large ovenproof pan, melt butter or margarine. Stir in the seasonings. Add the cubed bread. Stir to coat bread. Bake cubes for 1 hour or until crunchy. During baking, stir bread every 15 minutes. This helps prevent the bread from getting too brown.

Boone Tavern cornsticks©

2	cups white cornmeal
½	cup all-purpose flour
½	teaspoon salt

Makes 12 large corn sticks.
Preheat oven to 450 to 500 degrees. Sift together cornmeal, flour, salt and baking powder. Mix baking soda with buttermilk. Add to dry

1 teaspoon baking powder
½ teaspoon baking soda
2 cups buttermilk
2 eggs, well-beaten
4 tablespoons melted lard

ingredients. Beat well. Add beaten eggs and mix well. Add melted lard and mix well. Pour into a well-greased, smoking-hot corn stick pan that has been heated in the oven. Fill pans to level. Place on second shelf of oven and bake for 18 minutes or until well-browned.

It is important to heat the pan, well-greased, in the oven before filling with the corn stick mixture. This gives the corn sticks their crispy outside texture.

Our Best egg corn bread©

2 cups self-rising cornmeal
2 eggs
2 cups cold milk
½ cup melted shortening

Makes 6 to 8 servings.
Place cornmeal in a large bowl. Break eggs into cornmeal. Add milk and shortening. Stir together. Fry on well-greased skillet or griddle until lightly browned on both sides. Serve while hot.

Pittypat's Porch corn bread©

1¼ cups self-rising cornmeal
2½ cups all-purpose flour
½ cup sugar
¾ teaspoon salt
3 eggs, beaten
2 cups milk
1¼ cups sour cream
½ cup salad oil
4 tablespoons butter, melted

Makes 6 servings.
Lightly grease a 9-by-13-by-2-inch baking dish. Heat oven to 350 degrees.
In a large mixing bowl combine all ingredients. Stir until blended. Pour into prepared dish. Bake for 45 minutes or until a toothpick inserted near the center comes out clean.

Alligator Grille's jalapeno spoon bread©

2 cups all-purpose flour
2 cups yellow cornmeal
½ cup sugar
3 tablespoons baking powder
8 eggs
1 cup melted butter

Makes 8 to 10 servings.
In a medium-size mixing bowl combine flour, cornmeal, sugar and baking powder. Stir well to combine. Add eggs, melted butter, whipping cream, chopped jalapeno pepper and cilantro. Stir to blend. Pour into greased, 10-inch, cast-iron skillet. Bake in a preheated 350-degree

- ¾ cup heavy whipping cream
- 1 medium jalapeno pepper, seeded and diced
- ¼ cup chopped cilantro

oven. Check for doneness at 30 minutes. Bread should be very moist but not runny. Do not bake more than 40 minutes.

Country Crossroads' hush puppies©

- 1 cup self-rising cornmeal
- ⅓ cup self-rising flour
- ⅓ cup chopped onion
- 2 tablespoons sugar
  Dash garlic powder
- 1 egg, beaten
- ½ cup milk
  Oil for frying

Makes 25 hush puppies.
Mix all ingredients except oil together. Let set a few hours or overnight in the refrigerator. Drop with iced tea spoon into oil or lard heated to 350 degrees. Dip spoon into hot oil before each dipping to avoid batter sticking to spoon.

Dixie Crossroads' corn fritters©

- Oil for frying
- 2 cups all-purpose flour
- 1 tablespoon baking powder
- ½ teaspoon salt
- 4 tablespoon sugar
- 2 eggs, beaten
- 1 cup milk
- 4 tablespoons melted butter
- 1 cup whole kernel corn, drained
  Confectioners' sugar

Makes 30 to 35 fritters.
Heat oil (should be about 3-inches deep) in a pan to approximately 350 degrees.
Sift together flour, baking powder, salt and sugar. Combine eggs, milk and butter. Fold egg mixture into dry ingredients. Add corn. Stir to combine.
Drop by tablespoon into hot oil. Deep fry about 5 minutes or until golden brown. Sprinkle with confectioners' sugar. Serve warm.

Sourdough Bread©

Sourdough starter:
- 1 ¼-ounce package dry yeast
- 1½ cups warm water
- ¾ cup sugar
- 3 tablespoons instant potato flakes

Sourdough feeder:

To make starter: Mix dry yeast with ½ cup of the warm water. Combine sugar, remaining 1 cup warm water and potato flakes. Stir. Add yeast mixture. Stir. Loosely cover with foil or plastic wrap with a couple of air holes punched in it. Let stand all day. Refrigerate that night. After 3 days,

1 cup warm water
¾ cup sugar
3 tablespoons instant potato
  flakes
Sourdough bread:
¼ cup sugar
½ cup oil
1½ cups warm water
1 tablespoon salt
1 cup starter
6 cups bread flour

take out and feed.

To feed starter: Mix warm water, sugar and potato flakes. Add to starter. Allow starter to stand out of refrigerator all day. This shouldn't rise, but will start bubbling.

At the end of the day (or 12 hours), remove 1 cup of starter to use in making bread. Return remainder to refrigerator. Keep 3 to 5 days, then feed again.

If not making bread, give 1 cup of starter away or throw it away. Return remainder to refrigerator.

To make sourdough bread: Combine all ingredients in a large bowl. Stir with a wooden spoon until a stiff dough is formed. Oil another large bowl. Put dough in oiled bowl and turn it over so oiled side of bread is on top. Oil a large piece of wax paper. Place over bowl. Cover with a towel. Allow to stand overnight or until dough has doubled in volume.

Punch dough down. Knead 3 to 4 times (too much kneading releases the gases needed for rising). Divide into 2 equal portions. Place each portion into a greased 5-by-9-inch loaf pan. Let rise all day or until doubled.

Bake on bottom rack in a preheated 350-degree oven for 30 to 40 minutes. Remove from pans and brush with melted butter. Cool on rack. Wrap well to store. Can be frozen.

Makes 2 loaves.

   Note: If bread rises over sides of pan, next time make 3 loaves from this recipe.

Sourdough English muffins©

1	cup sourdough starter
1	cup milk
3½	cup all-purpose flour
1	tablespoon sugar
1½	teaspoons salt
¾	teaspoon baking soda
2 to 3	tablespoons cornmeal

Makes 12 muffins.

In a large glass mixing bowl, set the sponge by mixing together thoroughly the starter, the milk and 2 cups of the flour. Leave to rise, covered with a cloth, in a warm room overnight.

Mix ½ cup of the flour with the sugar, salt and baking soda. Blend into the sponge mixture to form a stiff dough. Flour a board or cloth with the remaining flour, turn out dough and knead several minutes, working in more flour until dough is no longer sticky. Roll out dough ½ inch thick. Cut circles 3 to 4 inches in diameter. (An empty tuna can makes a good cutter.) Place muffins on a cookie sheet sprinkled with cornmeal and dust more meal on top of muffins. Cover with wax paper and let rise in a warm place until light, which will take about an hour. Bake on moderately hot griddle, lightly greased, for 8 to 10 minutes on each side, turning once. You may serve immediately, or they keep well. To reheat, split in half. Spread lightly with butter and run under the broiler just until butter is melted and edges are slightly brown. Can be frozen.

Sourdough cinnamon rolls©

1	recipe for sourdough bread
4	tablespoons soft butter
¾	cup brown sugar
1	tablespoon cinnamon
	Glaze, recipe follows

Glaze:

1	cup confectioners' sugar
2	tablespoons melted butter

Makes 12 rolls.

Make one recipe for sourdough bread. Divide dough in half after first rising. Roll each half into a rectangle 12-by-9½-inches. Spread with soft butter. Mix brown sugar with cinnamon. Sprinkle over butter. Roll lengthwise like a jelly roll, pinching edges together. Using a thread, cut roll into 1-inch slices. Place each slice cut-side down into a

1   teaspoon vanilla
     Milk

greased 9-by-13-by-2-inch pan. Let rise until doubled.

Bake in a preheated 350-degree oven for 30 minutes. Glaze while hot.

To make glaze: Combine sugar, melted butter and vanilla. Add enough milk to make a spreadable glaze.

Sourdough kuchen©

1   recipe for sourdough bread

Fruit filling:
1   14.5-ounce can cherries, peaches or fruit of choice
     Sugar
3   tablespoons cornstarch
2   tablespoons cold water

Butter filling:
1   cup sugar
3   eggs
½   teaspoon vanilla
1   cup butter, melted

Cinnamon topping:
¼   cup butter
¼   cup brown sugar
½   cup flour
1   teaspoon cinnamon

After dough has gone through first rising, divide into 4 portions. Roll out and spread into four 8- or 9-inch greased cake pans. Cover with wax paper and a towel until doubled. Bake in a 350-degree oven for 10 minutes. Remove from oven and top with fruit, butter filling or cinnamon topping (recipes follow).

Return to oven to bake 10 to 15 minutes more or until crust is brown. Glaze edges while hot (glaze for cinnamon rolls).

To make fruit filling: Place fruit, including juice, in a heavy saucepan. Add sugar to taste.

Mix cornstarch with water (mixture will be stiff).

While stirring constantly, cook fruit mixture over medium heat, slowly adding 1 to 2 tablespoons cornstarch thickener. Cook until mixture is the consistency of pie filling. If needed, more thickener can be added. Pour on baked crust. Return to oven for additional 10 minutes of baking. Fills 1 kuchen.

To make butter filling: Beat together sugar, eggs and vanilla. Place over medium heat. Slowly beat in butter. Mixture will curdle if butter is added too fast. Continue whisking until mixture has thickened. Pour on baked crust. Return to oven for additional 10 minutes of baking. Tops 1 kuchen.

To make cinnamon topping: Combine all ingredients in a bowl using a pastry blender or 2 knives. Sprinkle over baked crust. Return to oven for additional 10 minutes of baking. Drizzle using recipe for cinnamon roll glaze. Tops 1 kuchen.

If you are not into making sourdough starter, you can use the following recipe to make kuchen using yeast dough.

Sweet homemade kuchen

6 tablespoons milk
2 tablespoons butter
¼ cup sugar
½ teaspoon salt
1 ¼-ounce package dry yeast
¼ cup warm water
(110 degrees)
1 egg
2 ½ cups all-purpose flour
Toppings (recipes follow)
Butter topping:
1 cup sugar
2 eggs
½ teaspoon vanilla
1 cup butter (melted) or oil
Cinnamon topping:
¼ cup butter or margarine
¼ cup brown sugar
½ cup flour
1 teaspoon cinnamon
Cherry topping:
1 21-ounce can cherry pie
filling
Cheese topping:
2 cups cottage cheese

Makes 3 9-inch kuchens.

Scald milk and add butter, sugar and salt. Dissolve yeast in warm water and add to milk mixture. Beat in egg then beat in flour. Place dough in bowl. Cover and let rise until double, about an hour. Divide into 3 pieces. Roll out into a 10 to 11-inch circle. Place in 9-inch cake pan (dough will come up sides of pan about ¼ to ¾ inch). Let rise 30 minutes or until double in size.

To make butter topping: Beat together sugar, eggs and vanilla. Slowly beat in melted butter or oil; add oil too fast and the mixture will curdle. Heat on top of stove until hot and pour on crust after it rises the second time. Bake 25 minutes in a preheated 375–degree oven. When cool, glaze edges and drizzle glaze on top. Makes topping for 1 kuchen.

To make cinnamon topping: Use a pastry blender or 2 knives to mix butter or margarine and brown sugar, flour and cinnamon. Sprinkle it over crust after it rises the second time. Dot with a bit more butter, if desired. Bake 20 minutes in a preheated 375-degree oven. Makes topping for 1

1   egg
½   cup sugar
    Cinnamon

Apple coffeecake:
3   apples, thinly sliced
    Cinnamon, nutmeg and
    sugar, to taste
1   tablespoon butter or
    margarine

Tea ring:
    Cinnamon, sugar and butter
    or margarine

Sugar glaze:
1   tablespoons butter, softened
½   cup confectioners' sugar
    Dash salt
½   teaspoon vanilla extract
1   tablespoon light corn syrup
1 to 2   tablespoons milk

kuchen.

To make cherry topping: Place pie filling in a sauce pan and heat on top of stove. Spread on crust after it rises the second time. Bake in preheated 375-degree oven for 20 minutes. Makes topping for 1 kuchen.

To make cheese topping: Mix cottage cheese, egg and sugar in a blender until creamy. Place in saucepan and heat slowly until warm. Pour on crust after second rising and sprinkle cinnamon on top. Bake 25 minutes in a preheated 375-degree oven. Makes topping for 1 kuchen.

To make apple coffeecake: Peel and slice apples. Sprinkle with cinnamon, nutmeg and sugar to taste. Roll the dough into a rectangle after it rises the first time. Place on a cookie sheet. Fill center of dough with the apple-cinnamon-nutmeg-sugar mixture. Dot with butter or margarine. Cut dough on both sides of the mixture into 1-inch wide strips. Bring the strips into the middle of the dough to form a cross-hatch pattern. Tuck in the ends. Bake 20 minutes in a preheated 375-degree oven. Cool and top with glaze.

To make tea ring: Roll dough into a rectangle about 2½ times longer than wide. Place on a cookie sheet. Sprinkle with cinnamon and sugar. Dot with butter or margarine. Starting with the long side, roll the dough in a spiral to enclose the cinnamon filling. Join the ends to form a circle. Use scissors to cut nearly through the dough at 1-inch intervals. Pull .the sections up and out to form a larger circle and expose the spiral interior. Let it rise until about double in size. Bake 15 minutes in a preheated 375-degree oven. Cool and top with glaze.

To make sugar glaze: Cream softened butter with confectioners' sugar. Add salt, vanilla, corn syrup and milk. Combine thoroughly.

Monkey bread©

This was always a favorite for breakfast when my boys were young and had friends over to spend the night. Easy and the boys can help by cutting up the biscuits.

½ cup butter or margarine
¾ cup brown sugar
3 12-ounce cans (10 biscuits to a can) refrigerated biscuits
¾ cup granulated sugar
2 teaspoons cinnamon
Nuts, optional
Raisins, optional

Makes 6 to 8 servings.
Preheat oven to 350 degrees.
Melt butter with brown sugar.
Cut each biscuit into fourths. Place granulated sugar and cinnamon in paper bag. Drop biscuit pieces, a few at a time, into bag. Shake to coat. Layer in tube pan. If using nuts and raisins, sprinkle between layers of biscuits. Pour brown sugar and butter mixture over biscuits. Bake in preheated oven 30 to 40 minutes. Remove to a serving platter while hot.

Glazed doughnuts©

2 ¼-ounce packages yeast
1 cup lukewarm water
1 cup milk
½ cup butter or margarine
⅔ cup sugar
1 teaspoon salt
2 eggs, well beaten
Juice of one lemon
⅛ teaspoon nutmeg
7 cups flour
Oil for frying

Makes 2 to 3 dozen.
To make doughnuts: Pour lukewarm water (110 degrees) over yeast. Let stand 10 minutes. Stir well.
Scald milk (heat to just below boiling) and let cool to lukewarm. Cream together the butter, sugar, salt, eggs, lemon juice and nutmeg.
Add lukewarm milk to softened yeast and blend with 3 cups flour. Beat until smooth. Add butter mixture and rest of flour. Beat until dough is smooth and soft. This is very moist, not like bread dough.
Place in a lightly greased bowl, turn once so

Sugar glaze:
- 1½ **cups sugar**
- ¾ **cup water**
- 1 **tablespoon butter**

top of dough will be greased. Cover with a thin kitchen towel and let rise in a warm, draft-free place until double in bulk. Punch down and, on a lightly floured surface, roll into a sheet ⅓-inch thick. Cut into desired shapes. Place on lightly floured surface, cover with a thin kitchen towel and let rise again until double in bulk, about 45 minutes.

Pour 2 to 3 inches of oil in a deep pan and heat to 350 degrees using a thermometer. (See note.) Fry doughnuts a few at a time, keeping fat temperature constant, for about 3 minutes on first side then turn so second side can brown. Remove with slotted spoon and drain on absorbent paper. Cover with glaze or icing.

Note: To correctly fry in deep fat, you need a deep saucepan, a slotted spoon for removing the doughnuts as they brown and, the most important piece of equipment of all, a thermometer. Without the thermometer, your doughnuts may be underdone or burned. If you have an electric deep fryer controlled by a thermostat, you need no thermometer. Corn or peanut oil, lard or any of the canned, white solid vegetable shortenings can be used for deep frying.

To make glaze: Place all ingredients in a heavy saucepan. Cook until mixture forms a soft ball. Drop doughnuts in glaze or, if doughnuts have a hole in center, string 3 or 4 onto the handle of a wooden spoon, place spoon over a large bowl and pour glaze over doughnuts.

Glaze that accumulates in bowl can be used again. Drain doughnuts on wire rack.

The following recipe appeared in Heloise's column several years ago. It has been our favorite for pancakes and waffles since then – excellent.

Heloise's waffle-pancake mix©

2	cups biscuit mix
1	egg
½	cup vegetable oil
1⅓	cups club soda

Makes 3 to 4 waffles or 12 pancakes.
Mix ingredients together and then ladle some onto a hot waffle iron.
You can't store this batter but you can cook extra waffles and freeze them for later use. To make pancakes, ladle a scant ¼ cup of batter onto a lightly greased hot skillet. Cook until batter dries around outer edge. Flip and cook until golden.

Bristol Bar & Grille waffles©

Waffles:

1	cup all-purpose flour
1	teaspoon sugar
½	teaspoon salt
1	teaspoon baking powder
1	egg
½	cup milk
5	teaspoons salad oil
	Honey butter (recipe follows)
	Fresh strawberries or blue berries
	Whipped cream

Honey butter

½	cup butter
¼	cup honey

Makes 3 servings.
To make waffles: Place flour, sugar, salt, baking powder, egg, milk and salad oil in large bowl of electric mixer. Beat until no lumps are present. Bake on hot waffle iron according to manufacturer's directions.
Pour honey butter over hot waffles. Top with fresh strawberries or blueberries and whipped cream.
To make honey butter: Melt butter in a saucepan and add honey, stirring to combine and heating only until warm (honey and butter will separate if overheated).

Petunias' New Orleans Pain Perdu (French Toast)©

6	eggs
2	cups sugar
	Cinnamon, nutmeg, ginger

Makes 6 to 8 servings.
In a large bowl, beat eggs. While beating, slowly add sugar. Beat until lemon in color. Add spices. Beat. Add half-and-half and

and allspice (generous dashes of each, heavier on cinnamon)
3 cups half-and-half
¼ to ½ cup vanilla (see note)
1 long, stale loaf French bread, cut into 1-inch slices
Butter
Confectioners' sugar
Syrup of choice

vanilla. Stir to blend. Dip bread into egg mixture until it absorbs some of the liquid. Squeeze out excess liquid.
Heat 1 to 2 tablespoons butter on a grill or in a frying pan. Grill bread on both sides until golden. Serve immediately with condiments of confectioners' sugar, butter and syrup.

Note: I questioned the amount of vanilla when I received the recipe from Petunias. Chef Jay Loomis told me they use ½ cup but if I was reluctant to use that much, cut it in half. I used ¼ cup vanilla, but next time I make it, I'll try ½ cup.

Banana-pineapple nut bread©

3 cups flour
2 cups sugar
1 teaspoon baking soda
1 teaspoon salt
1½ teaspoon cinnamon
1 cup chopped nuts, optional
3 eggs, beaten
1½ cups vegetable oil
2 cups mashed, ripe bananas
1 8 oz. can crushed pineapple
2 teaspoons vanilla extract

Makes 2 9-by-5-inch loaves.
Heat oven to 350 degrees. Grease and flour two 9-by-5-by-3-inch loaf pans or four 5-by-2-inch loaf pans.
Combine flour, sugar, baking soda, salt and cinnamon. Stir in nuts and set aside.
Combine eggs, vegetable oil, bananas, crushed pineapple with juice and vanilla.
Add to dry ingredients, stirring just until moistened.
Spoon batter into prepared pans. Bake 50 to 60 minutes for larger loaves, or about 40 minutes for smaller loaves. A toothpick inserted into center of each should come out clean when loaves are done.
Cool 10 minutes before removing from pans. Remove to wire racks; cool completely.

Grapevine Pantry's carrot-pineapple bread©

3 eggs
2 cups sugar

Makes 2 large and 1 small or 5 small loaves.
Heat oven to 350 degrees. Grease and flour two 9-by-5-inch-by-3- and one 5-by-2--inch

1⅓ cups vegetable oil
2 cups grated carrots
1 cup drained crushed pineapple
2 teaspoons vanilla
3 cups all-purpose flour
1 teaspoon salt
2 teaspoons baking soda
2 teaspoons cinnamon
1 cup chopped pecans

loaf pans or five 5-by-2-inch loaf pans.
In a large mixing bowl combine the eggs, sugar and oil. Add grated carrots, crushed pineapple and vanilla.
Sift together flour, salt, baking soda and cinnamon. Stir in nuts. Add to egg mixture, stirring just until moistened.
Spoon batter into prepared pans. Bake 60 to 70 minutes for larger loaves, or about 40 minutes for smaller loaves. A toothpick inserted into center of each should come out clean when loaves are done.
Cool 10 minutes before removing from pans. Remove to wire racks; cool completely.

DeSha's date-nut bread©

2 cups chopped dates
2 teaspoons baking soda
2 cups boiling water
6 tablespoons butter
2 cups sugar
2 teaspoons vanilla
2 eggs
2⅔ cups all-purpose flour
1 cup chopped pecans

Makes 1 loaf.
Preheat oven to 325 degrees. Grease and flour a 9½-by-5-by-3-inch loaf pan.
Place dates in a medium-size mixing bowl. Sprinkle baking soda over dates. Pour boiling water over all. Set aside.
Cream butter with sugar. Add vanilla and eggs. Beat well. Add flour and mix well. Pour in date mixture and pecans. Mix.
Pour batter into prepared pan. Bake about 1 hour and 15 minutes or until a toothpick inserted near center comes out clean.

Pumpkin bread©

4 eggs
2½ cups sugar
2 cups pumpkin
1 cup vegetable oil

Makes 2 large or 6 small loaves.
Preheat oven to 300 degrees. Grease and lightly flour two 9-by-5-by-2½-inch or six 5-by-2-by-2-inch pans.
Beat the eggs with the sugar until lemon-

½ cup cold water
3½ cups all-purpose flour
1½ cups chopped dates
1½ cups raisins
1½ cups chopped nuts
2 teaspoons baking soda
1½ teaspoons salt
1 teaspoon cinnamon
1 teaspoon vanilla

colored. Fold in pumpkin. Set aside. Combine the oil and water. Set aside. Mix ½ cup of the flour with dates, raisins and nuts. Sift remaining flour with baking soda, salt and cinnamon. Add flour mixture alternately with oil mixture to the pumpkin mixture, blending after each addition. Fold in fruit and nut mixture and vanilla. Pour into prepared pans and bake for approximately 1¼ hours or until a toothpick inserted near center comes out clean.

Tips on making muffins©

There are a few tips we need to heed when mixing and baking muffins. First, there are two types of muffins, stirred and creamed.

Stirred muffins are the simplest. First, you thoroughly mix the dry ingredients with a spoon. The baking powder and baking soda must be evenly distributed. Then, in a separate bowl, you whisk together the wet ingredients (egg, milk, melted butter, etc.).

The next step is important: You fold the wet ingredients into the dry ingredients. This means you pour the wet ingredients into the well you made in the center of the bowl of dry ingredients. With a rubber spatula, you cut through the center of the mixture, turning it slightly up as you turn the bowl, approaching the side of the bowl nearest you. Continue cutting and turning until the dry ingredients are moistened.

Don't worry about a few lumps in the batter. They should be there.

Creamed muffins call for more fat and sugar and taste more like cupcakes. The butter and sugar are creamed together and the eggs are beaten into the creamed mixture.

The dry ingredients are combined, and added to the sugar mixture alternately with milk, beginning and ending with the dry ingredients. Mixing is not quite as crucial as with a stirred batter.

The second tip is that muffins bake best when placed in a hot oven on a rack in the middle of the oven – not too close to the top or bottom.

When you are putting the batter into the muffin tin, try using a ¼-cup measuring cup instead of a spoon. This eliminates a lot of mess.

Lemon poppy seed muffins©

1	egg
	Grated zest (yellow part of rind) of 2 small lemons
1	tablespoon fresh lemon juice
4	tablespoons melted butter
1	cup buttermilk
1	tablespoon poppy seeds
1	teaspoon vanilla
2	cups all-purpose flour
1½	teaspoons baking powder
½	teaspoon baking soda
5	tablespoons sugar
½	teaspoon salt

Makes 12 muffins.

Heat oven to 350 degrees. Grease 12 muffin cups.

Beat egg gently. Stir in lemon zest, juice, melted butter, buttermilk, poppy seeds and vanilla. Beat to blend. Combine the flour, baking powder, baking soda, sugar and salt. Add all at once to the buttermilk mixture. Stir briefly and gently with a rubber spatula until just blended – lumps will remain.

Ladle batter into muffin cups. Bake 20 to 25 minutes, or until the muffins pull away from the side of the tin.

Glorious morning muffins©

2	cups all-purpose flour
¼	cup oat bran
2	teaspoons baking soda
½	teaspoon salt
2	teaspoons ground cinnamon
1¼	cups sugar
1½	cups finely shredded carrot
2	large cooking apples, peeled, cored and shredded
¾	cup flaked coconut
½	cup raisins
½	cup chopped pecans
1	cup vegetable oil
3	eggs, slightly beaten
½	teaspoon vanilla extract

Makes 2 dozen.

Combine flour, oat bran, baking soda, salt and cinnamon in a large bowl. Stir in sugar. Add carrot, apples, coconut, raisins and pecans. Stir until blended. Make a well in the center of the mixture.

Combine oil, eggs and vanilla. Add to dry ingredients, folding just until moistened. Using a ¼-cup measuring cup, spoon batter into greased muffin tins, filling three-quarters full. Bake in a 375-degree oven for 18 to 20 minutes or until golden brown.

DeSha's sweet potato muffins©

Makes 4 dozen.

4	cups cooked and mashed sweet potatoes
4	cups self-rising flour
4	tablespoons cinnamon
3	cups salad oil
4	cups sugar
8	eggs
1½	cups chopped nuts

Boil sweet potatoes until fork-tender. Skin and mash. Set aside.

Sift flour and cinnamon together. In a separate bowl, combine oil, sugar and eggs. Beat until blended. Add mashed sweet potatoes. Stir until blended. Add flour and cinnamon mixture and nuts. Stir only until blended.

Spoon into muffin tins that have been lined with paper or foil. Bake in a 350-degree oven for 20 minutes or until a toothpick inserted near center comes out clean.

The following three recipes are for stirred muffins.

Chocolate muffins

Makes 12 muffins.

2	ounces unsweetened or semisweet chocolate
1¾	cups all-purpose flour
1	teaspoon baking soda
¼	teaspoon salt
1	cup buttermilk
1	teaspoon vanilla
½	cup butter
1	cup packed light brown sugar
1	large egg
1	cup semisweet chocolate chips

Grease and flour a 12-muffin pan or line with muffin pan liners. Heat oven to 350 degrees. In a saucepan over very low heat melt 2 ounces of chocolate. Set aside.

In a bowl combine flour, baking soda and salt. Set aside.

In another bowl, combine buttermilk and vanilla.

Beat butter until creamy. Gradually add brown sugar, beating until light and fluffy, 4 to 5 minutes. Add egg and beat to blend. Add melted chocolate and stir to blend. Add the flour mixture in 3 parts, alternating with the buttermilk mixture in 2 parts, stirring with a rubber spatula until smooth, scraping the sides of the bowl while mixing.

Coarsely chop chocolate chips. Stir into batter.

Divide batter among the muffin cups. Muffin cups will be almost full, and muffins will cook out onto pan. This part of the muffin is crunchy and chewy.

If you prefer, you can use a larger muffin pan or make a couple more muffins. Bake in hot oven 25 to 30 minutes or until a toothpick inserted in center comes out clean. Cool a few minutes before removing to cool completely on a rack.

Note: For a special treat, add a cup of nuts, some chopped raisins, dried cherries, coconut or chopped dates.

Peach muffins©

- ½ cup butter
- ¾ cup sugar
- 1 egg
- 1½ cups all-purpose flour
- 1½ teaspoons baking powder
- 1 cup sliced peaches, fresh or frozen
- 1 teaspoon vanilla
- ½ cup plain yogurt or sour cream
- 1 cup chopped pecans

Makes 12 muffins.

Heat oven to 350 degrees. Grease 12 muffin cups.

Cream the butter. Add sugar and beat until light. Add egg and beat again. Sift together flour and baking powder. Chop peaches into small pieces. Beat vanilla and yogurt or sour cream into butter mixture, then stir in flour mixture. Add peaches and nuts and stir briefly. Ladle into prepared muffin cups Bake 20 to 25 minutes or until nicely browned.

Vanilla muffins©

- 2 cups sugar
- 2 eggs, beaten
- 4 cups all-purpose flour
- 1 tablespoon plus 1 teaspoon baking powder
- 2 cups milk
- ½ cup butter, melted
- 1 tablespoon vanilla extract

Makes 3 dozen.

Combine sugar and eggs, beating well at medium speed of an electric mixer.

In a separate bowl, combine flour and baking powder, stirring to thoroughly blend flour with baking powder. Add to sugar mixture alternately with milk, beginning and ending with flour mixture, beating well after each addition. Stir in melted butter and vanilla.

Using a ¼-cup measuring cup, spoon batter into greased muffin pans, filling two-thirds full. Bake in a 400-degree oven for 18 to 20 minutes or until a toothpick inserted near center comes out clean.

Chocolate chip scones

2¾	cups all-purpose flour
⅓	cup sugar
¼	cup brown sugar
2	teaspoons baking powder
½	teaspoon salt
12	tablespoons unsalted cold butter
1	cup mini chocolate chips
1	tablespoon orange zest
1	cup cold heavy whipping cream
1	egg blended with 1 tablespoon water
	Coarse or granulated sugar

Makes 8 scones.
Preheat oven to 375 degrees. Line a baking sheet with parchment paper. Set aside. In a bowl combine flour, sugars, baking powder and salt. Stir to combine. Using a pastry blender, cut in butter. Add chocolate chips and orange zest. Toss to combine. Add cream and mix together until blended. Knead and pat dough into a circle; cut into wedges. Transfer to the prepared baking sheet, spacing wedges about 2 inches apart. Brush with egg and water mixture and sprinkle with coarse or granulated sugar. Bake 25 to 30 minutes, or until golden brown and set. Cool briefly on racks. Serve warm.

Vegetables

Vincenzo's vegetable torta©

4	medium baking potatoes, peeled and cut lengthwise
4	carrots, peeled and cut lengthwise
6	small zucchini, cut lengthwise
6	small yellow squash, cut lengthwise
½	cup diced celery

Makes 6 to 8 servings.
Boil the potato slices just until tender. Grill the carrots, zucchini and squash (or sauté in hot olive oil) until tender. Sauté celery, onion and garlic in butter until onion turns translucent.
Cover the bottom of a 9-by-13-by-2-inch dish with olive oil and then with tomato sauce. Layer grilled vegetables and roasted peppers, sautéed onion mixture and

1 cup diced onion
1 tablespoon crushed garlic
2 tablespoons butter
Olive oil
3 cups tomato sauce
3 large red peppers, roasted, peeled and cut into 1-inch strips (see note)
2 cups grated Parmesan cheese
1½ cups shredded mozzarella cheese
1 tablespoon salt, or to taste
1 tablespoon crushed red pepper, or to taste
½ cup fresh basil

potatoes. Between layers of vegetables, add a thin covering of tomato sauce and a sprinkling of the cheeses. Sprinkle with salt, crushed red pepper and basil. Continue this process three times, alternating the direction of the vegetables. Top with remaining cheese and tomato sauce. Bake in a 400-degree oven for 45 minutes. Let cool about 5 minutes to set then cut and serve.

Note: To roast red peppers, place them in a shallow pan under the broiler until the skin has blistered and blackened. Turn the peppers to blacken all sides. Remove and place in a paper bag to steam for about 10 minutes. The skin should slip off easily.

610 Magnolia's grilled asparagus©

2 pounds asparagus
1 teaspoon salt
¼ teaspoon pepper
1 cup extra-virgin olive oil
1 small garlic clove, crushed
Juice of ½ lemon

Makes 4 to 6 servings.
Blanch asparagus in rapidly boiling water just until color is set. Drop in ice water to halt the cooking process. Remove from water and dry.
Combine salt, pepper, olive oil, garlic and lemon juice. Stir until well-blended. Drop in asparagus, turning to coat completely. Marinate for 10 minutes. Grill under the broiler until singed.

Cauliflower mountain©

1 medium head cauliflower, trimmed and washed
1 cup mayonnaise
1 teaspoon dry mustard
1 tablespoon prepared mustard
4 ounces sharp Cheddar cheese, shredded

Makes 6 to 8 servings.
Place cleaned head of cauliflower, stem down, in an 8-inch glass pie plate. Cover with plastic wrap, leaving an opening to release steam. Microwave at high 8 to 9 minutes or until tender.
In a bowl mix remaining ingredients, stirring until well blended. Spread over cooked

cauliflower. Do not cover with plastic wrap. Microwave at high for 1 minute to melt cheese. Good hot or cold.

Mr. Ebermann's Boston baked beans

1   pound dry pea beans
½   teaspoon baking soda
½   pound salt pork
½   medium onion, chopped
⅓   cup molasses
¼   cup sugar
1   teaspoon dry mustard
2   teaspoons salt
¼   teaspoon black pepper

Makes 8 to 10 servings.
Cover beans with cold water and let soak overnight. In morning, pour off water and cover with fresh water. Add baking soda and bring slowly to boil; simmer 10 minutes. Drain and reserve bean liquid. Cut half the salt pork into 1-inch cubes. Place cubes in bottom of a 2-quart bean pot. Add onion. Pour in all of the beans. Mix remaining ingredients and 1 cup of reserved bean liquid. Pour mixture over beans. Score remaining piece of salt pork at ½-inch intervals. Push pork down into beans with fat side up until about ½-inch protrudes above beans. Add bean liquid to just cover beans. Bake uncovered at 300 for at least 4 to 5 hours. Add a little hot water as necessary to keep juice bubbling at top of pot during the entire baking time.

Cuisine Marche vegetarian eggplant©

1   medium eggplant
2   cups cooked rice (¾ cup uncooked)
½   small onion, finely chopped
1   clove garlic, minced
2 to 3   tablespoons olive oil
2   ounces mushrooms, sliced
1   medium tomato, diced
¼   teaspoon tahini
     Salt and pepper to taste
     Parmesan cheese (optional)

Makes 4 servings.
Wash eggplant and wipe dry. Peel leaves from top, keeping skin in place. Cut eggplant in half, lengthwise. Score flesh of eggplant ½- to 1-inch deep, being careful not to cut through skin. Brush with some of the olive oil. Bake, cut side down, on lightly oiled cookie sheet in a preheated 375-degree oven for 20 to 30 minutes or until tender all the way through. When cool enough to handle, scoop out and chop flesh, being careful not to tear skin of eggplant.

While eggplant is baking, cook rice according to package directions. Sauté onion and garlic in remaining olive oil until onion is translucent. Add mushrooms and tomato. Cook until liquid from mushrooms has evaporated. Combine with cooked eggplant, cooked rice, tahini and salt and pepper. Return this mixture to shell of eggplant. Sprinkle with Parmesan cheese, if desired. Return to oven and bake an additional 5 minutes. Scoop out servings or cut eggplant into serving-size pieces.

Le Relais' vegetarian pie©

Crust for 1 9-inch pie:
- 1 cup flour
- ¼ cup polenta or cornmeal
- ½ cup butter, cut in pieces
- 1 tablespoon ice water

Filling:
- ½ green pepper
- ½ red pepper
- 1 medium yellow squash
- 1 medium zucchini squash
- 1 small to medium eggplant
- 2 cups fresh spinach
- 1 medium onion
- 3 tablespoons olive oil
- 1 teaspoon cumin
- Salt and pepper to taste
- 2 eggs or ½ cup Eggbeaters
- ½ cup sour cream
- Grated Parmesan cheese

Smoked tomato sauce with basil:
- 3 tomatoes
- 1 tablespoon finely chopped fresh basil

Makes 8 servings.

To make the crust: Place all ingredients in a food processor. Process until mixture forms a ball. Remove from processor, wrap in plastic wrap or place in a bowl, cover and refrigerate for 1 hour.

Divide into 2 portions. Roll each portion into a circle to fit a 9-inch pie pan. Place 1 circle in bottom of pan. Reserve second circle for top of pie.

To make the filling: Wash and seed pepper halves. Wash squash and eggplant, removing stem and blossom ends from each. Dice into bite-sized pieces. Wash, dry and chop spinach. Peel and chop onion.

In a large skillet heat olive oil. Add cumin and salt and pepper. Add all vegetables except spinach and cook till tender. In the last couple of minutes, toss in the spinach. Drain off any excess liquid. Combine eggs or Eggbeaters with sour cream. Pour just enough egg mixture into pie shell to cover bottom. Pile vegetables 1 inch higher than pie shell. Cover with the remaining egg mixture. Sprinkle with Parmesan cheese. Place top circle of pie crust over vegetables. Prick several times with the tines of a fork to release steam while baking. Bake in a preheated 350-degree oven for 45 to 55 minutes or until top crust is lightly browned. To serve, drizzle with smoked tomato sauce.

To make the sauce: Cut tomatoes in half. Place skin-side down on top rack of smoker. Cook for half-hour. Place tomatoes in blender or food processor. Puree until smooth. Strain to remove skin and seeds. Place tomato liquid in saucepan. Add fresh basil and cook until reduced by one-fourth or to your desired thickness. Drizzle on pie just before serving.

Tomato-feta tart

Pastry shell:
- 1 cups all-purpose flour
- 2 teaspoons baking powder
- ½ teaspoon salt
- 1 teaspoon dried basil
- ½ cup shortening
- ½ cup sour cream

Filling:
- 3 medium tomatoes, peeled and sliced
- ¾ cup mayonnaise
- 1 cup (4 ounces) feta cheese
- 1 cup sliced fresh mushrooms
- 1 tablespoon chopped onion
- 1 tablespoon chopped green pepper (optional)
- 1¼ cups chopped fresh basil
  Season to taste with salt and pepper

Makes 1 9-inch tart.

To make pastry shell: Combine flour, baking powder, salt and basil. Cut in shortening with pastry blender until mixture resembles coarse meal. Add sour cream; stir with a fork. Shape into a ball. Chill. On a lightly floured surface, roll pastry to ⅛-inch thickness. Place in a 9-inch pie pan. Trim off excess pastry along edges. Fold edges under and flute.

To make filling: Arrange half of the tomato slices on bottom of pastry shell. Combine mayonnaise, feta, mushrooms, onion, green pepper and basil, stirring well. Spread half of mixture over tomato slices. Repeat layers with remaining tomatoes and mayonnaise mixture. Bake in a preheated 350-degree oven for 45 to 50 minutes on the low rack in the oven. Wait 5 to 10 minutes for tart to set before serving.

Phyllis George Brown's carrot soufflé from Cave Hill©

1 pound fresh carrots
3 eggs
⅓ cup sugar
3 tablespoons all-purpose flour
1 teaspoon vanilla
½ cup butter, melted
Dash nutmeg

Topping:
¼ to ½ cup crushed corn flakes or walnuts
3 tablespoons brown sugar
2 teaspoons soft butter

Makes 6 servings.
To make soufflé: Cook carrots until tender. Place in blender container with eggs. Puree. Add sugar, flour, vanilla, melted butter and nutmeg. Blend until smooth. Pour into a lightly greased 1½-quart oven-proof pan or soufflé dish.
Bake in a 350-degree oven for 40 minutes. Spread topping over soufflé and bake an additional 5 to 10 minutes or until lightly browned.
To make topping: Mash all ingredients together. Use to spread over top of soufflé.

Basic terrific carrots©

1 pound California-grown carrots
1 tablespoon butter (optional)
1 tablespoon brown sugar (optional)

Makes 4 servings.
Wash carrots. Peel if you want. Cut into 1-inch pieces. Place in a pan with a tight-fitting lid. Do **not** add water. Place over very low heat. It's most important that you keep the heat very low. As the carrots begin to cook, they will release some moisture, but this will evaporate too quickly if the heat is too high. Cook until fork tender, 30 to 40 minutes, depending on size of carrots. Add the butter and brown sugar, if desired. Stir over medium-low heat until sugar melts.

Ronnie Hudson's scalloped potatoes

8 medium Idaho potatoes, sliced
1 medium onion, sliced
⅓ to ½ cup all-purpose flour
Salt and pepper, to taste
2 to 2½ cups half and half
4 to 6 tablespoons butter

Makes 6 to 8 servings.
Preheat oven to 350 degrees.
Butter a 9-by-13-by-2-inch baking dish. Place a layer of potatoes on bottom of dish. Scatter a few onion rings on top. Sprinkle with flour and salt and pepper. Layer until dish is filled to about an inch from the top. Cut butter into thin slices.

Scatter over top of potatoes. Add enough half-and-half until you see it coming up the sides of the dish. Cover casserole with aluminum foil and bake about 45 minutes. Remove foil and continue to bake until potatoes are tender and liquid has thickened, about 15 to 30 minutes.

Apron Strings' Monterey Jack cheese and zucchini casserole©

Makes 10 to 12 servings.

1	cup uncooked rice
1	4-ounce can green chilies
1	pound Monterey Jack cheese
3	medium zucchini, cut in ¼-inch slices
3	large tomatoes, peeled and sliced
2	cups sour cream
1	teaspoon oregano
1	teaspoon garlic salt
4	tablespoons chopped green onion
4	tablespoons chopped green pepper, optional
1	tablespoon chopped parsley

Cook rice according to package directions. Spray a 9-by-13--by-2-inch casserole with non-stick spray. Spread cooked rice in bottom of casserole. Spread chilies over rice. Slice half the cheese into thin slices. Use to top chilies. Place a layer of zucchini over cheese, then a layer of tomatoes.

Mix sour cream with oregano, garlic salt, onion, green pepper (if desired) and parsley. Spoon over tomatoes.

Grate remaining cheese. Sprinkle over sour cream mixture. Bake uncovered for 30 to 45 minutes in a preheated 350-degree oven.

Broccoli and rice casserole

Makes 10 to 12 servings.

1	cup long grain rice
2	10-ounce packages frozen chopped broccoli
½	cup chopped celery
½	cup chopped onion
3	tablespoons butter
8	ounces sharp Cheddar cheese
1	10¾-ounce can cream of mushroom soup

Cook rice according to package directions. Cook broccoli and drain. Sauté celery and onion in butter. Add Cheddar cheese, mushroom soup and thyme, marjoram and rosemary. Add cooked broccoli.

Make a crust with the rice in a 2-quart shallow baking dish. Pour broccoli mixture in rice crust and sprinkle with paprika. Bake in a preheated 375-degree oven for 10 minutes or until hot and bubbly. Serve while hot.

¼ teaspoon each thyme, marjoram and rosemary

Note: May be made ahead of time and refrigerated. When ready to serve, bring to room temperature and bake a little longer at 375 degrees.

This recipe can also be made with packaged long grain and wild rice with seasonings.

Cabbage casserole©

1 medium head cabbage
1 10¾-ounce can cream of celery soup
¼ cup milk
1 cup shredded American or sharp Cheddar cheese
½ teaspoon salt
½ teaspoon pepper
2 tablespoons butter, melted
½ cup bread or cracker crumbs

Makes 8 to 10 servings.
Shred or cut cabbage into bite-size pieces. Place in boiling water just until tender. Drain. Place in a lightly greased 9-by-13-by-2-inch baking casserole.
Combine cream of celery soup, milk, shredded American or Cheddar cheese, salt and pepper.
Stir until blended. Pour over cabbage.
Melt butter and combine with crumbs.
Sprinkle over top of cabbage. Bake in a preheated 350-degree oven for 15 minutes or until hot.

Beaumont Inn's corn pudding©

8 level tablespoons all-purpose flour
1 teaspoon salt
4 rounded teaspoons sugar
4 tablespoons butter, melted
2 cups white whole-kernel corn, drained, or fresh corn cut off the cob
4 eggs
1 quart milk

Makes 8 servings.
Stir flour, salt, sugar and butter into corn. Beat eggs well. Pour into milk and then stir into corn mixture. Pour into a 2-quart, greased casserole.
Bake in a preheated 400-degree oven for 40 to 45 minutes, stirring vigorously with a long-tined cooking fork 3 times about 10 minutes apart.

Kimchi©

Makes 4 cups.

1½ to 2	pounds Chinese cabbage or bok choy, cut into 1½-inch pieces
4	cups water
½	cup salt
4	ounces daikon (Japanese white radish), peeled and cut into julienne strips (3/4 cup)
¼	cup carrot, cut into julienne strips
3	green onions, bias sliced into 1½-inch lengths
2	teaspoons shrimp paste or anchovy paste
2	cloves garlic, minced
½	teaspoon ground red pepper
½	teaspoon grated gingerroot
¼	teaspoon sugar

In a large bowl, combine cabbage or bok choy, water and salt. Let stand 4 hours. Rinse well. Drain, leaving some water clinging to the leaves. Stir in daikon, carrot, green onions, shrimp or anchovy paste, garlic, red pepper, gingerroot and sugar. Mix well.

Press into a 1-quart jar. Secure lid. Let stand in cool place (60 to 70 degrees) for 2 to 3 days. To store, cover and refrigerate.

Ratatouille

Makes 8 to 10 servings.

3	eggplant, peeled and cut into bite-size pieces
2 to 3	medium zucchini, peeled and cut into bite-size pieces
2 to 3	yellow squash, peeled and cut into bite-size pieces
1 to 2	onions, sliced thin Olive oil
2	cloves garlic, minced
6 to 8	ripe tomatoes, peeled and quartered
2	tablespoons rough chopped

If eggplant, zucchini and yellow squash are in season, I don't peel them. I do peel them if they have been shipped in from another state or country.

Cut eggplant, zucchini and squash into bite-size pieces. Peel and slice onion.

Heat about 3 tablespoons olive oil in a large, heavy skillet. Add onion. Cook until onion is translucent. Add garlic, eggplant, zucchini and squash. Stir-fry until vegetables are soft and beginning to brown (you may have to add more olive oil). Add tomatoes, fresh or

fresh basil or 1 teaspoon
dried
Salt and pepper, to taste
Parmesan, optional

dried basil and salt and pepper to taste.
Cover pan, lower heat so mixture simmers
and, stirring occasionally, cook 10 minutes.
You can serve at this time or you can pour
mixture into a buttered baking dish and bake
at 350 degrees for 30 minutes, until bubbly
and well heated. Serve immediately topped
with a grating of Parmesan cheese.

Ferd Grisanti Restaurant's vegetable Parmesan©

Makes 10 to 12 servings.

¼ to ⅓ cup pure or virgin olive oil
1 tablespoon chopped garlic
(optional)
1 large yellow or white onion,
sliced into large circles or
chunks
6 green peppers, cleaned,
washed and cut into strips
(for a more colorful dish, use
2 red and 2 yellow peppers in
place of 4 green ones)
2 medium yellow squash,
cleaned and sliced into
¼-inch disks
2 medium zucchini, cleaned
and sliced into ¼-inch disks
Salt and pepper, to taste
2 cups marinara sauce, see
note
½ cup Parmesan or Asiago
cheese, grated

In a large sauté pan, heat olive oil over
medium heat. Immediately add garlic, onion
and peppers. Stir-fry till tender. Add squash,
zucchini, salt and pepper. Continue to stir till
heated through. Add marinara sauce and stir
till hot. Place in serving bowl and top with
grated Parmesan or Asiago cheese. Serve
immediately.

Note: If marinara sauce isn't readily
available, use a 16-ounce can of chunky
tomato sauce and add 1 tablespoon each of
fresh chopped parsley and basil. Dried
herbs can be substituted, but use only ¾
teaspoon of each.

Boone Tavern onion tart©

Makes 6 to 8 servings.

1 9-inch unbaked pastry shell
2½ teaspoons vegetable oil
1 pound onions

Heat the vegetable oil in a cast-iron skillet over
low heat. Add onions and Italian seasoning.
Sauté until onions are golden.

1¼	teaspoons Italian seasoning	Combine the grated cheeses and set aside.
2	cups grated Swiss cheese	Whisk together the eggs, milk, flour, mustard,
1	cup grated Cheddar cheese	salt and pepper.
6	eggs	Spread half the grated cheeses on the bottom
1	cup milk	of the pie crust. Top with the onions. Spread
1¼	tablespoons all-purpose flour	remaining cheeses on top of onions. Pour the egg mixture over all.
1	teaspoon Dijon mustard	Bake in a preheated 350-degree oven for 45 to
1	teaspoon salt	60 minutes or until set.
	Black pepper, to taste	Serve with sautéed vegetables.

Lynn's Paradise Café onion casserole©

Makes 8 to 10 servings.

1	quart whipping cream	Pour cream into a large skillet or sauce pan.
2	cups freshly grated cheese (any combination of Parmesan, Gruyere or a good-quality Swiss)	Reduce slowly over medium heat, stirring often, until thick enough to coat a metal spoon. Whisk in 1¼ cups cheese. Add
	Dash nutmeg	nutmeg, cayenne pepper and salt to taste.
	Dash cayenne pepper	While cream is reducing, peel onions. Slice
	Salt to taste	thin. Layer onions in a buttered 9-by-13-by-
5 to 6	large yellow onions, sliced thin	2-inch casserole. Pour cream sauce over onions. Arrange bread slices on top and
6 to 8	thick slices white bread	sprinkle with remaining ¾ cup grated cheese.
		Bake in a preheated 400-degree oven for 40 to 50 minutes or until brown and bubbly.

Down under onion©

	Oil for frying	Heat oil in a large deep kettle or deep-fryer.
1	large (16 ounces) white onion	The kettle has to be large enough to hold the
1	cup all-purpose flour	onion after it opens and deep enough for oil
¼	teaspoon chili powder	to cover the onion.
1	teaspoon salt	Cut onion into 16-sections, being careful not
½	teaspoon garlic salt	to cut through to the bottom. Onion will
½	teaspoon onion salt	resemble a peeled orange with sections
⅛	teaspoon white pepper	slightly separated.
1	cup milk	Combine flour, chili powder, salts and pepper
Dipping sauce:		in a wide flat bowl. Stir to combine. Set

⅓ cup Dijon extra-strong
 mustard
⅓ cup chili sauce
⅓ cup mayonnaise

aside.
Dip onion into milk, then into flour mixture,
working flour down into cuts. Drop into hot
oil. Cook to a light golden color. Serve with
dipping sauce while hot.
Dipping sauce: Combine mustard, chili
sauce and mayonnaise. Blend thoroughly.
Makes 1 cup.

Bobby J's garlic potato flan©

12 large potatoes, peeled and
 cubed
1 bunch leeks (about 3)
½ pound butter
½ pound Swiss cheese, cubed
3 tablespoons fresh garlic
1½ cups Parmesan cheese
1 cup heavy cream
 Salt and pepper, to taste

Makes 10 servings.
Boil potatoes until tender. Drain. Chop
leeks. Wash and drain. In a large skillet,
melt butter. Add leeks and cook until tender.
Add Swiss cheese. Heat until cheese melts.
Stir into cooked potatoes. Add garlic,
Parmesan cheese, heavy cream and salt and
pepper. Stir to combine. Pour into a
greased 9-by-13-by-2-inch casserole. Cover
with foil and bake in a preheated 350-degree
oven for 30 minutes.

Deitrich's potatoes©

1½ teaspoons chicken base
8 tablespoons (1 stick) butter
½ cup sour cream
2 cups heavy cream
2 cups milk
1 teaspoon dry basil
1 teaspoon granulated garlic
2½ pounds potatoes

Makes 6 to 8 servings.
In a saucepan, combine chicken base,
butter, sour cream, heavy cream, milk, basil
and garlic. Heat until sauce thickens slightly.
Peel potatoes and slice ¼-inch thick
Butter a 9-by-13-by-2-inch casserole. Place
potatoes in dish. Pour sauce over potatoes.
Cover dish with foil. Bake in a preheated
400-degree oven for 1 hour or until potatoes
are tender.

Jack Fry's potato gratin©

1 pound sliced shiitake
 mushrooms

Makes 8 to 10 servings.
Sauté shiitakes, shallots and thyme in olive
oil just until tender. Set aside to cool.

1	cup chopped shallots
2	tablespoons chopped fresh thyme
½	cup olive oil
10	large Idaho potatoes, sliced thin
	Salt and pepper, to taste
1	quart heavy cream
2	pounds goat cheese
2	egg yolks
1	cup sour cream

Slice potatoes thin, lengthwise. Set aside.

In a deep casserole dish, approximately 9-by-13-by-2-inches, place a layer of potatoes, then a layer of mushroom mixture, and a sprinkling of salt and pepper. Continue layering, ending with a layer of potatoes. Pour the heavy cream over the top layer of potatoes. Cover with foil and bake in a hot 450-degree oven for 1 hour. Remove from oven to cool slightly.

Mix together goat cheese, egg yolks and sour cream.

Just before serving, spread goat cheese mixture over top of potatoes and heat about 15 minutes.

O'Callaghan's leek-and-potato flan©

Makes 8 servings.

3	tablespoons unsalted butter
4	medium potatoes, unpeeled
3	medium leeks
2	tablespoons water
2½	ounces Gruyère cheese, grated
2	large eggs
2	large egg yolks
1½	cups heavy cream
	Salt and freshly ground white pepper, to taste
½	ounce Parmesan cheese, grated

Butter a 6-cup-capacity rectangular baking dish with 1 tablespoon of the butter. Set aside.

Bring 2 cups water to a boil in a medium saucepan fitted with a vegetable steamer. Add the potatoes, reduce heat to medium-low and steam for 15 minutes. When cool enough to handle, peel and refrigerate potatoes.

Trim the leeks of all but 2½ inches of green. Wash thoroughly. Cut into thin slices.

Melt the remaining butter in a medium skillet. Add the leeks and 2 tablespoons water and bring to a boil. Reduce heat to low, cover and braise the leeks until tender, 5 to 8 minutes. Drain in a colander and transfer to a mixing bowl.

Add the grated Gruyere cheese to the leeks in the mixing bowl. Cut the potatoes into thin slices and add them to the mixing bowl.

Heat the oven to 350 degrees.

In another bowl, beat together the eggs, egg yolks and heavy cream until smooth. Pour the mixture into the mixing bowl and combine the ingredients. Season with salt and pepper.

Pour mixture into the prepared baking dish, spreading the potatoes and egg mixture evenly. Sprinkle with the Parmesan cheese and bake in the center of a preheated oven for 40 to 50 minutes or until the flan is set and lightly browned.

Remove from oven and cool for 10 minutes before serving.

O'Charley's potato skins©

4   medium-size baking potatoes
    Cooking oil
    Salt to taste
2   cups shredded Cheddar and Jack cheese
8   tablespoons bacon bits
    Sour cream
    Chopped chives

Makes 8 skins.

Prick potatoes with a fork in several places before placing them in a 400-degree oven to bake until fork-tender, about 45 minutes. When cool, cut potatoes in half length-wise. Using a soup spoon, scoop out the inside of each potato half, leaving about ¼ to ⅜ inch of potato meat in each skin.

In a deep pot, heat cooking oil to 350 degrees. Drop scooped skins, a few at a time, into hot oil. Cook until golden brown. Remove from oil and drain, skin side up. Turn skins over and salt lightly. Fill each skin with ¼ cup mixed shredded Cheddar and Jack cheese. Place on a foil-lined metal tray. Slide under the broiler until cheese is melted. Top each skin with 1 tablespoon bacon bits, a dollop of sour cream and a sprinkling of chopped chives.

The Peddler's twice-baked potatoes©

6 baking potatoes
¾ cup sour cream
½ cup shredded Cheddar
cheese
2 eggs
¾ teaspoon white pepper
¾ teaspoon granulated garlic
¾ cup crumbled bacon
Salt, to taste

Makes 6 large servings, 12 small ones.
Bake potatoes in a 400-degree oven until done. Cut in half lengthwise. Scoop out potato, leaving skins intact.
Combine potato, sour cream, Cheddar cheese, eggs, white pepper, garlic, bacon and salt. Mash with a potato masher until well-blended. Fill skins with heaping spoonfuls of filling. Rebake in a 325-degree oven 8 minutes (or until ingredients are hot in center).

Lyonnaise potatoes©

6 medium potatoes, unpeeled
¼ cup butter
½ pound onions, thinly sliced
Salt
Ground black pepper
Fresh chopped parsley

Makes 6 servings.
Boil potatoes in their jackets until done, about 30 minutes. Peel and slice.
Heat butter in a skillet. Add potatoes and fry until browned.
In a separate skillet, sauté onions in butter until translucent. Add to the potatoes. Sprinkle with salt and pepper and mix lightly.
Turn into a serving dish. Sprinkle with chopped parsley.

Grand Victoria Casino & Resort's mashed potatoes©

3 Idaho potatoes, peeled and diced
3 medium-size red potatoes, diced, not peeled
¼ cup butter, melted
1 cup half-and-half
1½ teaspoons dry ranch-style salad dressing mix

Makes 6 to 8 servings.
Wash and prepare potatoes. Cover potatoes with water. Bring to a boil. Cook until potatoes are tender. Drain, saving some water in case you want to make the mashed potatoes a bit thinner.
Melt the butter and heat the half-and-half. Beat the potatoes until they are well-mashed. Add the melted butter and warm half-and-

Salt and pepper, to taste (you may not need much)

half. Beat until well-blended. Add the dry ranch dressing mix, salt and pepper. Mix well. If a thinner mixture is desired, add some of the reserved potato water.

I was so excited when Sue Grafton, author of the Kinsey Millhone mysteries, a series of mystery books beginning with "A is for Alibi", wrote requesting the recipe for the following scalloped potatoes. The request was written on her postcard, "K" is for Killer – that postcard is one of my treasures.

Anne Axton's scalloped potatoes©

Makes 6 servings.

2	pounds new red potatoes
1 to 2	cloves garlic, chopped (optional)
4	tablespoons butter
1	teaspoon salt
½	teaspoon freshly ground pepper
½	cup grated mild Cheddar cheese
½	cup grated Monterey Jack cheese
1	cup milk

Heat oven to 350 degrees. Grease a 9-by-9-by-2-inch baking dish.
Peel and slice potatoes ⅛-inch thick. Layer half each of potatoes, garlic, butter, salt, pepper, Cheddar cheese and Monterey Jack cheese. Using remaining ingredients, add second layer in the same order. Pour milk over all. Bake in hot oven for 1½ hours or until potatoes are tender and milk is absorbed.

Mrs. Wilkes' sweet potato soufflé©

Makes 6 to 8 servings.

4	pounds sweet potatoes
1	teaspoon salt
1½	cups sugar
2	eggs, beaten
½	cup raisins
1	lemon (grated zest and juice)
½	teaspoon nutmeg
½	cup evaporated milk
½	cup chopped pecans
1	stick butter or margarine, melted
½	cup shredded coconut

Peel sweet potatoes and slice about ½-inch thick. Place in a saucepan. Cover with water. Add salt. Bring to boil and cook until tender. Drain. Mash potatoes then whip until smooth and fluffy.
Combine sugar, beaten eggs, raisins, grated lemon zest (yellow part of rind only) and juice, nutmeg, evaporated milk, pecans, melted butter or margarine and shredded coconut. Stir until blended. Mix with sweet potatoes.
Pour into a greased casserole dish. Bake in

Marshmallows

a 350-degree oven for 25 minutes. Remove from oven. Cover top with marshmallows. Return to oven for 5 minutes or until marshmallows have turned a light golden brown. Serve immediately.

Heron Park Grill's scalloped sweet potatoes©

Makes 4 to 6 servings.

5   medium-size sweet potatoes, peeled
2   cups heavy cream
¼   cup prepared horseradish
3   tablespoons butter
1   teaspoon salt
¼   teaspoon ground white pepper

Preheat oven to 350 degrees. Slice potatoes about 1½-inches thick. Combine cream, horseradish, 1 tablespoon butter, salt and pepper in a large bowl. Mix to combine. Add sliced sweet potatoes and toss to coat evenly. With the remaining 2 tablespoons butter, grease the bottom and sides of a 9-by-13-by-2-inch baking dish. Place sweet potatoes in dish. Pour remaining cream mixture over potatoes.

Bake in preheated oven 45 to 55 minutes or until potatoes are tender.

Salsify au gratin©

Makes 6 servings.

1   tablespoon vinegar
3   cups water
1½ pounds salsify, trimmed
1   egg, beaten
5   tablespoons butter
¾   cup soft bread crumbs
3   tablespoons all-purpose flour
    Pinch salt
¼   teaspoon celery salt
¼   teaspoon dry mustard
    Dash white pepper
1½ cups milk
½   teaspoon Worcestershire sauce
1½ cups shredded Cheddar

In medium bowl stir together vinegar and water. Peel salsify and cut into one-inch pieces and immediately place into water-vinegar mixture to prevent darkening.
In a 2-quart saucepan over high heat, bring one inch water to a boil. Add salsify and reduce heat to medium-low. Cover and cook 20 minutes or until fork-tender. Drain and place salsify in a large bowl.
Mash with a potato masher. Mixture will be chunky. Stir in beaten egg.
In same 2-quart saucepan over medium heat, melt the butter. Spoon off 2 tablespoons butter and toss with bread crumbs until well-coated. Set aside.

cheese
Paprika

To remaining butter, add flour, salt, celery salt, mustard and pepper. Stir until smooth. Gradually stir in milk and Worcestershire sauce until well-blended. Cook over medium heat, stirring constantly until mixture boils and thickens. Add cheese, stirring until melted.

Remove from heat. Stir in salsify mixture, then spoon into greased 8-by-8-by-2-inch baking dish. Sprinkle with buttered bread crumbs and paprika.

Broil 7 inches from heat source for 2-3 minutes or until golden brown. Turn off broiler. Place on lowest rack in oven and let stand 7 minutes before serving.

Mrs. Droppelman's creamed spinach

Makes 4 to 6 servings.

2 pounds fresh spinach
6 slices bacon
4 tablespoons all-purpose flour
2 cups reserved spinach water
Salt and pepper, to taste

Dice bacon into small pieces. Place in a large skillet and fry bacon until crisp. Crumble into bits. Remove bacon from skillet and place on paper towel to drain. Set bacon drippings aside.

Meanwhile, bring a large kettle of water to a rolling boil. Drop in cleaned spinach. Leave in hot water only until softened, 3 to 4 minutes. Remove spinach from water and drain, pressing out as much water as possible.

Add flour to bacon drippings in skillet. Cook, stirring, until flour and drippings are thoroughly combined. Slowly pour in reserved spinach water, stirring while pouring. Cook until mixture has the consistency of medium creamed sauce.

Pour sauce over spinach, stirring to combine. Top with bacon bits. Serve immediately.

The Feed Bag's spinach soufflé©

1   10-ounce package frozen chopped spinach
2   10¾-ounce cans cream of mushroom soup
½   pound bacon
4   eggs, beaten
½   cup chopped green pepper
1   cup grated mozzarella cheese
1   cup grated Monterey Jack cheese
½   cup chopped green onion

Makes 8 to 10 servings.

Thaw and drain spinach thoroughly. Place in a saucepan. Add cream of mushroom soup (or you can use half-and-half cream). Heat and stir until combined.

Fry bacon until crisp. Remove to drain on paper toweling. Crumble into bits. Pour excess grease from skillet.

Add beaten eggs and chopped green pepper to the skillet the bacon was cooked in. Cook until eggs are almost set. Combine egg mixture with spinach mixture. Pour into a lightly greased casserole dish. Top with cheeses, green onions and bacon bits. Bake in a preheated 350-degree oven for 25 minutes or until golden.

Schnitzelbank Restaurant's spinach casserole©

White sauce:
6   tablespoons butter
6   tablespoons all-purpose flour
2   cups milk
1¼   teaspoons salt
1   teaspoon white pepper
Casserole:
1½   pounds frozen spinach
      White sauce
2   tablespoons butter
1   medium onion, diced
6   eggs, beaten
4   ounces mushrooms, sliced
½   cup Hormel's Real Bacon Bits
½   pound provolone cheese

Makes 8 to 10 servings.

To make white sauce: In a saucepan, melt butter. Add flour and stir. Cook over medium-high heat 3 to 4 minutes. Combine milk and salt and pepper. Heat, but do not boil. Slowly add to flour mixture, stirring constantly. Cook until thickened. Makes 2½ cups.

To make casserole: Heat spinach until defrosted. Squeeze very dry. Add white sauce, a little at a time, to spinach until you have the appearance of creamed spinach. (If mixture seems too thick, thin by adding half-and-half.) Set aside.

In a skillet, melt 1 tablespoon butter. Add diced onion. Sauté until translucent.

In another skillet, melt remaining tablespoon of butter. Add beaten eggs. Gently stir over low heat until eggs start to set. Add cooked onion, mushrooms and Bacon Bits. Stir in spinach mixture. Place in a 9-by-13-by-2-inch baking dish. Top with cheese. Bake in a preheated 350-degree oven until hot and cheese has melted, about 20 minutes.

Timothy's sautéed spinach and Tuscan beans©

Makes 4 servings.

¼ cup olive oil
1 tablespoon butter
1 tablespoon plus ½ teaspoon crushed fresh garlic
1 teaspoon lemon juice
¼ cup dry white wine
8 ounces washed and stemmed spinach
Salt, to taste
1 tablespoon chopped fresh rosemary
1 cup cooked Great Northern beans
Lemon wedges

In a heavy skillet, heat 2 tablespoons olive oil and the butter. When butter has melted, add 1 tablespoon crushed garlic, lemon juice and wine. Sauté 1½ minutes. Add spinach. Sauté only until spinach is soft. Add salt to taste. Remove from pan to a heated plate. Do not overcook the spinach.
In a separate skillet, heat remaining 2 tablespoons olive oil. When hot, add rosemary and remaining ½ teaspoon garlic. Sauté about a minute. Add the beans and salt to taste. Cook until beans are heated through. Serve with a wedge of lemon as a side dish to the spinach.

The Feed Bag's zucchini lasagna with wild rice©

Makes 8 to 10 servings.

2 6.25-ounce boxes long grain and wild rice
1 4.25-ounce can green chilies
1 pound Monterey Jack cheese, thinly sliced
3 medium zucchini, sliced
4 tablespoons grated Parmesan cheese
3 large tomatoes
3 cups sour cream
1 teaspoon garlic salt

Cook long grain and wild rice according to package directions. Drain when done.
Spray a 9-by-13-by-2-inch pan with non-stick spray. Spread rice in bottom of pan. Top with a layer of chilies, a layer of half of the Monterey Jack cheese and a layer of sliced zucchini. Sprinkle with Parmesan cheese. Layer on sliced tomatoes and sprinkle again with Parmesan.
Mix sour cream, garlic salt, basil, oregano, thyme, peppers and onion together. Spread

1   teaspoon basil
1   teaspoon oregano
½   teaspoon thyme
¾   cup chopped red bell pepper
¾   cup chopped green pepper
¾   cup chopped green onion
1   teaspoon Spanish paprika

over tomatoes. Top with remaining slices of Monterey Jack. Sprinkle top with paprika. Bake in a preheated 350-degree oven for 45 minutes to 1 hour.

Derby Dinner Playhouse's stewed tomatoes©

Makes 4 to 6 servings.

1   14.5- or 16-ounce can tomatoes
1   tablespoon butter
1 to 2 tablespoons sugar, or to taste
1   teaspoon salt
½   teaspoon ground pepper
3 to 4 slices day-old bread or dinner rolls

Heat tomatoes, butter, sugar, salt and pepper until hot and bubbly. Tear bread or rolls into medium pieces. Add to tomato mixture. Stir well and serve.

Cunningham's stewed tomatoes©

Makes 4 to 6 servings.

1   1 pound 6-ounce can whole tomatoes
¼   cup sugar
4   tablespoons butter or margarine
6   pieces bread or toast

In a saucepan combine tomatoes, sugar and butter or margarine. Bring to a boil and cook 5 minutes. Break bread into pieces and add to tomatoes. Boil 5 more minutes. Serve immediately.

Fried green tomatoes©

I had never eaten fried green tomatoes until I was testing recipes for this column! For health reasons, I chose olive oil instead of bacon grease for frying. My son, Chris, thought the recipe sounded rather bland and suggested adding some chopped onion. Had it not been for the addition of the onion, I would have chucked fried green tomatoes.
Now, I'm looking forward to the next time – green tomatoes, onions and bacon grease.

Makes 4 to 6 servings.

4 to 5 green or under-ripe red tomatoes

Slice tomatoes into ¼-inch slices. Set aside. Chop onion and set aside. In a shallow bowl

¼ cup chopped onion
1 egg
1 tablespoon water
1½ cups cornmeal or all-purpose flour
Salt and pepper, to taste
Shortening (your choice)

beat egg with water. Combine cornmeal or flour and salt and pepper on a platter. Dredge tomato slices in cornmeal or flour, dip in egg and coat completely with cornmeal or flour.

Heat enough shortening to generously cover bottom of a large heavy skillet (you can use bacon grease, butter, olive oil, margarine, vegetable oil—your choice). Drop in about a tablespoon chopped onion. Add coated tomato slices. Cook until golden, 3 to 5 minutes per side. Remove to platter.

Science Hill Inn's turnip casserole©

Makes 6 to 8 servings.

4 slices bacon
6 medium-size purple top turnips, peeled and grated (about 5 cups)
1½ teaspoons salt
½ teaspoon freshly ground black pepper
3 tablespoons chopped fresh chives
½ cup plus 2 tablespoons fontina cheese
3 medium eggs
1½ cups half-and-half

Fry bacon until crisp. Drain on paper toweling. Crumble. Generously grease a 2-quart glass casserole with bacon drippings. In a bowl combine crumbled bacon, grated turnips, salt, pepper, chives and ½ cup of the cheese. In a small bowl beat eggs lightly, add cream and pour over the turnip mixture. Stir well to combine. Pour into prepared casserole.

Sprinkle remaining 2 tablespoons cheese over top. Bake in a 350-degree oven for 30 to 40 minutes or until a knife inserted near the center comes out clean.

Grits and Rice

Atlanticville Café's grits and shrimp©

Makes 4 servings.

Salt
1 cup grits
2½ to 3 cups milk
3 tablespoons butter

In a 2-quart pan, bring 2 cups water to a boil. Season to taste with salt. While water is boiling, stir in grits. Turn heat to low. Cook until grits thicken, stirring constantly to prevent

4 tablespoons olive oil
½ cup chopped onion
20 shrimp, peeled, deveined and cooked
¾ cup dark beer
¼ cup sun-dried tomatoes
½ cup chopped country ham
4 tablespoons chopped green onion
½ cup veal or chicken stock
½ teaspoon Montreal Steak Seasoning

sticking. After grits have thickened, add milk to loosen. Cook again until thick. Add butter and stir until butter has melted.

Heat olive oil in a skillet. Add onion and cook until translucent. Add shrimp, beer, tomatoes, country ham, green onion, veal or chicken stock and Montreal Steak Seasoning. Cook until heated through. Pour over hot, creamy grits.

Azalea's sun-dried tomato roasted garlic grits©

¾ cup sun-dried tomatoes
1 bulb garlic, roasted and removed from skin and shell
5 cups chicken stock
6 tablespoons butter
½ cup diced small onion
½ cup diced small celery
2 cups heavy whipping cream
2 cups coarse ground white corn grits
3 ounces cream cheese
2 tablespoons chopped fresh basil
Salt and pepper, to taste

Makes 8 to 10 servings.

Combine sun-dried tomatoes, roasted garlic and chicken stock in a sauce pan. Bring to a boil. Allow to simmer 5 to 10 minutes. Place in a blender or food processor and blend until coarse texture remains.

In a large, deep, heavy pan melt butter. Add onion and celery and cook until translucent. Add cream and reduce by a quarter.

Add sun-dried tomato mixture and bring to a boil.

Slowly add grits and begin to stir constantly. Cook until grits are tender. Check for doneness by tasting (be very careful, as grits get extremely hot). Add more chicken stock if grits retain excessive crunchiness.

Remove from heat and incorporate the cream cheese and basil. Season with salt and pepper. Serve while hot.

To roast garlic: Heat oven to 350 degrees. Cut about ¼ inch from stem end of garlic head, exposing cloves. Leave root end intact but remove the extraneous papery outer layers from the head. Place in a shallow roasting pan. Drizzle with enough olive oil to go through to the pan. Sprinkle with a little salt. Turn upside down (root end up) on pan. Bake 15 minutes. Turn heads over and roast another 10 minutes. All cloves should be soft.

Alligator Grille's portobello grits©

Makes 6 to 8 servings.

2	cups chicken stock
2	cups heavy cream
1	cup quick grits
1	tablespoon butter
1½	cups portobello mushrooms, diced
¼	cup grated Parmesan cheese
1	tablespoon chopped parsley
	Salt and white pepper, to taste

In a heavy saucepan bring chicken stock and cream to a boil. Slowly stir in grits. Reduce heat and cook covered for about 4 minutes, stirring occasionally.

In a skillet melt butter. Add diced mushrooms. Cook until mushrooms take on a translucent look. Add to grits along with the cheese, parsley and salt and white pepper to taste. Finish cooking the grits, about 3 minutes. Let stand 10 minutes before serving. Grits should be soft and a little on the runny side.

Best grits casserole©

Makes 6 to 8 servings.

1	cup uncooked grits
4½	cups chicken broth
2	teaspoons seasoned salt
½	cup butter
2	cups grated sharp Cheddar cheese
2	eggs, beaten

Heat oven to 350 degrees.

Cook grits according to package directions using chicken broth instead of water and seasoned salt in place of the salt called for in directions. Remove from heat and add butter, Cheddar cheese and beaten eggs. Stir until butter and cheese melt. Pour into a greased 2-quart casserole. Bake for 30 minutes or until a knife inserted near center comes out clean.

Benihana of Tokyo fried rice©

Makes 10 servings.

1	cup uncooked rice

Cook rice according to package directions.

5	tablespoons butter	
1	cup chopped onions	
1	cup chopped carrot	
⅔	cup chopped scallions	
3	tablespoons sesame seeds	
1	egg for every 2 people	
5	tablespoons soy sauce	
	Salt and pepper to taste	

In a large skillet melt butter. Add onions, carrot and scallions. Sauté until onions are translucent. Set aside.
Heat oven to 350 degrees. Place sesame seeds in a shallow pan. Bake until golden, shaking pan occasionally for even color.
Lightly grease another skillet. Beat eggs. Pour into hot skillet. Cook as you would scrambled eggs.
Combine rice, vegetables, sesame seeds and eggs. Add soy sauce. Stir. Add salt and pepper to taste.

Caillouet's dirty rice©

5	each: chicken gizzards, necks, livers and hearts
1	quart water
2	pounds hot sausage
1	large yellow onion, minced
2	ribs celery, minced
1	small hot red pepper, minced
½	bunch green onions, minced
½	cup cooked ham, chopped
4	tablespoons butter
1	tablespoon dried parsley
3 to 4	cups cooked rice

Boil gizzards, necks, livers and hearts in the water until tender. Reserve broth. Grind gizzards, livers, hearts and meat from necks and set aside.
In large, heavy pot, brown sausage. Remove and set aside. Remove all but 2 tablespoons sausage drippings. Add yellow onion, celery and red pepper to drippings and simmer 20 minutes. Add green onions and simmer 10 minutes more. Add ham, reserved sausage, butter, parsley and ground chicken. Use some of the reserved broth to make mixture moist. Add salt to taste and simmer for 15 minutes.
Fold in rice and serve immediately.

Porcini spring vegetable risotto©

Makes 6 to 8 servings.

5	cups chicken broth
3	tablespoons butter
2	tablespoons oil
2	tablespoons chopped shallot or onion
1½	cups Arborio rice

Place chicken broth in a pan. Bring to a simmer.
Place oil and 2 tablespoons butter in a skillet placed over medium heat. Add shallot or onion and sauté until translucent but not browned. Add rice and sauté lightly 3 to 5

¾ cup grated Parmesan cheese
Salt and pepper, to taste
4 ounces each of julienne zucchini, julienne yellow squash and julienne carrot
⅓ cup peas

minutes. Begin adding simmering broth, ½ cup at a time, to rice. As the rice absorbs the broth and becomes almost dry, add another ½ cup broth, stirring so it does not stick. Repeat this step until all of the broth is used. When rice is almost done, add the remaining tablespoon butter, grated Parmesan, the julienne vegetables and the peas. (The raw vegetables are cooked by the internal heat and steam.) Mix well. Add salt if needed.

LaCazuela Mexican rice©

3 tablespoons oil
3 tablespoons butter
3 cups uncooked white rice
2 cloves garlic, minced
1 small to medium onion
2 tomatoes, diced
1 banana pepper, diced
1 jalapeño pepper, diced
3 tablespoons tomato purée
6 cups chicken broth
Salt to taste

Makes 10 to 12 servings.
In a large kettle, heat the oil and butter. Add rice and stir-fry until just golden. Add garlic, onion, tomatoes and peppers. Fry for 1 to 2 minutes. Add tomato purée and chicken broth. Taste to check flavor. Add salt to taste.
Stir until mixture comes to a boil. Reduce heat to a simmer and cover with a tight-fitting lid. Let simmer until rice is dry, about 20 minutes.

Equus' wild rice©

1 cup wild rice
2 tablespoons butter
1 teaspoon shallots, minced
¼ teaspoon garlic, minced
⅓ teaspoon fresh rosemary
⅓ teaspoon fresh tarragon
⅓ teaspoon fresh dill
2 ounces sherry
1 ounce soy sauce
Salt and pepper to taste
Dash paprika

Makes 8 servings.
Wash rice well in several waters, pouring off the foreign particles that rise to the top. Drain. Stir slowly into 4 cups boiling water to which 1 teaspoon salt has been added. Cook without stirring about 40 minutes or until tender. Or cook rice according to package directions.
In a large skillet, melt butter. Add shallots and garlic. Cook until transparent. Add fresh rosemary, tarragon and dill. Cook 15 seconds. Add sherry, soy sauce and cooked

Dash cayenne

rice. Season to taste with salt and pepper, a dash of paprika and cayenne.

Dairy and Cheese

When making cheese it is a good idea to sanitize the tools you will be using. The following is an easy way to do this. You will need a pan, colander, strainer or slotted spoon and a large piece of muslin or several layers of cheesecloth. Before beginning the process of making cheese, sanitize these items in a solution of one quart of water to one tablespoon bleach. Don't be alarmed – this is a very easy process – place the water and bleach in the large pan and drop in the other items. Let set about a minute. Wring out the cloth. Line the colander with it and place over a large bowl or place colander in the kitchen sink. Remove the strainer or spoon from the pan. Empty the sanitizing solution. Place pan over low heat just to dry.

Iole Kohl's homemade ricotta cheese

Makes about 1½ pounds.

2   quarts whole milk
1   pint buttermilk
1   pint heavy whipping cream

Place milk, buttermilk and whipping cream in a large pot. Place over medium heat until mixture reaches a temperature of 165 to 170 degrees and curds begin to form and separate from the whey. Place a cheesecloth or bag in a strainer or colander. Gently lift curds and place in cheesecloth. Strain out whey by lifting sides allowing it to drain off. The cheese will form into a nice ball. Remove cheese from cloth and refrigerate.

Crème fraîche (one way)©

Makes 1 cup.

1   cup heavy whipping cream
1   teaspoon buttermilk

Combine whipping cream and buttermilk in a jar with a tight-fitting lid.
Shake or stir mixture, then set it aside to let it ferment at room temperature for up to 24 hours.
Refrigerate. This recipe may be multiplied as desired.
Sweetened crème fraîche: Add 1

tablespoon confectioners' or granulated sugar to the buttermilk-cream mixture before allowing it to ferment.

Sweetened whipped cream

1 cup heavy cream
¼ cup sifted confectioners' sugar
½ teaspoon freshly ground nutmeg, optional
½ teaspoon vanilla

Makes about 2 cups.
Just before serving pie or dessert, whip the cream in a chilled bowl with the confectioners' sugar and nutmeg, if using, and vanilla. Beat to soft peak stage. Do not overbeat.

Colonnade cheese fondue©

3½ cups bread cubes
2½ cups grated or ground New York sharp cheese
3 large or 4 small eggs
½ teaspoon salt
3 cups skim milk, scalded

Makes 6 servings.
Remove end crusts from 2-day old bread. Cut trimmed slices into ½-inch cubes. Place about ⅓ of the bread cubes in the bottom of an 8-by-8-by-2-inch baking dish.
Distribute ⅓ of the cheese over the bread. Repeat, making 3 layers of each.
Beat eggs and salt slightly. Gradually add the hot milk, stirring constantly. Pour the egg mixture over the bread and cheese, being careful to moisten all the bread.
Place baking dish in a larger pan and add hot water to about half the depth of the baking dish. (Make sure the water will not come over the sides of dish into the fondue during baking.)
Bake on the bottom rack of a 350- to 375-degree oven for about 45 minutes, or until fondue just becomes firm.
Serve with jelly or Creole sauce.

Sandwiches, Stuffings and Dressings

Louisville's most famous sandwich, the "Hot Brown" has been served at the Brown Hotel since the twenties. Shortly after I started as Assistant Food Editor at The Courier-Journal, I was sent the following recipes for the hot brown as made by the first three chefs at the Brown. The lady who sent them, Mrs. Juanita H. Clark, of Sellersburg, Indiana, was a very good friend of Mr. J. Graham Brown's secretary. They were members of the Girl's YWCA "IT Club", and would meet after work on Monday night, go to the Brown for a hot brown then on to the "Y" for a Club meeting and a swim. Mr. Brown's secretary worked for him while all three chefs were at the Brown - she had the recipes from each chef and shared them with the girls in the club.

The original Hot Brown by Laurent Gennari, the first chef at The Brown Hotel (1923 to 1927)

Makes 4 sandwiches.

- 4 slices white bread, toasted
- 4 slices baked turkey or chicken, cut from the breast about ¼-inch thick
- ¼ cup grated American cheese
- 8 strips bacon, fried crisp
- 4 tablespoons grated Parmesan cheese
- 2 cups cream sauce

Blend American cheese with cream sauce until cheese melts. Place a piece of turkey or chicken on each piece of toast. Cover with ¼ - ½ cup of sauce. Place 2 strips of cooked bacon on each sandwich. Sprinkle with 1 tablespoon of Parmesan cheese. Place sandwiches in pan under the broiler until the cheese melts and becomes golden brown. Serve at once.

Note: There was no recipe for the cream sauce. You can use one of the recipe's for the sauce given in one of the other two chefs' recipes—remember to add the ¼ cup grated American cheese—or use the sauce recipe from The Brown Hotel's hot brown (recipe follows the first three chefs' recipes).

The original Hot Brown by Fred Schmidt, second chef (1927 to 1930)

Makes 4 servings.

Mornay sauce:
- 4 ounces butter (¼ pound)
  Flour (about 6 tablespoons)
- 3¼ cups milk
- 1 egg, beaten
- ¾ ounce Parmesan cheese

To make sauce: In a saucepan, melt butter. Add enough flour to make a roux (not too thin – not too thick blend). Slowly add milk, beaten egg and cheese. Stir thoroughly. Bring to a boil. Boil one minute, or until sauce thickens. Remove from heat. Fold in

(Romano may be substituted)
1 ounce whipping cream
Salt and pepper, to taste

Sandwich:
8 slices white bread, toasted
8 slices roasted turkey ¼-inch thick
8 to 12 slices fried bacon

whipping cream and stir carefully until smooth. Add salt and pepper to taste.

To make sandwich: Place two slices toast on a metal dish. Cover with turkey slices and a generous amount of sauce. Heat under broiler until sauce is speckled brown and bubbly. Garnish with two or three slices of fried bacon. Serve immediately.

The traditional Hot Brown by Mr. Harter, third chef (1930 – Mrs. Clark didn't give the year Mr. Harter left the Brown)

Makes 4 servings.

Sauce:
¼ cup oil
⅓ cup flour
2 cups fresh milk
1 tablespoon salt
Pinch white pepper
Pinch of Monosodium Glutamate
3 tablespoons Parmesan cheese
2 eggs, beaten

Sandwich:
8 slices white bread, crust trimmed and toasted
8 slices white meat of turkey
Parmesan cheese
8 slices crisp bacon

To make sauce: Heat the oil over a slow fire. Add flour. Stir. Heat milk and, while stirring, add to flour mixture. Add salt, pepper, monosodium glutamate and Parmesan cheese. Stir. Remove from heat. Add a small amount of hot sauce to beaten eggs. Stir. Add more sauce until eggs are warm. Add eggs, while stirring, to hot sauce mixture. Stir to combine

To make sandwich: Place toast on plate (must be metal or oven tempered). Cover with turkey and sauce. Sprinkle cheese on top. Bake under flame or in oven at 425 degrees until brown. Place crisp bacon crosswise on sandwich. Serve immediately.

The Brown Hotel's hot brown©

Makes 4 to 6 servings.

4 ounces butter
Flour to make a roux (about 6 tablespoons)
3 to 3½ cups milk
6 tablespoons grated Parmesan cheese

Melt butter and add enough flour to make a reasonably thick roux (enough to absorb all of the butter). Add milk and Parmesan cheese. Add egg to thicken sauce, but do not allow it to boil. Remove from heat. Fold in whipping cream. Add salt and pepper to

1 beaten egg
1 ounce whipping cream (optional)
Salt and pepper, to taste
8 to 12 slices of toast (may be trimmed)
Slices of roast turkey
Extra Parmesan for topping
8 to 12 strips fried bacon

taste.

For each hot brown, place 2 slices of toast on a metal (or flame-proof) dish. Cover the toast with a liberal amount of turkey. Pour a generous amount of sauce over the turkey and toast. Sprinkle with additional Parmesan cheese. Place entire dish under a broiler until the sauce is speckled brown and bubbly. Remove from broiler, cross 2 pieces of bacon on top and serve immediately.

Black Forest Inn's veggie burgers©

When I tested this recipe I wasn't too interested in trying the burgers. Much to my surprise, these burgers are excellent. The Black Forest Inn is in Minneapolis, MN.

Makes 8 to 10 large patties.

1 tablespoon olive oil
½ cup brown lentils
½ cup white rice
½ cup oatmeal
½ teaspoon salt
2 tablespoons sesame seed
1 tablespoon fennel seed
2 cups water
1 potato, shredded
1 carrot, shredded
½ green pepper, finely diced
½ medium onion, finely diced
1 cup mushrooms, finely diced
2 cloves garlic, minced
1 cup walnuts, chopped
1 teaspoon salt
1 teaspoon pepper
1 teaspoon oregano
1 teaspoon cumin
2 dashes cayenne pepper
2 teaspoons olive oil
1 teaspoon Worcestershire sauce

Heat olive oil in a medium saucepan. Add lentils, rice, oatmeal, salt, sesame and fennel seeds. Cook over low heat until the mix begins to brown, shaking and stirring as needed. Remove the pan from the heat and carefully add the water. Bring to a boil, lower the heat to a simmer, cover and cook for 20 minutes. Remove from heat, stir, cover and let stand for 10 minutes.

While the grain is cooking, prepare the following:

Shred the potato and carrot into a large mixing bowl. Add the remaining ingredients except the flour. Add the grain mixture and blend well. Mix in the flour, ¼ cup at a time. Cover and chill for 1 hour. Shape into patties the size you desire.

To finish, cover the bottom of a heavy frying pan with ⅛ inch vegetable oil (less in a non-stick pan). Allow oil to reach moderate heat (about 3 minutes). Set patties into pan. Keep the heat at about 300 degrees (moderately bubbling). Cook about 4

1   cup flour
    Vegetable oil

minutes on each side. Drain on paper towel. Transfer to a preheated, 350-degree oven for 6 to 8 minutes. If desired, cover with a slice of cheese for the last couple of minutes. Serve with bread or on a bun and garnish with your choice of sprouts, tomato slices, onion, mustard, mayonnaise, cucumber, secret sauces or whatever you like.

The Blue Goose Country Store and Tea Shop's nutty goose sandwich©

Makes 2 to 3 sandwiches.

1   8-ounce package cream cheese, room temperature
1   8-ounce can crushed pineapple, drained and squeezed
1   cup confectioners' sugar
1   11-ounce can mandarin orange sections, drained and squeezed
½   cup pecans
¼   teaspoon cinnamon
½   teaspoon vanilla

Place all ingredients in a bowl. Mix thoroughly. Serve on raisin bread. (I think date-nut bread would be good.)

Baked ham and cheese sandwiches

Makes 6 servings.

12 slices white bread, crusts trimmed
6   slices ham
6   slices turkey
6   slices Cheddar cheese
5   eggs, beaten
2½ cups milk
½   teaspoon onion salt
½   teaspoon dry mustard
    Topping (recipe follows)
Topping:
2   cups crushed cornflakes (this

To make sandwiches: Make a single layer of 6 slices of bread in a greased 9-by-13-by-2-inch baking dish. Top each slice with ham, turkey and cheese; then put the 6 remaining slices of bread over them. Mix remaining ingredients and pour over the sandwiches. Refrigerate overnight.

To make topping: Mix all ingredients thoroughly and distribute evenly over sandwiches. Bake 1 to 1¼ hours at 350 degrees. Slice into 6 portions. While hot, grate some Parmesan cheese over

takes nearly a whole 6-ounce
box)

½ cup (1 stick) melted butter
Grated Parmesan cheese

sandwiches.

Bristol Bar and Grille's grilled cheese sandwich©

6 Middle Eastern breads or pita
bread
1 to 1½ pounds Havarti cheese
Sautéed vegetables (recipe
follows)
2 tablespoons oil
Leaf lettuce
Melon
Strawberries

Sautéed vegetables:
2 small zucchini
1 medium onion
1 red or green pepper
1 large tomato
½ pound mushrooms
1 bunch broccoli
¼ cup salad oil
2 tablespoons sweet-and-hot
chili sauce
1 teaspoon thyme
1 teaspoon white pepper
1 to 2 teaspoons hot sauce

Makes 6 to 8 servings.
To make sandwiches: Place 2 slices of
Havarti cheese in the middle of Middle
Eastern bread. (If you are using pita bread,
cut bread open so you have 2 flat rounds.)
Place vegetables on top of cheese. Place 2
slices of cheese on top of the vegetables.
Fold bread to form sandwich or top with
remaining round of pita.
Place oil in a skillet. When the oil is hot,
brown the sandwich on one side. Flip so
browned side is up. Place on cookie sheet.
Bake in 350-degree oven for 8 minutes.
Serve on an oval plate with fruit garnish.
To make vegetables: Cut vegetables into
bite-size pieces. Put oil in a large skillet.
When hot, add vegetables and sauté just
until crisp. Add sweet-and-hot chili sauce,
thyme, white pepper and hot sauce. Stir to
blend. Use as filling for grilled cheese
sandwiches.

The Café at the Louisville Antique Mall roasted vegetable sandwich©

2 loaves French bread
Roasted vegetables:
1 small eggplant, peeled and
sliced ¼ inch thick
1 medium zucchini, sliced ¼
inch thick

Makes 6 servings.
To make sandwich: Cut each loaf of
French bread into 3 equal portions. Slice
each lengthwise. Set aside.
To make roasted vegetables: Line a sheet
pan with parchment paper or liberally grease
the pan. Spread out vegetables onto pan.

3 portobello mushrooms, sliced ¼ inch thick
1 large red pepper, julienne slices
¼ cup olive oil or vegetable oil spray
  Seasoned salt, to taste

Red onion relish:
1 large red onion, sliced ¼ inch thick
½ cup vegetable oil
3 tablespoons soy sauce
1 tablespoon cider vinegar
⅓ cup brown sugar

Sandwich:
1 cup fresh spinach leaves
6 slices Swiss cheese
12 slices ripe tomato

Spray or drizzle oil lightly on vegetables. Sprinkle with seasoned salt. Roast in a hot 350-degree oven until tender, about 15 to 20 minutes.

Set aside to cool.

To make relish: Sauté red onion in vegetable oil over medium heat. Once onion begins to wilt, add soy sauce, vinegar and brown sugar. Cook until sauce thickens. Set aside.

To make sandwich: Line a 15½-by-10½-by-1-inch pan with parchment paper or wax paper that has been lightly greased. Build 6 individual piles of vegetables, beginning with eggplant, then zucchini, portobello mushroom, red pepper, red onion relish, spinach leaves and Swiss cheese. Place pan in a hot 400-degree oven until cheese melts, about 5 minutes. Remove from oven. Place a stack of vegetables on each bottom portion of French bread. Top with tomato slices and top portion of bread. Serve immediately.

Pippin's Monte Cristo sandwich©

Makes 2 sandwiches.

2 eggs, beaten
¼ teaspoon vanilla
¼ teaspoon cinnamon
¼ teaspoon sugar
2 tablespoons milk
4 slices white sandwich bread
4 ounces turkey
4 ounces ham
4 slices Swiss cheese
¼ cup sour cream
¼ cup strawberry preserves

Combine eggs, vanilla, cinnamon, sugar and milk. Whip until well-blended. Dip both sides of bread into egg mixture. Grill one side of each slice of bread. When golden, flip. Layer turkey, ham and cheese onto grilled side of 2 slices of bread. Top each with a slice of bread, grilled-side down.
When bottom bread is golden, flip sandwich and grill top slice of bread, having all sides of bread grilled. Serve with sour cream and strawberry preserves.

Uptown's portabella mushroom sandwich©

Marinade:
- 1½ teaspoons cumin
- 1½ teaspoons thyme
- 1 chipotle canned pepper
- 2 tablespoons adobo sauce (from the canned pepper)
- 4 cloves garlic, crushed
  Juice of 3 limes
- ¼ cup cranberry juice
- ⅓ cup balsamic vinegar
- 1¼ cups olive oil

Sandwich:
- ½ pound bacon
- 6 portabella mushrooms
- 1 red bell pepper, cut into strips
- 1 green bell pepper, cut into strips
- 1 red onion, sliced thin
- ½ cup dry red wine
- ¼ pound arugula salad green (you can use half arugula and half fresh spinach)
- 4 6-inch French rolls
  Butter
- ½ pound feta cheese

Makes 4 sandwiches.

To make marinade: In the bowl of a food processor, combine cumin, thyme, chipotle pepper, adobo sauce and garlic. With processor running, add lime juice, cranberry juice and vinegar. Very slowly, with processor running, add olive oil. Process several seconds. Set aside.

To make sandwich: In a large skillet, fry bacon. When crisp, remove from pan and place on paper towel to drain.

Slice mushrooms, peppers and onion into thin strips. Place in a bowl and cover with the marinade. Let set for ½ hour. Place half the mushroom mixture, along with a small amount of the marinade, into a large, hot sauté pan. As vegetables soften and mixture begins to stick to pan, deglaze by adding half the wine. Cook until wine evaporates. Remove from heat and add half the arugula. Clean the pan and repeat procedure with remaining mushroom mixture and the arugula.

Lightly spread cut side of French roll with butter. Place buttered side down in a hot skillet or grill just long enough to toast. Top toasted French roll with mushroom mixture. Garnish with crumbled bacon and feta cheese. Repeat with each roll.

Stuffings and Dressings

Back Home's corn bread dressing©

- 1 pan sweet corn bread
- 5 hamburger buns
- 6 tablespoons butter

Makes 10 to 12 servings.

Crumble corn bread and buns into a large bowl. Melt butter in a skillet. Add onion, celery and sage. Cook until onion is

½ cup diced onion
½ cup diced celery
1 tablespoon dried sage
2 cups chicken broth
1 10¾-ounce can cream of chicken soup

translucent. Add chicken broth and chicken soup. Mix until well-blended. Pour over corn bread mixture. Stir until all is moistened. Pour into a well-greased 9-by-13-by-2-inch baking dish. Bake in a hot, 350-degree oven for 30 minutes or until hot. Serve immediately.

Chestnut stuffing©

4 cups boiled, shelled and peeled chestnuts, coarsely chopped
4 slices crisp-cooked bacon, crumbled
2 tablespoons drippings from cooked bacon
1 cup chopped onion
1 cup chopped celery
½ cup raisins
4 cups tart, diced apples
6 cups firm white bread, "torn" or cubed
¼ cup chopped parsley
1½ teaspoons fresh sage or ½ teaspoon dried sage
1½ teaspoons fresh thyme or ½ teaspoon dried thyme
Salt and pepper to taste
2 eggs
1 cup warm milk or broth

Makes 1 gallon dressing.
Put all ingredients except eggs and milk in a large bowl. Toss to combine.
Mix together eggs and milk or broth and add to bread mixture, tossing lightly to mix.
Use to stuff turkey, duck, pheasant or crown roast of pork. Cook according to appropriate timetable for the meat.
  Note: Recipe can be halved. Extra dressing can be baked separately.

Homer's Pub's corn-bread dressing©

1 gallon broth, chicken, turkey or pork
4 cups chopped onions

Makes 12 to 16 servings.
To make dressing: In a large kettle, combine broth, onions, celery and sage. Boil until vegetables are tender. Cool.

4 cups chopped celery
½ cup dried sage
⅓ cup corn oil
3 eggs, beaten
1 teaspoon salt, or to taste
1 teaspoon black pepper, or to taste
⅔ of the corn bread (recipe follows)
1 28-ounce loaf white bread

Corn bread:
1½ cups self-rising flour
Pinch salt
2 cups yellow self-rising cornmeal
1⅓ cups sugar
2 tablespoons baking powder
1¾ cups milk
4 eggs
2 tablespoons corn oil

When cool, add remaining ingredients. Stir to combine. Pour into a lightly greased 9-by-13-by-2-inch casserole. Bake in a 400-degree oven for about 1 hour.

When serving, add a little hot broth to top of dressing.

To make corn bread: Heat oven to 450 degrees.

Combine flour, salt, cornmeal, sugar and baking powder. Mix thoroughly. Add milk, eggs and corn oil. Mix until blended.

Grease corn-stick pans with melted butter. Fill pans and bake for about 15 minutes. Makes 3 pans of corn sticks, 9 sticks to the pan.

Marinades and Sauces

TGI Friday's Jack Daniel's marinade and glaze©

White wine and butter marinade:
¼ cup Chablis cooking wine
1 cup butter, melted
¼ cup lemon juice
¼ cup water
Salt and pepper, to taste

Glaze:
1 teaspoon onion powder
1 tablespoon Tabasco sauce
2 tablespoons red wine vinegar
¼ cup Jack Daniel's whiskey
2 cups brown sugar

To make marinade: In a container combine wine, melted butter, lemon juice and water. Add salt and pepper to taste. Use as a marinade for meat, poultry or seafood before grilling and as a basting sauce during grilling.

To make glaze: Combine all ingredients in a saucepan and bring to a boil. Reduce heat and simmer for 15 minutes. Allow to cool. Use as a glaze on meat, poultry and seafood just before removing from grill.

To prepare chicken breasts: Use two 4-ounce breasts for each serving. Marinate for

¼ cup water
2 beef bouillon cubes
2 tablespoons Worcestershire
  sauce

5 to 10 minutes in white wine and butter marinade. Place chicken on the grill or in a sauté pan. While cooking, baste often with marinade. When cooked to your satisfaction, brush liberally with glaze. Remove immediately to serving dish. Glaze burns quickly and can be difficult to remove from grill or pans if left to burn onto surface.

Easy hollandaise sauce©

3 tablespoons butter
2 tablespoons all-purpose flour
1 cup hot water
½ teaspoon salt
  Few grains cayenne pepper
2 tablespoons lemon juice
2 egg yolks, well-beaten

Makes about 1½ cups.
Melt butter in top of a double boiler. Add flour and blend well. Add hot water gradually, stirring continuously until thickened and smooth. Add salt, cayenne and lemon juice. Place over hot but not boiling water until ready to serve. While stirring, pour mixture slowly over well-beaten egg yolks. Reheat quickly and serve at once.

Hungry Pelican's sauce©

⅓ cup chili sauce
⅓ cup Dijon mustard
⅓ cup mayonnaise

Makes 1 cup.
Mix all ingredients well. Refrigerate.

Café Mimosa/The Eggroll Machine's Mimosa sauce©

1 7-ounce bottle pure fish
  sauce
1⅓ cups water
⅔ cup sugar
⅓ teaspoon crushed garlic
2½ tablespoons orange juice
2½ tablespoons vinegar
1 tablespoon lemon or lime
  juice

Makes 2½ cups.
In a large saucepan combine the fish sauce, water, sugar and crushed garlic. Bring to a boil, stirring occasionally. After mixture comes to a boil, remove from heat and let cool. Add the orange juice, vinegar, juice from lemon or lime and crushed red pepper flakes to taste.

Crushed red pepper flakes, to taste

Key West Grill's basil pesto sauce©

Makes 4 servings.

- 4 ounces fresh basil leaves
- 3 fresh garlic cloves, chopped
- ¼ cup olive oil
- ½ cup grated Parmesan cheese
- ½ teaspoon ground black peppercorns

Combine all ingredients in a blender or food processor. Smoothly puree and pour into medium saucepan. Warm on medium-low heat. Pour over pasta and serve. This makes a wonderful side dish for beef, poultry or seafood.

Kunz's beurre blanc sauce© (for poultry, seafood, vegetables and eggs)

Makes about 2 cups.

- 2 ounces chopped shallots
- 1 cup white wine
- 2 cups heavy cream
- Pinch of salt and pepper
- ½ cup butter, room temperature

In a saucepan, bring chopped shallots and white wine to a boil. Reduce heat to medium and simmer until wine is reduced by half. Whisk in heavy cream, salt and pepper; add butter a little at t time. Let this slowly reduce by one-third. Sauce will thicken while it reduces. Strain before serving.

Sarah's remoulade sauce© (for cold meat, fish, shellfish and pasta salad)

Makes about 1 quart.

- 3 cups Hellman's mayonnaise
- 2 tablespoons Dijon mustard
- ½ cup capers, drained
- 2 tablespoons fresh parsley
- 1 teaspoon cayenne pepper
- 1 tablespoon lemon juice
- 1 clove garlic, crushed
- Dash hot pepper sauce
- Dash A-1 Steak Sauce
- ⅛ teaspoon horseradish

Place all ingredients in the container of a food processor. Process until well-blended. Place in a container with a tight-fitting lid. Serve with cold meat, fish and shellfish. Keep refrigerated.

Note: Great mixed with pasta salad.

Alfredo sauce©

½ cup butter, room temperature
1⅓ cups whipping cream
1½ cups grated Parmesan cheese

Makes 2 cups.
In a heavy skillet melt butter. Add cream. Bring to a simmer. Cook until mixture reduces to consistency you desire (you can boil cream to make a nice thick sauce but you **CAN NOT** boil milk). Cook over medium heat until butter has melted and mixture is hot. Slowly add cheese. Stir until cheese melts and sauce has thickened.

Velouté sauce©

2 tablespoons butter
2 tablespoons all-purpose flour
2 cups chicken or beef stock
    Pinch nutmeg
    Salt and white pepper, to taste

Makes 1½ cups.
In top of a double boiler, not over water, melt butter. Stir in flour. When blended, gradually add chicken or beef stock.
Stir over low heat until well-combined and thickened. Place top pan in bottom pan of double boiler and simmer over boiling water about 1 hour, stirring occasionally. Add pinch of nutmeg and season to taste.
    Note: Do not cook this in an aluminum pan – it will discolor the sauce.

Sauce diable© (for meat or seafood)

3 tablespoons finely minced onion
2 tablespoons butter
2 tablespoons all-purpose flour
1 teaspoon soy sauce
1 tablespoon Worcestershire sauce
2½ teaspoons Dijon mustard
1 cup boiling water
1 rounded teaspoon instant beef bouillon (or 2 bouillon cubes)

Makes about 1½ cups.
In a skillet, sauté onion in butter until transparent and soft. Mix in flour to form smooth paste. Add remaining ingredients except the hot green pepper. Cook over medium heat, stirring constantly, until sauce thickens. If desired, add the hot green pepper, minced fine.
This is a **"red hot"** sauce to be used with any meat or seafood. Serve hot or cold.

2 dashes Tabasco sauce
½ cup red wine vinegar
1 canned hot green pepper,
chopped (optional)

Lemon sauce© (for chicken)

Makes about 1 cup.

½ cup lemon juice
½ cup water
½ cup sugar
2 tablespoons cornstarch

In a saucepan, mix lemon juice and water. Combine sugar with cornstarch. Stir into lemon juice mixture. Bring to a boil. Cook until thickened. Serve over chicken.

The Egg Roll Machine's sweet and sour sauce©

Makes 4 cups.

½ cup pineapple juice
½ cup peach juice
Juice of ½ lemon
Juice of ¼ orange
1 teaspoon tomato paste
¾ cup vinegar
3 to 3½ cups water
1¼ cups sugar, more or less to taste
Red food coloring
4 tablespoons cornstarch
4 tablespoons cold water

In a large sauce pan combine pineapple juice, peach juice, juice from half a lemon and fourth of an orange, tomato paste, vinegar and water. Add sugar to desired level of sweetness. Bring to a boil stirring occasionally. Let mixture boil for 1 to 2 minutes. Add red food coloring if desired. If served immediately, add cornstarch mixed with cold water to make a slurry to reach desired thickness. If stored, do not add cornstarch immediately. Wait until ready to serve, then heat sauce and add cornstarch mixed with cold water.
Sauce should be served warm. Will store for about 2 weeks in the refrigerator.

Sweet and sour sauce

Makes about 1½ cups.
In a saucepan combine all ingredients. Simmer to desired thickness.

½ cup vinegar
½ cup sugar
1 8-ounce can crushed pineapple
1 tablespoon soy sauce
1 to 2 tablespoons cornstarch

Mayonnaise-mustard sauce

1 cup mayonnaise
1 tablespoon yellow mustard
1 teaspoon dry mustard
4 ounces Cheddar cheese

Makes 1 cup.
In a bowl combine all ingredients. Pour over cooked vegetables such as broccoli or cauliflower. Heat a few seconds to warm sauce. Serve immediately.

Camille Glenn's favorite barbecue sauce©

The pickled ginger makes this a terrific sauce.

¾ cup apple cider or rice vinegar
2 tablespoons imported pickled ginger
1¼ cups best-quality ketchup
5 tablespoons Lea & Perrins Worcestershire sauce
1 cup light brown sugar, firmly packed
4 thin slices of lemon (seeds discarded)
3 to 4 tablespoons unsalted butter
Salt, to taste
Lemon juice, to taste
(optional)

Makes 2½ to 3 cups.
Combine the vinegar, ginger, ketchup, Worcestershire sauce, brown sugar and lemon slices in a processor for several seconds. Pour into a non-reactive saucepan and bring to a low boil. Simmer over low heat 6 to 8 minutes. The heat must be low, or use a flame tamer. This sauce will burn easily. Watch it closely.
Add the butter and simmer a few minutes longer. Add salt to taste and a little lemon juice, if desired.
Allow the sauce to stand for several hours or overnight.
Strain into a clean jar and store in the refrigerator. It will keep under refrigeration for several weeks, but does not freeze well.
  Note: This sauce will burn and blacken the meat if used for long-term basting. Go easy. Rice vinegar is more delicate in flavor than apple cider vinegar.

Hasenour's barbecue sauce©

2	15-ounce cans tomato sauce
1	12-ounce can tomato paste
1	32-ounce bottle ketchup
¼	cup granulated sugar
2	tablespoons mustard
2	tablespoons Worcestershire sauce
1	teaspoon Tabasco
2	cloves fresh garlic, crushed
4	teaspoons salt
½	cup brown sugar
2	teaspoons horseradish
½	cup soy sauce
¼	cup vinegar
1	quart water

Makes 3 quarts.
In a large kettle combine all ingredients. Bring to a simmer and cook 15 minutes. Store in refrigerator. Use with pork, ribs and chicken.

   Notes: For a smoky flavor, add 1 tablespoon liquid smoke.
For a hotter sauce, add 1 tablespoon dry mustard, 1 tablespoon chili powder and Tabasco to taste.
For still another flavor, add 1 lemon, sliced thin. Remove after simmering.
   Note: Do not use *creamy* horseradish

Barbecue Sauce minus the tomato©

1	quart water
1	pint vinegar
1	tablespoon Worcestershire sauce
½	cup salt
2	tablespoons sugar
1	teaspoon pepper
1	pound butter or margarine
½	cup chopped onion
	Garlic, to taste, optional

Combine all ingredients. This is enough sauce for grilling 8 medium chickens.

Jezebel sauce©

¾	cup pineapple preserves
¾	cup apple jelly
2 to 3	tablespoons horseradish
1 to 2	tablespoons dry mustard
⅛	teaspoon white pepper

Makes about 1½ cups.
Thoroughly blend all ingredients. Let stand at least four hours. Keeps indefinitely in refrigerator. Excellent with pork, beef, lamb, egg rolls or chicken.
   Note: Pineapple preserves is difficult to find – I use pineapple ice cream topping.

Morrison's tartar sauce©

¼ pound cabbage
1 small onion
1 thin strip green bell pepper
¼ cup dill relish
1 cup plus 2 tablespoons mayonnaise

Makes 2 ½ cups.
Place cleaned cabbage, onion and pepper in blender or food processor. Process to a fine pulp. Add relish and mayonnaise. Stir to blend. Place in a covered container. Refrigerate overnight before serving.

Equus tartar sauce©

¼ cup capers
¼ cup chopped parsley
1 tablespoon garlic
1 tablespoon shallots
Juice from 1 lemon
Juice from 1 lime
1½ cups mayonnaise
Tabasco sauce to taste
Salt and pepper to taste

Makes 2 cups.
Combine all ingredients in food processor and puree. Taste and adjust seasonings.

Entrees

Trellis Café's beef tips and noodles©

1 1-pound package egg noodles
Butter
Salt and pepper
Dill, fresh or dried
1 pound beef tips, preferable from the tenderloin or New York sirloin

Makes 6 servings.
Cook noodles according to directions on package. Add butter, salt and pepper to taste and a sprinkling of fresh or dried dill (if using dried, sprinkle sparsely). Keep warm. Dredge beef tips in flour. Shake off excess. Heat oil or butter in pan. When hot, add beef tips. Cook until well-browned, about 3 to 4 minutes. Remove from pan. Add

Flour for dredging
¼ cup cooking oil or clarified butter
½ pound fresh mushrooms, sliced
1 medium onion, diced
½ cup beef broth
½ cup white wine
1 teaspoon Worcestershire sauce
1 cup sour cream
Salt and freshly ground black pepper
Fresh parsley or chervil
Tomato wedges

mushrooms and onion to pan and sauté until tender, about 4 to 5 minutes. Add broth, wine and Worcestershire. Cook, stirring, until liquid is reduced by half.

Reduce heat and stir in sour cream. When sour cream is heated (do not boil), return beef to pan. Season with salt, if necessary, and a little freshly ground black pepper. Place noodles either on individual serving plates or on a serving platter. Spoon beef tips over noodles. Garnish with chopped parsley or chervil and small, thin tomato wedges.

The Upper Crust's meatloaf©

Makes 8 to 10 servings.

1½ pounds lean ground beef
4 eggs
1 medium onion, finely chopped
½ cup finely chopped green pepper
½ cup finely chopped celery
1½ cups bread crumbs
1 cup ketchup
1 teaspoon garlic powder
1 teaspoon thyme
Salt and pepper, to taste

Combine ground beef with remaining ingredients, mixing until well-blended. Shape into a loaf. Place in a lightly greased oven-proof pan. Bake in a 350-degree oven for 1 hour. Let cool 5 to 10 minutes before slicing.

Atomic Café's ropa vieja or Cuban pot roast©

Makes 6 to 8 servings.

2 tablespoons olive oil
1 large onion, chopped
1 green pepper, seeded and chopped
4 cloves garlic, minced

In a large stockpot heat the olive oil. When hot, add the chopped onion, chopped green pepper and minced garlic.
Sauté until tender but not brown.
Rub the beef with the salt and pepper. Add

2½   **pounds flank steak, brisket or stew beef**
1   **teaspoon salt**
1   **teaspoon black pepper**
1   **cup water**
2   **cups tomato sauce**
3   **tablespoons sliced green olives**
1   **tablespoon capers**

to the pot. Brown on both sides, about 10 minutes on each side. Add water, tomato sauce, olives and capers. Stir well. Bring mixture to a simmer. Lower heat and cook 2 to 3 hours or until meat shreds easily when pulled with a fork.

Blue Boar's Salisbury steak©

1   **large onion**
⅛   **green pepper**
⅛   **red pepper**
2   **pounds lean ground beef**
1   **teaspoon salt**
⅛   **teaspoon white pepper**
½   **cup cracker meal**
1   **egg, beaten**
⅓   **cup beef broth**
Mushroom sauce;
  Drippings from beef patties
3   **tablespoons all-purpose flour**
1½   **cups beef broth**
½   **cup water**
1   **cup mushrooms**
  Salt and pepper to taste

Makes 6 servings.
To make patties: Clean and chop onion and peppers. Place in a blender or food processor. Process until finely chopped. Mix ground beef with pepper-onion mixture, salt, pepper, cracker meal, beaten egg and ⅓ cup of the beef broth. Mix until well-blended.
Form beef into patties. Brown on both sides in frying pan. (Leave drippings in pan to use when making sauce.) Place patties in casserole. Cover with mushroom sauce. Bake in a 400-degree oven for 10 minutes.
To make mushroom sauce: Heat drippings from beef patties in frying pan. (Add vegetable oil or margarine to the drippings if you don't have enough fat in the skillet to total 3 tablespoons.) Add flour. Stir until flour has browned. Slowly add cold beef broth and water, stirring constantly to prevent lumps. Add mushrooms and salt and pepper to taste. Cook until desired consistency is reached.
Pour over beef patties and cook according to previous directions. Makes about 2½ cups.

Morrison's short ribs©

This is an excellent way to prepare short ribs. It's a two-day process but will worth the effort

8	pounds beef short ribs
1	tablespoon salt
¼	teaspoon pepper

Gravy:

	Drippings from short ribs
1	cup all-purpose flour
2	1-ounce packages au jus gravy mix
4	cups beef stock
4	cups diced onions
1	14.5-ounce can tomatoes, crushed

Makes 8 servings.

To prepare ribs: Rub ribs with salt and pepper. Place on baking sheet in a single layer, evenly spaced. Bake at 450 degrees until all sides are well-braised. Remove from oven and reserve drippings.
Place ribs on a rack placed over another pan and drain for about 45 minutes.
Cool and then chill overnight.

To make gravy: In a cast-iron skillet, heat drippings. Add flour and cook and stir until very dark.
Prepare gravy mix according to package directions. Add beef stock and gravy mix to flour mixture. Stir to make a thin gravy. Strain lumps.
Place short ribs in a roasting pan. Spread onions over top and add crushed tomatoes. Pour gravy over short ribs. Mix carefully. Cover with lid and bake at 350 degrees for 2 to 3 hours, or until meat is tender. Adjust seasonings, if necessary.

Kentucky pepper steak©

2	pounds boneless steak cut 1 to 1½ inches thick
¼ to ½	cup peppercorns, or very coarse, cracked black pepper
3	tablespoons butter
¼	cup whiskey or brandy
1	cup cream
	Watercress (nice, but optional)

Makes 4 servings.

Use a rolling pin or pepper mill to crack peppercorns, or use coarsely ground pepper. Press into both sides of steak with heel of hand.
Heat the butter in a heavy skillet until it foams.
Add the steak and brown on both sides. Lower the heat and cook to the desired doneness.
Transfer to a hot platter.

Pour off the fat. Return steak to skillet. Add liquor and ignite with a match. When flame has died down, return the steak to the platter.

Pour cream into skillet while stirring the particles from the bottom of the pan and cook until reduced by half. Pour sauce over steak. Serve with a generous amount of watercress, if desired.

Steak au poivre©

1 2-pound sirloin, chuck or favorite cut, at least 1½ inches thick
  Whole black peppercorns, coarsely crushed to equal about ¼ cup (see note)
4 tablespoons butter, divided
  Drop of oil
½ cup dry white wine
1 tablespoon brandy

Makes 4 servings.

Cover both sides of the steak generously with crushed peppercorns. Pound the pepper firmly into the meat with the heel of your hand.

Heat half the butter and a drop of oil in an iron skillet over high flame. Brown both sides of the steak, cooking to desired doneness. Remove to a hot platter.

Stir the wine and brandy into the pan juices. Simmer the sauce for two minutes. Add remaining butter and pour over the steak.

   Note: Place peppercorns in a heavy sealable plastic bag and crush with a rolling pin or potato masher.

Bristol Bar & Grille filet mandarin©

1 cup honey
1 cup soy sauce
1½ cups salad oil
¼ cup vinegar
¼ cup Mandarin Napoleon liqueur
½ cup minced onion
2 tablespoons garlic powder
2 tablespoons ground ginger
6 prime filets

Makes 6 servings.

Combine all ingredients except filets. Stir until well-blended. Place filets in a flat glass dish. Cover with marinade. Let sit for at least an hour.

Grill filets, basting with marinade, to desired doneness.

Rubino's grilled sirloin steak©

1	12-ounce center-cut sirloin steak

Basting sauce:
1½	cups yellow mustard
1	cup granulated sugar
½	cup brown sugar
2	cups cider vinegar
⅓	cup Cajun seasoning for steak
1	tablespoon granulated garlic
2	tablespoons Worcestershire sauce
2	tablespoons soy sauce
2	tablespoons butter

Makes 1 to 2 servings.
To make sauce: In a saucepan, combine yellow mustard, granulated sugar, brown sugar, vinegar, Cajun seasoning, garlic and Worcestershire sauce. Stir or whip until sugar is dissolved. Cook over low heat 10 minutes. Remove from heat. Stir in soy sauce and butter. Refrigerate. Makes 5 to 6 cups.
To make steak: Place steak in a shallow pan. Cover with basting sauce. Marinate about 30 minutes. Grill first side 3 to 4 minutes while basting often with sauce. Grill second side 3 to 4 minutes while basting often. Steak will be rare. Repeat process if you desire more doneness.
   Note: For the Cajun seasoning, Rubino's uses Chef K-Paul's Meat Magic Seasoning. This can be purchased through specialty catalogs. When I tested the recipe, I used McCormick's Cajun quick Blackened Steak Seasoning.

Iron Kettle meat loaf (family size)©

2	pounds ground beef
1	cup chopped onion
1	cup chopped green pepper
½	teaspoon garlic salt
1	teaspoon salt
1	teaspoon pepper
1	tablespoon celery seed
½	cup ketchup (or barbecue sauce)
1 to 2	tablespoons Tabasco sauce, or to taste
¼	cup Worcestershire sauce

Makes 6 servings.
Mix all ingredients together. Mold into a long, slim loaf. Place in a low baking dish, not a loaf pan. Bake in a 350-degree oven for 1 hour and 15 minutes.

½ cup quick oats
½ cup plain flour
4 eggs, beaten
½ cup milk

John's meat loaf

2 pounds lean ground beef
½ pound breakfast sausage
1 egg
½ to ¾ cup chopped onion
¾ cup ketchup
2½ cups crushed saltine crackers
⅓ cup Worcestershire sauce
½ teaspoon black pepper
1 teaspoon salt

Makes 6 to 8 servings.
In a big bowl combine all ingredients except ¼ cup of the ketchup. Mix, using your hands, until all the ingredients are evenly distributed. Gather the mixture together and place in a baking dish (not a loaf pan). Form into a loaf, patting together until the mixture is firm.
Bake in a 350-degree oven for 45 minutes. After a crust forms on the outside of the loaf, pour the remaining ¼ cup of ketchup over the meat loaf and bake an additional 45 minutes.
   Note: We often make 2 loaves, cutting the baking time to 35 minutes instead of 45 minutes. We have one for dinner and freeze the other for another time. Excellent.

John's roast beef

1 8- to 10-pound sirloin tip roast
2 cloves garlic, sliced
4 tablespoons melted margarine
1 tablespoon dry mustard
   Fresh ground black pepper
¼ cup lightly browned all-purpose flour
1 flattened piece beef suet, to cover
6 ounces dry red wine

Makes 10 to 12 servings.
Insert the tip of a sharp knife into beef in several places. Insert thin slices of garlic into pockets. Spread melted margarine over outside of beef. Sprinkle or rub with mixture of dry mustard, pepper and flour which you have lightly browned in a heavy skillet. Tie flattened layer of beef suet over the top of the roast.
When ready to roast, place the meat on a rack over a roasting pan and brown in preheated 425-degree oven for 15 minutes. Reduce oven to 325 degrees and add red

wine to pan. Continue to roast, basting frequently. Allow 18 minutes per pound for rare, 22 minutes per pound for medium or 25 minutes per pound for well done. When meat is finished cooking, turn off oven, open door and let meat set next to open door for 20 minutes before carving. Make gravy out of drippings in roasting pan.

Hint: Let roast stand outside refrigerator 2 hours before putting in oven.

J. Graham's beef, chicken or shrimp stir-fry©

Makes 8 to 10 servings.

2 to 3 cups uncooked rice
Oriental sauce (recipe follows)
1 cup thinly sliced boneless, skinless chicken breast, trimmed round steak or peeled and deveined raw shrimp
2 tablespoons sesame oil or corn oil
1 cup bias-cut celery
1 cup julienne-cut carrots
1 cup bias-cut bok choy or thinly sliced cabbage
1 cup broccoli florets
1 cup bean sprouts
1 cup bamboo shoots
1 cup sliced water chestnuts
1 cup sliced mushrooms
1 cup julienne-cut red pepper
1 cup julienne-cut green pepper
1 teaspoon chopped garlic
Dash soy sauce

Cook rice according to package directions. Set aside.

Prepare Oriental sauce. Keep warm.

Prepare meat of your choice. Heat a large wok or skillet until hot. Add sesame oil and meat. Brown quickly over high heat, turning frequently. Reduce heat and add celery, carrots, bok choy, broccoli, bean sprouts, bamboo shoots, water chestnuts, mushrooms, red and green peppers, garlic and soy sauce. Stir fry for 2 to 3 minutes until vegetables are just tender.

To serve, place rice on plate. Spoon meat and vegetables over rice. Top with Oriental sauce. Garnish with 1 or more of the garnishes.

To make sauce: In a saucepan, combine chicken stock, pineapple juice, soy sauce, ginger, garlic, sesame oil, sesame seeds and brown sugar. Bring to a boil.

Combine cornstarch with water. Pour slowly into boiling mixture, stirring constantly. When mixture reaches desired thickness, lower heat until ready to serve.

1   cup Chinese noodles,
    chopped scallions, cashews,
    peanuts or julienne-cut leeks
    or crepes (for garnish)

Makes 4 cups.

Oriental sauce:

2   cups chicken stock
2   cups pineapple juice
¼   cup soy or teriyaki sauce
¼   teaspoon ground ginger
¼   teaspoon chopped garlic
1   tablespoon sesame oil
1   teaspoon sesame seeds
    (optional)
¼   cup brown sugar
2   tablespoons cornstarch
2   tablespoons cold water

O'Callaghan's boeuf a la bourguignon©

Makes 6 servings.

6   ounces jowl bacon
1   tablespoon olive oil
3   pounds rump roast, cut into
    2-inch cubes
2   thickly sliced carrots
1   large onion, diced
1   teaspoon salt
¼   teaspoon pepper
2   tablespoons all-purpose flour
3   cups full-bodied, young red
    wine
3   cups beef stock
1   tablespoon tomato paste
2   cloves mashed garlic
½   teaspoon thyme
1   crumbled bay leaf
4   tablespoons butter
18 to 24   pearl onions
1   pound fresh mushrooms,

Remove rind from bacon and set aside. Cut bacon into thin sticks about ¼-inch thick and 1½ inches long. Simmer rind and bacon for 10 minutes in 1½ quarts of water. Drain and dry.

Heat oven to 450 degrees. Sauté simmered bacon in olive oil over moderate heat in a 9- to 10-inch oven-proof casserole that is at least 3 inches deep. Cook until lightly brown, 2 to 3 minutes. Remove bacon and set aside, leaving the fat in the casserole. Turn heat to high until fat is almost smoking before you sauté the beef.

Dry beef in paper towels – it will not brown if damp. Sauté a few pieces at a time in the hot oil and bacon fat until nicely browned on all sides. Add it to the bacon.

In the same fat, brown the vegetables. Remove and set aside. Pour out fat and

quartered
1 bunch parsley, chopped fine
and allowed to dry a bit

wipe inside of casserole with a paper towel. Return beef and vegetables to the casserole and toss with salt and pepper. Sprinkle flour and toss again to coat the beef lightly with flour.

Set casserole, uncovered, in middle position of oven for 4 minutes. Toss the meat and return to oven for 4 minutes more (this browns the flour and covers the meat with a light crust). Remove the casserole and turn the oven down to 325 degrees.

Stir in the wine and enough stock so the meat is barely covered. Add the tomato paste, garlic, herbs and bacon rind. Bring to a simmer on top of the stove. Cover the casserole and set in lower third of oven. Regulate heat so the liquid simmers very slowly for 3 to 4 hours. The meat is done when a fork pierces it easily.

In a skillet, melt butter. Add onions and brown. Remove from skillet and set aside. Add mushrooms; cook until tender; set aside until needed.

When the meat is tender, pour the contents of the casserole into a fine mesh sieve set over a saucepan. Wash out the casserole and return the beef mixture. Distribute the mushrooms and onions over the meat. Bring the liquid in the saucepan to a boil. Pour over the meat and return to the oven for 30 minutes. Remove from oven, sprinkle with parsley and serve.

Baked pot roast©

2 to 3 tablespoons vegetable oil
2½ to 4 pound top or bottom round
roast

Makes 4 to 6 servings.
Place vegetable oil in a heavy Dutch oven over medium-high heat. When oil is hot, add meat. Brown on all sides. Salt and pepper

Salt and freshly ground
pepper, to taste
1 carrot
1 rib celery
1 onion
1 to 2 cups beef stock
1 to 2 tablespoons all-purpose flour
½ cup cold water

roast well. Add vegetables and beef stock to cover ¾ of the roast.

Cover and place in a 300-degree oven 3 to 4 hours or until meat is tender. Remove from oven. Discard vegetables and skim extra fat. Remove meat to a platter. Place Dutch oven over medium-high heat to bring liquid to a boil.

To make gravy: Combine flour with water to make a slurry. Add to boiling liquid. Cook 3 to 4 minutes or until thickened.

Blue Boar's beef-stuffed peppers©

1 pound cooked beef
½ cup finely chopped onion
¼ cup finely chopped celery
1 tablespoon shortening
½ cup uncooked rice
⅓ cup ketchup
1 teaspoon salt
4 large green peppers

Creole sauce:
1 tablespoon shortening
1 medium onion, diced
½ green pepper, diced
½ cup celery, diced
Dash garlic powder
1⅓ cups beef or chicken stock
1 cup canned tomatoes
½ cup tomato puree
1 teaspoon sugar
½ teaspoon salt
¼ teaspoon white pepper
¼ teaspoon vinegar
1 tablespoon cornstarch
¼ cup water

Makes 4 servings.

To make peppers: Trim all fat and gristle from cooked beef. In a skillet sauté finely chopped onion and celery in shortening until translucent but not brown. Grind the trimmed beef and sautéed onion and celery together. Cook rice according to package directions. Drain but do not wash.

Combine meat mixture with cooked rice, ketchup and salt. Mix well.

Cut pepper in half, remove stem and seeds and steam until partially done, about 10 minutes. Fill each pepper with meat mixture. Place filled peppers on a baking sheet. Bake in a preheated 350-degree oven 15 to 20 minutes. Serve with Creole sauce.

To make sauce: Melt shortening in a heavy 2-quart saucepan. Add onion, green pepper, celery and garlic powder. Sauté until onion is translucent but not brown. Add stock, tomatoes, puree, sugar, salt, pepper and vinegar. Simmer gently for 30 minutes. Dissolve cornstarch in water. Add to sauce and cook until clear. Serve while hot. Makes approximately 4 cups.

Joe Huber Family fried chicken livers©

1 pound chicken livers
1 12-ounce can beer
2 cups all-purpose flour
1½ teaspoons seasoned salt
1½ teaspoons black pepper
Vegetable oil for frying

Makes 3 to 4 servings.
Rinse chicken livers well. Marinate in beer for approximately 10 minutes.
Combine flour, seasoned salt and black pepper. Dip chicken livers in the flour mixture. Redip in beer and again in the flour. Deep-fry for approximately 3 to 4 minutes or until golden brown in 350-degree vegetable oil.

O'Callaghan's lemon chicken©

4 whole skinless, boneless chicken breasts, halved lengthwise
10 to 12 lemons
8 tablespoons unsalted butter
2 tablespoons olive oil
1 cup all-purpose flour
¼ teaspoon garlic powder
¼ teaspoon black pepper
¼ teaspoon onion salt
¼ cup packed brown sugar
1 cup chicken stock
Salt and pepper, to taste
Fettuccine or rice (optional)
Chopped fresh parsley, for garnish

Makes 6 to 8 servings.
Place chicken breasts in a glass or plastic mixing bowl. Squeeze enough lemons to cover the chicken with juice. Cover with plastic wrap and let marinate in the refrigerator for at least 8 hours; overnight is preferred.
Melt butter in a large cast-iron skillet over medium-high heat and add the olive oil.
Mix flour, garlic powder, pepper and onion salt in a bowl. Dredge each breast in the flour mixture, reserving the lemon juice.
Place chicken breasts in hot butter and brown lightly on both sides. After browning, arrange breasts in an oven-proof casserole. Set aside.
To the hot skillet add the reserved lemon juice, brown sugar and chicken stock. Allow to simmer 3 to 5 minutes. While mixture is simmering, cut the end off 1 lemon and then cut lemon lengthwise. Slice each half as thinly as possible, starting with the end that already has been cut. Discard remaining ends. Add the lemon slices to the skillet and let simmer 2 more minutes. Taste sauce. Add salt and pepper to taste.

Pour sauce over chicken breasts and bake for 30 minutes in a 350-degree oven. Remove from oven and serve over buttered fettuccini or rice. Garnish with parsley.

Chestnut Street Café's roasted Cornish hen dijonnaise©

Makes 6 servings.

1	teaspoon fresh rosemary
2	teaspoons Montreal Steak Seasoning
2	teaspoons olive oil
3	whole Cornish hens, split in half
¾	cup white wine
1½	teaspoons honey
2	cups chicken stock
½	cup heavy cream
½	cup Dijon mustard (Grey Poupon)
1½	tablespoons cornstarch
	Salt and pepper, to taste

Mix together rosemary, steak seasoning and half a teaspoon olive oil. Rub this mixture over the Cornish hens 2 hours before cooking. Marinate in the fridge until baking. In a saucepan combine the wine, honey and chicken stock. Bring to a boil, reduce heat and cook to reduce by half. Drizzle remaining olive oil onto a baking sheet. Place Cornish hens on the sheet. Bake in a hot, 375-degree oven 45 to 60 minutes. To finish reduced sauce, add cream and mustard. Cook another 15 minutes. Mix cornstarch with 3 tablespoons cold water. Add to sauce. Stir to blend. Season to taste with salt and pepper. Cook another 15 minutes or until sauce has thickened. Serve over the Cornish hens.

El Rey Sol's chicken chipotle©

Makes 5 servings.

Chipotle sauce:

2	tablespoons vegetable oil
1	pound tomatoes, chopped
½	pound onions, chopped
8	chipotles adobados (canned chipotle chilies in adobo sauce)
8	ounces port wine
2	bay leaves
½	cup brown sugar
	Pinch black pepper

To make sauce: In sauce pan heat oil. Add tomatoes, onions and chipotles. Sauté about 8 minutes. Add wine and bay leaves. Bring to a boil. Simmer until tomato is very soft and breaks apart. Add brown sugar and pepper. Boil 5 minutes. Remove bay leaves. Blend mixture in a food processor. Press sauce through a sieve into a sauce pan. Bring to a boil and cook 3 minutes, stirring constantly. Mixture will thicken as it reduces. Remove from heat and set aside.

Chicken:
- 5 tablespoons vegetable oil
- 5 boneless chicken breasts
- 5 boneless chicken thighs
- 5 ounces brandy
- 20 ounces port wine
- Brown sugar (optional)
- 1⅔ cups heavy whipping cream

To prepare chicken: Heat oil in large skillet over medium-high heat. Add chicken and sear on both sides. Carefully stir in brandy and ignite. After flames have died, carefully add wine. Flambé and cook about 3 minutes until reduced.

Stir in chipotle sauce. If sauce is not sweet enough, add brown sugar to taste. Cook over medium heat for 5 minutes until reduced, constantly bathing the chicken with the sauce. Add cream and reduce until sauce thickens, about 5 minutes. Remove to serving plates and top each portion with sauce.

Oldenberg's Tuscan chicken©

- 1 10-ounce skinless, boneless whole marinated chicken breast (marinade recipe follows)
- 2 tablespoons herb butter (see note)
- ¼ cup sun-dried tomatoes, chopped
- 1 ounce goat cheese
- ¼ cup loose-packed chopped basil

Marinade:
- 1 cup vegetable oil
- ½ cup beer
- ¼ cup white vinegar
- 1½ teaspoons salt
- ¾ teaspoon pepper
- 1⅛ teaspoons sugar
- ¾ teaspoon chopped onion

Makes 1 serving.

To make chicken: Grill marinated chicken breast until done (internal temperature should register 170 degrees on instant-read thermometer). Place cooked chicken on serving plate. Top with herb butter, sun-dried tomatoes, goat cheese and fresh chopped basil. Serve immediately.

Note: Herb butter is butter that has been seasoned with dried herbs, to taste. When I tested the recipe, I used 2 tablespoons butter and ⅛ teaspoon each of thyme, basil and oregano.

To make marinade: Place all ingredients in a bowl and stir to combine. Add chicken and marinate at least 24 hours.

Makes about 1¾ cups marinade.

Rubino's chicken tetrazzini©

Makes 4 servings.

12	ounces linguine
12	ounces boneless, skinless chicken breasts
1 to 2	tablespoons olive oil
	Italian herb seasoning (mixture of ½ teaspoon each basil, thyme and oregano)
2	tablespoons butter, room temperature
2	tablespoons all-purpose flour
½	cup chicken stock
3	cups heavy cream
1	cup sliced mushrooms
	Salt and pepper to taste
1	teaspoon thyme
1	teaspoon basil
1½ to 2	cups freshly grated Parmesan cheese (more if you like)
½	cup chopped scallions
	Ground pepper for garnish

Cook linguine in boiling water until al dente. Drain and set aside.

While linguine is cooking brush chicken breasts with olive oil. Sprinkle with Italian herb seasoning. Place under broiler, turning once, until chicken is done. Cut chicken into ½-inch strips. Set aside.

Mix butter with flour to form a roux. Heat chicken stock. Add to roux in small amounts to form a paste, or veloute.

Heat cream in a large skillet. Slowly stir in chicken veloute. Add mushrooms, salt, pepper, thyme and basil. Bring to a boil. Add Parmesan cheese. Mix thoroughly. Cook for 30 seconds. Add linguine and toss. Add cooked chicken and toss. Add scallions and toss. Served garnished with freshly ground black pepper;.

Cheesy chicken divan with rice©

Makes 6 to 8 servings

6 to 8	boneless, skinless cooked chicken breasts
1	large bunch broccoli
1	cup long grain rice
½	cup chopped onion
½	cup chopped celery
3	tablespoons butter
¼	teaspoon each thyme, marjoram and rosemary
1	10 ¾-ounce can cream of

Bake chicken breasts until juices run clear – do not over bake. When cool enough to handle, cut on the diagonal into half-inch slices. Set aside.

Rinse and clean broccoli. Cut into bite-size pieces (you can also use the stalk portion of the broccoli). Cook in salted water until bright green, about 5 minutes. Drain and set aside.

Bring 2½ cups salted water to a boil. Add

mushroom soup
1   8-ounce jar Cheez Whiz
    Paprika

rice and stir. Turn heat to low and simmer covered 15 minutes. Set aside.
Sauté onion and celery in butter. Add thyme, marjoram and rosemary. Stir. Add mushroom soup and Cheez Whiz. Stir to blend.
Lightly grease a 2-quart shallow pan. Make a crust with rice. Place sliced chicken over rice. Pour broccoli mixture over chicken and sprinkle with paprika. Bake in a hot, 350-degree oven for 15 minutes or until hot and bubbly.
   Note: This dish can be prepared in advance and refrigerated or frozen. If frozen, thaw in the refrigerator. Bake 35 to 40 minutes or until hot and bubbly. Baking dish should be freezer-to-oven safe.

Columbia's chicken and yellow rice©

Makes 4 servings.

1   3-pound frying chicken
½   cup olive oil
2   onions, chopped
1   green pepper, chopped
2   medium tomatoes, peeled, seeded and chopped
2   cloves garlic, minced
1   bay leaf
2   cups long-grain rice
4   cups chicken broth
½   teaspoon saffron
1   tablespoon salt
½   cup small green peas (frozen of canned)
4   asparagus tips
¼   cup white wine
2   canned pimentos, cut in half

Cut fryer into quarters. In a skillet, sauté chicken in olive oil until skin is golden. Remove chicken and place in 3-quart casserole.
In the same oil, sauté onion, green pepper, tomatoes, garlic and bay leaf for 5 minutes. Spray a 9-by-13-by-2-inch pan with a non-stick spray. Place uncooked rice in bottom of pan. Place chicken pieces on top of rice. Pour onion mixture over chicken. Mix the chicken broth, saffron and salt together. Pour over chicken. Cover pan with aluminum foil. Bake in a 350-degree oven 40 to 50 minutes or until chicken is tender and rice is cooked.
While chicken is baking, defrost peas or drain if using canned. Steam asparagus just until tender. After removing chicken from

oven, sprinkle with wine and garnish with peas, pimentos and asparagus tips. Serve while hot.

Ferd Grisanti's chicken formaggio©

Makes 6 to 8 servings.

6   6- to 8-ounce whole boneless chicken breasts, cut in half
3   eggs, beaten
2   cups bread crumbs
    Olive oil (to coat bottom of sauté pan ¼-inch deep)

Sauce:
4   ounces (1 stick) butter
4   ounces (1 cup) all-purpose flour
2   teaspoons salt, optional
½   teaspoon white pepper
3   cups milk (heated to 160 degrees)
1¾   cups grated Parmesan cheese
1   cup half-and-half cream (heated to 160 degrees)

To make chicken: Rinse chicken breasts with cold water and drain. Dip in beaten egg. Coat with bread crumbs.

Heat oil in skillet to 350 degrees (drop in a few bread crumbs; if oil crackles, it's hot enough). Sauté chicken till done. Set aside on paper towels to drain.

To make sauce: Melt butter in a large saucepan. Immediately add flour, salt and pepper, stirring with a whisk. Cook over medium heat for about 3 minutes. (This mixture is called a roux.)

Slowly add heated milk, incorporating it into the roux. After all the milk has been added, let the mixture thicken, then slowly add the grated cheese. Stir again for a few minutes till mixture is thickened. Now slowly add half-and-half; cook for a few minutes on high heat while stirring constantly. The sauce is done when it coats a spoon.

Pour some of the cheese sauce in the bottom of a baking dish (enough to coat ⅛-inch thick). Lay chicken on top of sauce, arranging all the pieces in 1 layer. Cover chicken with remainder of sauce. Bake at 400 degrees for 10 to 15 minutes.

  Note: You can prepare the chicken and the sauce in advance, refrigerate them, then put them together later for less last-minute preparation. If this is done, the cheese sauce will thicken and perform better when putting the dish together.

Biltmore Estate's chicken breasts in lemon sauce©

Makes 4 servings.

Chicken:

½	cup margarine
½	cup butter
4	chicken breast halves, boned and skinned
1	cup white bread crumbs
1½	teaspoons paprika
1	teaspoon salt
½	teaspoon white pepper

Lemon sauce:

2	tablespoons butter, clarified
1	cup chicken stock or broth
¼	cup lemon juice
2	tablespoons all-purpose flour
	Salt and white pepper, to taste

To make chicken: Melt margarine and butter together. Dip chicken in butter mixture. Combine bread crumbs, paprika, salt and white pepper. Roll chicken in seasoned bread-crumb mixture. Place on greased pan and drizzle butter mixture over top. Bake in a 350-degree oven 15 to 20 minutes or until done. Keep warm.

To make sauce: To clarify butter, melt over low heat. Let stand a few minutes, allowing the milk solids to settle to the bottom. Skim the butterfat from the top and strain the clear yellow liquid into a container.

Heat stock and lemon juice together to a simmer. Heat clarified butter in a separate saucepan. Add flour, stirring to make a roux. Cook roux a few minutes but do not brown. Add stock mixture to roux, stirring until thickened and smooth. Strain if necessary. Add salt and pepper to taste.

Serve chicken topped with lemon sauce.

The Tea Leaf's chicken cordon bleu©

Makes 8 servings.

8	boneless chicken breast halves
8	thin slices Kentucky country ham
4	slices Monterey Jack cheese
8	teaspoons diced, fresh tomato
	Melted margarine
1	cup Parmesan cheese
1	cup parsley flakes
1	cup seasoned dry bread crumbs

Wash, skin and flatten chicken breasts by pounding with a mallet or plate edge. Place a thin slice of country ham, half a slice of Monterey Jack cheese and a teaspoon diced tomato on each chicken breast half. Fold so ham, cheese and tomato are encased within the chicken.

Dip in melted margarine.

Combine Parmesan cheese, parsley flakes and bread crumbs. Roll chicken breasts in crumb mixture. Place in buttered casserole. Bake in a preheated 350-degree oven 45 to 50 minutes.

Uptown Café's honey pecan chicken©

Makes 8 servings.

8 boneless skinless chicken breast halves

2 eggs, lightly beaten
Tabasco to taste
Pecan flour (recipe follows)

1 cup (2 sticks) butter, clarified (see note)

6 tablespoons chopped leeks

3 tablespoons minced garlic

1 cup plus 2 tablespoons brandy

5 cups chicken stock

2 tablespoons Dijon mustard

½ cup honey

4 tablespoons pecan pieces
Butter, cut into pats

Pecan flour:

2½ cups pecan halves

2½ cups all-purpose flour

1 tablespoons black pepper

1 tablespoon paprika

2¼ teaspoons cayenne pepper

1½ teaspoons white pepper

To make chicken: Dip chicken breasts into a mixture of eggs lightly whipped with 2 to 3 shakes Tabasco. Remove breasts. Drain off excess egg. Dip breasts into pecan flour mixture. Coat both sides evenly. At this stage, chicken can be either sautéed or fried. Cook until just slightly underdone.

Start pan sauce by heating clarified butter in a sauté pan. Add leeks and garlic. Cook for about 1 minute. Add brandy. **Caution:** Brandy is highly flammable so you may want to remove pan from burner before adding brandy. If brandy doesn't ignite, light it with a match. After brandy has flamed off, add chicken stock, mustard, honey and pecan pieces.

Boil down sauce to reduce. As sauce reduces, it will begin to thicken. Just before desired thickness is reached, place chicken breasts in sauce and allow to finish cooking. To finish, add several small pats of cold butter to enrich the sauce.

To make flour: Place pecans in container of food processor. Pulse until they are as fine as possible. If they are over processed, they will become oily and stick together. After pecans have been processed, mix all ingredients together. Store in an airtight container. Refrigerate.

Makes 5 cups.

   Note: To clarify butter, melt it slowly in a heat-proof glass measure in a pan of hot water. As the butter melts, the white solids will drop to the bottom, with the clear, yellow clarified butter remaining on top. Strain the clear butter into a container and discard the solids. Refrigerate.

Romano's Macaroni Grill's scaloppini de pollo©

Makes 2 servings.

4	ounces angel-hair pasta
1	chicken breast (2 halves)
½	pound butter
½	cup all-purpose flour, seasoned to taste with salt and pepper
½	cup sliced mushrooms
1	teaspoon capers
½	cup artichoke hearts
2	teaspoons rendered pancetta (see note)
½	cup white wine
½	cup heavy cream
	Juice of lemon

Cook angel-hair pasta according to package directions.

Meanwhile, pound chicken breast to even thickness. Cut into 4 pieces.

Heat a heavy skillet with enough butter to coat bottom of pan.

Coat chicken lightly with seasoned flour. Sauté in butter until lightly browned. Add mushrooms, capers, artichoke hearts and pancetta. Sauté until golden. Add white wine. Let reduce by half. Add heavy cream and continue to cook until thickened.

Remove from heat. Add lemon juice and remaining butter. Swirl pan to melt butter. Serve over angel-hair pasta.

Note: Pancetta is Italian bacon cured with salt and spices but not smoked. It's available at specialty supermarkets and some grocery stores.

Showley's risotto with smoked chicken, sun-dried tomatoes and pine nuts©

Makes 8 servings.

Risotto:

2½	tablespoons butter
2½	tablespoons olive oil
1	small onion, peeled and chopped
2	cups uncooked rice
2-3	saffron threads or a pinch of powdered saffron (optional)
1¼	cups white wine
2	teaspoons salt
4 to 6	cups chicken stock

To make risotto: In a large kettle, heat butter and olive oil. Add onion and cook until translucent. Add rice and continue to cook until the rice begins to color and loses the starch from the outside. Add the saffron, wine and salt and pepper, to taste. Stir until the rice begins to stick on the bottom of the pan. Add the chicken stock a little at a time, stirring constantly. Each time the rice begins to stick, add more stock. When you have used 4 cups of stock, taste the rice. It

⅛ teaspoon ground white pepper

To finish dish:
2 whole chicken breasts, skinned, boned and smoked or sautéed
2 to 3 tablespoons olive oil
1 pound white mushrooms, cut into quarters
1 red bell pepper, seeded and diced
¼ cup sun-dried tomatoes, cut into slivers
¼ cup pine nuts
2 cups chicken stock
½ cup whipping cream, optional
1 cup grated Parmesan cheese
Salt and pepper, to taste

should be crunchy in the middle but cooked on the outside. (If the rice has not reached this point, continue to add chicken stock and cook until it reaches this point.)

Remove from heat and spread risotto onto a large cookie sheet to allow it to cool immediately and stop cooking. Once the rice has cooled, put it in a covered container and chill until ready to use.

To finish dish: If using uncooked chicken breasts, cut into large cubes. In a large kettle, heat olive oil until hot but not smoking. Add chicken breasts. Cook until tender. Add mushrooms and cook until slightly colored. (If using smoked chicken, add to hot oil when adding mushrooms.)

Add 4 cups cooked rice and cook for 30 seconds to allow the rice to warm. Add the peppers, tomatoes, pine nuts, chicken stock and whipping cream. Stir constantly until the liquid has been absorbed by the rice. Add the Parmesan cheese and taste for seasoning. Pour onto heated plates and serve immediately.

Joe Huber's Family Restaurant's Grandma's chicken and dumplings©

1 chicken, boiled for broth
Fresh parsley or parsley flakes
1 cup all-purpose flour
⅛ teaspoon baking powder
¼ teaspoon salt
1 teaspoon lard
1 egg
1 tablespoon water

Makes 4 to 6 servings.

Place chicken in a deep pot with enough water to cover. Add parsley to water. Cook until chicken is done, about 45 minutes. Remove chicken from broth. When cool enough to handle, pull chicken from bones. Discard bones and return chicken to broth. In a bowl, combine flour, baking powder and salt. Using a pastry blender or 2 knives, cut in lard.

Combine egg and water. Add to flour mixture. Stir to combine. If dough is too stiff, add a bit more water. Place on a lightly floured surface. Knead 8 to 10 times. Roll, as you would for pie crust, to about ⅛-inch thickness. Cut into 1-inch squares. Drop into boiling broth. Cook about 15 minutes or until dumplings are tender.

O'Callaghan's sauté of chicken thighs with leeks and mushrooms©

2	small leeks
¼	pound fresh morels or other mushrooms
4	chicken thighs (about 1⅓ pounds)
	Salt and pepper
2	tablespoons butter
½	cup white wine
¼	cup chicken stock
½	cup heavy cream
⅛	teaspoon nutmeg

Makes 4 servings.
Cut green leaves from leeks. Thoroughly rinse leeks and morels. Cut leeks into julienne strips. Trim tough stems from mushrooms and halve very large mushrooms.
Sprinkle chicken with salt and pepper. In a large frying pan, heat butter. Sauté chicken, skin side down, over medium heat until golden. Turn and sauté until golden on second side. Add leeks and cook until soft (about 3 minutes). Add wine and stock. Bring to a simmer. Cover pan and gently simmer, turning chicken once until done (about 10 minutes). Remove chicken. Keep warm.
Add mushrooms to pan. Cook over high heat until sauce is slightly thickened. Lower heat. Stir in cream. Simmer gently until sauce thickens enough to coat the back of a spoon. Season with nutmeg, salt and pepper, to taste.
Spoon sauce over chicken before serving.

Buffalo chicken wings©

24	(about 4 pounds) chicken wings
	Salt and pepper, to taste

Makes 4 to 6 servings.
To make wings: Cut off and discard small tip of each chicken wing.
Cut at joint, dividing wing into 2 pieces.

4 cups peanut, corn or
vegetable oil
¼ cup butter
2 to 3 tablespoons hot pepper
sauce
2 to 3 teaspoons white vinegar
Celery sticks

Blue cheese dressing:
1 cup mayonnaise
2 tablespoons finely chopped
onion
1 teaspoon minced garlic
½ cup sour cream
2 tablespoons chopped parsley
2 to 3 teaspoons lemon juice
2 to 3 teaspoons white vinegar
¼ cup crumbled blue cheese
Salt (optional)
Freshly ground black pepper
Cayenne pepper

Season with salt and pepper.
Heat oil in deep fryer or deep heavy skillet to 375 degrees. Add half the wings and fry about 10 minutes, until golden brown and crisp. Remove wings and drain well. Repeat frying with remaining wings.

Melt butter in a saucepan. Add hot sauce (more may be added; let your taste buds decide) and vinegar.

Place wings on a warm platter and pour butter mixture over them.

Serve with blue cheese dressing and celery sticks.

To make dressing: Combine mayonnaise, onion, garlic, sour cream, parsley, lemon juice, vinegar and blue cheese in a mixing bowl.

Season to taste with salt, pepper and cayenne.

Mix and chill 1 hour or longer before serving. Makes about 1½ cups.

O'Callaghan's chicken tetrazzini©

Makes 6 to 8 servings.

8 ounces uncooked noodles
2 cups chicken broth
2 tablespoons butter or
margarine
1 tablespoon olive oil
2 tablespoons grated onion
1 cup sliced mushrooms
1 medium green pepper, diced
1 medium sweet red pepper,
diced
4 tablespoons all-purpose flour
2 egg yolks, lightly beaten

Cook noodles according to package directions. Drain and set aside. Start heating chicken broth.

Heat butter and olive oil. Add onion, mushrooms and peppers. Sauté until onion becomes translucent. Stir in flour to make a roux. Cook, stirring 3 to 4 minutes.

Whisking constantly, slowly add ¼ cup hot chicken broth to egg yolks. Slowly return mixture to hot chicken broth, whisking constantly. Continue whisking while adding cream. Combine with roux, whisking until

½ cup whipping cream
2 to 3 cups diced chicken or turkey
Chopped parsley
Salt and pepper, to taste
½ cup toasted almonds
Parmesan cheese

smooth and thickened. Add chicken, parsley and noodles.
Season to taste with salt and pepper. Turn mixture into a greased 3-quart casserole. Sprinkle with almonds and Parmesan cheese. Bake at 350 degrees until hot..

Jack Fry's lamb chops©

4 lamb chops
2 ounces veal or chicken stock
1 teaspoon butter
1 teaspoon mustard
1 teaspoon chopped fresh rosemary

Makes 1 serving.
Grill chops to desired tenderness. While chops are grilling, prepare demi-glace by combining veal stock, butter, mustard and rosemary in a sauté pan. Heat until butter has melted and all ingredients are thoroughly mixed together. Serve immediately.

Jack Fry's pork chops©

5 to 6 tablespoons olive oil
4 12-ounce center-cut pork loin chops
1 yellow onion, diced
1½ teaspoons sugar
2 cups chicken stock
8 blanched garlic cloves
5 ounces shiitake mushrooms, stemmed and sliced
2 slices bacon, finely diced
½ cup vermouth
¼ teaspoon rosemary
12 ounces new red potatoes, quartered
12 spears fresh asparagus, cut into 2-inch pieces

Makes 4 servings.
Heat 2 tablespoons olive oil in a sauté pan. Add chops and sear until golden on both sides. Remove to a 400-degree oven. Bake for 20 minutes for medium to medium-well; 25 minutes for well-done.
Combine onion, sugar and 1½ teaspoons olive oil in a sauté pan. Add ½ cup chicken stock and simmer until syrupy. Set aside. Dip garlic cloves in boiling water for 3 to 4 minutes. Remove to ice water to chill. Do this 3 or 4 times or until garlic reaches the consistency of cooked potato. Heat 1 teaspoon olive oil in a sauté pan. Add peeled garlic cloves and cook until golden brown. Set aside. Sauté mushrooms in 1 tablespoon olive oil until soft. Set aside. Sauté bacon until crisp. Drain on paper towel. Reserve some of the fat in the pan. Deglaze pan with vermouth (be very careful

– vermouth is highly flammable). Cook until it reduces by half. Add remaining 1½ cups chicken stock and rosemary. Simmer and adjust seasonings.

Sauté potatoes in 2 to 3 tablespoons olive oil until golden brown. Remove potatoes from pan and add a bit more olive oil. Add asparagus. Sauté just until crisp tender. Combine onion mixture, garlic, shiitake mushrooms, bacon, potatoes and asparagus in a large pan. Keep warm until ready to serve with the pork chops.

Autumn pork chops©

1   tablespoon butter
6   center-cut pork chops
     Salt and pepper, to taste
3   tart apples, peeled and
     quartered
12   dried figs
1   tablespoon brown sugar
     Dash nutmeg
¼   teaspoon cinnamon

Makes 6 servings.
In a large, heavy skillet, melt butter. Sprinkle chops with salt and pepper. When butter has melted, place chops in skillet. Brown on both sides. Arrange apples and figs around chops. Combine brown sugar, nutmeg and cinnamon. Sprinkle over chops. Cover skillet and simmer 30 minutes or until chops are done.

Simple pork roast©

1   3- to 4-pound boned pork loin
     roast
     Salt and pepper, to taste
1   teaspoon rosemary leaves or
     sage
1   clove garlic, thinly sliced,
     optional

Makes 8 to 10 servings.
Sprinkle pork roast liberally with salt and pepper then with rosemary or sage.
If you choose to use garlic, slice into thin slivers. Using the pointed end of a sharp knife, make several punctures into pork. Insert a sliver of garlic into each puncture. Place pork on a rack in a roasting pan that has been sprayed with a non-stick spray. Bake in a hot 450-degree oven for 20 minutes.
Lower heat to 350 degrees and bake an

additional 50 to 60 minutes or until a meat thermometer inserted into the center of the pork reads 155 degrees.
Remove from oven and allow to rest at least 10 minutes before serving. Temperature should rise to 160 degrees.

Baked pork tenderloin©
When preparing pork tenderloin, a very tender, delicious cut of meat, the oven is heated first to 450 degrees. The meat is cooked 30 minutes and removed to rest 10 minutes before slicing.

Yen Ching's double-cooked pork

1½	pounds pork
½	cup wine
2	thin slices fresh ginger, chopped
3	green onions, chopped
¼	head cabbage
1	green pepper
1	red pepper
½	pound carrots
3	garlic cloves
6	tablespoons vegetable oil
1	tablespoon water
2	tablespoons sweet soybean paste
1	tablespoon hot bean paste
2	tablespoons soy sauce
2	tablespoons sugar

Makes 6 servings.

Simmer the whole piece of pork (starting with cold water) with the wine, ginger and green onions for about 20 minutes or until the pork is thoroughly cooked. Remove from water. Cool. Slice across the grain into thin slices. Cut the cabbage into diamond shapes 1 by ½-inch. Remove seeds from green and red peppers and cut into 1-inch squares. Slice carrots on the diagonal into 1-inch pieces. Slice garlic.

Heat 3 tablespoons oil in wok. Add cabbage. Add 1 tablespoon of water. Stir-fry over high heat. Remove when cabbage starts to turn soft.

In a small bowl mix the sweet soybean paste, hot bean paste, soy sauce and sugar. Set aside.

In a wok, heat 3 tablespoons of oil. Fry pork slices until the grease is extracted from the fat. Add garlic, green and red pepper, cabbage and carrots. Stir-fry several seconds. Remove from wok. Use the remaining oil to fry the soybean mixture for several seconds. Return the pork slices and the vegetables. Stir well and serve.

Donna Gill's pork tenderloin with mustard sauce©

Makes 6 servings.

12 slices pork tenderloin, cut ¾ inch thick
Salt and freshly ground pepper
All-purpose flour
5 tablespoons butter
⅓ cup white wine vinegar
8 black peppercorns, crushed
2 cups heavy cream
½ cup Dijon mustard

Place each slice of pork tenderloin between 2 sheets of wax paper and pound until flattened to ½-inch thick. Sprinkle with salt and pepper and dust with flour.
In a skillet, melt 3 tablespoons of the butter. Sauté the pork on both sides until just done. Transfer to a platter and keep warm.
Add the vinegar and crushed peppercorns to the skillet. Bring to a boil and deglaze the pan, scraping up the browned bits that cling to the bottom of the pan, boiling until the liquid is reduced by two-thirds. Add the heavy cream and simmer until thickened. Remove from the heat and stir in the mustard and the remaining 2 tablespoons butter. Season to taste and pour over the pork.

Pork Dijonnaise©

Makes 6 to 8 servings.

1½ to 2 pounds pork tenderloin
Oil
1 cup butter
½ cup Grey Poupon Dijon mustard
⅓ cup packed light brown sugar

Place tenderloin on a rack in a shallow baking pan. Brush with vegetable or olive oil. Bake in a preheated 325-degree oven for 1 hour or until the internal temperature reaches 170 degrees on a meat thermometer.
In a skillet, melt butter over low heat. When melted, add mustard. Stir and cook 2 to 3 minutes. Add sugar. Cook and stir another 2 to 3 minutes.
Slice cooked tenderloin on the diagonal. Pour sauce over pork.

Savory pork roast©

Makes 8 to 10 servings.

1 teaspoon salt
1 teaspoon pepper

Combine salt, pepper, saffron, marjoram, basil, cumin and garlic. Mix to combine

1 teaspoon ground saffron or crushed saffron threads
½ teaspoon marjoram
½ teaspoon basil
½ teaspoon cumin
3 garlic cloves, finely chopped
1 3- to 4-pound boned pork loin roast
1 cup white wine
3 tablespoons grated onion
½ teaspoon salt
¼ teaspoon pepper
2 tablespoons finely chopped fresh parsley
½ cup cold water

thoroughly. Rub into the pork. Wrap pork in plastic wrap and refrigerate overnight.
Place the pork in a roasting pan and roast in a hot 400-degree oven for 30 minutes. Reduce the heat to 350 degrees. Slowly pour the wine over the roast, being careful of splattering, and continue to roast for a total of 20 to 25 minutes per pound or to an internal temperature of 155 degrees. Baste frequently with the pan juices.
Transfer the roasted pork to a warm platter. Degrease the roasting juices and combine in a saucepan with the onion, salt, pepper, parsley and cold water. Bring to a boil and cook over low heat for 2 minutes.
Carve the pork and serve the sauce in a separate gravy boat.

Pork chop-rhubarb casserole©

Makes 6 servings.

4 tablespoons butter
6 loin or rib chops cut ¾-to 1-inch thick
1¼ teaspoons salt
⅛ teaspoon pepper
2 cups toasted soft bread cubes
½ cup brown sugar
½ cup granulated sugar
3 tablespoons all-purpose flour
½ teaspoon cinnamon
6 cups sliced rhubarb, about 1½ pounds

Melt 2 tablespoons butter in a large skillet. Add chops that have been seasoned with about 1 teaspoon salt and the pepper. Brown chops on both sides. Remove to a platter.
Toast bread and cut into ¼-inch cubes. Add remaining 2 tablespoons butter to drippings in skillet. When butter melts, add bread cubes and remaining ¼ teaspoon salt. Toss. Set aside.
In a bowl combine sugars, flour and cinnamon. Stir to blend. Add rhubarb. Stir. Lightly grease an oven-proof, 3-quart casserole. Place half of the bread mixture in the bottom of the casserole. Spoon half of the rhubarb over the bread. Arrange chops on top of rhubarb. Place remaining rhubarb

over chops.
Cover tightly with foil and bake in a
preheated 350-degree oven for 40 minutes.
Remove from oven and top with remaining
bread mixture. Bake an additional 10
minutes.

Silo Microbrewery's pecan-crusted pork chops©

Makes 6 servings.

6	7-ounce center cut butterflied pork chops
	Milk
10	ounces pecan pieces ground fairly fine
¼	cup vegetable oil (for frying)
3	cups heavy whipping cream
3	tablespoons pureed chutney
3	ounces brandy
1	Granny Smith apple, diced

Dip chops in milk and then in pecans,
pressing firmly so pecans adhere to chops.
Heat oven to 400 degrees.

In a heavy skillet heat oil. Add chops. Fry
on each side until pecans are golden.
Transfer chops to an oven-proof dish. Finish
cooking in oven to desired doneness, usually
internal temperature of 140 degrees, or
about 30 minutes.

In a saucepan combine heavy cream, pureed
chutney, brandy and diced apple. Bring to a
simmer and cook until mixture is reduced by
half. Sauce should have a syrupy
consistency. Spoon sauce over chops
before serving.

Boil-baked country ham©

1	country ham
	Water to cover
1	cup vinegar
1	cup dark brown sugar
	Whole cloves
¼	cup dry mustard
½	cup packed dark brown sugar
2	tablespoons cornmeal

Three days before serving, in a large roaster
or stock pot, soak ham overnight in enough
cold water to cover. In the morning remove
ham, place in sink and scrub with a brush
under running water until it has been cleaned
of any clinging debris.

Wash roaster or stock pot, place ham in it
and cover with water.

Add vinegar and brown sugar to ham water
and bring to a boil, immediately reducing
heat to low.

Simmer 20 minutes per pound for older ham,

15 to 18 minutes per pound for quick-aged ham, or until the small bone in the hock can be pulled out with the fingers. Let cool in cooking water overnight.

Place cooked ham on rack to drain. Trim fat to about ½-inch thickness, score and stud with cloves.

Mix dry mustard, brown sugar and cornmeal. Apply uniformly over ham. Place ham on an open baking pan with a rack. Bake in a 375-degree oven 20 to 30 minutes or until evenly browned. Remove from oven and cool on rack.

Refrigerate overnight before serving. Slice paper-thin. Served on beaten biscuits, it feeds a crowd.

John E's barbecued ribs©

1 slab ribs (3 pounds or less before trimming)
½ cup barbecue spice (recipe follows)
½ cup your favorite rich and thick barbecue sauce

Barbecue spice:
1½ cups sugar
6 tablespoons salt
¼ teaspoon turmeric
½ teaspoon coarse ground pepper

To make ribs: Rub both sides of slab with barbecue spice. Let stand 15 minutes. Rub on barbecue sauce. Let stand in refrigerator for 2 hours or longer.

Lay slab, meat side up, on rack over pan containing a small amount of water. Cook in a 375-degree oven until done (about 1 hour), turning once after meat side is richly browned. (Replace water as needed.)

Slice ribs when cool. The meat can be cooked ¾ done in the oven and then finished on an outdoor grill.

To make spice: Combine all ingredients and stir to blend. Store in airtight container. Makes about 2 cups.

Best way to roast a turkey©

1 12- to 14-pound turkey
2 cups salt

Makes 6 to 8 servings.
Remove giblets, neck and tail from the bird and rinse. Rinse bird inside and out.

½ **cup butter, melted**
½ **cup all-purpose flour**

Place turkey in a non-reactive (stainless steel, plastic, ceramic, etc.) pot or container large enough to hold it. Rub salt all over the turkey and into the body cavities. Add cold water to cover. Stir water until salt dissolves. Set turkey in refrigerator or other cool location for at least 4 hours or overnight (I prefer overnight).

When ready to cook, remove turkey from salt water and rinse it several times so that all traces of salt water are gone.

Remove liver from giblets and return to refrigerate (or, if you don't like liver, toss). Put remaining giblets, neck and tail piece in a large saucepan. Add water to cover. Bring to a boil, skimming foam from surface as necessary. Simmer, uncovered, for 1 hour. Strain broth. Cool to room temperature and refrigerate until ready to use.

Remove the meat from the neck and tail. Chop meat and giblets into medium-fine dice. Refrigerate until ready to use.

Preheat oven to 400 degrees. Bring turkey legs together by trussing (tying them together). Brush the entire breast side of the turkey with the melted butter. Place the turkey, breast side down, on a rack (v-rack is best). Brush back of turkey with butter.

Lower oven rack to second-lowest position in oven. Place turkey in oven and roast 45 minutes. Brush the turkey with a little more butter and some of the pan drippings. Add some water to the pan. Roast another 30 minutes, basting occasionally.

Remove turkey from oven and turn it breast side up. Roast until a meat thermometer stuck in the deepest part of the thigh registers 165 degrees, about 30 minutes. Transfer turkey to platter and allow to rest 15 to 20 minutes before carving.

To make gravy: Place the roasting pan over a burner set on medium heat. Scrap drippings from bottom of pan. Add flour. Stir and cook, scrapping the drippings into the flour. Let cook 1 to 2 minutes – don't let it get too brown. Add reserved broth (if you don't have enough broth, add some water) and stir. Add the chopped meat and giblets. Return to a boil, lower heat and simmer until broth thickens slightly. Serve with turkey.

   Note: If you want, you can cook the liver and add it to the gravy. I usually toss the liver from turkey..

Deep-fried turkey©

1   **10- to 12–pound turkey**
    Salt and pepper
    Cayenne pepper
    Oil for frying

Makes 6 to 8 servings.

Remove the giblets from the turkey. Rinse inside and outside of the turkey. (You can soak the bird in brine as above but dry the bird thoroughly before lowering it into the hot oil. If you soak the bird in salted water, don't salt before frying – it won't need it.) If you have not soaked the bird, sprinkle the bird with salt, pepper and a bit of cayenne pepper.

Use an extra-large pot for cooking the bird – remember when you lower the bird into the oil, the level of the oil is going to rise. The oil is very hot – if the bird has any water on it, the oil will splatter and pop. This is kind of messy so if possible, cook the turkey outside. Heat the oil to just below smoking – about 375 degrees. Carefully lower the bird into hot oil. Fry 4 minutes to the pound. Remove from oil, drain and serve. Delicious.

Bravo Gianni's veal scaloppini a la Pitino©

Makes 4 servings.

12	veal scaloppini (medallions of veal sliced very thin)
12	thin slices Italian prosciutto
6	tablespoons butter
½	cup light sherry or dry Marsala
2	teaspoons capers
1	teaspoon fresh garlic, finely chopped
8	cups fresh spinach
4	hard-boiled eggs, sliced
4	tablespoons Parmesan cheese

For each patty, pound 3 veal scaloppini and 3 thin slices prosciutto together to form a patty. Heat 4 tablespoons butter in a heavy skillet until hot. Add veal patties. Cook until veal is brown on one side. Remove from skillet. Pour off butter and clean pan. Add light sherry or dry Marsala and a teaspoon of capers to skillet. Return veal patties, cooked side up. Cook slightly (veal should be medium-rare when served). Remove patties to a hot platter. Add remaining 2 tablespoons butter to skillet. When melted, add garlic. Sauté several seconds. Add spinach. Cook just until limp. Divide spinach among 4 oven-proof serving dishes. Top each serving with a veal patty. Top veal with several thin slices of hard-boiled egg. Sprinkle each serving with a tablespoon of grated Parmesan cheese and several capers. Run under the broiler for several seconds or until cheese has turned golden. Serve immediately.

Porcini's veal piccata©

Makes 1 serving.

1	tablespoon olive oil
3	slices (2 ounces each) veal scaloppini
½	cup all-purpose flour
2	ounces white wine
1	tablespoon lemon juice
1	teaspoon nonpareil capers
2	ounces veal or chicken stock
1½	teaspoons unsalted butter
	Pinch fresh chopped parsley

In a sauté pan heat the oil. Dredge the scaloppini slices in the flour, then place in the hot oil. Sauté gently about 45 seconds to 1 minute on each side. Drain excess oil. Deglaze the pan with white wine. Add the lemon juice, capers and stock. Simmer about a minute. Place the veal slices on a serving plate. Add the butter and parsley to the wine mixture. Reduce it by half its volume, about another minute or so. Pour sauce over scaloppini and enjoy.

Parakeet Café's veal Prudhomme©

4 ounces veal scaloppini
¼ cup all-purpose flour, seasoned with salt and pepper to taste
1 tablespoon olive oil
½ cup fresh sea scallops
½ cup zucchini, cut in sticks
1 cup heavy cream
Frank's Louisiana hot sauce, to taste
¼ cup chopped green onions

Makes 1 serving.
Dredge veal in seasoned flour. Heat olive oil in skillet. Add veal and sauté lightly, 1 to 2 minutes on each side. Remove veal to a platter and keep warm. Add scallops to skillet. Sauté 2 minutes. Add zucchini. Sauté 1 minute. Add cream and hot sauce. Reduce to sauce consistency.
Place veal on serving plate and top with sauce. Garnish with chopped green onions.

Fish and Seafood

Seafood burritos©

3½ pounds boneless whitefish (cod)
10 whole imitation crab sticks
2 pounds popcorn shrimp, cooked
1 pound fresh mushrooms, sliced
8 ounces unsalted butter
5 sprigs fresh parsley, chopped, reserve stems
2 tablespoons dried chives or 3 tablespoons fresh
2 teaspoons crushed fresh garlic
10 12-inch flour tortillas
Seafood sauce:
8 ounces butter
1 cup all-purpose flour

Makes 10 large servings.
Place fish in an oven-proof dish. Cover with foil. Bake in a preheated 350-degree oven 20 to 30 minutes or until flaky. Remove from oven and set aside.
While fish is baking, cut each crab stick into four 1-inch pieces. Cook shrimp in boiling water just until pink, drain and set aside. Sauté mushrooms in 4 ounces of the butter until tender; set aside.
In a skillet, melt 4 ounces of the butter. To the melted butter add fresh chopped parsley, chives and garlic. Add the cooked seafood. Remove from heat and cover to keep warm.
To make sauce: In a 3-quart saucepan melt 8 ounces butter. Stir in the flour to make a roux. Add lobster base, paprika, lemon juice and white pepper. While stirring, slowly add half-and-half and reserved parsley stems.

4 ounces lobster base (see note)
1 teaspoon Spanish paprika
Juice of 1 lemon
¼ teaspoon white pepper
2 quarts half-and-half
5 whole fresh parsley stems (use reserved stems)

Stir with a wire whisk until sauce simmers and is smooth and creamy. Remove parsley stems and keep sauce warm.

To assemble: Place ½ to ¾ cup of seafood mixture in center of tortilla. Fold sides in first; roll toward front. Place folded-side down in a glass baking dish. When all burritos are made, add any remaining seafood to the sauce. Ladle some seafood sauce over top, cover with foil and bake at 350 degrees for 15 to 20 minutes. Before serving, ladle remaining seafood sauce over burritos. Garnish with additional fresh chopped parsley and paprika.

Porcini cappellini con pesce©

Red clam sauce:

4 cups clam juice or stock
2 cups crushed tomatoes
1 teaspoon minced garlic
¼ teaspoon dried basil
¼ teaspoon dried thyme
⅛ teaspoon dried oregano
⅛ teaspoon dried marjoram
¼ teaspoon crushed red pepper flakes (less for milder sauce)
½ cup white wine
⅓ cup corn starch

Con pesce:

12 ounces uncooked cappellini
16 littleneck clams, washed and rinsed
12 large sea scallops
12 large shrimp, peeled and deveined
16 mussels, debearded
6 ounces squid, tubes and tentacles cleaned

Makes 4 servings.

To make sauce: In a saucepan, combine clam juice, tomatoes, garlic and seasonings. Bring to a rapid boil for 5 to 6 minutes. Reduce to simmer and continue to cook an additional 10 to 15 minutes. Combine wine and cornstarch. Stir until cornstarch dissolves. To thicken sauce, while stirring, add this mixture in four stages. After each addition, allow mixture to come back to a boil. When desired thickness is achieved, remove from heat. If necessary, discard any remaining wine mixture. Strain to remove the herbs and garlic. Discard.
Makes about 1 quart.

To make con pesce: Cook pasta according to package directions.
While pasta is cooking, heat clam sauce to simmering in a large saucepan or stockpot. Add clams. Bring back to simmer and cook 3 to 4 minutes. Add sea scallops. Bring mixture back to simmer and cook 1 to 2

Chopped parsley (optional)

minutes. Add shrimp and mussels and poach 1 to 2 minutes.
Remove from heat and add the squid. Let stand 1½ to 2 minutes.
To serve, divide pasta among 4 large plates. Divide seafood equally among plates.
Ladle any remaining red clam sauce equally over seafood and pasta.
Garnish with chopped parsley. Serve immediately.

Scalloped oysters

Makes 4 to 6 servings

8	ounces fresh oysters, reserve oyster liquor
3	cups coarse-crushed saltine crackers
4	tablespoons butter
	Salt and pepper, to taste
1 to 1½	cups half-and-half or whole milk

Preheat oven to 375 degrees. Lightly grease a 1½ quart casserole. Place a layer of crushed crackers on bottom of casserole. If oysters are large, cut into pieces about an inch long. Place randomly over crackers (not in a solid layer). Dot with butter and salt and pepper. Continue to layer until casserole is filled to about 1-inch from top. Add milk or half-and-half to oyster liquor to make 1 to 1½ cups. Pour over crackers until you can just see the liquid coming up the side of the dish. Bake in a preheated oven for 45 minutes. Serve while hot.

Jack Fry's shrimp and scallop bow-tie pasta©

Makes 1 serving.

3½	ounces uncooked pasta
½	teaspoon dried tarragon
½	teaspoon fresh garlic
¼	teaspoon shallots
½	cup white wine
1	cup heavy cream
½	cup chicken stock
	Salt and pepper to taste

Cook pasta according to package directions. Combine tarragon, garlic, shallots and wine. Simmer and reduce by one half. Add cream, chicken stock and salt and pepper. Reduce by one-fourth. Thicken with ½ teaspoon roux. Sauté shrimp and scallops with small amount of butter. Toss with pasta and sauce.

4 large shrimp, peeled and
cleaned
4 large scallops
Butter

To make roux: Combine 1 tablespoon each
of butter and flour. Stir into a smooth paste.
Refrigerate until ready to use. Can be used
to thicken any cooked sauce or gravy.

Linguine with white clam sauce©
This has been a favorite of my family for years.

1½ cups thoroughly degreased
fresh or canned chicken
stock
1½ cups dry white wine
3 shallots, diced
3 celery tops with leaves, diced
4 sprigs parsley, chopped
1 bay leaf
10 black peppercorns
3 dozen clams, shelled (see
note)
White sauce (recipe follows)
2 pounds linguine noodles,
cooked (recipe follows)

White sauce:
¼ cup butter
5 tablespoons all-purpose flour
2 cups reserved reduced clam
stock
¾ cup milk
2 egg yolks
¼ to ½ cup whipping cream
Salt
White pepper
Garlic powder
Few drops lemon juice

Linguine:
2 pounds linguine noodles
Water
2 tablespoons vegetable oil

Makes 6 to 8 servings.
To make clam sauce: Combine stock,
white wine, shallots, celery, parsley, bay leaf
and peppercorns in 2-quart saucepan. Over
high heat, bring to boiling point. Reduce
heat and simmer, uncovered, 20 minutes.
Strain liquid into 12-inch skillet. Discard
vegetables. Add clams to liquid. Cover and
simmer 3 minutes. With a slotted spoon,
transfer clams to a large mixing bowl and
quickly reduce remaining stock to 2 cups.
Reserve stock for white sauce.
  Note: Two to three 6.5 ounce cans of
minced clams may be used if fresh clams are
not available.
To make white sauce: Melt butter in 2-
quart saucepan. Stir in flour. Cook over low
heat 1 minute, stirring constantly. Remove
pan from heat and gradually stir in reduced
clam stock and milk, whisking constantly.
Return to heat and cook until sauce begins to
boil and thicken. Reduce heat and simmer 1
minute.
In a small bowl, combine egg yolks and ¼
cup cream. Add 2 tablespoons of heated
sauce to egg mixture. Blend. Whisk heated
egg mixture back into remaining sauce in
pan. Bring to boil while constantly whisking.
Boil 30 seconds or until sauce coats a metal
spoon.
Remove from heat and season to taste with

½   cup butter
    Salt
    White pepper
¼   cup grated Parmesan cheese

salt, pepper, garlic powder and lemon juice. If sauce becomes too thick, thin with remaining cream.

Discard any juices that have accumulated under clams in bowl and stir clams into ⅔ cup sauce. Return to remaining sauce and blend well.

To make linguine: Fill a large stockpot or spaghetti cooker three-fourths full of water. Add oil. Bring water to a good rolling boil. Drop linguine into boiling water. Bring water back to rolling boil. Cover pot with a tight fitting lid and remove from heat. Allow to sit the same amount of time as the packaged directions say to boil linguine, approximately 10 minutes. Drain completely.

In a large skillet, melt butter. Add cooked, drained linguine and sauté lightly. Season to taste with salt and white pepper. Spoon into well-greased individual baking dishes. Top with white clam sauce mixture. Sprinkle with grated Parmesan cheese and place under broiler for 30 seconds to brown.

Jumbo lump crab cakes with chipotle sauce©

Mayonnaise:

1½   **cups vegetable oil, plus more for sautéing**
½   **cup finely diced red, green and yellow bell peppers**
¼   **cup finely diced onion**
2   **egg yolks**
2   **tablespoons freshly squeezed lime juice**
2   **tablespoons Dijon mustard**
1   **teaspoon Tabasco**
1½   **teaspoons Vietnamese fish sauce**

Prepare a saucepan of boiling water and a bowl of ice cubes and cold water.

To make mayonnaise: Put ½ cup of oil in a saucepan with peppers and onion. Cook over medium heat until oil simmers and vegetables are tender, about 7 minutes. Meanwhile, in a metal bowl whisk together yolks, lime juice, mustard, Tabasco and fish sauce. Add vegetables to yolk mixture, along with ½ cup hot oil, by droplets, whisking steadily until mixture is smooth and slightly thickened. Season with salt and

Salt and freshly ground white pepper

Crab cakes:

- 1 pound jumbo lump crab meat, picked over to remove cartilage
- ½ to ⅔ cup fresh bread crumbs
- 2 tablespoons each of roughly chopped fresh dill, chives and parsley
- 1 cup panko (Japanese bread crumbs)

Sauce:

- 1 chipotle pepper with 1½ teaspoons adobo sauce
- 1 teaspoon finely chopped garlic
- 1 teaspoon finely chopped shallot
- ¼ cup (packed) roughly chopped cilantro leaves
- ¼ cup seasoned rice vinegar
  Juice of ½ lemon
  Salt and pepper to taste
  Coleslaw, homemade or store-bought, for serving (optional)
  Vegetable oil for frying

white pepper.

Put bowl over pan of boiling water, and while whisking, cook 1 minute. Transfer bowl to ice-water bath. When mayonnaise is cool, cover and refrigerate until thoroughly chilled.

To make crab cakes: Place crab meat in a large bowl. Gently fold in 1 cup of the mayonnaise and ½ cup bread crumbs. Mixture should lightly bind. If necessary, fold in more bread crumbs. Fold in herbs. Dust a plate with panko. Place a 2-inch diameter ring mold, 1½ inches high, on panko, and pack mold with crab meat. Dust top with panko, and tamp down crab meat, pressing hard. Remove mold, and transfer crab cake to another plate; repeat with remaining mixture. Cover crab cakes and chill for at least 1 hour.

To make sauce: Place chipotle, garlic, shallot, cilantro, rice vinegar and lemon juice in a small food processor and pulverize. While machine runs, gradually pour in remaining 1 cup vegetable oil, blending until sauce is emulsified. Add salt and pepper to taste. Refrigerate. Bring to room temperature before serving.

Heat oven to 350 degrees. Pour vegetable oil into a large sauté pan until it reaches ¼ inch, and set over medium heat. When oil is hot, slip crab cakes into pan. Cook about 2 minutes on one side until brown, then transfer to a baking pan. Bake 5 minutes. Spoon coleslaw, if using, on each plate. Surround with chipotle sauce, and top with two crab cakes.

North China's crab Rangoon©

Makes 1 serving.

2 to 3	tablespoons cream cheese
	Milk
3	tablespoons fresh crab meat
	Onion, diced, to taste
	Salt and white pepper, to taste
6	won-ton skins
1	egg, beaten
	Vegetable oil for frying

Combine cream cheese with enough milk to make a smooth paste. Add crab meat, onion, salt and white pepper.

Place about a tablespoon of crab mixture in center of won-ton skin. Moisten edges of skin with beaten egg. Bring points to center. Press diagonal edges together, forming a shape resembling a star or crab. Pinch center together. (Edges must be sealed before frying.) Heat oil to 325 degrees. Drop rangoon into hot oil, 2 or 3 at a time. Cook until golden brown, 3 to 5 minutes.

Morrison's fish almondine©

Makes 6 servings.

2½	pounds whitefish
	Salt and pepper, to taste
½	cup all-purpose flour
1	egg
½	cup milk
½	teaspoon almond extract
1	2-ounce package slivered almonds
1 to 1½	cups crushed crackers
	Vegetable oil
	Butter or margarine
	Lemon, optional
	Fresh parsley, optional

Season fish with salt and pepper. Roll fish in flour to coat, shaking off excess. To make egg wash, mix together egg, milk, almond extract and salt and pepper. Set aside.

Crush 2 tablespoons of the almonds and add to crushed crackers.

Dip floured fish in egg wash and then in cracker-almond mixture. Pat lightly to ensure mixture adheres to fish.

Heat oil to 300 to 325 degrees. Fry fish until golden brown. Remove to serving platter. Garnish top with liberal amount of remaining slivered almonds and butter or margarine. If desired, top with lemon cut into sections and fresh parsley.

Vincenzo's salmon with apple butter cream sauce©

Makes 4 servings.

4   **8-ounce filets of fresh salmon**
    Olive oil (good quality)
2   **tablespoons minced shallots**
1   **tablespoon capers**
2   **Granny Smith apples**
¼   **cup white wine**
½ to ¾   **cup cream**
    Salt and white pepper to taste
1   **tablespoon butter, room temperature**

Cook salmon on the grill or in a hot sauté pan. (If using sauté pan, add just enough olive oil to lightly coat the bottom of the pan.) In sauté pan cook shallots in olive oil, using just enough oil to coat pan, until translucent. Rinse capers and add to shallots.

Peel and core apples. Cut 1¼ of the apples into ½-inch cubes. Add to shallots. When apples become translucent, deglaze pan with white wine. Cook to reduce by half and add cream. Let rise to bubble; add salt and white pepper to taste. Add butter; remove from heat. Serve over salmon.

Cut reserved portion of apple into 12 thin slices. Garnish plates by fanning apple slices on side of fish.

Blue Boar's salmon croquettes©

Makes 6 to 8 servings.

1   **14.75-ounce can salmon**
1   **pound cooked fish**
1   **large onion, finely chopped**
1½   **cups broken pie shells or crushed saltine crackers**
3   **eggs**
6   **tablespoons liquid margarine**
1   **tablespoon milk**
½   **cup all-purpose flour**
2½   **cups cracker meal**
    Oil for frying

Cream sauce:
4   **tablespoons butter**
4   **tablespoons flour**
2   **cups milk**

To make croquettes: Drain liquid from salmon. Remove round bones. Set aside. Place cooked fish, finely chopped onion and broken pie shells or saltine crackers in the bowl of a food processor. Process until thoroughly blended.

Beat 2 of the eggs with a wire whisk until yolks and whites are well-blended. Add to fish mixture along with liquid margarine and salmon. Mix until well-blended. Place in refrigerator to chill for easier handling. When thoroughly chilled, form into croquettes. Beat remaining egg with milk. Roll croquettes in flour, dip in egg mixture and roll in cracker meal.

½   teaspoon salt
1   chicken bouillon cube
½   cup frozen peas

Place enough oil to cover croquettes in a deep fryer or pan. Heat oil to 350 degrees. Drop croquettes into hot oil, 3 or 4 at a time, allowing ample space for even frying around each. When golden brown, remove croquettes to drain on paper towel. Prepare cream sauce and serve with croquettes.

To make sauce: In a heavy saucepan, melt butter. Add flour. Stir and cook 2 to 3 minutes. While stirring, slowly add milk, salt and chicken bouillon. Stir and cook until mixture thickens to desired consistency. Add peas and cook an additional minute. Makes 2 to 2½ cups.

Parakeet Café's salmon with sautéed spinach and mushrooms©

Makes 1 to 2 servings.

1   8- to 10-ounce fresh salmon filet
1   tablespoon olive oil
½   cup sliced fresh mushrooms
1   teaspoon fresh garlic
2   cups fresh baby spinach
    Kosher salt
    Coarse ground black pepper

Dijon-dill sauce:
6   tablespoons Dijon mustard
2½ teaspoons sugar
2½ tablespoons white wine vinegar
1½ teaspoons dry mustard
6   tablespoons olive oil
¼   cup chopped fresh dill

Prepare salmon to your liking – fried, grilled or baked. In a sauté pan, heat olive oil. Add mushrooms and garlic. Sauté 2 minutes. Add spinach. Season with salt and pepper to taste. Sauté for 1 minute.

Place spinach mixture on serving plate and top with salmon. Garnish with Dijon-dill sauce.

To make sauce: Combine all ingredients. Mix thoroughly. Makes 1 cup.

Porcini salmon©

Makes 4 servings.

2   tablespoons olive oil
½   cup all-purpose flour

In large skillet heat oil until hot. While oil is heating, dredge salmon fillets in flour. Cook

4 8-ounce salmon filets
¼ cup Grand Marnier or other orange liqueur
¼ cup white wine
¼ cup golden raisins
¼ cup orange juice concentrate
2 tablespoons unsalted butter (optional)

gently in heated oil about 4 to 5 minutes on each side. Drain oil, leaving fillets in pan. Add orange liqueur, white wine, raisins and orange juice concentrate. Bring liquid to a simmer and reduce by half. Add butter, if using. Stir until incorporated. Spoon sauce equally over salmon. Serve immediately.

Jack Fry's shrimp and grits with red-eye gravy©

Makes 6 portions.

Grits:
1 cup uncooked grits
4 cups milk
1 cup whipping cream
1 cup grated Parmigiano Reggiano cheese
Salt and pepper, to taste

Red eye gravy:
2 tablespoons butter
3 ounces country ham, minced
½ cup sliced shiitake mushrooms
½ cup minced onion
¾ cup green pepper
1 tablespoon minced fresh thyme
¼ cup Madeira wine
½ cup strong freshly brewed coffee
½ cup tomatoes, peeled, seeded and chopped
1 teaspoon hot sauce (Tabasco)
1 teaspoon cornstarch
1 cup cold chicken broth

Shrimp:
3 tablespoons butter

To make grits: In a 3-quart saucepan combine the grits, milk and whipping cream. Over medium heat, bring to a low boil. Reduce heat to low. Simmer, stirring frequently, until grits are creamy, about 10 minutes. Whisk in the Parmigiano cheese and salt and pepper to taste.

To make red-eye gravy: In a large skillet over high heat melt the butter. Add ham and brown. Add shiitakes, onion, green pepper and fresh thyme. Sauté until onion becomes translucent. Add wine, coffee, tomatoes and hot sauce. Bring to a slight boil. Combine cornstarch and chicken broth. Stir into gravy mixture. Reduce heat and cook another couple of minutes.

To prepare shrimp: In a large skillet over high heat, melt 2 of the 3 tablespoons butter. Add shrimp and cook until shrimp are just pink.
Add red-eye gravy. Finish sauce with remaining 1 tablespoon butter stirred in. Divide warm grits among 6 plates and top each with a portion of shrimp and gravy. Garnish with freshly grated Asiago cheese and fresh chopped parsley.

1½ pounds shrimp
    Asiago cheese, for garnish
    Fresh chopped parsley, for
    garnish

Uptown Café's fusilli with sea scallops©

Makes 6 servings.

1   pound fusilli
2   cloves fresh garlic
1   large Spanish onion, diced
1   tablespoon olive oil
1   cup fresh basil or 2
    tablespoons dried basil
1   quart cream
2   tablespoons chicken base or
    2 bouillon cubes
    Black pepper to taste
    Tabasco sauce to taste
1   cup milk
2¼ pounds sea scallops (6
    ounces per serving)
    Diced tomatoes
    Parmesan cheese

Cook fusilli in boiling salted water until al dente. Cool in cold water. Drain. Oil lightly. Sauté garlic and onion in olive oil. Add basil, cream and chicken base. Reduce heat. Cook until chicken base is dissolved. Season with black pepper and Tabasco. Add milk. Cook 8 to 10 minutes.

Add scallops and diced tomatoes. Simmer, stirring constantly, until sauce thickens (will coat back of spoon) and scallops are done. Add pasta. Cook a couple of minutes just to heat pasta.

Before serving, garnish with freshly grated Parmesan cheese.

Chesapeake House sautéed shrimp©

Makes 4 to 6 servings.

2   pounds medium shrimp
1   teaspoon Lawry's Seasoned
    Salt
4   ounces (1 stick) butter
1   clove fresh garlic, chopped
¼   cup white wine

Peel and devein shrimp. Remove tails. Season shrimp with Lawry's.
In a 12-inch sauté pan, heat butter over medium heat. Add garlic and shrimp. Toss shrimp lightly for even cooking. If butter begins to burn, reduce heat. When shrimp become pink and firm, add white wine. (Caution: Wine may flame up.) Toss shrimp. Remove from pan and serve immediately.

Jack Fry's lemon shrimp cappelini©

Makes 1 serving.

2 to 3	ounces uncooked pasta
8	shrimp (16 – 20 count), shelled
¼	cup all-purpose flour
2	tablespoons olive oil
1	teaspoon chopped fresh garlic
½	teaspoon crushed red pepper flakes
¼	red bell pepper, diced
2	tablespoons fresh lemon juice
2	tablespoons chicken stock
2	scallions, chopped
	Romano cheese

Cook pasta according to package directions. Drain and set aside.

Lightly flour shrimp. Heat olive oil in large sauté pan. When oil is hot, add shrimp. Cook 1 to 2 minutes. Turn shrimp and add garlic, red pepper flakes, red bell pepper, lemon juice and chicken stock. Cook until shrimp are bright pink. Add cooked pasta. Toss.

Transfer to serving plate. Garnish with chopped scallions and desired amount of Romano cheese.

Porcini's shrimp and scallops©

Makes 4 servings.

1	pound linguini pasta
3	tablespoons virgin olive oil
12	large raw shrimp, peeled and deveined
12	large raw sea scallops
½	cup all-purpose flour
1	large clove finely minced garlic
½	cup dry white wine
4	cups white clam juice
3	tablespoons pesto (recipe follows)
	Salt and white pepper to taste
4	ounces freshly grated Reggiano Parmesan cheese
2	ounces toasted pine nuts

Cook pasta according to package directions for al dente.

In a large sauté pan heat olive oil. While oil is heating, lightly dust shrimp and scallops in flour. Sauté in hot oil about 45 seconds to 1 minute on each side. Remove from pan and set aside.

Add garlic to sauté pan and cook about 15 seconds. Drain oil from pan, being careful not to lose any garlic. Deglaze pan with white wine. Add clam juice and pesto. Season to taste with salt and white pepper. Add cooked and drained pasta to sauce and toss thoroughly. Add shrimp and scallops to pasta. Heat just until seafood is hot. Divide equally among 4 plates. Garnish with

(see note)
1   small Roma tomato, diced
    into ¼-inch cubes
1   small yellow tomato, diced
    into ¼-inch cubes
    Fresh basil

Pesto:
3   cups fresh basil leaves,
    washed and patted dry
6   large cloves garlic, peeled
    and chopped
1   cup pine nuts or English
    walnuts
1   cup good-quality olive oil
1   cup freshly grated Parmesan
    cheese (optional)

grated Parmesan, toasted pine nuts, tomatoes and fresh basil.

Note: To toast pine nuts, spread on a cookie sheet. Bake in a 350-degree oven until lightly toasted. Watch carefully; nuts brown quickly.

To make pesto: Combine basil, garlic and nuts in the bowl of a food processor or half of each in a blender container. (Chop roughly, in 2 batches, if using a blender.) With motor running, add olive oil in a steady stream. Add cheese, if desired, and blend. Freezes well. Multiply the recipe as desired.

Ragtime Tavern's coconut batter fried shrimp©

1   cup beer
1   cup club soda water
        Dash Worcestershire sauce
2 to 3 dashes Tabasco sauce
        Salt and pepper to taste
2   cups all-purpose flour
2 to 3 pounds fresh shrimp
3   cups sweetened flaked
        coconut (approximate)

Honey-mustard sauce:
⅔   cup salad oil
¼   cup honey
¼   cup Dijon Country or stone-
    ground mustard
1   tablespoon chives, finely
    chopped
1   tablespoon fresh ginger,
    grated
¾   teaspoon dill weed

Combine first five ingredients. Add flour until mixture resembles thick cream or pancake batter.

Peel shrimp, leaving tail intact. While holding shrimp by the tail, dip into batter. Roll in coconut. Fry in hot oil (350 to 400 degrees) until golden brown. Serve with honey-mustard sauce.

To make honey-mustard sauce: In a large bowl, combine all ingredients. Whisk until well-blended. Serve with shrimp.
Makes about 2 cups.

¾ teaspoon paprika
1 tablespoon fresh garlic, minced
½ cup red wine vinegar
1 tablespoon soy sauce
1 tablespoon lemon juice

Shrimp J Timothy©

16 slices bacon
32 large raw shrimp, peeled, with tails
1 teaspoon curry powder
½ teaspoon granulated garlic
1 10- to 12-ounce jar chutney
¼ pound butter
Cooked rice, approximately 4 cups
Parsley, for garnish

Makes 4 servings.
Start with all ingredients at room temperature. Slice bacon in half and wrap neatly around each shrimp. Sprinkle with curry powder and granulated garlic. Broil 5 to 6 inches under broiler for about 7 to 8 minutes, turning so bacon cooks evenly.
For the sauce, chop chutney. Place in a saucepan with butter and heat just until butter melts.
Divide rice among 4 serving plates. Arrange shrimp on top. Pour sauce over shrimp and garnish plates with parsley.

Equus crab cakes©

¼ cup vegetable or soy oil
10 to 12 scallions, finely diced
1 red onion, finely diced
8 ounces lump crab
1 teaspoon capers
1 teaspoon minced garlic
1 teaspoon shallots
Juice of 1 lemon
1 teaspoon Dijon mustard
6 tablespoons white wine
½ cup shrimp stock
½ cup heavy cream

Makes 4 servings.
To make crab cakes: In large sauté pan heat oil. Add scallions and onion. Sauté until translucent. Add crab, capers, garlic, shallots, lemon juice, Dijon mustard, white wine, shrimp stock, heavy cream, cream cheese, enough cornstarch to thicken mixture and enough bread crumbs to bind. Chill before forming cakes.
After mixture has chilled, form into 8 2-ounce cakes. Lightly flour crab cakes. Dip in beaten egg and lightly bread with remaining bread crumbs. Lightly fry cakes in vegetable

4 ounces cream cheese
  Cornstarch to thicken
3 cups bread crumbs
  All-purpose flour
6 eggs, beaten
  Vegetable oil
  Tartar sauce, recipe follows

Tartar sauce:
¼ cup capers
¼ cup chopped parsley
1 tablespoon garlic
1 tablespoon shallots
  Juice from 1 lemon
  Juice from 1 lime
1½ cups mayonnaise
  Tabasco sauce to taste
  Salt and pepper to taste

oil.
Serve topped with tartar sauce.
To make tartar sauce: Combine all ingredients in food processor and puree. Taste and adjust seasonings. Makes approximately 2 cups.

Casseroles, Eggs and Quiches

George Long's Derby breakfast egg casserole

6 to 8 hard-boiled eggs
2½ cups crushed saltine crackers
6 tablespoons butter
  Salt and pepper, to taste
1½ to 2 cups milk

Makes 4 to 6 servings.
Butter a 8-by-8-by-2-inch casserole. Sprinkle a thin layer of crushed crackers over the bottom of casserole. Slice a layer of eggs over crackers. Dot with butter and sprinkle with salt and pepper. Continue with layers until you have used the eggs and crackers. Pour milk over all until you can see the milk coming up the sides of the casserole. Bake in preheated 350-degree oven for 30 to 40 minutes or until crackers turn golden. Serve while hot.

The Brown Hotel's hot brown casserole©

1   cup butter
¾   cup all-purpose flour
2   eggs, beaten
6   cups milk
1   cup grated Parmesan cheese
¼   cup heavy whipping cream
      Salt and pepper, to taste
16   slices white bread, toasted
16   slices roast turkey
      Paprika
1   cup bacon bits (½ to ¾ pound uncooked bacon)
1   cup tomato, seeded and diced
¼   cup chopped parsley

Makes 8 servings.

In a large saucepan, melt butter. Add flour, stirring to make a roux. Cook 2 to 3 minutes. Thoroughly beat eggs. Beat into milk. While stirring, very slowly add milk mixture to butter mixture. Cook until mixture thickens but do not boil. This will take 30 to 45 minutes. Mixture should heavily coat spoon. Stir in ¾ cup Parmesan cheese. Remove from heat. Fold in whipping cream and add salt and pepper to taste.

Trim crust from bread. Toast in a regular toaster or place in pan under broiler until golden. Do both sides. Line the bottom of a 9-by-13-by-2-inch casserole and an 8-by-8-by-2-inch casserole. (I used 6 slices of toasted bread to line a 9-by-13-by-2-inch casserole and 4 slices for an 8-by-8-by-2-inch casserole.) If your casserole dish is large enough to accommodate 10 slices of bread, use only one casserole.

Top with slices of turkey. Cover with sauce, dividing the sauce between the 2 casseroles, or if using one casserole, spread all of the sauce over the turkey. Sprinkle with remaining Parmesan cheese and paprika. Place in a preheated 350-degree oven for 15 minutes or until golden brown.

While casserole is baking, fry bacon. When crisp, remove from pan and place on paper toweling to drain. When cool, break into bits. Toast remaining 6 slices of bread. Cut in half on the diagonal.

After removing the casserole from the oven, place toasted bread around outer edge, point side up. Garnish with bacon bits and diced tomatoes. Sprinkle with chopped parsley. Serve while hot.

Planning ahead: I would not freeze any part of this dish, but you can do the grocery shopping, prepare the sauce, fry the bacon, chop the tomato and parsley and get out the casseroles a day in advance. I would wait to toast the bread until just before assembling the casserole. Prep time would be 15 minutes at the most. If ingredients are cold, increase the baking time to 30 to 35 minutes or until golden brown.

Sausage-egg casserole

8 slices white bread
2 pounds link sausage, browned
6 large eggs
2½ cups milk
1 teaspoon dry ground mustard
1 10¾-ounce can cream of mushroom soup
2 cups grated Cheddar cheese

Makes 10 to 12 servings.
Grease a 9-by-13-by-2-inch baking casserole.
Line the bottom of casserole with bread.
Place a layer of browned sausage over bread.
Beat eggs. Add milk and mustard. Stir to blend. Pour over sausage. Cover and refrigerate overnight.
Spread soup over top of casserole. Sprinkle cheese over soup. Bake in a preheated 325-degree oven for 50 to 60 minutes.

Old House scrambled eggs

8 eggs
½ cup whipping cream
6 tablespoons butter
½ cup sliced onion
½ cup diced celery
½ cup diced green pepper
½ cup chopped tomatoes
½ teaspoon salt

Makes 4 servings.
Beat eggs slightly with cream. Melt butter in sauté pan. Add vegetables, sauté until tender. Season with salt, pepper and garlic. Stir. Add ham. Cook until warm. Add eggs and cook until desired doneness.

¼ teaspoon coarsely ground
black pepper
1 clove garlic, minced
1 cup cold diced ham

Kunz's eggs Benedict for one

1 toasted English muffin
2 slices cooked Canadian
bacon
2 poached eggs
Hollandaise sauce for 1 serving:
4 egg yolks
1 teaspoon water
1 teaspoon white wine
(optional)
Pinch salt and cayenne
pepper to taste
Squeeze of lemon
3 tablespoons clarified butter

Makes 1 serving.
To make eggs: Split English muffin. Place under broiler until light golden. Top each half with a slice of Canadian bacon and a poached egg. Cover with Hollandaise sauce.
To make sauce: Over very low heat, whip egg yolks, water, wine, seasonings and lemon until eggs start to peak. Remove from heat and whip in clarified butter, 1 tablespoon at a time. Pour over eggs Benedict.

The Irish Rover's Scotch eggs©

12 large, hard-boiled eggs
1½ pounds bulk pork sausage
Dipping batter (recipe
follows)
Colman's English mustard
Dipping batter:
1 cup all-purpose flour
½ cup cornmeal
1 teaspoon baking soda
1 teaspoon salt.
1 12-ounce can beer

Makes 6 servings.
Place eggs in a pan. Cover with cold water. Place pan over medium heat. Bring water to boiling point. Remove from heat. Cover pan with a tight-fitting lid and wait 15 to 20 minutes.
When the time is up, immediately run the eggs under cool water (or put 10 to 12 ice cubes in the pan, cover and shake – the shells will crack and come off easily).
Wrap sausage meat about ¼ to ½ inch thick around each egg. Dip in batter. Fry in hot oil (375 degrees) until brown, 4 to 5 minutes, depending on thickness of sausage. Sausage should be cooked thoroughly. Drain on paper towels. Serve at once with

hot mustard.

To make batter: Combine flour, cornmeal, baking soda and salt. Stir. Add beer to make a thin batter. (You may not need all the beer). Makes about 2 cups.

Back Porch black bean casserole©

Beans:

2	cups (1 pound) black beans
1¼	teaspoons salt
1	bay leaf
1½	teaspoons dried oregano
1½	teaspoons dried thyme
1½	teaspoons garlic

Sauce:

1½	cups chopped onions
1	tablespoon plus 1½ teaspoons chopped garlic
1	cup diced red pepper
1	cup diced green pepper
3	tablespoons oil or butter
1	cup white wine
1	cup chicken or vegetable stock
¼	teaspoon salt or to taste Dash black pepper
¼	teaspoon red pepper flakes
1	tablespoon plus 1 teaspoon ground cumin
1	cup yellow raisins
1	cup slivered, blanched almonds
1¾	cups cooked rice
1	pound Monterey Jack cheese
⅓	cup bread crumbs

Makes 10 to 12 servings.

Check beans for stones. Rinse. Soak overnight in water to cover.

Drain beans and place in a large pan. Cover generously with water. Add salt, bay leaf, oregano, thyme and garlic. Cook over medium heat until beans are soft and liquid is reduced to just covering beans. (I added more water as the beans cooked. It took about 2 hours.) Remove bay leaf.

You may freeze the beans at this point to be thawed for use later or you may finish the dish.

Sauté onions, garlic and red and green pepper in oil or butter until soft. Add cooked black beans, wine, chicken stock, salt, black pepper, red pepper flakes, cumin, raisins, almonds and cooked rice. Cook until simmering and liquid is reducing. You want some liquid left at this point because the beans, rice and raisins will continue to absorb it after removal from the heat.

Spray a 9-by-13-by-2-inch casserole with no-stick cooking spray. Line dish with part of the grated or sliced Monterey Jack cheese. Fill with beans. Top with remaining cheese and bread crumbs. Bake in a 400-degree oven until top is crusty and beans bubble.

Miller's Cafeteria's eggplant casserole©

Makes 8 to 10 servings.

1 large eggplant
2 cups chicken broth
1 10¾-ounce can cream of
  mushroom soup
1 8-ounce package stuffing mix
3 tablespoons Parmesan
  cheese
1 small green pepper, chopped
½ cup diced onion
1 tablespoon butter
  Olive oil
  Salt and pepper, to taste
½ teaspoon crushed anise seed
1 to 1½ cups mixed shredded
  Cheddar and mozzarella
  cheese

Peel and dice eggplant. Soak in salt water 30 minutes.

Combine chicken broth and cream of mushroom soup. Add stuffing mix and Parmesan cheese. Stir until stuffing is moistened.

Sauté green pepper and onion in butter and 1 tablespoon olive oil. Remove pepper and onion from pan and drain. Add 2 or more tablespoons olive oil to drippings in pan. Add eggplant. Sauté until tender. Season with salt, pepper and anise. Stir. Add to stuffing mixture.

Pour mixture into a buttered 9-by-13-by-2-inch baking dish. Top with cheese. Bake in a preheated 350-degree oven 30 to 45 minutes.

Flagship's mushroom and cheese quiche

Makes 4 entrée or 8 appetizer servings.

1 10-inch unbaked pie shell
6 ounces sliced fresh
  mushrooms
2 tablespoons butter
2 cups grated Gruyere or Swiss
  cheese
4 eggs, lightly beaten
1¾ cups heavy cream
  Salt and pepper to taste
  Pinch nutmeg

Line pie shell bottom with foil and place enough dried beans to weight the bottom. Bake in a preheated 400-degree oven for 15 minutes.

While shell is baking, sauté mushrooms in butter. Set aside to cool.

Remove shell from oven and remove foil with beans from shell.

Mix cheese with mushrooms and place in bottom of pie shell.

Blend lightly beaten eggs with heavy cream. Add salt and pepper to taste. Pour over mushroom and cheese mixture. Sprinkle lightly with nutmeg.

Place pie on a baking sheet. Bake in 400-degree oven 35 minutes or until custard is set.

Gilroy meat-and-potatoes quiche©

Crust:

1   pound ground beef
¾   cup bread crumbs
1   egg
1   clove fresh garlic, minced
2   tablespoons Worcestershire sauce
2   tablespoons fresh basil
½   teaspoon pepper

Filling:

3   cloves fresh garlic, minced
½   cup diced onion
2   tablespoons oil
3   medium potatoes, peeled, cooked and sliced
4   ounces Cheddar cheese, in small cubes
1   4-ounce can green chilies
1   teaspoon salt
½   teaspoon pepper

Topping:

½   cup potatoes, mashed with ½ cup milk
2   ounces Cheddar cheese, grated
3   cloves fresh garlic, minced
1   egg
1   teaspoon dry mustard

Makes 8 servings.

To make crust: Combine beef, bread crumbs, egg, garlic, Worcestershire sauce, fresh chopped basil and pepper. Press into a 9-inch pie pan. Bake in a preheated 350-degree oven for 15 minutes. Remove from oven and set aside.

To make filling: Sauté garlic and onion in oil for 5 minutes. Combine potatoes (reserving ½ cup mashed for topping) and cheese with garlic and onion, chopped chilies, salt and pepper. Mix well and spread over the beef crust.

To make topping: Combine all the topping ingredients and pour over the filling. Bake in 350-degree oven for 25 to 30 minutes.

Pasta and Pizza

Perfect pasta al dente every time

I cook all pasta this way – always perfect. The following restaurant recipes call for the pasta to be cooked according to the directions given to me by the chef – this is a better way of doing it.

Bring a large pot of water to a rolling boil. Add salt to taste. Stir pasta into boiling water. Bring water back to a rolling boil. Stir. Remove from heat. Cover pot with a tight-fitting lid. Set aside for 10 to 12 minutes or the amount of time suggested in the package directions. This method gives you perfect pasta every time – pasta with flavor. Drain and set aside.

Homemade egg noodles

3	egg yolks
1	whole egg
3	tablespoons water
1½	teaspoons olive oil
¾	teaspoon salt
1¾ to 2	cups all-purpose flour

Makes about ¾ pound.

To make noodles: Beat to blend the egg yolks, egg, water, olive oil and salt.
Place 1½ cups flour into a large mixing bowl. Make a hole in the center. Pour in the egg mixture and stir with a fork until flour is well moistened. Form into a ball.
Sprinkle some of the remaining flour on board or smooth surface and knead dough until it is very smooth and elastic, 5 to 10 minutes. The dough should just hold together and have a smooth uniform texture. Place dough in a bowl, cover with a damp cloth and allow to rest for at least 15 minutes (or chill for about an hour).

To shape noodles by hand: Divide dough into 4 equal portions. On a floured surface, roll out one portion at a time into a rectangle about 4 inches wide and as thin as possible, about 1/16 inch thick. Cut this length into two lengths. Starting at the narrow end, roll up each strip in jellyroll fashion and cut the width of noodle you want. Unfurl the coil. Lay out on a floured surface or hang on a pasta drier to dry about 30 minutes. At this point, the noodles can be cooked or packaged in plastic bags and frozen.

To cook homemade egg noodles: Drop noodles into 2 to 4 quarts rapidly boiling salted water (the amount of water depends on how many noodles you are cooking). Bring water back to a boil. Cover pan and remove from heat. Allow to sit 3 to 4 minutes or until noodles are al dente. These noodles can be used in any dish calling for egg noodles.

John Colombo's pasta e fagioli

Makes 6 servings.

1	beef marrow bone
1½	pounds soup meat
2	quarts canned tomato juice (or 2 quarts water and 6 teaspoons tomato paste)
1	large onion, chopped
2	cloves garlic, smashed
3	tablespoons olive oil
1	15.5-ounce can chili hot beans
4	tablespoons fresh chopped parsley
½	cup dry red wine
1½	teaspoons salt
	Ground black pepper, to taste
1	teaspoon oregano
	Cayenne pepper, to taste
8	ounces elbow macaroni (see note)
	Parmesan cheese

In a large pot combine beef marrow bone, soup meat and tomato juice. Bring to a boil. Lower heat, cover and simmer two hours. Remove bone and meat. Dice meat and return to pot.

Chop onion. Press garlic to release flavor. Place in a skillet with the olive oil. Cook until onion is translucent (do not let the garlic burn – it will become bitter). Add to the simmering pot along with the chili hot beans, parsley, red wine, salt, pepper, oregano and cayenne pepper. Simmer for 20 minutes.

Add macaroni and continue cooking until macaroni is al dente. Serve sprinkled with grated Parmesan cheese.

Note: For a juicier dish, cook macaroni separate from main ingredients and add before serving.

Rigatoni a la Pitino©

This dish is served at Bravo Gianni's in New York. The owner, Bravo Gianni Garavelli, named the dish for Rick Pitino, who eats there often when he goes to New York. Mr. Garavelli doesn't have a recipe but happily shared the list of ingredients along with the method of preparation. The following is a close approximation of this winning dish.

Makes 4 servings.

1	16-ounce package rigatoni
¼	cup olive oil
3	cloves garlic
1	dozen large ripe plum

Cook pasta al dente.

In a large skillet, heat olive oil. When hot, add garlic (chop, but not too fine). Stir and cook until garlic starts to turn golden. Add

tomatoes, chopped
Red pepper flakes, to taste (optional)
Salt, to taste
2 cups fresh basil
¼ cup grated Parmesan cheese
¼ cup grated Romano cheese

coarsely chopped tomato and pepper flakes, if desired. Add salt to taste. Cook 7 to 8 minutes.
Remove the garlic. Add cooked rigatoni and mix. Cook 1 to 2 minutes. Remove from heat. Add fresh basil (do not chop basil – you don't want to bruise it). Stir lightly. Mix Parmesan and Romano cheeses and sprinkle over pasta. Serve immediately.

Sentimental's Tea Room and Akin Back Farm's pasta bleu©

Makes 6 to 8 servings.

3 boneless, skinless chicken breasts
4 to 6 sprigs fresh rosemary
4 to 6 sprigs fresh thyme
1 pound ziti
¾ cup unsalted butter
¼ cup fresh lemon juice
1 cup Gorgonzola cheese, shredded
Salt and freshly ground pepper to taste
3½ cups fresh spinach torn into bite-size pieces
Nasturtiums
Edible flowers in season

Grill chicken with fresh rosemary and thyme. Place the herbs on the chicken and on the coals. Cut cooked chicken into strips. Set aside.
Prepare ziti according to package directions. While ziti is cooking, melt butter in a large skillet. Slowly stir in lemon juice and cheese. Turn heat to low and continue stirring until cheese has melted. Season to taste with salt and pepper.
Add cooked ziti and torn spinach leaves to cheese mixture. Heat through. Toss. Top with strips of grilled chicken. Garnish with nasturtium petals and other edible flowers.
   Note: Blossoms from the following plants are edible: day lily, rose, lavender, sage, dill, fennel, basil, marigold, rosemary, marjoram, mint, violet, pansy and yucca.

The Crow's Nest pasta Florentine©

Makes 8 servings, 3 shells per serving.

1 12-ounce box jumbo pasta shells
2 10-ounce packages frozen chopped spinach, thawed and thoroughly drained

In a large kettle, bring 5 quarts water to a rolling boil. Add pasta shells and cook 15 to 20 minutes or until al dente. Drain and rinse under cold water to cool rapidly.
Thaw spinach. Drain thoroughly. Mix with

1 16-ounce carton cottage
   cheese
2 8-ounce packages cream
   cheese, softened
½ cup grated Swiss cheese
½ cup grated Parmesan cheese
1 teaspoon white pepper
1 teaspoon garlic powder
6 cups marinara sauce,
   homemade or canned
2 cups grated mozzarella
   cheese

Marinara sauce:
1 8-ounce can tomato sauce
2 tablespoons tomato paste
¼ cup olive oil
½ cup chopped onion
1 minced garlic clove
1 teaspoon basil
1 teaspoon oregano
½ teaspoon thyme
   Dash salt and pepper

cottage, cream, Swiss and Parmesan cheeses, white pepper and garlic powder. When mixing this, it's best to use your hands so the cream cheese is evenly distributed throughout the filling.

Stuff each pasta shell with approximately ¼ cup of filling. Line up shells in a glass or stainless steel baking pan. Top with marinara sauce and bake in a preheated 350-degree oven for 10 minutes. Top with mozzarella cheese and bake an additional 5 to 10 minutes or until cheese is melted and lightly browned. Serve immediately.

To make sauce: The Crow's Nest used a purchased marinara sauce. The following recipe is from The Courier-Journal's files. Combine ingredients in a small saucepan. Bring to a boil and simmer gently, uncovered, 10 minutes.
Makes 1½ to 2 cups.

Le Relais angel hair pasta with fried Kentucky goat cheese©

Makes 6 to 8 servings.

¾ cup cooked tomato Provencal
   (recipe follows)
1 heaping tablespoon pesto
   (recipe follows)
¾ pound spinach, sautéed
1½ pounds Kentucky goat cheese
5 green onions, chopped
⅓ sheet of puff pastry
1 egg
2 tablespoons water or milk
1 to 1½ cups bread crumbs
   Olive oil for frying
1 pound angel hair pasta

Prepare Provencal. Set aside. Prepare pesto (recipe follows). Set aside. Wash spinach. Remove stems, tearing leaves. Set aside.
Mix the goat cheese and green onions. Form into 12 medallions. For each medallion, roll 1 square inch of puff pastry paper thin. (Sprinkle some flour on counter and rolling pin to keep pastry from sticking.) Wrap puff pastry around each medallion of goat cheese, being careful to close all corners so cheese is totally wrapped. Beat egg with water or milk. Dip medallion in

¼ cup olive oil
1 quart heavy cream
¼ cup Parmesan cheese
½ cup cooked, sliced, button mushrooms
   Salt and pepper to taste
2 to 4 tablespoons Pernod (licorice-flavored liqueur), or to taste
   Diced tomatoes (optional)
   Parsley (optional)

Tomato Provencal:
1 tablespoon olive oil
1 tablespoon chopped onion
1 clove garlic, chopped
2 tomatoes, peeled, seeded and chopped
1 tablespoon oregano
   Salt and pepper to taste

Pesto:
3 cups fresh basil leaves, washed and patted dry
6 large cloves garlic, peeled and chopped
1 cup pine nuts or English walnuts
1 cup good quality olive oil
1 cup freshly grated Parmesan cheese

egg wash then in bread crumbs. Add about ⅛ inch olive oil to heavy skillet. Heat and fry medallions over medium heat until golden brown. Set aside. Add a little more olive oil to the skillet and when hot, sauté spinach. Remove and set aside. Cook the angel hair pasta according to package directions. Drain. Rinse with cold water. Add ¼ cup olive oil. Toss to keep pasta from sticking together. Set aside. Pour heavy cream into a large skillet. Bring to a boil and reduce by one-fourth. Add Parmesan cheese, sautéed mushrooms, tomato Provencal, pesto, salt and pepper. Reduce again by one-fourth. Add pasta and toss. Add spinach and Pernod. Place pasta in serving dish. Top with fried goat cheese packets. If desired, garnish with diced tomatoes and parsley.

To make tomato Provencal: Heat olive oil in a heavy skillet. Add onion and garlic. Cook one minute. Add tomato, oregano and salt and pepper. Cook gently for 15 minutes.
Makes about 1 cup.

To make pesto: Combine basil, garlic and nuts in the bowl of a food processor, or half of each in a blender container. Chop roughly, in two batches if using a blender. With motor running, add olive oil in a steady stream. Add cheese and blend. Freezes well. Multiply the recipe as desired. (Cheese may be omitted.)

Vincenzo's fettuccine Alfredo©

Makes 4 to 6 servings.
1 pound fettuccine, dry or fresh
1 tablespoon salt, or to taste

Bring 4 quarts water to a boil. Add salt and olive oil. Drop in pasta. Cook to al dente.

1   tablespoon olive oil
1   quart heavy cream
2   tablespoons unsalted butter
½   cup chicken stock
6   tablespoons freshly grated
    Parmesan cheese
½   teaspoon white pepper
    Fresh chopped parsley

Drain. Set aside.
In a large sauté pan, bring cream to a boil.
Add cooked pasta, unsalted butter and
chicken stock. Stir. Gradually add cheese
and white pepper. Stir with a wooden spoon.
Sprinkle with fresh chopped parsley. Serve
immediately.

Zephyr Cove's basil Alfredo©

    Pasta of choice
1   pint heavy cream
½   pound Parmesan cheese,
    grated
½   teaspoon white pepper
½   teaspoon ground nutmeg
½   teaspoon Kosher salt
3 to 4 sprigs fresh basil, or to taste
2   ounces cornstarch (optional)

Makes 4 servings.
Cook pasta according to package directions.
While pasta is cooking, heat cream in a
heavy saucepan over medium heat until the
cream starts to boil. Add grated Parmesan
cheese, white pepper, nutmeg and salt.
Reduce to low heat and stir vigorously to
thoroughly incorporate the cheese. Reduce
this sauce until desired consistency is
reached. Add chopped fresh basil just
before serving.
   Note: If using cornstarch to thicken, toss
all dry ingredients together, including the
cheese, and follow same directions.

Angelo's Fettuccini Caterina©

4   ounces fettuccini or linguine
4   tablespoons olive oil
1   teaspoon chopped garlic
1   tablespoon fresh parsley,
    chopped
7   ounces bay scallops
5   ounces shrimp, diced
10 ounces fresh mushrooms,
    sliced
1   lemon, peeled and diced

Makes 2 servings.
Cook pasta according to package directions.
Set aside.
Using a large skillet, heat olive oil, garlic,
parsley, scallops, shrimp, mushrooms, diced
lemon and capers. Cook over high heat
about 5 minutes or until shrimp and scallops
are cooked. Add flour, white wine, salt and
pepper and dash of lemon juice. Add cooked
pasta. Toss lightly until blended. Serve
immediately.

1 tablespoon capers
1 tablespoon all-purpose flour
2 tablespoons dry white wine
  Salt and white pepper, to
  taste
  Dash lemon juice

Ferd Grisanti's cavatelli formaggio©

Makes 4 servings or appetizers for 10 to 12.

1	pound pasta (fettuccini, linguine, rotini, fusilli or medium-size shells)
2½	tablespoons olive oil
1 to 2	cloves garlic, crushed
1	cup mushrooms
½	cup chopped broccoli, lightly steamed
2	tablespoons butter
1	teaspoon all-purpose flour (this can be eliminated if one uses heavy cream instead of half-and-half)
1	pint half-and-half
1	cup Parmesan or Asiago cheese, grated
	Salt and white pepper, to taste

Cook pasta according to package directions. (One pound of dry pasta will make 2 pounds when cooked.)
Heat olive oil in pan. Add crushed garlic. Sauté till slightly brown. Add mushrooms. Sauté 3 to 5 minutes.
Slightly steam broccoli. Drain.
Melt butter in a 4-quart saucepan. Do not let butter separate. When butter has just melted, slowly whisk in flour until smooth. *Slowly* add half-and-half, whisking continuously. Bring mixture to a boil and add cooked pasta. Reduce heat. Add grated cheese and mix. Add sautéed mushrooms and steamed broccoli. Add salt and white pepper to taste.
You may have to increase or decrease the sauce, depending on how long you cook the pasta. (Pasta cooked to al dente will absorb the sauce and become dry and sticky.) This dish should be rather saucy. If your pasta absorbs most of the sauce, add more half and half and heat thoroughly.

Roy and Nadine's white lasagna©

Makes 12 to 15 servings.

5	cooked chicken breast halves
15	lasagna noodles

Place chicken breasts in a pan with enough water to cover. Bring to a simmer. Cook 15

1½ quarts cream
3 tablespoons chicken base
¾ pound grated Parmesan cheese
½ cup cornstarch
½ cup water
1 pound shredded provolone cheese
1½ pounds ricotta cheese
3 eggs
¾ pound sliced mushrooms
2 cups grated mozzarella cheese

minutes. Cover. Set aside until ready to use.

Cook lasagna noodles according to package directions. Drain.

While noodles are cooking, bring cream and chicken base to a boil. Whisk in Parmesan cheese. Mix cornstarch with water. Add to cream mixture. Whisk until mixture thickens. Set aside.

In a bowl, combine provolone, ricotta and eggs.

Remove chicken from broth. Drain. Cut into bite-size pieces.

Grease an ovenproof 9-by-13-by-2-inch pan. Spread a thin layer of cream sauce in bottom of pan. Alternate layers of noodles, provolone mixture, sliced mushrooms, chopped chicken and cream sauce until all of the ingredients have been used. (You should have 5 layers of pasta and 4 layers each of provolone, mushrooms, chicken and cream sauce.) Sprinkle mozzarella over top. Cover with foil and bake in a preheated 425-degree oven for 10 minutes or until cheese has melted and begins to brown. Remove from oven. Let rest 10 minutes before serving.

The Fishery Restaurant 'Old Florida Waterfront Dining' V.L.T. linguine©

Makes 2 to 3 servings.

⅓ cup butter
½ teaspoon minced garlic
1 cup sliced fresh mushrooms
1 cup chopped scallions
4 to 5 cups cooked linguini
1 cup chopped fresh tomatoes
  Pinch of salt

In a heated skillet, melt butter. Add garlic, sliced mushrooms and scallions. Stir until slightly cooked. Add cooked linguini. Toss until mixed. Add tomato and a pinch of salt. Toss again. Season to taste with salt and pepper. Serve immediately.

214

Salt and pepper, to taste

Mamma Grisanti's linguine carbonara©

Makes 1 serving.

3	strips pancetta or bacon, chopped
3	ounces (dry weight) linguine
6	ounces heavy cream
1	ounce fresh Parmesan, grated
	Salt and white pepper, to taste
½	egg, beaten
	Fresh parsley or diced tomatoes

In a skillet, fry chopped bacon until crisp. Drain, reserving grease.

Cook linguini in salted, boiling water until al dente. Drain.

Meanwhile, place cream and cheese in a heavy saucepan. Bring to a boil, stirring constantly. Continue stirring until mixture is just thick enough to coat spoon. Add cooked bacon, ½ to ¾ teaspoon bacon grease, and salt and pepper, if desired. Stir to blend. Add drained pasta to sauce. Toss lightly. While stirring, add beaten egg to pasta mixture. As soon as egg is incorporated, remove from heat. Place on serving dish, garnish with parsley or chopped tomato.

Mick's broccoli linguine©

(The Peasant Restaurants)

Makes 6 to 8 servings.

1	quart heavy whipping cream
½	pound grated Parmesan
1	teaspoon salt
1½	teaspoons white pepper
2	tablespoons fresh garlic, finely chopped
1½	teaspoons thyme
1	tablespoon pesto
1½	pounds fresh spinach linguine
1	quart steamed broccoli florets
½	cup chopped walnuts

In a large pan combine heavy cream, Parmesan, salt, white pepper, garlic, thyme and pesto. Bring to a boil. Cook until slightly thickened.

Cook linguine in salted water until tender but firm to the bite.

Meanwhile, steam the broccoli.

To serve, place cooked linguine on a serving platter or on individual plates. Top with broccoli. Ladle sauce over broccoli. Sprinkle with walnuts. Serve immediately.

Colonnade's macaroni and cheese©

1   tablespoon salt
¼   teaspoon vegetable shortening
9¼   ounces macaroni
10   ounces grated New York Cheddar
3   cups white sauce (recipe follows)
½   teaspoon salt, or to taste

White sauce:
5   tablespoons butter
5   tablespoons flour
3   cups hot milk
     Salt and white pepper, to taste

Makes 8 to 10 servings.
To make macaroni: In a large pan bring 2½ quarts water to a boil. Add 1 tablespoon salt, vegetable shortening and macaroni to the boiling water. Cook according to package directions – the macaroni should be soft but not collapsed. Immediately add a large quantity of cold water to the kettle. Let settle and pour off most of the water, leaving the macaroni in the kettle. Repeat until macaroni water runs clear. Drain well.

Combine 8 ounces of grated cheese with white sauce. Add cheese sauce to drained macaroni. Mix thoroughly. Taste for salt. Add more if necessary. Pour into a 9-by-9-by-2-inch pan that has been sprayed with non-stick vegetable spray. Sprinkle remaining 2 ounces of cheese over top of macaroni. Bake on upper rack in a hot, 350- to 375-degree oven until browned and heated through, about 15 minutes.

To make sauce: In a thick-bottomed saucepan, melt butter. Stir in flour and, stirring constantly, cook for 3 to 4 minutes or until mixture cooks through but does not take on color. Add hot milk and cook, stirring constantly, until the mixture is thick and smooth. Season to taste with salt and white pepper.

Makes about 3 cups.

Afro-German Tearoom's pesto pasta©

Makes 2 servings.

½	pound linguine
1	tablespoon butter
2	medium cloves garlic, finely minced
2	tablespoons sun-dried tomatoes
¼	cup pesto (recipe follows)
½	cup cream

Pesto:

5	cups fresh basil leaves
4	large cloves garlic
8	tablespoons pine nuts
8	tablespoons Parmesan cheese
1	bunch Italian parsley
	Olive oil to make smooth paste, approximately 1 cup

Cook linguine according to package directions.

In a medium skillet, heat butter until it foams. Add garlic and sauté just until translucent. Add softened sun-dried tomatoes (if tomatoes are dry, not in oil, pour hot water on them to soften them, then discard water). Stir. Add pesto and cream. Cook a minute. Add cooked pasta. Toss to coat pasta. Serve immediately.

To make pesto: Place all ingredients in the bowl of a food processor. Process to a smooth paste. Extra pesto may be frozen. Makes 1½ to 2 cups.

Pizza Pronto's cappellini con pesto©

Makes 4 to 6 servings.

1	pound angel hair pasta
4	tablespoons extra virgin olive oil
1	cup chopped fresh tomato
½	cup chopped sun-dried tomatoes
8	chopped pepperoncini
½	cup pesto (recipe follows)
	Parmesan cheese, grated

Pesto:

½	pound fresh basil
1	cup extra virgin olive oil
2 to 3	cloves garlic
2	tablespoons grated

To make cappellini: Cook pasta according to package directions. Heat olive oil in a large skillet. Add fresh tomato, sun-dried tomato, pepperoncini and pesto. Bring to a boil and cook 2 minutes.
Add cooked and drained pasta. Stir until blended and hot. Sprinkle with Parmesan cheese and serve immediately.

To make pesto: Place all ingredients in container of blender or food processor. Blend until thoroughly mixed. Will keep refrigerated for up to a year. Makes 2 cups.

Parmesan cheese
¼ cup pine nuts

Anytime pizza

2¼ cups all-purpose flour
1 teaspoon sugar
1 ¼-ounce package active dry yeast
½ teaspoon salt
¾ cup plus 2 tablespoons very hot tap water

Sauce:
1 tablespoon vegetable or olive oil
2 cloves garlic, minced
1 15-ounce can tomato sauce
1 teaspoon dried basil
½ teaspoon dried oregano
½ teaspoon Italian seasoning
½ teaspoon fennel seed

Topping suggestions:
Italian sausage, pepperoni, diced ham, bacon bits, Canadian bacon, diced chicken or ground beef
Diced tomatoes, green peppers, onion, zucchini, yellow squash, eggplant,
½ cup fresh sliced mushrooms
½ green pepper, diced , optional
Green or black olive rings, optional
¼ cup diced onion
Shredded mozzarella cheese, goat cheese or cheese of choice

Makes 1 14-inch pizza.

To make crust: In a small bowl combine flour, sugar, yeast and salt. Stir to mix, then add hot tap water and stir well. Place dough on lightly floured surface and, with floured hands, knead about five minutes. Place back in bowl, cover with a light film of vegetable oil and set in a sink basin containing about 3 inches of very hot tap water. Let set until double in bulk.

While dough is proofing, prepare toppings and sauce.

To make sauce: In a saucepan heat the oil. Add garlic and cook briefly. Add tomato sauce, basil, oregano, Italian seasoning and fennel seed. Simmer about 10 minutes. Set aside.

To prepare toppings: You can use any topping you prefer – these are just a few suggestions. It's fun to be creative and try different things such as fresh vegetables, some fruits or different cheeses – goat cheese is a favorite of mine.

In a skillet, brown sausage or any raw meat. Drain on paper towels.

Brush the dirt off the mushrooms and slice. Core and dice tomatoes and green pepper. Peel onion and slice into very thin slices. Whatever toppings you are using, have them ready before dough is placed on a cookie sheet, pizza pan or stone.

Assembling pizza: If using a cookie sheet or pizza pan, grease lightly. If using a pizza stone, follow manufacturer's directions. Roll, stretch or press dough to desired thickness. Cover with a thin layer of sauce, sprinkle toppings on, one at a time. Add the sausage or whatever meat you choose. Top with cheese. Bake in a preheated 475 degree oven until crust is golden and cheese browns and bubbles, about 20 to 25 minutes.

Hometown Pizza's white chicken pizza

1 12-inch pizza crust

White sauce:
- 2 cups heavy whipping cream
- 1¼ cups fresh grated Parmesan cheese
- ½ teaspoon chicken base
- 1 tablespoon parsley flakes
- ¼ teaspoon salt

Pizza topping:
- ½ cup white sauce, or to taste
  Red onion, sliced thin
  Fresh spinach
- 1 cup grilled mesquite chicken strips
- ½ cup cooked bacon, crumbled
- 16 ounces diced mozzarella cheese

Makes 1 12-inch pizza.

To make sauce: Place cream in a heavy saucepan. Over medium heat bring to a boil. Simmer 10 to 15 minutes or until reduced by a third. Add Parmesan cheese; stir to incorporate cheese. It takes a while for the cheese to melt, so continue to beat with a whisk every few minutes until mixture cools and begins to thicken. Add chicken base, parsley flakes and salt. Stir. Pour sauce into a bowl. Refrigerate until cold, about 4 hours.

To make pizza: Spread sauce over pizza crust. Add onion and torn spinach to taste. Sprinkle chicken evenly around pizza. Top with crumbled bacon and mozzarella cheese. Place on bottom rack of a hot 475-degree oven. Cook until cheese is golden and bubbles, about 25 minutes. Serve while hot.

Nationality Foods

Knaidel (a German dressing ball)

My friend, Mary Ann Feger, shared this recipe. Her mother served knaidel with red cabbage.

- 10 slices stale bread
  Salt and pepper, to taste
- 1 beaten egg
- 2 tablespoons all-purpose flour

Makes 4 balls.

Dip bread lightly in bowl of water. Tear into pieces. Add salt, pepper and egg. Sprinkle flour over all. Mix well so no chunks of bread remain. Form into balls about the size of baseballs. Cover and refrigerate for about 2 hours.

When ready to cook, fill a large pot half full of water. Add a teaspoon of salt. Bring to boil. Drop balls into boiling water. Cover and cook slowly 15 to 20 minutes. Remove and serve as is or with red cabbage, gravy or in rich chicken broth.

Note: If making lots, don't crowd pot. You can add chopped onions and/or 2 tablespoons chopped parsley.

Spaetzle (a German dish of tiny noodles or dumplings)©

Makes 6 servings.

3½ **cups sifted all-purpose flour**
3 **teaspoons salt**
5 **eggs, slightly beaten**
½ **cup water, more or less**

In a large mixing bowl, combine flour and salt. Make a well in center. Add eggs and half the water. Beat until a stiff dough forms, adding remaining water a little at a time. The dough should be thick, firm and come away easily from the sides of the bowl.

Turn out on lightly floured surface. Knead until smooth. Return to bowl, cover with damp cloth and let rest for 30 minutes.

Heat a kettle of salted water to boiling. With a sharp knife or scissors, cut off thin slivers of dough (or put through a spaetzle cutter) and drop into boiling water. Do not crowd kettle. Spaetzle will rise to surface when cooked, in about 5 minutes.

Remove with slotted spoon to a colander. Continue adding dough to the water until all is cooked.

Variation: While spaetzle is cooking, melt 8 tablespoons butter or margarine in a large skillet. Fry 2 cups of soda crackers broken into small pieces until very lightly browned. Pour over spaetzle and serve hot.

Colombo's Italian meat sauce©

This is an excellent sauce that can be used with any kind of pasta, as topping for pizza, as a sauce in calzones, for lasagna, ravioli, tortellini – its uses are endless.

Makes 6 quarts.

3	pounds lean ground beef
1 to 2	tablespoons olive oil
1	large onion, chopped
3	cloves fresh garlic, crushed
1 to 2	pounds sweet Italian sausage, in links
6 to 8	15-ounce cans Hunt's tomato sauce
1	12-ounce can Hunt's tomato paste
2	tablespoons fresh, chopped parsley
2	tablespoons brown sugar
1	tablespoon dried oregano
¼ - ½	teaspoon cayenne pepper
1	tablespoon dried basil
1	teaspoon paprika
2	bay leaves
1	tablespoon tarragon
1	tablespoon onion salt
3	chicken bouillon cubes
3	beef bouillon cubes
	Ground black pepper, to taste

In a large pot brown the beef until no longer pink. Drain.

In the same pot heat olive oil. Add onion. Cook until translucent. Add garlic and cook until soft. Return beef to pot. Add the uncooked sausage links and remaining ingredients.

Cook covered 3 to 4 hours.

Note: When cool, sauce can be frozen in containers the size of your choice.

Colombo's lasagna©

Makes 12 to 15 servings.

1	1-pound package lasagna noodles
1	teaspoon salt
1	tablespoon cooking oil
1	1-pound carton ricotta or dry cottage cheese
2	eggs

Cook lasagna noodles. I use my oval roasting pan because the noodles fit so nicely in it. Fill ¾ full of water. Add salt and about a tablespoon of oil. Bring to a boil. Add noodles. Bring back to boiling. Cover pan and turn off heat. Allow noodles to sit covered for 10 to 12 minutes. Drain.

2 cups Asiago or Parmesan cheese, grated
2 tablespoons chopped fresh parsley
1 pound cooked Italian sausage (cooked in meat sauce)
1 to 1½ quarts meat sauce
1 pound mozzarella cheese, sliced thin

Place ricotta cheese, eggs and about ½ cup of the Asiago or Parmesan cheese in blender or food processor. Process until smooth. Stir in parsley. Set aside.

Slice the cooked Italian sausage into ⅛-inch thick rounds.

Spray a 9-by-13-by-2-inch baking dish with non-stick spray. Place a thin layer of meat sauce in bottom of dish. Add a layer each of noodles, ricotta cheese mixture, thin sliced mozzarella cheese, a few pieces of sausage, a thin layer of sauce and a light sprinkling of Asiago or Parmesan cheese.

Repeat layers till dish is filled or you run out of noodles. I like lasagna that is moist but not soupy. (The amount of sauce you use between the layers determines how moist your dish will be.) Sprinkle remaining Asiago or Parmesan cheese over top. (At this point, the dish may be covered with plastic, wrapped in aluminum foil and frozen. It also could be refrigerated overnight.)

When ready to serve, bake in a preheated 350-degree oven until hot and bubbly, about 30 minutes. Allow to set for 10 minutes before cutting. If the dish has been frozen, allow to thaw in refrigerator and add 15 to 20 minutes to the baking time.

Colombo's ravioli

Basic ravioli pasta dough:
4 cups all-purpose flour
1 teaspoon salt
5 large eggs
2 tablespoons olive oil
1 egg beaten with 2 tablespoons water

Makes 200 small ravioli.
To make dough: Combine 3½ cups of flour with salt, eggs and oil. Stir until mixture forms a stiff ball. Turn out onto a work surface sprinkled with some of the remaining flour.

Knead, working in the loose particles, until the dough is well blended and pliable. This

Beef and spinach filling:

- 1 tablespoon olive oil
- 1 small onion, chopped
- 1 clove garlic, mashed
- 1 pound lean ground beef (may use pork or veal)
- 1 pound fresh spinach, washed, cooked and drained, or 1 10-ounce package frozen, chopped spinach, thawed
- ¼ teaspoon thyme
- ¼ teaspoon marjoram
- ¼ teaspoon crushed rosemary
- 1 teaspoon salt
- ½ teaspoon black pepper
- 2 eggs
- 1 cup fresh bread crumbs
- 1 cup grated Parmesan cheese

takes about 5 minutes. Add flour as needed. Form into a ball. Place in a bowl and cover with a damp towel. Let rest 30 minutes.

To make filling: In a large frying pan, heat the oil. Add onion and garlic. Sauté until onion is limp. Add meat and cook until brown and crumbly. Drain liquid from meat. Add spinach. (If using frozen, allow to thaw and squeeze out excess liquid.) Add seasonings. Remove from heat and add the eggs, bread crumbs and cheese. Mixture should be thick enough to handle. Mix well.

To form ravioli using a mold: Sprinkle mold lightly with flour.

Roll a small piece of dough on a floured surface into a very thin strip about 6 inches wide and 12 inches long, or to a size that is the approximate dimension of your ravioli mold.

Place the bottom layer of dough on mold. Depending on size of pockets, fill each with portion of filling - ravioli may burst if overfilled.

Roll out a second piece of dough about the same size as the first. Brush with egg wash. Place over filling, egg-wash-side down. With a rolling pin, roll over mold with heavy pressure. Remove excess dough along sides. Turn out ravioli on a surface sprinkled with cornmeal. If all ravioli do not separate, go over the places with a small knife or pastry wheel. May be cooked immediately or placed on a cookie sheet and frozen. After freezing, place ravioli in a plastic bag and return to freezer.

To make free-form ravioli: Roll out a long thin strip of dough. Mark dough with a ravioli cutter or the rim of a glass, pressing into dough without going through it. Spoon filling in center of marking. Roll out a second strip of dough. Brush with egg wash. Place over first strip and fillings, egg-wash-side down. Cut through double layers of ravioli with cutter. Remove excess dough and save scraps for future rolling. If ravioli do not seal properly, crimp edges with tines of a fork. Place each ravioli on a surface sprinkled with cornmeal. Repeat rolling strips of dough until filling is used.

May cook immediately or be placed on a cookie sheet and frozen. When frozen, place in a plastic bag and return to freezer.

To cook ravioli: Bring a large pot of salted water or chicken broth to a rolling boil. Drop in ravioli. When water returns to a boil, cover pot and lower heat so water is just simmering. Cook 25 to 30 minutes or until ravioli are tender. Cooking in this manner prevents ravioli from falling apart.

To serve: Place some heated sauce (we use our meat sauce) in bottom of a oven-proof bowl. Place a layer of ravioli on top of sauce. Sprinkle with some grated Parmesan cheese. Add another layer of ravioli, sauce and cheese. Continue layering until bowl is filled or all the ravioli has been used. Cover bowl with foil and place in oven set at lowest temperature (my oven goes down to 170 degrees) or a warming oven until ready to serve. Plan on 8 to 10 per serving, if using as an entrée.

Colombo's calzone©

Sauce:
 1 **pound spicy Italian sausage**
 1 **tablespoon vegetable or olive oil**

Makes 10 large calzone.
To make sauce: Brown sausage in skillet. Drain on absorbent paper.
Heat oil in saucepan. Add garlic, green pepper and onion. Cook briefly. Add tomato

2	cloves garlic, minced
½	green pepper, diced
1	medium onion, diced
1	15-ounce can tomato sauce
1	teaspoon basil
½	teaspoon oregano
½	teaspoon fennel seed

Crust:

2¼	cups flour
1	teaspoon sugar
1	¼-ounce package active dry yeast
½	teaspoon salt
1	cup minus 2 tablespoons very hot tap water
	Vegetable oil

To fill calzone:

	Olive oil
	Prepared sauce
8 to 10	ounces mozzarella or provolone cheese, grated

sauce, basil, oregano and fennel seed. Simmer until slightly thickened, 45 minutes to an hour.

To make crust: In a small bowl combine flour, sugar, yeast and salt. Stir to mix. Add hot tap water and stir well. Place dough on lightly floured surface and, with floured hands, knead about five minutes. Return to bowl. Cover with a light film of vegetable oil. Place plastic wrap over top of bowl and set in a sink basin containing about 3 inches of very hot tap water for approximately 15 minutes. Dough should rise to about double in bulk.

Punch down dough and divide into four portions. Place one portion at a time on a lightly floured surface. Roll out to about ⅛-inch thickness or the thickness of pie crust. Cut into 8-inch circles.

To assemble: Brush each circle lightly with olive oil to within ½-inch of edge. Spread 2 to 3 tablespoons of sauce over half the dough circle to within ½ inch of edge. Sprinkle 2 to 3 tablespoons of cheese over sauce.

Fold plain half over filling to within ¼ inch of opposite edge. Roll bottom edge up over top edge; pinch or crimp with the tines of a fork to seal. Place on a lightly greased baking pan, flipping calzone as you place it on pan so overlapped crimped edge is on the bottom. Brush top with olive oil. Prick once with fork to allow steam to escape.

Repeat procedure until all dough and sauce have been used. Bake in a 500-degree oven for 6 minutes, or until golden brown.

Rubino's Mamma Maria meatballs©

2	cloves fresh garlic, chopped
	Dash salt
1	tablespoon pepper
½	ounce fresh Italian parsley, chopped
2	cups (6 ounces) freshly grated Parmesan cheese
2	eggs
8	slices white bread, crust removed
2½	pounds lean ground beef

Makes 14 meatballs.

Mix together garlic, salt, pepper, parsley, Parmesan cheese and eggs.

Moisten bread with water. Squeeze out excess water. Add bread to egg mixture. Mix.

Add ground beef. Combine thoroughly. Shape into 14 meatballs. Place meatballs on a jelly roll pan lined with oiled parchment paper. Bake in a 375-degree oven until brown, about 15 minutes.

Note: If meat mixture seems too soft to shape into balls, sprinkle bread crumbs into meat mixture until balls hold their shape.

Gnocchi (Italian dumplings)©

3	cups mashed potatoes (directions follow)
2 to 3	cups all-purpose flour
1½	teaspoons salt
1	tablespoon olive oil
2	eggs, slightly beaten
	All-purpose flour
	Boiling salted water
2 to 3	tablespoons melted butter
1½	cups shredded cheese

Makes 4 to 6 main dish servings or 8 first course servings.

Measure potatoes into a bowl and add about 2 cups flour, salt and oil. Blend with a fork. Add eggs and blend thoroughly. Turn dough out onto a floured board and knead gently, adding more flour until mixture no longer sticks to your fingers. Knead gently about 15 times. Shape into a fat loaf and set on a floured area to prevent sticking.

When ready to form mixture into individual gnocchi, cut off a piece of dough about the size of a baseball. With the palm of your hands roll on a very lightly floured board into a cord 3/8-inch thick. Cut cord into 1¼-inch lengths. Roll each segment in the center lightly under your forefinger to give the piece a bow shape. Set shaped gnocchi aside on a lightly floured pan such as a baking sheet; the pieces should not touch.

Note: Gnocchi can be frozen at this point. I place the baking sheet with the gnocchi on it into the freezer. When frozen, the gnocchi can be placed in a plastic bag – they won't stick if they are frozen.

To cook gnocchi: In a large kettle, bring about 3 quarts salted water to a boil. Drop about a third of the gnocchi into the boiling water. After the gnocchi returns to the surface, cook about 5 minutes. (Stir gently if they haven't popped up in about a minute). Keep water at a slow boil.

Remove gnocchi from water and drain well. If you are cooking all the gnocchi, place the cooked gnocchi in a shallow pan (such as a jelly roll pan) and mix gently with melted butter. Cover tightly with foil and keep in a warm place while you cook remaining gnocchi.

You can hold the gnocchi in a 170 degree oven for as long as 3 hours, keeping them well covered to retain moisture. Flavor is best if they don't cool after cooking.

To serve, arrange a layer of about half the gnocchi in a wide, shallow rimmed, oven-proof dish. Top with about half the hot sauce and half the cheese. Top with remaining gnocchi, sauce and cheese. Heat in a 375-degree oven for about 10 minutes or until cheese melts and gnocchi are piping hot.

To make mashed potatoes: You can use dehydrated instant mashed potatoes or fresh potatoes. Cook peeled potatoes until tender in unsalted boiling water and drain thoroughly, then rub through a fine wire strainer or mash.

To prepare instant dehydrated mashed potatoes, heat the amount of water called for on package to make 6 to 8 servings; stir in potatoes as directed. Add no seasonings or other ingredients. Measure 3 cups; use at once.

Bleu cheese sauce: Bring 2 cups cream to a boil. Add 2 or 3 chopped sun-dried tomato pieces. Continue to cook until cream is reduced to about half. Add crumbled bleu cheese to taste. Pour over cooked gnocchi.

Polenta

Makes 6 to 8 servings.

1	cup yellow corn meal
4	cups cold water
1 to 2	tablespoons chicken base

In a heavy pot combine corn meal, water and salt. Bring to a boil – lower heat – mixture will pop if the heat is too high. If using, add

(optional)
1   teaspoon salt

chicken base to taste (if you are using chicken base, you may want to add the salt after tasting). It takes about 30 minutes to cook – the corn meal should be soft.

Note: I like to use the chicken base – gives a lot of flavor to the polenta.

Porcini lasagna©

3   tablespoons extra virgin olive oil
4 to 5   cloves garlic
¼   pound ground chuck
¼   pound ground veal
½   pound hot Italian sausage, ground
3   tablespoons red wine, preferably Chianti
1   teaspoon each basil, oregano and ground fennel
1   15-ounce can tomato sauce
12   lasagna noodles
1   15-ounce carton ricotta cheese
1   cup grated Gruyère cheese
1   cup grated mozzarella cheese

Makes 6 to 8 servings.
Heat oil in skillet. Add garlic and sauté half a minute. Add chuck, veal and sausage. Cook over medium heat until browned, about 10 to 12 minutes. Drain grease. Add wine and herbs. Cook until liquid has evaporated. Add tomato sauce and simmer for 5 minutes. Cook lasagna noodles according to package directions. Drain.
Grease an ovenproof dish and alternate the layers of pasta, ricotta and meat sauce until all of the ingredients have been used (you should have 4 layers of pasta and 3 layers of ricotta and meat sauce). Sprinkle Gruyere and mozzarella cheese over top. Bake in a 375-degree oven for 40 to 45 minutes or until cheese turns an even golden brown.

Pierogi (a small Polish turnover)©

2   cups all-purpose flour
1   teaspoon salt
1   egg
½   cup water
    Filling (recipes follow)
    Boiling water
½   cup butter

Makes 25 to 30 pierogi.
To make pierogi: In a bowl combine the flour and salt. Add egg and enough water to make a medium-soft dough. Turn out on lightly floured surface and knead until smooth, about 5 minutes. Return to bowl and cover with a damp cloth. Allow to rest for about 10 minutes.

1 large onion, chopped

Potato-cheese filling:

4 to 5 Idaho potatoes

Salt and pepper to taste

½ to 1 pound Longhorn cheese, cubed

Cottage cheese filling:

2 cups dry cottage cheese, drained

1 egg, beaten

Salt to taste

Sugar (optional)

Lekvar (prune) filling:

1 pound dried, pitted prunes

¼ to ½ cup sugar

Divide dough into 4 equal portions. Roll a portion at a time to a thickness comparable to that of pie crust. Cut into 3-inch squares or circles. Place 2 or 3 tablespoons of filling on one half of dough (the amount of filling used depends on size of square or circle). Fold opposite half over filling. Crimp edges with tines of fork.

Drop three or four pierogi at a time into rapidly boiling water. Cook 3 to 4 minutes. Using a slotted spoon, remove from water, drain, then place in serving bowl. Meanwhile, in a heavy skillet, melt the butter. Add onion and cook until lightly browned. Pour butter mixture over cooked pierogi.

To make potato-cheese filling: Peel potatoes and cook in boiling water until tender. Drain completely. Add salt, pepper and cheese to taste to hot potatoes. With an electric mixer or potato masher, beat until cheese has melted and potatoes are free of lumps. Check seasoning. If desired, more cheese may be added. Beat until cheese has melted. Potatoes should be quite stiff when used as filling for pierogi.

To make cottage cheese filling: Combine cottage cheese, egg, salt and sugar, if using. Beat until smooth.

Lekvar (prune) filling: Cover prunes with cold water. Bring to boiling point. Reduce heat and simmer gently about 20 minutes. Add sugar to taste. Cook about 10 minutes longer. Drain, reserving liquid. Chop or mash prunes. If needed, add enough liquid to form a soft paste.

Colombo's burritos©

Refried beans:
- ½ pound lean bacon, diced
- 1 medium onion, chopped
- 1 clove garlic, minced, or garlic salt to taste
- 2 15-ounce cans pork-flavored pinto beans

Meat filling:
- 2 pounds ground beef
- 2 medium onions, chopped
- Chili powder, to taste
- 1 teaspoon oregano
- 1 teaspoon paprika
- 1 teaspoon salt
- 1 tablespoon Worcestershire sauce
- 1 15-ounce can tomato sauce
- Few drops hot sauce

Additional ingredients:
- 2 16-ounce jars taco sauce
- Shredded Monterey Jack cheese
- Shredded Cheddar cheese
- 1 to 2 packages (1 pound 4 ounces) large flour tortillas

To make beans: Place diced bacon in a large skillet and fry until crisp. Remove bacon and set aside. Add onion. Fry until onion softens. Add garlic and cook until onion is transparent - garlic should not burn. Add beans. When beans are hot, mash with a potato masher. Stir in bacon bits. (If using garlic salt in lieu of fresh garlic, add to taste.) Set aside.

To make filling: In a large pan or skillet brown ground beef and onions. Drain well. Add seasonings and sauce. Heat thoroughly. Mixture should be thick.

To assemble burritos: Preheat oven to 350 degrees.

Before you start to fill tortillas, place a thin layer of taco sauce in bottom of an oven-proof casserole.

Place tortillas, one at a time, briefly on a warm griddle to make pliable. Place on a flat surface or plate. Place a spoonful of beans in the center of the tortilla. Add a spoonful of meat sauce and a spoonful each of Monterey Jack and Cheddar cheese. Fold the tortilla envelope-style. Place in casserole, folded side down. When layer is completed, top with additional cheese and taco sauce. Bake in a preheated 350-degree oven until hot and bubbly and cheese has melted. If desired, serve topped with any of the following.

Garnishes: Shredded lettuce, chopped tomatoes, chopped onions, sour cream, additional Monterey Jack and Cheddar cheeses.-

Paul's Fruit Market's chicken enchiladas©

Makes 10 to 12 enchiladas or 6 to 8 burritos.

1 chicken or 6 chicken breasts
Enchilada sauce (recipe follows)
¾ cup sour cream
1 teaspoon chili powder
½ teaspoon cumin
½ teaspoon oregano
½ teaspoon salt
¼ cup chopped cilantro (optional)
½ medium onion, finely chopped
8 flour tortillas (see note)
2 cups grated Monterey Jack or Chihuahua cheese

Enchilada sauce:
1 tablespoon butter
1 tablespoon flour
½ cup chicken stock
1 15-ounce can crushed tomatoes
1 tablespoon diced green chilies
1 teaspoon chili powder
½ teaspoon cumin
½ teaspoon oregano
½ teaspoon salt

To make enchiladas: Place chicken in a large kettle with 3 cups water. Cook until chicken is tender, 30 to 40 minutes. Remove chicken to a platter to cool. Strain stock and set aside (you can use ½ cup in the following sauce then freeze the remainder for later use). While chicken is cooking, prepare the enchilada sauce.

When chicken has cooled, shred. Add sour cream, chili powder, cumin, oregano, salt, cilantro and onion. Heat tortillas briefly in a microwave (20 seconds) to soften. Before rolling, sprinkle each tortilla with Monterey Jack or Chihuahua cheese before topping with the chicken mixture. Roll to close. Place in a lightly greased 9-by-13-by-2-inch ovenproof dish. Pour sauce over enchiladas and sprinkle lightly with Monterey Jack or Chihuahua cheese. Cover loosely with foil and bake in a hot, 350-degree oven until sauce is bubbly and cheese is melted.

   Note: Use the 6-inch tortilla for enchiladas and the 10-inch for burritos.

To make sauce: In a saucepan melt butter. Add flour, stirring to combine. Add remaining ingredients and simmer until thickened. If sauce becomes too thick, thin with a little more chicken stock.

Oriental Dishes

Notes: It is important to remember that Chinese cooking is done very quickly. This is why it is critical that all ingredients be prepared before the actual cooking and that the wok is heated to a high temperature, 350 degrees. Also, although it appears that a lot of oil is used, it is needed to ensure that the ingredients are cooked quickly and fully.

Wonton Express sweet and sour chicken©

8	boneless, skinless chicken breast halves
2¼	cups self-rising flour
2	tablespoons vegetable oil
2	tablespoons cornstarch
½	teaspoon salt
¼	teaspoon ground white pepper
1	egg
1½ to 2	cups water
	Vegetable oil for frying
2	tomatoes
2	green peppers
1	8-ounce can pineapple chunks in heavy syrup
	Sweet and sour sauce (recipe follows)

Sweet and sour sauce:

¼	cup cornstarch
1¾	cups water
¾	cup sugar
½	cup vinegar
	Reserved syrup from 8-ounce can pineapple
1 to 2	drops orange food coloring (optional)

Makes 4 to 5 servings.

To make sweet and sour chicken: Cut chicken into 1-inch cubes. Combine flour, oil, cornstarch, salt, pepper and egg. Add water gradually to make a thick batter. Stir to blend thoroughly. Add chicken pieces. Stir until chicken is well-coated.

Heat 2 inches of oil in skillet or wok to 360 degrees. Fry chicken pieces until golden. Remove chicken and drain on paper towels. Cut tomatoes and green peppers into bite-size pieces. Drain pineapple; reserve juice for sweet and sour sauce.

When ready to serve, layer tomatoes, green peppers and pineapple chunks on a platter. Place cooked chicken pieces over the uncooked vegetables. Pour hot sweet and sour sauce over top. Serve at once.

To make sweet and sour sauce: Combine cornstarch and ¼ cup water. Stir until well-blended. Set aside. In a saucepan, combine remaining 1½ cups water, sugar, vinegar, pineapple, syrup and orange food coloring, if desired. Heat to boiling. Turn off heat. Slowly stir in the cornstarch mixture. Continue stirring until mixture thickens. Makes about 2½ cups.

Golden Dragon War Su gai©

1	whole chicken breast
½	teaspoon salt
1	cup bread crumbs
¼	cup sliced almonds
½	cup all-purpose flour
1	egg, beaten
3	cups vegetable oil for frying

Makes 1 serving.

To make War Su gai: Remove bones and skin from chicken breast. Cut whole chicken breast in half at center. Butterfly each half by slicing breast from outer edge, part way through, to open like a book. Sprinkle with ½ teaspoon salt.

Combine bread crumbs with sliced almonds.

Gravy (recipe follows)

Gravy:

1¼ cups chicken broth
2 tablespoons cornstarch
1 teaspoon mirin rice wine
1 tablespoon soy sauce

Coat each piece of chicken with flour, dip in egg and press on crumb mixture.

Fry in hot oil (375 degrees) for 4 minutes or until golden brown. Cut chicken into bite-size pieces.

Prepare gravy.

To make gravy: In a saucepan, combine all ingredients. Bring to a full boil, stirring constantly. Pour over chicken and, if desired, top with toasted, slivered almonds. Serve immediately.

Yen Ching's moo goo gai pan©

Makes 6 to 8 servings.

3 pounds boneless, skinless chicken breasts
4 egg whites
½ teaspoon salt
1½ teaspoons cornstarch
1 teaspoon cooking wine
¾ cup chicken broth or water
1 tablespoon white wine
2 teaspoons cornstarch
1½ teaspoons sesame oil
1 teaspoon salt
½ teaspoon monosodium glutamate
½ teaspoon sugar
⅛ teaspoon black pepper
1 pound mushrooms, thinly sliced
1 pound snow-pea pods
1½ pounds napa cabbage
2 medium carrots, thinly sliced
1 8-ounce can bamboo shoots
3 cups vegetable oil for cooking

Slice chicken breasts into thin slices. Set aside.

Combine egg whites, salt, 1½ teaspoons cornstarch and cooking wine. Place chicken slices in batter and marinate for a half-hour.

Combine chicken broth, white wine, 2 teaspoons cornstarch, sesame oil, salt, monosodium glutamate, sugar and black pepper. Stir to combine. Set aside.

Slice mushrooms. Remove strings and ends from snow-pea pods. Clean napa and cut into 1½–inch pieces. Peel carrots and slice into thin slices. Set aside.

In a wok, heat cooking oil to 365 degrees. Add chicken slices. Fry till chicken is almost done. Remove from oil. Drain.

Pour oil from wok. Return 1 tablespoon of oil to wok. Heat. Add mushrooms, snow-pea pods, napa, carrots, bamboo shoots and the chicken-broth mixture. Stir-fry until sauce has thickened. Add cooked chicken slices. Serve immediately.

James Tavern Oriental chicken stir-fry©

Makes 2 servings.

2 tablespoons clarified butter
½ pound boneless chicken breast, cut into strips
3 cups vegetable medley (a mixture of julienne carrots, celery, zucchini and yellow squash and broccoli florets)
3 tablespoons soy sauce (preferably light, low sodium)
20 snow peas
½ teaspoon herb or seasoned salt
1 cup cooked rice

In a large skillet heat butter over medium-high heat. Add chicken strips and sauté until cooked through and lightly brown. Add vegetable mix and cook until just tender. Add soy sauce, snow peas and salt. Toss and continue cooking for 1 minute or until snow peas are cooked through but still crisp. Serve over cooked rice.

Dela Torre's paella© (a Spanish dish of saffron-flavored rice)

Makes 6 servings.

½ cup lima beans
¼ to ½ pound fresh green beans
1 cup olive oil
Salt to taste
1 chicken cut into 12 pieces
1 medium onion, peeled and chopped
1 clove garlic, peeled and chopped
2 vine-ripened tomatoes, cored and chopped
½ green pepper, chopped
1 tablespoon Spanish paprika
¼ teaspoon crushed saffron
4 small clams
½ pound medium shrimp, peeled
8 mussels
½ cup peas (preferably fresh)
1 cup long-grain rice

Bring 5 cups water to boil in a stockpot. Add lima beans, reduce heat and simmer 30 minutes. Add green beans and cook 10 minutes more. Strain and save liquid.
Heat olive oil in paella pan or a wide, shallow skillet. Salt the chicken pieces and add to skillet. Brown well, about 15 minutes, turning occasionally. Add onion and cook stirring often, over high heat, about 2 minutes. Add garlic, then tomatoes and green pepper. Cook over fairly high heat, stirring often, about 5 minutes. Add paprika, saffron, limas and green beans. Stir to mix; add clams, medium shrimp and mussels.
Add the water used to cook the beans (about 4 cups), or use chicken stock or other meat stock, if desired. Simmer 10 to 20 minutes. Add peas. Push contents of pan to either side so there's a place cleared down the middle. Add rice in a line down the middle of

4   large shrimp or prawns

the pan. Use a spoon to gently distribute it evenly. Let the mixture boil rapidly, uncovered, about 8 minutes, then add unpeeled shrimp or prawns in a spiral fashion in the middle of the pan. Cook 6 minutes more, flipping the prawns once, or until rice is cooked and liquid is absorbed.

Cakes

Spring angel food cake©

Angel food cake:
1   cup sifted cake flour
1½   cups confectioners' sugar
12   egg whites, about 1½ to 2 cups
1½   teaspoons cream of tartar
¼   teaspoon salt
1   cup granulated sugar
1½   teaspoons vanilla
½   teaspoon almond extract

Filling and icing:
1   pint strawberries, more or less
3   cups heavy whipping cream
¼   cup sugar
1   cup lemon curd (see recipe)

Lemon curd:
4   tablespoons unsalted butter
½   cup sugar
½   cup freshly squeezed lemon juice
4   egg yolks
1   tablespoon grated lemon zest (yellow part only of peel)

Makes 10 servings.

To make cake: Preheat oven to 350 degrees.

Sift flour and confectioners' sugar 3 times. Place egg whites in large bowl of electric mixer. Add cream of tartar and salt. Beat until whites are frothy. Add sugar 2 tablespoons at a time, beating at high speed until stiff, glossy peaks form. Add flour mixture a little at a time, folding flour in after each addition. Blend in vanilla and almond extract.

Spoon batter into ungreased 10-inch angel food cake pan. Pull a metal knife through the batter once to break up the large air bubbles. Bake 35 to 40 minutes, or until cake is golden and springs back when lightly touched with your fingers. Invert the tube pan on a funnel or bottle to cool. When completely cooled, gently run a knife around edge and center to remove cake. Place cake on plate.

To make filling and icing: Wash and hull strawberries. Chop them but not too small. Beat whipping cream in a bowl until fluffy.

Slowly add sugar while beating until stiff peaks form. Put 2 to 3 cups of whipped cream in a smaller bowl and add strawberries. Fold them in; set aside.

Use a serrated knife to slice cake horizontally in 3 equal layers. Set bottom layer on a decorative serving plate and spread it with half of the lemon curd. Top with a layer of strawberry cream. Top berries with middle layer of cake. Repeat lemon curd and strawberry layers. Top with remaining cake layer, pressing gently. Use remaining sweetened whipped cream to ice cake.

Note: The cake slices more easily if it's allowed to stand several hours. Use a serrated knife and a sawing motion to slice cake. Don't be surprised if you need to wipe the knife frequently as you slice.

Easy variations: Use only 1 cup of heavy whipping cream for the strawberry layer and serve the cake without icing.

You can also leave out the lemon curd, though it is delicious

To make lemon curd: In a heavy non-aluminum saucepan (or the top of a non-aluminum double boiler), combine butter, sugar, lemon juice and egg yolks. Cook over lowest heat (or simmering water), stirring constantly, until mixture thickens enough to heavily coat the back of a spoon. Do not let the mixture boil or it will curdle. Pour the lemon curd into a small bowl and stir in the lemon zest. Refrigerate until ready to use. Makes 1 cup.

Cottage Café's apple harvest cake©

4 cups chopped apples (Golden Delicious or Arkansas Black)
2 cups sugar
2 eggs
1 cup vegetable oil
3 cups all-purpose flour
2 teaspoons baking soda
½ teaspoon salt
1 teaspoon vanilla
1 cup English walnuts

Caramel applejack brandy sauce:
3 ounces cream cheese, room temperature
⅓ cup whipping cream
1 cup granulated sugar
⅓ cup water
2 tablespoons applejack brandy

Makes 12 to 15 servings.

To make cake: Peel, core and chop apples. Combine with sugar and let stand 2 hours or overnight at room temperature.

Add eggs and oil to apple mixture. Mix thoroughly. Add flour, baking soda, salt, vanilla and walnuts. Mix well. Pour into a greased and lightly floured 9-by-13-by-2-inch baking dish. Bake in a preheated 350-degree oven for 40 minutes or until a toothpick inserted near the center comes out clean. Serve with warm applejack brandy sauce.

To make sauce: Place cream cheese and whipping cream in bowl of electric mixer and beat until smooth. Set aside.

Place sugar and water in heavy saucepan over medium-high heat. Stir just to dissolve the sugar; let the mixture cook without stirring until it reaches 300 degrees on a candy thermometer. Remove pan from heat and carefully pour in the cream mixture. It will foam up. Over low heat, whisk the mixture just until smooth. Stir in brandy. Sauce will hold well, covered, in the refrigerator for 5 to 7 days. Warm over very low heat, stirring often.

Makes about 1½ cups.

Cheddar Box caramel cake©

Cake:
3 cups all-purpose flour
1 tablespoon baking powder
½ teaspoon salt

Makes 16 servings.

Cake: Preheat oven to 350 degrees. Combine flour, baking powder and salt. Cream butter. Slowly add sugar, ¼ cup at a time and, when well-mixed, add eggs 1 at a

1   cup butter
2   cups sugar
5   eggs
1½ cups heavy cream
2   tablespoons vanilla

Icing:
½   cup butter
1   cup brown sugar
4   tablespoons cream
3⅔ cups confectioners' sugar
½   pound cream cheese
2   teaspoons vanilla

time. Then add dry ingredients alternately with cream and vanilla, beginning and ending with flour.
Bake in 2 greased and floured 9-inch cake pans at 350 degrees for 35 minutes.
Icing: In a saucepan, melt butter and add brown sugar. Bring to a boil. Cook 1 minute. Add cream and boil another minute. Remove from heat. Add confectioners' sugar and beat in cream cheese and vanilla.

O'Callaghan's carrot cake©

3   cups flour
3   cups sugar
½   teaspoon salt
1   tablespoon baking soda
1   tablespoon cinnamon
1½ cups corn oil
4   eggs, slightly beaten
1   tablespoon vanilla
1½ cups chopped walnuts
1½ cups (3½-ounce can) coconut
1⅓ cups (15-ounce can) canned carrots, mashed
¾   cup (8-ounce can) crushed pineapple
    Frosting (recipe follows)

Frosting:
1   8-ounce package cream cheese, room temperature
6   tablespoons butter, softened
1   teaspoon vanilla
    Juice of ½ lemon
4 to 6 cups confectioners' sugar

Makes 16 servings.
To make the cake: Grease and flour 2 9-inch cake pans. Set aside. Heat oven to 350 degrees.
In a large bowl combine all ingredients. Stir until blended.
Pour into prepared pans. Bake 35 to 40 minutes or until a toothpick inserted near the center comes out clean.
Allow cake to cool in pans 10 to 15 minutes. Loosen sides by running a knife around the inside of the pan and turn out onto cooling racks. Cool completely before frosting.
To make the frosting: Cream butter with cream cheese. Add vanilla and lemon juice. Slowly add confectioners' sugar. Beat until smooth. Add confectioners' sugar until frosting reaches the consistency you desire.

Chocolate Fudge Cake©

This cake has been my family's favorite for at least the past 35 years. It's always the cake everyone wants for birthdays and, when I was doing wedding cakes, it was always chosen as one of the tiers or for the groom's cake. It's very moist but you must use the ingredients listed – cake flour is a must. It takes a bit more time but it's worth the effort.

Makes 16 servings.

3 1-ounce squares unsweetened baking chocolate
2¼ cups sifted cake flour
2 teaspoons baking soda
½ teaspoon salt
½ cup (1 stick) butter, room temperature
2¼ cups firmly packed light brown sugar
3 large eggs, room temperature
1½ teaspoons vanilla
1 cup dairy sour cream
1 cup boiling water

Chocolate fudge frosting:
4 squared unsweetened baking chocolate
½ cup (1 stick) butter
1 pound (4 cups) confectioners' sugar
½ cup milk
2 teaspoons vanilla

To make cake: Melt chocolate in a double-boiler over hot, not boiling water; cool. (I use the microwave to do this. I melt for 30 seconds and stir. If the chocolate isn't completely melted, do in increments of 5 to 10 seconds, stirring after each increment until chocolate is melted. Watch carefully - chocolate burns quickly.)

Grease and flour three 9-by-1½-inch or three 8-by-1½-inch layer-cake pans; tap out excess flour. Preheat oven to 350 degrees. Sift flour and measure. Sift again with baking soda and salt onto wax paper. Set aside.

In a large bowl, beat butter until soft. Add brown sugar and eggs. Beat with electric mixer at high speed until light and fluffy, approximately 5 minutes. Beat in vanilla and cooled melted chocolate.

Stir in dry ingredients alternately with sour cream, beating well with a wooden spoon after each addition until batter is smooth. Stir in boiling water. This batter is thin. Pour at once into prepared pans.

Bake in preheated oven 35 minutes or until a cake tester inserted near center comes out clean. Cool layers in pans for 10 minutes. Remove from pans and cool completely. Frost with chocolate fudge frosting.

To make frosting: In a heavy saucepan combine chocolate and butter. Place over low heat until melted; cool.

In a bowl combine sugar with a small amount of the milk. Mix to form a paste. Slowly add remaining milk and vanilla. Stir until smooth. Add melted chocolate mixture. Set bowl in a pan of ice, being careful not to get any moisture into chocolate mixture. Beat with wooden spoon until frosting is thick enough to spread and hold its shape.

Desserts by Helen Friedman's chocolate truffle cake (flourless)©

Makes 12 to 16 servings.

18 ounces semisweet chocolate, divided
1½ cups plus 6 tablespoons butter, divided
6 large eggs
1½ cups sugar
¾ cup amaretto
3 tablespoons corn syrup

Heat oven to 350 degrees and line a 9-inch springform pan with foil.

Melt 12 ounces chocolate and 1½ cups butter in a saucepan.

Beat together the eggs and sugar. Add the amaretto. Stir to blend. Add the melted chocolate.

Pour into prepared springform pan – batter will be thin. Bake 40 minutes. Refrigerate before removing from foil.

Make a glaze by melting the remaining 6 tablespoons butter. Remove from heat and add remaining 6 ounces chocolate.

Stir until smooth. Add corn syrup and stir. Pour over cake and sides.

German chocolate cake©

Makes 12 to 16 servings.

¼ pound sweet cooking chocolate
½ cup boiling water
1 cup butter, margarine or shortening
2 cups sugar
4 egg yolks, unbeaten
1 teaspoon vanilla
2½ cups sifted cake flour

To make the cake: Preheat oven to 350 degrees. Grease the bottoms of three 8- or 9-inch cake pans and line them with wax paper.

Melt chocolate in boiling water (yes, melt the chocolate in the boiling water). Cool. Cream butter and sugar until light and fluffy. Add egg yolks, one at a time, beating after each addition. Add vanilla and melted chocolate.

1	teaspoon baking soda
½	teaspoon salt
1	cup buttermilk
4	egg whites, stiffly beaten

Coconut pecan frosting:

1	cup evaporated milk or half-and-half
1	cup sugar
3	egg yolks
1	cup butter or margarine
1	teaspoon vanilla
1	cup flaked coconut
1	cup chopped pecans

Mix until blended.

Sift flour with baking soda and salt. Add sifted dry ingredients alternately with buttermilk to creamed mixture, beating after each addition until batter is smooth. Fold in stiffly beaten egg whites.

Pour batter into prepared pans. Bake in preheated oven for 35 to 40 minutes. Cool and remove from pans.

When completely cooled, frost top and between layers with coconut pecan frosting.

To make the frosting: In a saucepan, combine milk, sugar, egg yolks, butter and vanilla. Cook over medium heat for 12 minutes, stirring constantly, until mixture thickens. Remove from heat.

Add coconut and pecans. Beat until cool and of spreading consistency. Makes enough to cover tops of three 9-inch layers. Do not frost sides of cake.

Red Velvet Cake©

½	cup butter
1½	cups sugar
2	eggs
2	ounces red food coloring (¼ cup)
3	tablespoons cocoa
1	cup buttermilk
2½	cups sifted cake flour
½	teaspoon salt
1	teaspoon vanilla
1	tablespoon white vinegar
1	teaspoon baking soda

Frosting:

3	tablespoons flour
1	cup milk

Makes 12 to 16 servings.

To make cake: Grease and lightly flour two 8-inch cake pans. Set aside. Preheat oven to 350 degrees.

In the large bowl of an electric mixer combine butter and sugar. Beat until creamy. Add eggs one at a time, beating after each addition.

Make a paste of food coloring and cocoa. Add to creamed mixture. Add alternately buttermilk and sifted flour and salt, beginning and ending with flour. Add vanilla. Place vinegar in a cup. **While holding vinegar over the mixing bowl, add the soda. Mixture foams.** Add to cake mixture, blending instead of beating.

1 cup granulated sugar
1 cup butter
1 teaspoon vanilla

Pour into prepared pans. Bake 25 to 30 minutes or until a toothpick inserted near center comes out clean. Remove from oven. Invert pans. Cool 10 minutes. Remove cake from pans. When completely cooled, split each layer into 2 layers.

To make frosting: In a saucepan combine flour with a small amount of milk to make a paste. Slowly add remaining milk, stirring to prevent lumps from forming. Cook over medium to low heat, stirring constantly, until very thick. Cover and cool completely in refrigerator.

With an electric mixer, cream the sugar, butter and vanilla until very light and fluffy. Add cooled milk mixture to creamed sugar and beat until well-blended. It should have the texture of whipped cream.

Frost between the cake layers and the top and sides.

   Note: If you don't want to use ¼ cup red food coloring, a more modern recipe for red velvet cake calls for mixing 3 tablespoons cocoa, 1 teaspoon red coloring and 2 tablespoons water instead of all food coloring.

Creamy coconut cake©

1 cup butter, room temperature
2 cups sugar
5 eggs, separated
2 cups all-purpose flour
1 teaspoon baking soda
¼ teaspoon salt
1 cup buttermilk
2 teaspoons vanilla

Makes 16 servings.

To make cake: Grease and flour 3 9-inch cake pans. Preheat oven to 350 degrees. Cream butter with sugar until light and fluffy. Add egg yolks one at a time, beating well after each addition.

Combine flour, baking soda and salt. Add to creamed mixture alternately with buttermilk, beginning and ending with flour mixture. Stir

⅛ teaspoon cream of tartar

Coconut filling:
1 6-ounce package fresh frozen coconut
1 8-ounce carton sour cream
2 cups granulated sugar

Whipped cream frosting:
1 pint whipping cream
⅔ cup sugar
1 teaspoon vanilla
1 cup coconut filling

in vanilla.

Have egg whites at room temperature. Beat until frothy. Add cream of tartar and continue beating until egg whites are stiff but not dry. Fold into batter.

Spoon batter into prepared pans. Bake for 25 to 30 minutes, or until a toothpick inserted near center comes out clean.

Invert cake in pans on cooling racks. Cool 10 minutes. Remove cake from pans and cool completely.

Split each layer to form 2 layers, making a total of 6 layers. Set aside.

To make coconut filling: Combine all ingredients, mixing thoroughly. Refrigerate 30 minutes. Remove 1 cup of mixture and reserve for whipped cream frosting. Spread remaining filling between layers of cake.

To make whipped cream frosting: Begin whipping cream with mixer on high speed. When cream starts to thicken, slowly add sugar and vanilla. Continue whipping until firm. Add reserved one cup coconut filling, mixing thoroughly. Frost top and sides of cake. Store in refrigerator for 2 to 3 days.

Captain Anderson's feud cake©

6 egg whites
1½ cups granulated sugar
2½ tablespoons all-purpose flour
1 teaspoon baking powder
3 cups finely ground pecans
1 pint whipping cream
¼ cup granulated sugar
1 teaspoon vanilla

Makes 12 servings.

Grease and line with wax paper two 8- or 9-inch cake pans. Grease wax paper and flour lightly. Set aside.

Heat oven to 350 degrees.

Beat egg whites (by hand) for 15 minutes adding sugar gradually. (I used an electric mixer, beating 5 to 7 minutes, gradually adding sugar.) Add flour and baking powder, sifted. Fold in pecan meal.

Pour into prepared pans and bake in

preheated oven for 30 minutes. Remove pans from oven. Let cool 10 minutes. Run knife around edge of cake to loosen. Invert pans, on a cooling rack and leave 5 minutes. Cake should drop out of pan. Remove wax paper.

Place whipping cream in large bowl of electric mixer. While beating, gradually add sugar and vanilla. Beat until stiff.

Put layers together with whipped cream. Pile thick between layers, sides and top. Sprinkle with ground pecans.

Alice Colombo's fruitcake

Makes 1 large 10-inch cake or two smaller ones.

½ pound candied red cherries
½ pound candied green cherries
½ pound candied pineapple
½ pound candied mixed fruit
1 pound medium pecan pieces
2 cups all-purpose flour
½ teaspoon baking powder
1 cup butter
1 cup granulated sugar
5 eggs
4 tablespoons bourbon, brandy or lemon juice
1 tablespoon pure vanilla extract
½ cup corn syrup
½ cup water
Extra whole pieces of fruit and nuts for garnish

Grease one 10-inch tube pan or two 9-by-5-by-2½-inch loaf pans. Line with parchment paper and grease again. Set aside.

In a large bowl combine fruit and nuts with ¼ cup flour. Set aside.

In a separate bowl, cream butter. Gradually add sugar. Beat until light and fluffy. Add eggs one at a time, beating after each addition. Add baking powder to remaining 1¾ cups flour. Stir. Add to butter mixture. Stir just until blended. Add bourbon or other liquid, vanilla and fruit and nut mixture. Stir until blended. Fill prepared pan with batter to about 1 inch from the top. Place on center shelf in a cold oven. Place a pan of water on lower shelf of oven. Turn oven temperature to 275 degrees. Bake tube cake 2½ hours; loaf cakes, 2 hours, or until cake, when pressed lightly with a finger, comes back into shape. Cool 20 to 30 minutes on a rack. Remove from pan. Peel away paper; rack cool until free of heat.

Make a glaze by combining corn syrup and water. Bring to a rolling boil. Remove from heat. Brush over top of cake. Dip pieces of fruit and nuts in glaze and arrange on top of cake. Allow to dry.

Storing fruitcakes: Soak a linen towel or several layers of cheesecloth in bourbon, brandy or wine. Wrap around the cake. Wrap in foil. Store in tightly covered tin in a cool place. (Alcohol keeps cake from molding.)

Dark fruitcake

Makes about 5 pounds.

8	ounces candied cherries
6	ounces pitted dates
20	ounces candied mixed fruit
4	ounces raisins
4	ounces chopped walnuts
4	ounces chopped pecans
¼	cup all-purpose flour
1	cup shortening
½	cup sugar
½	cup honey
5	eggs, well beaten
1½	cups sifted flour
1	teaspoon salt
1	teaspoon baking powder
1	teaspoon allspice
½	teaspoon ground cloves
½	teaspoon nutmeg
¼	cup bourbon

Cut cherries in half. Chop dates. Dredge mixed fruit, cherries, dates, raisins and nuts in ¼ cup flour.

Cream shortening and sugar. Add honey and eggs. Beat well.

Sift 1½ cups flour with salt, baking powder, allspice, cloves and nutmeg. Add alternately with bourbon to shortening mixture. Beat thoroughly. Pour batter over floured fruits and nuts. Mix well.

Grease and line with wax paper two 8½-by-4½-by-2½-inch loaf pan. Pour batter into pans – do not flatten. Bake in a preheated 250 degree oven for approximately 3 hours. Before placing cakes into oven, place a pan containing 2 cups water on bottom shelf. A cake baked with water in oven has greater volume, moist texture and a smooth, shiny glaze. If decoration of nuts and cherries is used, place on cake at end of 2 hours. Store in a covered container in a cool place.

Hummingbird cake©

1   cup butter
½   cup shortening
2   cups sugar
3   eggs
3   cups all-purpose flour
2   teaspoons baking soda
½   teaspoon salt
1½ teaspoons cinnamon
1   8-ounce can crushed
    pineapple, drained
2   cups chopped bananas
    (about 5 bananas)
1   teaspoon vanilla
1   cup chopped nuts (pecans,
    English walnuts or black
    walnuts)

Makes 16 servings.
Grease and lightly flour 3 9-inch cake pans.
Preheat oven to 350 degrees.
Cream butter, shortening and sugar until light
and fluffy. Add eggs, one at a time, beating
after each addition.
Sift together flour, baking soda, salt and
cinnamon. Add to creamed butter mixture
along with drained pineapple, mashed
bananas, vanilla and nuts. Mix until blended.
Divide batter evenly between the three
prepared pans. Bake in preheated oven 30
to 35 minutes or until a toothpick inserted
near center of layers comes out clean. Invert
pans onto cooling racks. Allow to cool about
10 minutes. Remove cake from pans.. Cool
completely before frosting with your favorite
cream cheese, butter or caramel frosting.

Italian Cream Cake©

1   cup butter
2   cups sugar
5   eggs, separated (room
    temperature)
2   cups sifted all-purpose flour
1   teaspoon baking soda
½   teaspoon salt
1   cup buttermilk
1   cup angel-flake coconut
1   cup chopped pecans or
    walnuts
Frosting:
8   ounces cream cheese, room
    temperature

Makes 16 servings.
To make cake: Grease and flour three 9-
inch cake pans. Set aside. Preheat oven to
350 degrees.
Using an electric mixer, blend butter and
sugar. Beat till light and fluffy. Add egg
yolks one at a time, beating after each
addition.
Sift flour and measure. Sift again with baking
soda and salt. Add the flour and buttermilk
alternately, beginning and ending with flour.
Stir till blended after each addition. Stir in
coconut and nuts.
Beat egg whites until stiff. Fold into batter.
Pour batter into prepared pans and bake in

6 tablespoons butter, softened
1 teaspoon vanilla
½ teaspoon grated lemon zest
(only yellow part of peel)
Juice of ½ lemon
Dash salt
4 to 5 cups confectioners' sugar

preheated oven for 35 minutes or until a toothpick inserted near center comes out clean. Remove from oven. Invert pans onto cooling racks. Allow to cool about 10 minutes. Remove from pans. Cool completely before frosting.

To make frosting: Cream butter with cream cheese. Add vanilla, lemon zest, lemon juice and dash of salt. Slowly add confectioners' sugar. Beat until smooth. Add confectioners' sugar until frosting reaches the consistency you desire.

Three-jam cake ©

1 cup butter
1 cup sugar
5 eggs, separated
1 cup strawberry jam
1 cup apricot jam
1 cup seedless blackberry jam or jelly
3 cups all-purpose flour
1 tablespoon cinnamon
½ teaspoon nutmeg
1 tablespoon baking soda
1 cup buttermilk
1 cup chopped walnuts
1 teaspoon vanilla

Makes 12 to 16 servings.
Heat oven to 350 degrees. Grease and flour 3 9-inch cake pans.
Cream butter and sugar until light and fluffy. Beat egg yolks well. Add to creamed mixture. Mix well. Add the jams and mix well.
Sift flour, cinnamon and nutmeg together. Dissolve baking soda in buttermilk. Add flour mixture to creamed mixture alternately with buttermilk, beginning and ending with flour. Stir in nuts and vanilla.
Beat egg whites until stiff. Fold gently into batter.
Pour into prepared pans. Bake 35 to 40 minutes, or until a toothpick inserted near the center comes out clean.
Invert pans onto racks. Cool 10 minutes. Remove from pans. Cool completely before frosting with your favorite white frosting or caramel icing.

Executive West Hotel's frozen lemon meringue cake©

Look at the weather forecast. If the humidity is too high, your meringues will not dry out enough. Save for another day.

Makes 8 to 10 servings.

Lemon butter:
- 2 large eggs
- 2 egg yolks
- 1 cup sugar
- 6 tablespoons unsalted butter
- ⅓ cup lemon juice
- 2 tablespoons grated lemon zest (yellow part of peel only)
- ⅛ teaspoon salt

Meringues:
- 3 egg whites, room temperature
- ⅛ teaspoon cream of tartar
- ⅓ cup sugar
- ¾ teaspoon vanilla
- 3 cups vanilla ice cream

To make lemon butter: In a heavy saucepan combine the whole eggs, egg yolks, sugar, butter, lemon juice, lemon zest and salt. Heat slowly over moderate heat, while stirring, until butter is melted and the mixture is thick enough to coat a spoon. Do not boil. Transfer to a bowl to cool.

To make meringues: Line a large baking sheet with parchment paper and, using a 7-inch cake pan or plate as a guide, trace 2 circles on paper. Heat oven to 250 degrees. In a large mixing bowl beat the egg whites with the cream of tartar until they hold soft peaks. Beat in the sugar adding a tablespoon at a time, and vanilla. Beat until the meringue is shiny and very stiff. Divide the meringue between the 2 circles, smooth it evenly with a rubber spatula. Place in the middle of the oven for 1 hour. Turn the oven off and let the meringue stand in the oven for 2 hours or until dry.

Place 1 meringue on a serving plate. Spread with 1 cup of ice cream, leaving a ¼-inch border. Freeze until the ice cream is firm. Spread half the lemon butter over the ice cream. Freeze until the lemon butter is firm. Top with 1 cup ice cream and freeze again until firm. Spread the remaining lemon butter over the ice cream and freeze again until firm. Top with the remaining ice cream and the remaining meringue. Freeze. When ready to serve, cut into wedges.

248

Mincemeat Cake©

- 2½ cups all-purpose flour
- 2 teaspoons baking powder
- 1 teaspoon baking soda
- 1 teaspoon salt
- ½ teaspoon cloves
- ½ teaspoon nutmeg
- ½ teaspoon cinnamon
- ½ cup butter, room temperature
- 1½ cups sugar
- 3 eggs
- 1 cup milk
- 2 teaspoons vanilla
- 1½ cups mincemeat
- 1 cup chopped nuts

Makes 16 servings.

Heat oven to 350 degrees. Grease and flour three 9-inch cake pans. Set aside.

Sift together flour, baking powder, baking soda, salt, cloves, nutmeg and cinnamon. Set aside.

Cream butter until light and fluffy. Slowly add sugar. Beat until creamy. Add eggs one at a time, blending after each addition. Combine milk and vanilla. By hand, stir into creamed mixture alternately with the dry ingredients, starting and ending with the dry. Blend thoroughly after each addition. Add mincemeat and nuts. Stir to blend.

Pour into prepared pans. Bake at 350 degrees for 35 minutes or until a toothpick inserted near center comes out clean. Remove from oven. Invert pans onto cooling racks. Leave for 10 minutes. Remove cake from pans and cool completely. Frost with caramel or your favorite frosting.

Pumpkin cake©

- 2 cups sugar
- 2 cups all-purpose flour
- 2 cups pumpkin or pie filling
- ½ teaspoon salt
- 1 cup corn oil
- 4 eggs
- 2 teaspoons baking soda
- 2 teaspoons baking powder
- 2 teaspoons cinnamon
- 1 cup chopped nuts

Cream cheese frosting:
- 1 16-ounce box confections' sugar

Makes 12 to 15 servings.

To make the cake: Grease and lightly flour a 9-by-13-by-2-inch baking pan. Heat oven to 350 degrees.

In a large bowl combine sugar, flour, pumpkin, salt, corn oil, eggs, baking soda, baking powder and cinnamon. Mix until well-blended. Stir in nuts.

Pour batter into prepared dish. Bake 30 to 35 minutes or until a toothpick inserted near the center comes out clean. Cool completely before frosting.

To make frosting: Combine all ingredients. Mix until thoroughly blended.

1 8-ounce package cream
cheese, room temperature
½ cup butter, softened
2 teaspoons vanilla

Note: I use a 30-ounce can of pumpkin pie filling along with all the spices called for in the recipe – great.

French walnut cake©

1 cup butter
2½ cups brown sugar, sifted
4 eggs, separated
1½ cups cake flour
1 cup milk
3 cups black walnuts
1½ cups shredded coconut
4 tablespoons extra flour mixed
with 1½ teaspoons baking
powder
Frosting:
3 to 4 cups confectioners' sugar
4 tablespoons melted butter
4 tablespoons orange juice
4 tablespoons lemon juice
Walnuts (optional)

Makes 12 to 16 servings.
To make cake: Grease and flour 2 9-inch cake pans. Preheat oven to 350 degrees. Cream butter with the sifted brown sugar (sifting the brown sugar makes it easier to cream with the butter) until light and fluffy. Add well-beaten egg yolks and beat again. Add flour alternately with milk.
Fold in walnuts and coconut. Mix in the extra 4 tablespoons flour sifted with the baking powder. Beat the egg whites until stiff. Fold into batter. Pour batter into prepared pans. Bake in preheated oven for 30 to 40 minutes or until a toothpick inserted near center comes out clean. Cool completely.
To make frosting: Cream together the sugar and butter. Add orange and lemon juices. Continue to stir until well-blended. Frost cooled cake. Add chopped walnuts to the top and sides of cake, if desired.

Beaumont Inn's white cake©

1 cup butter, room temperature
2 cups sugar
3½ cups cake flour, sift before
measuring
3½ teaspoons baking powder
1 cup milk
Pinch salt
8 egg whites, room
temperature

Makes 16 servings.
To make cake: Grease bottoms and sides of 3 8-inch pans or 2 9-inch pans. Line bottoms of pans with wax paper. Grease paper. Heat oven to 375 degrees.
In the large bowl of electric mixer cream butter and sugar until fluffy. Sift flour before measuring. Sift flour with baking powder 3 times. Add flour mixture to butter mixture alternately with milk, beginning and ending

1   teaspoon vanilla

Cathy Nichols' white icing

1   teaspoon clear vanilla or ½
     teaspoon regular vanilla
¾   cup shortening, room
     temperature
1   pound confectioners' sugar
     Cold water
     Pinch salt

with flour. Add pinch of salt.

Beat egg whites until stiff but not dry. Fold into above mixture. Stir in vanilla.

Pour into prepared pans. Bake 8-inch layers 20 to 25 minutes; 9-inch layers 25 to 30 minutes. Cool in pans 5 minutes. Run a knife between cake and edge of pans. Turn out onto racks to cool completely. Cover with frosting.

To make icing: In medium mixing bowl combine vanilla with shortening (I used butter and pure vanilla but if you want a pure white icing, use pure vegetable shortening and clear vanilla) until creamy. Slowly mix in confectioners' sugar, ½ cup at a time. Add water as needed for creamy, fluffy consistency. Add pinch of salt and mix well. Makes frosting to cover 1 cake.

Brown sugar pound cake©

1   cup butter
½   cup vegetable shortening
1   (16-ounce) box light brown
     sugar
1   cup granulated sugar
5   large eggs
3   cups all-purpose flour
½   teaspoon salt
½   teaspoon baking powder
1   cup milk
1   cup chopped walnuts
2   teaspoons vanilla
1   cup amaretto (optional)

Makes 16 to 20 servings.

Heat oven to 325 degrees. Grease a 10-inch tube pan.

Cream butter, shortening and light brown sugar. Beat well. Add granulated sugar. Beat until light and fluffy. Add eggs, 1 at a time, beating well after each addition. Beat an additional 3 minutes.

Sift together flour, salt and baking powder. Add to creamed mixture alternately with milk, beginning and ending with flour. Add vanilla and nuts. Stir just until blended. Pour into prepared pan. Bake for 1 hour and 30 minutes or until a toothpick inserted near the center comes out clean.

Cool cake in pan for 10 minutes. Remove

from pan. Brush with amaretto, allowing it to soak into cake. When completely cool, wrap in aluminum foil. Store in refrigerator. More amaretto may be added if desired. Will keep a couple of weeks.

Chocolate bar pound cake©

Makes 16 to 20 servings.

7 (1.55-ounce) chocolate bars, melted
2 cups sugar
1 cup butter
4 eggs
1 (16-ounce) can chocolate syrup
2½ cups sifted all-purpose flour
¼ teaspoon salt
1 cup buttermilk
½ teaspoon baking soda
1 teaspoon vanilla

Liberally grease a 10-inch tube pan. Preheat oven to 325 degrees.

Melt chocolate bars in the top of a double boiler over hot (not boiling) water. Remove from heat. Set aside.

Cream butter with sugar. Add eggs 1 at a time, beating after each addition. Add syrup. Beat until blended.

Add salt and baking soda to sifted flour. Add dry ingredients alternately with buttermilk to butter mixture, beginning and ending with flour. Add vanilla and melted chocolate bars. Mix just until well-blended.

Pour batter into prepared pan. Bake 1 hour and 20 minutes or until a toothpick inserted near the center comes out clean. Cool in pan.

My chocolate tea cake©

Makes 8 to 10 servings.

Cake:
1¾ cups all-purpose flour
½ cup cocoa
1½ teaspoon baking soda
1 teaspoon baking powder
½ teaspoon salt
½ cup butter, room temperature
1½ cups sugar
3 large eggs
1 cup sour cream

To make the cake: Grease and flour a 9-by-5-by-3-inch loaf pan. Preheat oven to 350 degrees.

Sift together flour, cocoa, baking soda, baking powder and salt. Set aside.

In the bowl of an electric mixer, beat butter and sugar until light and fluffy. Add eggs, 1 at a time, beating well after each addition. Stir in dry ingredients alternately with sour cream, beginning and ending with flour

1 teaspoon vanilla
½ cup boiling water

Syrup:
⅔ cup chocolate chips
4 tablespoons butter
2 cups confectioners' sugar
Dash salt
¾ cup evaporated milk
1 teaspoon vanilla

mixture. Add vanilla and boiling water. Stir until combined. Pour at once into prepared pan.

Bake 45 to 50 minutes or until a toothpick inserted near center comes out clean. Remove cake from pan while hot and place on aluminum foil.

To make the syrup: Combine chocolate chips, butter, sugar, salt and evaporated milk. Cook and stir over medium heat until mixture boils and chocolate chips melt. Reduce heat and cook for 5 minutes. Remove from heat. Add vanilla and stir. Pierce the hot cake with the tines of a fork. While spreading cake slightly with the tines, spoon syrup over the top, allowing it to run down into the cake. Pour any remaining syrup over top. Place in refrigerator until syrup sets. Cover with foil. Refrigerate overnight. For maximum flavor, allow cake to sit at room temperature for about an hour before serving.

Coconut tea cake©

Cake:
1¼ cups all-purpose flour
1 teaspoon baking powder
½ teaspoon salt
1 cup sugar
½ cup butter, room temperature
3 eggs
½ cup buttermilk
1 teaspoon coconut flavoring
1 cup coconut

Syrup:
½ cup sugar
½ cup water

Makes 8 to 10 servings.

To make cake: Grease and flour an 8-by-4-by-3-inch loaf pan. Preheat oven to 350 degrees.

Sift together flour, baking powder and salt. Set aside.

In a large mixing bowl of electric mixer, cream sugar and butter. Add eggs, one at a time, beating thoroughly after each addition. Add buttermilk alternately with dry ingredients, beginning and ending with dry ingredients. Stir in flavoring and coconut. Pour into prepared pan. Bake 45 to 50 minutes or until a toothpick inserted near

1   **teaspoon coconut flavoring**

center comes out clean. Remove cake from pan while hot and place on aluminum foil.

To make syrup: Combine sugar and water in saucepan. Place over low heat until mixture reaches low boil. Add flavoring. Remove from heat.

Pierce the hot cake with the tines of a fork. While spreading cake slightly with the tines, spoon syrup over the top, allowing it to run down into the cake.

Wrap hot cake in foil. Chill overnight. For maximum flavor, allow cake to sit at room temperature for about an hour before serving.

Lemon tea cake©

Cake:
- ½   **cup butter, room temperature**
- 1   **cup sugar**
- 2   **eggs, beaten**
- 1½   **cups all-purpose flour**
- 1   **teaspoon baking powder**
- ¼   **teaspoon salt**
- ½   **cup milk**
- 1   **teaspoon lemon zest**
-   **Juice of 1 lemon**

Syrup:
- ½   **cup sugar**
- ¼   **cup water**
- 1   **teaspoon lemon zest**
-   **Juice of 1 lemon**

Makes 8 to 10 servings.

To make cake: Grease and flour an 8-by-4-by-3-inch loaf pan. Preheat oven to 350 degrees.

In the bowl of an electric mixer, cream butter with sugar. Add eggs. Beat until light lemon in color.

Sift together flour, baking powder and salt. Add alternately with milk to sugar mixture, beginning and ending with flour mixture. Stir in lemon juice and zest. Pour into prepared pan. Bake 45 to 50 minutes or until a toothpick inserted near the center comes out clean.

Remove cake from pan while hot. Place on aluminum foil.

To make syrup: Combine sugar, water, zest and lemon juice. Heat just until sugar melts. Pierce the hot cake with the tines of a fork. While spreading cake slightly with the tines, spoon syrup over the top, allowing it to run down into the cake. Immediately wrap in foil and refrigerate while hot. Chill overnight. For maximum flavor, allow cake to sit at room temperature for about an hour before serving.

Dream cake©

Cake:

1	18.25-ounce package white or yellow cake mix
1	envelope Dream Whip
4	eggs well beaten
1	cup water

Fluffy white frosting:

4	tablespoons flour
1	cup cold milk
4	tablespoons butter or margarine, room temperature
4	tablespoons shortening
1	cup granulated sugar
1	teaspoon vanilla

Makes 12 to 15 servings.

To make cake: Lightly grease a 9-by-13-by-2-inch baking dish. Set aside. Preheat oven to 350 degrees.

In a mixing bowl combine cake mix and Dream Whip. Stir to combine. Add beaten eggs and water. Stir to thoroughly combine. Pour into prepared pan. Bake in preheated oven 30 minutes or until a toothpick inserted near the center comes out clean. Cool completely before frosting.

To make frosting: In a small saucepan combine flour and milk. Cook over medium heat until thick. Chill several hours or overnight. When very cold, combine with butter (it is important the butter be at room temperature), shortening, sugar and vanilla. Beat until you can feel no more sugar grains. Mixture should look like whipped cream. Spread on cooled cake.

Easy cake©

1	18.25-ounce box lemon or yellow cake mix
2	tablespoons unflavored bread crumbs
1	3-ounce package instant vanilla pudding
4	eggs
1	cup vegetable oil
1	cup sour cream

Makes 12 to 16 servings.

Preheat oven to 350 degrees. Generously grease a 10-inch bundt pan with vegetable shortening. Sprinkle with unflavored bread crumbs.

In a large bowl of an electric mixer combine cake mix, instant pudding, eggs, oil and sour cream. Beat for 3 minutes. Pour half the batter into prepared pan. Sprinkle with half the chocolate chips and nuts and all the

- 1 cup semisweet chocolate chips
- 1 cup miniature marshmallows
- 1 cup chopped nuts

marshmallows. Pour in remaining batter. Top with remaining chips and nuts. Bake 1 hour. Remove from oven. Cool completely in pan (overnight is great). DO NOT TURN PAN UPSIDE DOWN WHILE COOLING. Cake will flip out when completely cool.

German chocolate upside down cake

Makes 16 to 20 servings.

- 1 18.25-ounce box German chocolate cake mix
- 1 cup coconut
- 1 cup chopped pecans
- 1 8-ounce package cream cheese
- ½ cup butter
- 4 cups (1 pound) confectioners' sugar

Generously grease a 9-by-13-by-2-inch baking pan. Preheat oven to 350 degrees.
Sprinkle coconut and pecans over bottom of pan.
Prepare cake mix according to package directions. Pour over coconut and pecans.
Melt cream cheese with butter. Stir in confectioners' sugar.
Pour over cake mixture.
Bake in preheated oven 45 to 50 minutes. Let cool 15 minutes. Turn out onto a serving plate.

The Feed Bag's mandarin orange cake©

Makes 12 to 16 servings.

Cake:
- 1 18.25 ounce yellow cake mix
- 1 11-ounce can mandarin orange sections
- ½ cup chopped pecans
- 4 eggs
- ½ cup vegetable oil

Frosting:
- 1 8 ounce package cream cheese
- 2 tablespoons milk or butter
- 4 cups confectioners' sugar

To make cake: Grease and flour two 9-inch cake pans or one 9 by-13-by-2-inch oven-proof dish. Heat oven to 350 degrees.
In large bowl of electric mixer, combine cake mix, orange sections, pecans, eggs and vegetable oil. Blend at low speed until moistened. Beat at medium speed for 2 minutes. Pour batter into prepared pan. Bake 9-inch layers 30 minutes. If using the 9-by-13-by-2-inch pan, bake 35 minutes. Cool completely before frosting.
To make frosting: In large bowl of electric mixer, combine cream cheese, milk or butter and confectioners' sugar. Beat until creamy.

Spread frosting between layers and on top and sides of layer cake; frost top of 9-by-13-by-2-inch cake.

Rum cake

Cake:

½ cup chopped pecans
1 18.25 yellow cake mix
1 3-ounce package instant vanilla pudding
½ cup oil or melted butter
½ cup water
½ cup rum or apricot brandy
4 eggs

Rum sauce:

1 cup sugar
¼ cup water
¼ cup rum or apricot brandy
¼ cup butter

Makes 12 to 16 servings.
To make cake: Grease and flour a 10-inch bundt pan. Sprinkle with nuts.
In a large bowl combine cake mix and pudding mix. Add oil or butter, water, rum or brandy and eggs. Beat thoroughly. Pour into prepared pan. Bake in a preheated 350-degree oven for 1 hour. Remove cake from pan and, while still hot, insert the blade of a knife into the cake in several places. Pour the warm rum sauce down the blade and over the cake into the holes   Let stand at least 30 minutes before serving.
To make sauce: In a small saucepan combine all ingredients. Bring to a boil and cook 3 minutes. Spoon over hot cake.

Frostings, Fillings, Sauces and Syrups

Chocolate mocha icing

2 tablespoons butter
3 tablespoons cocoa
1½ cups confectioners' sugar
3 tablespoons hot black coffee

Makes frosting for 1 cake.
Melt butter over hot water. Add cocoa. Stir until smooth. Add confectioners' sugar and hot coffee. Beat well and spread on the cake.

Plehn's Bakery's chocolate icing©

6 cups confectioners' sugar
6 tablespoons butter

Makes 3 cups.
To make icing: Slowly combine sugar, butter, cocoa and salt. Add hot water, simple

¾ cup plus 2 tablespoons cocoa
   Dash salt
½ cup hot water
4 tablespoons simple syrup
1 teaspoon vanilla

Simple syrup:
¼ cup cold water
½ cup sugar

syrup and vanilla. Stir until smooth. If icing is too thick, add a little more water; if too thin, add confectioners' sugar.

To make simple syrup: Place water and sugar in a small saucepan. Bring to boil. Cook until sugar is dissolved.

Lemon curd©

4 tablespoons unsalted butter
½ cup sugar
½ cup freshly squeezed lemon juice
4 egg yolks
1 tablespoon grated lemon peel

Makes 1 cup.

In a heavy non-aluminum saucepan (or the top of a non-aluminum double boiler), combine butter, sugar, lemon juice and egg yolks. Cook over lowest heat (or simmering water), stirring constantly, until mixture thickens enough to heavily coat the back of a spoon. Do not let the mixture boil or it will curdle.

Pour the lemon curd into a small bowl and stir in the lemon peel. Refrigerate until ready to use.

Wedding cake frosting

¾ cup butter
¾ cup shortening
1 envelope Dream Whip
2 teaspoons vanilla or ¼ teaspoon almond extract
½ to ⅔ cup milk
2 pounds confectioners' sugar

Makes 5 to 6 cups.

In the large bowl of electric mixer combine butter, shortening, Dream Whip and vanilla. Beat on high speed (or #6 on a Kitchenaid mixer) for 8 minutes or until mixture looks like whipped cream. Add milk alternately with sugar. Beat until light and creamy. Do not over beat.

Jack Fry's warm caramel syrup©

1¾ cups heavy cream
4 ounces (1 stick) butter

Makes about 4 cups.

In a small saucepan, heat the cream and butter with the vanilla bean until the butter is

1   vanilla bean, split and
    scraped
¼   cup white corn syrup
2   cups sugar

melted and the mixture is hot. Keep warm over low heat.

In a deep, heavy saucepan, heat the corn syrup over medium heat just until it bubbles. Sprinkle enough sugar on top of the bubbling corn syrup to cover the surface completely (about ⅓ cup). Stir with a wooden spoon to incorporate and thin out. Stir constantly. Add the rest of the sugar in batches of the same size. The mixture will get very stiff. Continue cooking and stirring vigorously until a thread of syrup drizzled from the lifted spoon is runny and straw-colored. Remove from heat.

Remove vanilla bean from hot cream and butter mixture. Add cream and butter mixture to syrup in 4 portions, stirring well after each addition. The mixture will bubble up and be very hot, so be careful when doing this.

Return the mixture to high heat and boil for 2 to 3 minutes, stirring gently. The caramel will become thick and will be a pale color. If needed, add up to another ¼ cup cream to get the desire consistency for the syrup. Keep caramel in the refrigerator. Heat over low flame or in the microwave before using.

Bourbon sauce©

1   cup brown sugar
2   tablespoons cornstarch
¼   teaspoon salt
1½ cups boiling water
4   teaspoons butter
1   teaspoon vanilla
½   cup bourbon

Makes about 2½ cups.

In a small saucepan, mix brown sugar, cornstarch and salt. Add the boiling water and cook over low heat for 5 minutes or until thickened, stirring occasionally.

Remove from heat and add butter. Stir until melted. Add vanilla and bourbon. Serve warm.

The best hot fudge sauce

3	squares unsweetened chocolate
4	tablespoons butter
2	cups confectioners' sugar
	Dash salt
1	5-ounce can evaporated milk
1	teaspoon vanilla

Makes 1¾ cups.

In a saucepan, combine chocolate, butter, sugar, salt and evaporated milk. Cook and stir over medium heat until mixture boils and chocolate melts. Reduce heat to low and cook 5 minutes only, stirring often. Remove from heat and add vanilla. Stir.
Store in refrigerator. To serve – heat over hot water, stirring often until smooth and hot. Great over ice cream.

Amick's Family Restaurant's cinnamon Sauce©

3	cups sugar
4	cups water
3	tablespoons flour
1	teaspoon cinnamon
½	teaspoon nutmeg
¼	teaspoon red food coloring, optional

In a 2-quart saucepan, combine sugar, water, flour, cinnamon and nutmeg. Bring to a boil and simmer one hour. Add food coloring, if desired. Serve while hot over your favorite apple pie. Store in refrigerator.

Hot, bubbly butter sauce©

1	cup sugar
1	tablespoon all-purpose flour
½	cup cream
1	tablespoon vinegar
½	cup butter
1	teaspoon vanilla

Makes about 1½ cups.

In a saucepan combine sugar and flour. Stir. Add cream, vinegar and butter. Heat, beating well, over high heat until hot and bubbly. Add vanilla. Stir. Serve warm over cake.

Kentucky sauce©

1	cup brown sugar
1	cup white sugar
1	cup water
1	cup pecans, broken
1	cup strawberry preserves

Makes over a quart.

Combine sugars with the water. Cook over medium heat until syrup reaches about 240 degrees on candy thermometer, or until it will almost, but not quite, spin a thread. Remove from heat and stir in pecans and preserves.

1	orange
1	lemon
1	cup bourbon

Using a potato peeler remove orange part and yellow part of rind from orange and lemon. Chop fine. Cut off and discard white membrane from orange and lemon. Cut sections into small pieces. Add cut-up rind, fruit and the bourbon to the first mixture. Set in refrigerator to ripen – keeps indefinitely and is wonderful served over ice cream.

Rum raisin sauce©

Makes 1½ cups.

½	cup raisins
¾	cup dark rum
1	cup granulated sugar
¼	teaspoon cinnamon
⅛	teaspoon nutmeg
½	cup water
¼	cup (½ stick) butter

Place raisins in a bowl with half the rum. Let soak for 1 hour, or until plumped.

Put the sugar, cinnamon, nutmeg and water into saucepan and bring to a boil. Stir to dissolve the sugar, then cook over moderate heat for 5 minutes, or until mixture is darkened and syrupy.

Remove from heat and add the remaining rum and the soaked raisins. Gradually stir in the butter and set aside to cool.

Norma Hudson's chocolate gravy©

Makes 6 to 8 servings.

2	level tablespoons Hershey's cocoa
2 to 3	ounces (4 to 6 tablespoons) sugar
2	tablespoons all-purpose flour
	Dash salt
2	cups milk
1	teaspoon vanilla
1	teaspoon butter

Mix dry ingredients together; while stirring, slowly add milk and vanilla, stirring well to make a smooth, creamy mixture, as you would for white sauce. Bring to a slow boil and then add butter. Serve while hot.

Fruits

Kentucky fruit compote©

1	21-ounce can cherry-pie filling
1	11-ounce can Mandarin oranges, drained
1	8-ounce package mixed dried fruit
⅓	cup brown sugar, well packed
½	cup Kentucky bourbon
½	teaspoon cinnamon
⅛	teaspoon nutmeg

Makes 8 to 10 servings.

Mix cherry-pie filling, Mandarin oranges and dried fruit. Add brown sugar, bourbon, cinnamon and nutmeg. Stir until sugar dissolves and spices are thoroughly wet. Place in a covered, oven-proof casserole. Bake in a 350-degree oven for 45 minutes. Serve warm.

Cumberland House scalloped pineapple©

4	cups bread chunks (French-style bread is best)
1	20-ounce can pineapple chunks, drained
3	eggs
2	cups sugar
1	cup melted butter

Makes 8 to 10 servings.

Place bread chunks in the bottom of a well-greased 9-by-13-by-2-inch dish. Spread drained pineapple chunks over bread. Beat eggs slightly. Mix in sugar and melted butter. Pour over chunks of bread and pineapple.
Bake in a 375-degree oven for about 40 minutes, or until sugar is melted.

'Country Kitchen Cook Book' caramel candy apples©

6	medium-sized apples
6	wooden skewers
½	cup granulated sugar
½	cup brown sugar
2	tablespoons light corn syrup
⅓	cup water
½	teaspoon salt
1	teaspoon butter

Makes 6 apples.

Wash and dry apples. Insert skewers in stem ends of apples. Set aside.
In a heavy 3-quart saucepan, combine sugars, corn syrup, water, salt and butter. Stir over medium heat until sugar is dissolved. Cover and cook for 3 minutes without stirring. This washes down any sugar crystals that may form on the sides of

1   cup chopped nuts

the saucepan. Remove cover and continue cooking without stirring until candy thermometer registers 250 degrees F. (hard ball in cold water). Remove from heat. Hold each apple by skewer and dip in syrup. Let excess syrup drain off. Roll in chopped nuts. Set on wax paper or greased baking sheet to harden.

'American Home All-Purpose Cookbook' red candy apples©

8   large red apples
8   wooden skewers
3   cups sugar
½   cup light corn syrup
½   cup water
1   teaspoon cinnamon extract
1   teaspoon red food coloring

Makes 8 apples.
Wash and dry apples. Insert skewers in stem ends of apples. Set aside.
Combine sugar, corn syrup and water in heavy 3-quart saucepan. Stir over medium heat until sugar is dissolved. Cover and cook for 3 minutes without stirring. This washes down any sugar crystals that may form on the sides of the saucepan. Cook without stirring until candy thermometer registers 285 degrees F. (soft-crack stage). Remove from heat. Add cinnamon extract and coloring. Stir only enough to mix. Let mixture settle a few minutes.
Hold each apple by skewer; quickly twirl in syrup, tilting pan to cover apples with syrup. Allow excess to drip off. Place on lightly buttered cookie sheet to cool. Store in cool place.

The Depot's fried apples©

2   pounds fresh unpeeled apples
4   tablespoons butter or margarine

Makes 6 to 8 servings.
Wash, core and slice apples. In a large skillet, melt butter or margarine. Add apples, brown sugar, cinnamon, nutmeg and orange juice. Simmer, covered, for 15 minutes.

6 tablespoons light brown sugar
2 teaspoons ground cinnamon
1 teaspoon ground nutmeg
¼ cup orange juice

Remove cover and cook over low heat until thick and bubbly, stirring occasionally.

Brennan's Bananas Foster©

¼ cup (½ stick) butter
1 cup brown sugar
½ teaspoon cinnamon
¼ cup banana liqueur
4 bananas, cut in half lengthwise, then halved
¼ cup white rum
4 scoops vanilla ice cream

Makes 4 servings.
Combine the butter, sugar and cinnamon in a flambé pan or skillet. Place the pan over low heat either on an alcohol burner or on top of the stove, and cook, stirring, until the sugar dissolves. Stir in the banana liqueur, then place the bananas in the pan. When the banana sections soften and begin to brown, carefully add the rum. Continue to cook the sauce until the rum is hot, then tip the pan slightly to ignite the alcohol (if you are cooking on electric, you probably will have to ignite the alcohol by using a match or long-handled lighter). When the flames subside, lift the bananas out of the pan and place 4 pieces over each portion of ice cream. Generously spoon warm sauce over the top of the ice cream and serve immediately.

Blueberry-lemon lush©

Lemon lush:
¾ cup sugar
¼ cup cornstarch
3 egg yolks, beaten
2 cups milk
Zest and juice of 2 lemons
2 tablespoons butter

Makes 6 servings (about 375 calories per serving).
To make lemon lush: Place sugar and cornstarch in a saucepan and stir to combine.
In a bowl, beat egg yolks. Slowly add milk. Stir until well-blended. While stirring, add to sugar mixture. Place over medium heat. While stirring, bring mixture to a boil. Cook

1 teaspoon vanilla
Blueberry sauce:
2 cups fresh blueberries
4 tablespoons sugar
1 tablespoon cornstarch
Juice of half lemon
2 tablespoons water
Topping:
½ cup heavy whipping cream (optional)
6 sprigs of mint (optional)
6 fresh blueberries (optional)

until mixture thickens. Remove from heat. Add zest, lemon juice, butter and vanilla. Stir until butter melts and mixture is well-blended. Refrigerate while preparing sauce.

To make blueberry sauce: In a saucepan, combine sugar and cornstarch. Stir. Add lemon juice, water and blueberries (reserve 6 blueberries for garnish). Bring mixture to a boil. Cook until thickened. Remove from heat.

Layer lemon lush and blueberry sauce in champagne or parfait glasses. Refrigerate until ready to serve. Top each serving with 2 tablespoons whipped cream, a sprig of mint and a blueberry.

No-fat lemon lush with blueberries©

¾ cup sugar
¼ cup cornstarch
1½ cups skim milk
1 4-ounce carton Egg Beaters (or other egg substitute)
1 teaspoon pure vanilla extract
Juice and zest of 2 lemons
2 cups fresh blueberries

Makes 6 servings, about 177 calories per serving.
In a saucepan, combine sugar and cornstarch. Stir. Add skim milk and egg substitute. Stir. Cook over medium heat, while stirring, until mixture comes to a boil and thickens. Remove from heat. Add vanilla, lemon juice and zest. Layer lemon lush and blueberries in champagne or parfait glasses. Refrigerate 4 to 6 hours or until set.

Hot cranberry salad©

3 cups chopped apples, peeled
2 cups whole, raw cranberries
1½ teaspoons lemon juice
1½ cups sugar
1⅓ cups quick-cooking oatmeal
1 cup chopped walnuts
⅓ cup brown sugar, packed
1 stick butter, melted

Makes about 6 servings.
Oil a 2-quart casserole. Place the chopped apples and cranberries in the casserole. Sprinkle with lemon juice. Cover with sugar. In a medium mixing bowl, blend just to moisten the oatmeal, walnuts, brown sugar and melted butter. Pour crumb mixture over fruit. Bake uncovered at 325 degrees for 1¼ hours.

Strawberries with Rebecca sauce©

2 quarts fresh strawberries
1 pint sour cream
½ cup brown sugar
1 tablespoon vanilla
1 tablespoon dark rum or
   bourbon (optional)

Makes about 3 cups sauce.
Wash berries. Drain on paper toweling. Place in a decorative bowl or basket. Combine sour cream, brown sugar, vanilla and rum or bourbon. Stir to mix well. Refrigerate until ready to use. Recipe may be doubled.

Pies and Tarts

Plain pastry shell or piecrust

(Adapted from Better Homes and Gardens)

Single crust:
1¼ cups all-purpose flour
¼ teaspoon salt
⅓ cup shortening
3 to 4 tablespoons ice water
Double crust:
2 cups all-purpose flour
⅔ cup shortening
1 teaspoon salt
5 to 7 tablespoons ice water

Single crust makes 1 9-inch pie shell. Double crust makes 2 9-inch pie shells or 1 9-inch pie shell and top.
To make pie crust: Place flour, salt and shortening in a large bowl. Stir to mix. Using a pastry blender or two knives, cut shortening into flour until crumbly. Add ice water a tablespoon at a time. Cut in with pastry blender or knives. Add only enough water to hold mixture together. Form into a ball. Let rest 15 to 20 minutes. Flatten on lightly floured surface by pressing with edge of hand. Using a rolling pin, roll from center to edge in both directions to ⅛-inch thickness.
To bake single-crust pie shell: Fit pastry into pie plate; trim ½ to 1 inch beyond edge; fold under and flute edge by pressing dough with forefinger against wedge made of finger and thumb of other hand. Prick bottom and sides well with fork. Bake in a preheated 450-degree 12 to 15 minutes or until light golden

To make lattice-top pie: Fit bottom pastry into pie plate. Trim lower crust ½ inch beyond edge of pie plate. Roll remaining dough ⅛ inch thick. Cut strips of pastry ½ to ¾ inch wide with pastry wheel or knife. Lay strips on filled pie at 1-inch intervals. Fold back alternate strips as you weave cross strips. Trim lattice even with outer rim of pie plate; fold lower crust over strips. Seal; flute edge

For double-crust pie: Fit pastry into pie plate; trim lower crust even with rim of pie plate. Roll out pastry for top crust. Lift pastry by rolling it over rolling pin and then unroll loosely over well-filled pie. Trim ½ inch beyond edge. Tuck top crust under edge of lower crust. Flute edge of pastry as desired

Graham cracker crust

1½   cups fine graham–cracker crumbs
6   tablespoons sugar
6   tablespoons butter or margarine, melted

Makes 1 9-inch pie shell.
Combine graham-cracker crumbs, sugar and melted butter. Mix; press into a 9-inch pie plate. Bake in a preheated 375-degree oven 6 to 8 minutes or until edges are browned; cool.
For unbaked crust, chill 45 minutes; fill.

Chocolate wafer crust

1½   cups fine chocolate wafer crumbs
2   tablespoons sugar
6   tablespoons butter or margarine, melted

Makes 1 9-inch pie shell.
Mix together chocolate wafer crumbs, sugar and melted butter or margarine. Press firmly into a 9-inch pie plate. Chill before serving.

Coconut crust

1   3½-ounce can angel flake coconut
2   tablespoons butter or margarine
¼   cup chopped pecans, optional

Makes 1 9-inch pie shell.
Combine coconut, melted butter or margarine and pecans. Mix thoroughly. Press into a 9-inch pie pan. Bake in a preheated 325-degree oven for 12 to 15 minutes, or until coconut is light golden brown.

Pretzel crust

1½   cups pretzel crumbs
7   tablespoons butter, melted
4   tablespoons sugar

Makes 1 9-inch pie shell.
Combine crushed pretzels and melted butter with sugar. Press into the bottom and sides of a 9-inch pie pan. Chill.

I use the following pudding as a dessert, filling between layers of cake, fruit trifle, custard cannoli filling and cream pies.

Basic pudding

1   cup sugar
4   tablespoons cornstarch
¼   teaspoon salt
3   eggs, separated
2   cups milk, scalded
1   teaspoon vanilla
2   tablespoon butter

Makes 1 pie.
To make pudding: In top of a double boiler that has been placed over simmering water, combine sugar, cornstarch and salt. Stir to combine. Using a fork or whisk, beat egg yolks while adding a small amount of scalded milk. When enough hot milk has been slowly added to yolks to warm them, combine yolks with remaining milk. Slowly stir into sugar mixture. Cook, stirring frequently until thick. This is a slow process so be patient (if you have a candy thermometer, temperature should reach 170 degrees). Add vanilla and butter. Stir until butter melts and vanilla is incorporated into pudding.
Coconut pie: Add 1 cup angel flake or

shredded coconut. Top with meringue and bake until meringue is golden.

Banana cream pie: Cover bottom of baked pastry shell with pudding. Cover with thin slices of banana. Top with pudding and another layer of banana until pastry shell is full, ending with pudding. Top with meringue and bake until meringue is golden.

Peanut butter pie: Add 1 cup peanut butter. Stir to thoroughly combine. Pour into baked pastry shell. Top with meringue and bake until meringue is golden.

Meringue

1	tablespoon cornstarch
8	tablespoons sugar
⅓	cup water
3	egg whites
⅛	teaspoon salt

Makes meringue for 1 pie.

In a small saucepan, mix cornstarch, 2 tablespoons sugar and water. Cook over low heat until mixture has thickened and is clear. Remove from heat.

Place egg whites in bowl of electric mixer. Beat to soft peak stage. While slowly beating, add cornstarch mixture. Beat until creamy. Add salt and remaining 6 tablespoons sugar. Beat until fluffy. Pile on pie and bake in a 350-degree oven until meringue is golden, about 20 to 25 minutes.

Alice's perfect apple pie

1	recipe for double-crust pie shell
6 to 8	Macintosh apples, pared, cored and thinly sliced (6 cups)
	Juice of half lemon
¾ to 1	cup sugar
3	tablespoons tapioca

Makes 8 servings.

Prepare recipe for plain double crust. Divide into two portions. Roll one portion out and place in a deep 9-inch pie pan. Roll remaining portion out to cut into strips for lattice top.

Peel, pare, core and thinly slice apples. Place in a saucepan. Add lemon juice, sugar, tapioca, cinnamon, ginger and nutmeg. Stir.

½ to 1 teaspoon cinnamon
   1 tablespoon chopped
      crystallized ginger (optional)
      Dash grated fresh nutmeg
   2 tablespoons butter
      Cream and sugar for top of
      pie

Cook over medium heat until apples are soft. Pour into prepared crust. Dot with butter. Top with lattice strips. Brush with cream and a sprinkling of sugar.
Bake in preheated 400-degree oven for 50 minutes or until crust is golden.

Grapevine Pantry's apple strudel cheese pie©

   1 unbaked 9-inch pastry shell
4 to 5 tart apples, peeled and sliced
   1 cup sugar, divided
   1 teaspoon cinnamon
   2 8-ounce packages cream
      cheese, softened
   2 eggs
   1 teaspoon vanilla
Topping:
   2 tablespoons butter
   5 tablespoons sugar
   2 tablespoons flour
   ½ teaspoon cinnamon

Makes 8 servings.
Peel and slice apples. Toss with ½ cup of sugar and cinnamon. Set aside.
Using an electric mixer blend cream cheese, remaining ½ cup sugar, eggs and vanilla until smooth.
In a separate bowl, make topping by cutting butter into dry ingredients until well-blended and crumbly. Set aside.
Pour cream cheese mixture into unbaked pastry shell. Place apple slices on top, laying them out in a spiral fashion and sprinkle with topping.
Bake in preheated 450-degree oven for 10 minutes. Reduce temperature to 350 degrees and continue baking an additional 30 minutes or until set. Cool and chill for at least 1 hour before serving.

Blue Boar sugarless apple pie©

   1 double-crust 9-inch pastry
      shell, unbaked
   4 apples, cored, peeled and
      sliced
   ⅓ cup orange juice,
      unsweetened
   1 cup water, divided
   1 teaspoon cinnamon

Makes 8 servings.
In a saucepan, combine apples, orange juice, ⅔ cup of the water and cinnamon. Cook until apples are tender.
Combine gelatin with remaining ⅓ cup water. When gelatin has dissolved, add to apple mixture along with the sugar substitute. Stir until blended.

1 ¼-ounce envelope unflavored gelatin
1½ teaspoons sugar substitute
Sweetening mist (recipe follows)

Place filling in unbaked shell and add top crust. Cut several slits in top crust or cut top crust into strips and make a lattice top. Bake in a 350-degree oven 40 to 45 minutes or until crust is golden brown.

Sweetening mist: In a spray bottle, combine 1 teaspoon sugar substitute with ⅓ cup water. Shake to dissolve. Spray mist lightly on top of baked pie.

The Country Kitchen's apricot pie©

Makes 8 servings.

1 unbaked double-crust pie shell
4 cups canned apricots, drained
1 cup sugar
3 tablespoons tapioca
1 teaspoon lemon juice
Milk or cream and sugar for top crust

Roll dough and line bottom of a 9-inch pie pan. Set aside. Roll remaining dough for top of pie.

Drain and discard juice from apricots. Chop apricots coarsely. Add sugar, tapioca and lemon juice. Stir to combine. Pour into prepared unbaked pie shell.

Top with remaining rolled dough (this can be a full crust with slits cut into it or you can cut into strips to form a lattice top). Trim edges and crimp. Brush top of crust with milk or cream and sprinkle with sugar. Bake in a preheated 400-degree oven for 50 to 60 minutes or until crust is golden.

Maple syrup pie©

Makes 8 servings.

1 9-inch unbaked pastry shell
2 eggs
⅓ cup real maple syrup
1 cup brown sugar
½ cup heavy cream
2¼ teaspoons soft butter
Additional cream for serving

Combine the eggs. Beat the eggs with the maple syrup, brown sugar, cream and butter. Pour into pastry shell, leaving ¼ inch of crust above the filling. Bake in a 350-degree oven for 40 minutes, or until golden brown.

When ready to serve, place a slice of pie on a serving dish. Pour cream over the pie until a shallow pool forms.

The Feed Bag's German chocolate pie©

- 1 unbaked 9-inch pastry shell
- 1½ cups sugar
- 2 tablespoons cornstarch
- 3 tablespoons all-purpose flour
- 3 tablespoons cocoa
- Pinch salt
- 3 eggs
- 4½ tablespoons melted butter
- 1 cup milk
- 1 cup coconut
- 1 cut nuts
- 2 teaspoons vanilla

Topping:
- 1 cup chocolate chips
- 2 teaspoons vegetable oil

Makes 8 servings.

To make pie: In a large bowl combine sugar, cornstarch, flour, cocoa and salt. Stir to blend. Add eggs and melted butter. Stir until well blended. Slowly add milk while stirring. Add coconut, nuts and vanilla. Stir to thoroughly combine. Pour into pastry shell. Bake in a preheated 350-degree oven for 45 minutes.

To make topping: After removing pie from oven, prepare topping. In the top of a double-boiler over warm water, melt chocolate chips. Stir in vegetable oil. Pour over top of baked pie, spreading to cover completely.

Just plain, good chocolate pie

- 1 baked 9-inch pastry shell (see recipe for plain pastry)
- 1½ cups sugar
- 6 tablespoons all-purpose flour
- 6 tablespoons cocoa
- ½ teaspoon salt
- 3 cups milk
- 4 eggs, separated
- 2 tablespoons butter
- 1 teaspoons vanilla

Meringue:
- 1 tablespoon plus 1 teaspoon cornstarch
- 3 tablespoons sugar
- ½ cup water
- 4 egg whites
- Dash salt
- 8 tablespoons sugar

Makes 8 servings.

Prepare pastry according to plain pastry recipe at beginning of Pies section.

To make filling: In the top of a double-boiler, combine sugar, flour, cocoa and salt. Stir to combine. Slowly add milk, stirring to incorporate dry ingredients. Cook over simmering water, stirring occasionally, until thick (this is a slow process so be patient – pudding must reach 170 degrees on a candy thermometer). Remove from heat. Add, while stirring, ¼ cup hot filling to slightly beaten egg yolks. Continue adding hot pudding until yolks are very warm. Add warmed yolks to remaining filling, stirring to incorporate. Add butter and vanilla. Stir until butter melts. Pour into baked pastry shell. While hot, top with meringue.

To make meringue: In a saucepan, mix

cornstarch with 3 tablespoons sugar and water. Cook over low heat until mixture is clear. Remove from heat. Beat egg whites until peaked then slowly add cornstarch mixture, beating until creamy. Add salt and the 8 tablespoons sugar, 2 tablespoons at a time, beating until fluffy. Pile on pie and bake in a preheated 350-degree oven until meringue is golden, about 15 to 20 minutes.

Note: To cut down on time, I heat the milk in the microwave for 2 to 3 minutes - **do not boil.** When I am in a hurry, I don't use a double boiler but you **MUST** stir constantly. This cuts the prep time to about a fourth of what it takes to use a double boiler.

Apron Strings chocolate buttercrunch pie©

Makes 8 servings.

Crust:
- 1 cup all-purpose flour
- ⅓ cup brown sugar
- ¼ teaspoon salt
- 5 tablespoons butter
- ¼ cup chocolate chips
- ¾ cup finely chopped pecans
- 2½ tablespoons water
- 2½ teaspoons vanilla

Filling:
- 2 cups whipping cream, divided
- 1 cup brown sugar
- 4 teaspoons cocoa
- 4 eggs, separated
- 4 teaspoons vanilla
- 3 1-ounce squares unsweetened chocolate
- 8 tablespoons (1 stick) butter, softened

Curst: Preheat oven to 350 degrees. Combine flour, sugar and salt in food processor. Add butter and process to coarse meal. Remove and place in a mixing bowl. Place chocolate chips and pecans in processor and process slightly. Add to flour mixture. Add water and vanilla. Stir till well-blended. Press into pie pan, covering rim. Bake until golden. Cool crust completely.

Filling: Place 1 cup of the whipping cream in top of double boiler. Combine brown sugar and cocoa. Add to cream along with beaten egg yolks. Heat over simmering water to 160 degrees (this kills salmonella), stirring constantly. Remove from heat. Add vanilla and chocolate. Stir till chocolate melts. Place pan in ice water. Stir till mixture begins to firm slightly. Pour into bowl of electric mixer. Beat at high speed, adding butter a tablespoon at a time, beating after

¼ cup confectioners' sugar
Grated bittersweet chocolate

each addition until blended. Add egg whites and continue beating at high speed (10 to 15 minutes) or until mixture reaches the consistency of whipped cream. Mound into crust. Cover and refrigerate several hours. Before serving, whip remaining 1 cup cream with sugar until stiff peaks form. Place on top of pie and garnish with grated chocolate.

Porcini coconut cream tart ©

Sable dough (for crust):
½ pound margarine (see note)
½ cup sugar
1 egg
1 teaspoon pure vanilla extract
3 cups flour

Filling:
1¾ cups sugar
½ teaspoon salt
¼ cup cornstarch
4 egg yolks
2 cups milk
1½ cups toasted coconut (see note)
1 teaspoon pure vanilla extract

Topping:
2 cups heavy whipping cream
1 cup confectioners' sugar
1 teaspoon coconut extract
1 teaspoon Malibu rum
Toasted coconut, for garnish

Makes 1 12-inch tart or 8 4–inch tarts.
To make sable dough crust: Cream margarine and sugar until light and fluffy. Add egg and vanilla. Mix well. Mix in flour until well-blended. Refrigerate 1 hour. Press into tart pan and bake in a preheated 350-degree oven for 10 to 15 minutes or until golden brown. Cool.

To make filling: In a saucepan combine sugar, salt and cornstarch. Beat yolks. While beating, slowly add milk. Beat until well-blended. Add to sugar mixture, stirring sugar mixture while adding milk. Place over medium heat. Bring to a boil, stirring constantly. Boil 1 minute. Remove from heat and add coconut (reserving a small amount to garnish top of pie) and vanilla. Cool to lukewarm. Pour into cooled tart.

To make topping: Whip cream to soft peak. Add sugar, coconut extract and rum. Whip to stiff peak. Place flavored whipped cream on top of cooled filling. Garnish with toasted coconut.

About margarine: Check the label on the package. It should say "margarine"; if it doesn't, then it isn't. By law, "margarine" must be 80 percent fat, the same as butter.

If it is not, you may sacrifice flavor, texture and appearance for a few calories.

To toast coconut: Spread coconut on a cookie sheet. Place in a preheated 350-degree oven. Bake, stirring frequently until coconut starts to turn golden. Watch closely; coconut burns quickly.

Azalea's banana cream pie©

Pastry shell:

2	cups all-purpose flour
¼	cup cake flour
¼	teaspoon baking powder
¼	teaspoon salt
1	cup cold butter
6	teaspoons water

Filling:

3½	cups half-and-half cream
1	cup sugar
¾	cup cornstarch
5	egg yolks
6	tablespoons butter
½	teaspoon vanilla
4	bananas
3	teaspoons banana liqueur
1	cup heavy whipping cream
	Semisweet chocolate, garnish

Makes 1 12-inch pie.

To make pastry shell: Sift flours, baking powder and salt into a large bowl. Using a pastry blender or 2 knives, cut butter into flour mixture until it resembles coarse cornmeal. Add water until dough just comes together. Wrap and let rest for 30 minutes. On a lightly floured surface, roll pastry to fit a 12-inch pie pan. Place pastry in pan. Crimp edges.

Bake in a preheated 450-degree oven for 10 to 12 minutes or until golden. Cool before filling.

To make filling: In a heavy saucepan, bring 2¾ cups half-and-half to a boil.

In the large bowl of an electric mixer, combine sugar and cornstarch. Add egg yolks. Turn mixer to low speed and add remaining half-and-half. Beat until thoroughly mixed. With mixer on slow speed, slowly add hot half-and-half to egg mixture. Strain into saucepan. Return to medium heat and cook until thick. Add vanilla and butter. Stir to blend. Cool. Add sliced bananas and banana liqueur. Gently stir to combine.

Pour filling into baked pastry shell. Whip cream to soft peak stage. Spread over top of

pie. Garnish with shaved chocolate.
Refrigerate until ready to serve.

Shoofly pie©

1 unbaked 8- or 9-inch pastry shell
1½ teaspoons baking soda
¾ cup boiling water
½ cup dark corn syrup
1 egg yolk, well-beaten
¾ cup all-purpose flour
½ cup brown sugar
⅛ teaspoon nutmeg
⅛ teaspoon ginger
⅛ teaspoon cloves
½ teaspoon cinnamon
¼ teaspoon salt
2 tablespoons butter

Makes 6 to 8 servings.
Make favorite pastry crust, roll out and fit into pie pan, fluting the edges. (The 8-inch pastry shell makes a thicker, more delightful pie.) Preheat oven to 400 degrees.
Dissolve baking soda in boiling water; combine with dark corn syrup. Add the beaten egg yolk; mix well. Mix all the dry ingredients together and work in the shortening with the fingertips or a pastry blender until it is like coarse meal.
Place alternate layers of the liquid mixture and the crumb mixture in unbaked pastry shell, having the crumbs as a final layer.
Bake in preheated oven until the edges of the crust begin to brown, 20 to 25 minutes. Reduce the heat to 300 degrees and bake until firm, about 20 to 25 more minutes.

Butterscotch meringue pie©

1 9-inch pastry shell, baked
½ cup light brown sugar
½ cup dark brown sugar
5 tablespoons cornstarch
½ teaspoon salt
2 cups milk
4 eggs, separated
½ cup (1 stick) butter
1 teaspoon vanilla

Makes 8 servings.
Prepare your favorite pastry shell and bake.
To make filling: In the top of a double boiler, stir together sugars, cornstarch and salt. Continue stirring as you slowly add milk. Cook over boiling water 10 minutes or until mixture thickens. Remove from heat. Beat egg yolks slightly. While stirring, slowly add half the hot mixture to the yolks. When smooth, stir eggs into the rest of hot mixture. Return to heat and cook 3 to 5 minutes or until thick. Add butter and vanilla. Stir until

Meringue:

4	egg whites
¼	teaspoon cream of tartar
¾	cup sugar
½	teaspoon vanilla

well blended. When slightly cooled, pour into baked pastry shell. Top with meringue.

To make meringue: Beat egg whites until frothy. Add cream of tartar. Gradually add sugar, beating constantly until egg whites are stiff but not dry. Beat in vanilla.

Spread on pie, being sure to seal meringue to pastry at edges. Bake in a 350-degree oven 15 to 20 minutes or until delicately browned.

O'Charley's caramel pie©

1	9-inch graham cracker crust
1	14-ounce can sweetened condensed milk
1	cup whipping cream
3	tablespoons granulated sugar
¼	teaspoon vanilla
⅓	cup pecans, chopped Chocolate curls or shaved chocolate

Makes 8 servings.

Place unopened can of sweetened condensed milk in a pan of water, being sure water completely covers can. Bring water to a boil. Reduce heat. Simmer for 5 hours, adding water as needed. Keep can completely submerged. Remove can from water. Place in refrigerator to chill overnight. Prepare your favorite graham cracker crust or purchase one already prepared. Remove chilled caramel from the can and place in bowl of an electric mixer and beat until smooth. Pour into prepared pie shell. Whip cream, gradually adding sugar and vanilla while beating. When stiff, spread over caramel filling. Sprinkle with pecans and garnish with chocolate curls or shaved chocolate. Chill several hours before serving.

Warning: The U. S. Department of Agriculture Extension Service says that boiling an unopened can of condensed milk can be dangerous, and the manufacturers of sweetened condensed milk do not recommend the practice. Here are the manufacturer's recommended methods for

caramelizing sweetened condensed milk.
Oven method: Pour the sweetened
condensed milk into a 9-inch pie plate, cover
with aluminum foil and place pie plate in a
shallow pan. Fill pan with hot water. Bake at
425 degrees for 1½ hours.
Microwave method: Pour condensed milk
into a 2-quart glass measure. Microwave at
50 percent power (medium) for 4 minutes,
stirring every 2 minutes until smooth. Then
microwave on 30 percent power for 12 to 18
minutes, until caramel colored, stirring every
2 minutes.

My favorite cherry pie

1	9-inch double-crust pastry shell, unbaked
2	15-ounce cans red tart cherries in water
1½	cups sugar
¼	cup tapioca
½	teaspoon pure almond extract (optional)
1	tablespoon butter
	Milk or cream and sugar for top of pie

Makes 8 servings.
Preheat oven to 425 degrees.
Prepare one recipe for double crust. Divide
into two portions. On a well-floured surface,
roll out one portion of crust. Place in 9-inch
pie pan.
Drain cherries. Place in a large bowl. Add
sugar, tapioca and almond extract. Stir to
combine. Pour cherry mixture into pastry
shell. Dot with butter. Roll out second
portion of crust. Cut into strips and place on
top of cherries to form a lattice top. Brush
with milk or cream and sprinkle with sugar.
Bake in preheated oven for 10 minutes.
Reduce heat to 350 and bake an additional
40 to 50 minutes or until golden brown.

Cherry custard pie©

1	fully baked 10-inch pastry shell
1	cup sugar, divided
4	tablespoons cornstarch,

Makes 8 to 10 servings.
Measure out the cup of sugar and set aside 2
tablespoons of it. Combine remaining sugar
with 3½ tablespoons cornstarch and the egg
yolks in a heavy saucepan. Mix well with a

divided
4   egg yolks from extra-large eggs (or 5 from large eggs)
4   cups milk
2   tablespoons butter or margarine
1   teaspoon vanilla extract
½   teaspoon almond extract (optional)
1   15-ounce can pitted cherries (NOT pie filling)
    Few drops red food coloring (optional)
¼   cup slivered almonds

whisk, fork or electric mixer.

Stir in milk, butter and extracts. Stirring constantly, cook this custard filling over medium heat until thick – about 10 or 15 minutes. Don't try to rush the process by raising the heat, even if it seems to be taking too long to cook.

When the pudding is ready, a spoonful dropped back into the pot will maintain a raised impression for about a minute. Allow the pudding to cool in the pot somewhat, stirring often to prevent a skin from forming. While it's still warm but not boiling hot, pour filling into pastry shell. Cover the surface with a piece of wax paper so a skin won't form. Refrigerate.

Drain the canned cherries in a strainer set over a small saucepan. Set the fruit aside and add the remaining 2 tablespoons of sugar and ½ tablespoon (1½ teaspoons) of cornstarch to the cherry juice.

Stir until both sugar and starch are completely dissolved. Add red food coloring if you wish. Heat over medium heat, stirring often, until liquid boils and cornstarch mixture clears and thickens. Immediately stir in the reserved cherries and stir until they are hot, but not really cooked.

Remove the wax paper from the top of the pie and spoon the cherry mixture over the custard filling. Sprinkle on the almonds and return pie to the refrigerator. It will take several hours for the pie to set completely. This pie may be prepared a day before it's to be served, as long as the cherry topping is covered well.

   Note: Even without a crust or cherry topping, this recipe makes a delicious homemade pudding.

Uncle Vincent's chess pie©

1   unbaked 9-inch pastry shell
¼   cup butter
1½ cups sugar
3   eggs
1   tablespoon cornmeal
1   tablespoon vinegar
1   teaspoon vanilla

Makes 8 servings.
Prepare pastry shell. Set aside.
Preheat oven to 350 degrees.
In a saucepan, over low heat, melt butter.
Remove from heat. Add sugar and eggs.
Blend thoroughly. Add cornmeal, vinegar
and vanilla. Mix; pour into unbaked pastry
shell. Bake in preheated oven for 35 to 45
minutes or until filling sets.

Chocolate chess pie©

1   unbaked 9-inch pastry shell
2   eggs
1   5-ounce can evaporated milk
4   tablespoons butter, melted
1   teaspoon vanilla
1½ cups sugar
3   tablespoons baking cocoa
    Whipped cream (optional)

Makes 6 to 8 servings.
Whisk eggs, milk, butter and vanilla in a bowl
until well blended. Mix sugar and cocoa
together. Add to egg mixture. Mix well.
Pour into pastry shell. Bake in a hot, 350-
degree oven 30 to 45 minutes or until a knife
inserted near center comes out clean. Top
each serving with a dollop of whipped cream,
if desired.

Gertrude's lemon chess pie©

1   9-inch unbaked pastry shell
2   cups sugar
⅛   teaspoon salt
1   tablespoon flour
1   tablespoon cornmeal
4   eggs
¼   cup melted butter
¼   cup milk
2   tablespoons grated lemon
    zest
¼   cup lemon juice

Makes 8 servings.
In a large bowl combine sugar, salt, flour and
cornmeal. Thoroughly beat in eggs. Add
melted butter, milk, lemon zest and juice.
Stir till blended.
Pour into prepared pastry shell and bake in
preheated 350-degree oven 50 to 60 minutes
or until set.

Peach chess pie©

1 9-inch pastry shell, unbaked
4 to 5 fresh peaches, peeled and halved
1 cup sugar
⅓ cup butter or margarine, softened
⅓ cup all-purpose flour
1 egg, slightly beaten
¼ teaspoon vanilla

Makes 8 servings.
Peel peaches and cut in half. Place in bottom of unbaked pastry shell, cavity side down. The number of peaches needed will depend on their size.
Cream together sugar and butter or margarine. Work flour into this mixture. Add egg and beat until blended. Add vanilla and stir to blend. Spread over top of peaches. Bake in a 375-degree oven for 30 minutes. Puncture crust that has formed on top of pie. Lower heat to 300 degrees and bake an additional 30 minutes. Custard should be slightly firm.
   Note: Drained canned peach halves may be used instead of fresh peaches.

Corner Café's coconut pie©

1 9-inch baked pastry shell
Filling:
1 cup sugar
4 tablespoons cornstarch
2 tablespoons flour
Pinch salt
3 cups milk
4 eggs, separated
1 teaspoon vanilla
6 tablespoons margarine
½ cup coconut
Meringue:
4 egg whites
Pinch salt
⅛ teaspoon cream of tartar
6 to 8 tablespoons sugar
1 tablespoon coconut

Makes 6 to 8 servings.
Prepare pastry shell. Set aside.
To make filling: Combine sugar, cornstarch, flour and salt in a saucepan. While stirring, slowly add milk. Cook over medium heat until filling coats the back of a wooden spoon.
Beat egg yolks. While stirring, slowly add about a cup of cooked filling to yolks. Stir; return to filling. Cook, stirring constantly, until filling thickens and spoon leaves a trail in filling when stirred. Add vanilla, margarine and coconut. Stir until margarine melts. Pour into baked pastry shell.
To make meringue: Beat egg whites until fluffy. Add salt and cream of tartar. While beating, slowly add sugar, a tablespoon at a time. Beat at high speed until smooth and standing in high peaks. Spread over top of

pie, being careful to seal the edges. Sprinkle top with coconut.

Bake in a preheated 350-degree oven for 15 to 20 minutes or until golden. Let cool at room temperature away from drafts.

Note: For chocolate pie, add 3 tablespoons cocoa to dry ingredients. For peanut butter pie, stir in 4 heaping tablespoons peanut butter before pouring into pastry shell.

The Depot's French coconut pie©

1	unbaked 9-inch pastry shell
1	cup flaked coconut
1½	cups sugar
3	eggs, beaten
1	tablespoon vinegar
½	cup melted margarine
1	teaspoon vanilla

Makes 8 servings.

In a bowl combine coconut and sugar. Add beaten eggs, vinegar, melted margarine and vanilla. Stir to combine thoroughly. Pour into unbaked pastry shell. Bake in a preheated 325-degree oven for 35 to 45 minutes or until a knife inserted near center comes out clean.

Patti's boo boo pie©

3	cups shredded coconut
1	14-ounce can sweetened condensed milk
½	cup margarine
3	1-ounce squares unsweetened chocolate
¾	cup sugar
½	cup all-purpose flour
3	eggs
1	tablespoon vanilla

Makes 8 servings.

Grease a deep 9-inch pie plate or a 10-inch regular pie plate. (This recipe does not call for a pastry shell.)

Combine shredded coconut and sweetened condensed milk. Set aside.

In a small pan over low heat melt margarine and chocolate (can also be done in microwave). Combine with sugar, flour, eggs and vanilla. Pour into greased pie plate. Spoon coconut mixture around top edge of pie. Bake in a preheated 325-degree oven for 25 minutes. Chill before serving.

Note: This pie is very rich – you may want to cut the servings in half.

Best chocolate chip nut pie©

1	9-inch unbaked pastry shell
2	eggs, beaten
¼	cup cornstarch
1	cup sugar
½	cup butter, melted
2	tablespoons bourbon
1	cup chopped pecans
1	cup (6-ounce) package chocolate chips

Topping:
1	cup whipping cream
	Sugar, to taste
1 to 2	teaspoons bourbon

Makes 8 servings.

To make filling: In a small bowl, beat eggs. Combine cornstarch with sugar. Gradually add to eggs. Mix until blended. Add melted butter and bourbon. Stir in pecans and chocolate chips. Pour into unbaked pastry shell. Bake in a preheated 350-degree oven for 45 to 50 minutes.

Cool 1 hour. Serve warm topped with bourbon-flavored topping.

Bourbon-flavored topping: Place whipping cream in bowl of electric mixer. While beating, slowly add sugar, to taste. Beat until soft peaks form. Flavor with bourbon. Refrigerate until ready to serve.

Imitation fried pies©

I call them "imitation" because we like them baked better than fried.

Fried-pie pastry
2	cups all-purpose flour
1	teaspoon salt
⅔	cup vegetable shortening
5 to 7	tablespoons ice water
	Cream (optional)
	Vegetable shortening (only necessary when frying pies)

Glaze for fried pies:
1	tablespoon butter, room temperature
	Pinch salt
1	cup confectioners' sugar
1	tablespoon liqueur (see note)
1	tablespoon water

Makes 16 to 20 pies, depending on thickness of crust and size of pies..

To make pie pastry: In a large bowl, combine flour and salt. Stir. Using a pastry blender or 2 knives, cut in shortening until pieces are the size of small peas. Sprinkle ice water, a couple of tablespoons at a time, over the mixture. Cut in as you did the shortening. Work enough water into flour to form a ball. Cover and set aside for 30 minutes.

To make pies: Dust a pastry sheet or smooth surface with flour. Pinch off a piece of dough about the size of a ping-pong ball for a 6-inch circle (a bit larger for larger pies). Form into a nice little ball. Roll from center to edge to about ⅛-inch thickness (try to get a nice circle about 6 to 8 inches in diameter –

you can use a saucer or plate as a guide). Brush edge with a bit of water. Fold circle of dough almost in half; so you will have about ¼ inch of extended dough on lower half. Pinch at fold about 1 inch up on each side, forming a "cup". Place about 1½ tablespoons (depending on size – may use more) of filling in "cup". Don't overfill – filling may cook out. Fold the edge of extended dough over top edge. Crimp edges with the tines of a fork, making sure the edges are staying together.

If you are baking, heat oven to 350 degrees. Place pies on baking sheet, folded edge under. Brush tops of pies with cream (gives pies a nice color and shine). Bake 25 to 30 minutes or until golden. Frost with glaze while warm.

If you prefer frying, heat a small amount of shortening in a heavy skillet. Over very low heat, fry pies until golden. Frost with glaze while warm.

To make glaze: The glaze for the pies is optional but excellent. It can be flavored with vanilla, almond extract, fruit juice or a liqueur. Work butter and salt into confectioners' sugar. Stir. Add water or half water and half liqueur to make a glaze. Stir to blend. Brush lightly over warm pies.

Makes enough glaze for 16 to 20 small pies.

  Note: If using vanilla, use ½ to 1 teaspoon. If using almond extract, use ⅛ to ¼ teaspoon. Add water to equal about 2 tablespoons liquid. If using lemon juice, use 1 to 2 teaspoons and enough water to equal about 2 tablespoons. If using orange juice, use 2 tablespoons. You can enhance the flavor by adding some zest (colored part only of peel) of lemon or orange.

Fried apple pies©

1	recipe for fried-pie pastry
12	ounces dried apples
2	cups water
1 to 1½	cups sugar
	Pinch salt
3	very thin slices unpeeled lemon
3	very thin slices unpeeled orange
1½	tablespoons cornstarch
1½	tablespoons water
4	tablespoons butter
¼	cup Grand Marnier, a liqueur flavored with orange peel (optional, but delicious)
	Glaze (see recipe above)

Makes 14 to 16 pies.
Make pie pastry. Set aside.
Place apples in a saucepan. Cover with water. Add sugar, salt, lemon and orange slices. Stir. Bring mixture to a boil. Reduce heat to simmer and cook until apples are tender. The amount of time required to cook the apples will vary. Mine cooked for 45 minutes. However, it may only take 15 minutes.

When apples are tender or after cooking for 20 minutes, remove orange and lemon slices. Discard.

Combine cornstarch and water. Stir. Add to apple mixture. Cook until thickened. Add butter and Grand Marnier. Stir. Set aside to cool.

See above instructions for making pies.

Mediterranean fried apple pies©

1	recipe for fried-pie pastry
4	cups cooking apples, like Pippin, Granny Smith, Jonathan or McIntosh, peeled, cored and diced
½	cup golden seedless raisins
⅔ to 1	cup sugar, depending on tartness of apple
½	teaspoon cinnamon
⅛	teaspoon freshly grated nutmeg
⅔	cup water
	Dash salt
1	tablespoon fresh lemon juice
1	tablespoon cornstarch mixed with 1 tablespoon water

Makes 14 to 16 pies.
Make pie pastry. Set aside.
To make filling: In a saucepan combine apples, raisins, sugar, cinnamon, nutmeg, water and dash salt. Cook until apples are tender, about 15 minutes. Add lemon juice and cornstarch mixture. Cook until thickened, about 5 minutes. Add butter, pine nuts and brandy. Stir to combine.

See above instructions for making pies.

2   tablespoons butter
¼   cup pine nuts
2   tablespoons Calvados brandy
     (optional, but excellent)
     Glaze (see recipe above)

Blueberry fried pies©

1   recipe for fried-pie pastry
1   15-ounce can wild Maine
     blueberries (or other
     blueberries)
⅓   cup sugar
     Pinch salt
1½   tablespoons cornstarch
1½   tablespoons water
2   tablespoons butter
2   tablespoons Chambord, a
     raspberry liqueur
     Glaze (see recipe above)

Makes 14 to 16 pies.
Make pie pastry. Set aside.
To make filling: In a saucepan, combine blueberries, sugar and salt. Mix cornstarch with water and add to blueberry mixture. Cook over medium heat until thickened. Remove from heat and add butter and Chambord. Stir until well-blended.
See above instructions for making pies..

Red tart cherry fried pies©

1   recipe for fried-pie pastry
1   15-ounce can red tart
     cherries
¾   cup sugar
1½   tablespoons cornstarch
1½   tablespoons water
2   tablespoons butter
¼   teaspoon almond extract
1   tablespoon Kirsch, a cherry
     brandy
     Glaze (see recipe above)

Makes 14 to 16 pies.
Make pie pastry. Set aside.
To make filling: In a saucepan, combine cherries and sugar. Mix cornstarch with water. Add to cherry mixture. Cook over medium heat until thickened. Remove from heat. Add butter, almond extract and Kirsch. Stir until well-blended.
See above instructions for making pies.

Chocolate fried pies©

1   recipe for fried-pie pastry
1   cup sugar
⅓   cup cocoa powder
    Pinch salt
3   tablespoons cornstarch
1   cup cream
1   cup milk
3   egg yolks
2   tablespoons butter
1   teaspoon vanilla
    Glaze (see recipe above)

Makes 14 to 16 pies.
Make pie pastry. Set aside.
To make filling: In the top of a double boiler, combine sugar, cocoa powder, salt and cornstarch. Stir until well-blended. While stirring, slowly add cream and milk. Place over simmering water. Cook, stirring frequently, until thickened, about 25 minutes. (Spoon should leave a trail in pudding.) Beat egg yolks. Add several spoonfuls of hot mixture to egg yolks. Stir. Return egg mixture to chocolate mixture. Return to heat and cook 3 to 4 minutes. Remove from heat and add butter and vanilla. Stir until well-blended. Set aside to cool.
See above instructions for making pies.

Lemon cream fried pies©

1   recipe for fried-pie pastry
1   cup sugar
4   tablespoons cornstarch
    Pinch of salt
½   cup fresh lemon juice
3   egg yolks
1   cup whipping cream
1   cup milk
    Zest of two lemons
2   tablespoons butter
    Glaze (see recipe above)

Makes 14 to 16 pies.
Make pie pastry. Set aside.
To make filling: In the top portion of a double boiler, combine sugar, cornstarch and salt. Stir thoroughly to combine. Add lemon juice. Stir well. Add egg yolks. Stir until well-blended. Slowly stir in cream and milk. Combine thoroughly. Place over simmering water. Cook until spoon leaves a trail in filling. Remove from heat. Add zest of lemons (yellow part only of rind) and butter. Stir until butter has melted and is thoroughly blended. Pour into a non-corrosive dish. Chill until ready to use.
See above instructions for making pies.

My lemon cream meringue pie©

Makes 8 servings.

1   9-inch baked deep-dish
pastry shell (recipe follows)

Filling:
1½   cups sugar
¾   cup all-purpose flour
Dash salt
2   cups whipping cream
1   cup milk
6   eggs, separated
½ to ¾   cup fresh lemon juice
Zest of 2 lemons (yellow part of rind)
2   tablespoons butter
Meringue (recipe follows)

Pastry shell:
2   cups flour
1   teaspoon salt
⅔   cup vegetable shortening
5 to 7   tablespoons ice water

Meringue:
¾   cup water
2   tablespoons cornstarch
1   cup sugar, divided
6   egg whites, room temperature
⅛   teaspoon salt

To make filling: Combine sugar, flour and salt in the top of a double boiler. Slowly add cream, stirring to prevent lumping. Add milk, beaten egg yolks, lemon juice and zest, stirring constantly to prevent lumping. Cook, stirring over boiling water, until thick (170 degrees on a candy thermometer). Add butter and stir until butter melts.

Pour prepared, cooked filling into baked shell. Top with meringue. Bake in a preheated 350-degree oven 18 to 20 minutes or until golden. Cool to room temperature. Chill until ready to serve.

To make pastry shell: In a large bowl, combine flour and salt. Stir. Using a pastry blender or two knives, cut in the shortening until pieces are the size of small peas. Sprinkle ice water, a couple of tablespoons at a time, over the mixture. Cut in the mixture, as you did the shortening. Work enough water into the flour to form a ball. Cover and set aside for 30 minutes. Dust a pastry sheet or smooth surface with flour. Roll out dough 2 inches larger than the pie pan and then fit the dough loosely into the pan. Crimp or flute the edges. Prick the bottom dough all over with a fork and bake the shell for 15 to 18 minutes in a preheated 425-degree oven.

To make meringue: In a small saucepan, mix the water with the cornstarch and 4 tablespoons of sugar; cook over low heat until mixture is clear. Remove from heat. In a bowl, whip egg whites until peaked, then slowly add the cornstarch-sugar mixture and beat until creamy. Add salt and the rest of the sugar, one tablespoon at a time, beating after each addition until fluffy.

Pile on the pie and bake in a preheated 350-degree oven until meringue is golden, 18 to 20 minutes.

Pippin's lemon meringue pie©

1 9-inch baked pastry shell
Filling:
1½ cups sugar
½ cup cornstarch
¼ teaspoon salt
1¾ cups water
4 large egg yolks, beaten
½ cup lemon juice
Grated zest (yellow part of rind) of 1 lemon
2 tablespoons margarine
Meringue:
4 egg whites
¼ teaspoon salt
½ cup sugar

Makes 8 servings.

Make your own favorite pie pastry (or the one at the beginning of the section), roll out and bake. Let cool.

To make filling: In a saucepan, combine sugar, cornstarch and salt. Stir to blend well. Add water. Bring to boil and cook 1 minute. Mix a small amount of hot mixture into beaten egg yolks and then stir egg yolks into hot mixture. Bring back to boil and cook 2 minutes, stirring constantly.

Remove from heat and add lemon juice, zest and margarine. Stir until smooth. Allow to cool.

To make meringue: Place egg whites in bowl of electric mixer. Add salt and beat until frothy. With mixer running, slowly add sugar. Beat until stiff but not dry.

Pour cooled lemon filling into baked pie shell. Top with meringue, spreading it over all the filling, being careful to seal edges of pie. Bake in a preheated 400-degree oven for 15 minutes.

Peach cream pie©

1 9-inch baked pastry shell
2 cups milk
6 tablespoons all-purpose flour
1 cup sugar
¼ teaspoon salt

Makes 8 servings.

Prepare and bake pastry shell. Let cool. Heat milk in a double boiler. In a saucepan, mix flour, sugar and salt. Add hot milk slowly, stirring constantly. Bring to a boil. Cook 2 to 3 minutes. Beat egg yolks with a

3 egg yolks
1½ teaspoons vanilla
2 pounds peaches, peeled and sliced
1 cup heavy cream
2 to 3 tablespoons confectioners' sugar

fork. Slowly add 1 cup of the hot mixture to the beaten egg yolks while beating. Return egg mixture to remaining hot-milk mixture. Pour into double boiler and cook, stirring, about 15 minutes or until the mixture coats back of spoon. Cool and add vanilla. Chill in refrigerator several hours.

Peel and remove pits from peaches. Slice. Sweeten peaches, if desired, but keep in mind that the cream filling is sweet.

Beat heavy cream with an electric mixer or rotary beater just until it mounds slightly and soft peaks form when the beaters are lifted. Sweeten to taste with confectioners' sugar. Beat chilled pie filling thoroughly. Pour into baked 9-inch pie shell. Top with peaches. Garnish with whipped cream.

Everyday peach pie©

1 double-crust 9-inch pastry shell
½ to ¾ cup sugar
3 tablespoons all-purpose flour
¼ teaspoon cinnamon
¼ teaspoon nutmeg
¼ teaspoon almond extract (optional)
6 cups sliced peaches
1 tablespoon milk
1 tablespoon granulated sugar

Makes 8 servings.

Prepare pastry and set aside. Heat oven to 375 degrees.

In a large mixing bowl combine sugar, flour, cinnamon, nutmeg and almond extract. Add peaches. Toss till peaches are coated with sugar mixture. Pour into 9-inch pastry-lined pie plate. Cut slits in top crust. Place over peaches. Seal and flute edges. Brush top with milk. Sprinkle with sugar. Cover edge with foil.

Bake 25 minutes. Remove foil. Bake for 20 to 25 minutes more or until top is golden and fruit is tender.

The Feed Bag's peanut-butter-candy pie©

1   9-inch pastry shell, unbaked
3   eggs
½   cup sugar
1   cup light corn syrup
1   teaspoon vanilla
¼   teaspoon salt
½   cup peanut butter
1   cup semisweet chocolate
    morsels
1   tablespoon vegetable oil

Makes 8 servings.
Heat oven to 350 degrees.
In a large bowl beat eggs until creamy.
Gradually add sugar. Mix well. Add corn
syrup, vanilla, salt and peanut butter. Blend
thoroughly. Pour into an unbaked pastry
shell. Bake 40 to 45 minutes.
When pie is almost done, heat chocolate
morsels with vegetable oil. Remove the pie
from the oven and pour chocolate mixture
over the top of the hot pie. Set aside to cool.

Jessie's Family Restaurant peanut butter pie©

1   10-inch or 2 8-inch baked
    pastry shells
2   cups sugar
6   tablespoons cornstarch
4   cups milk
5   eggs, separated
1   cup peanut butter
1   teaspoon butter
1   teaspoon vanilla
Meringue:
5   egg whites
¼   teaspoon cream of tartar
½   cup sugar
    Crushed peanuts (optional)

**A 10-inch pie makes 8 large servings.
Each 8-inch pie will make 6 regular
servings.**
To make filling: In a heavy saucepan,
combine sugar and cornstarch. Stir till well-
blended. Beat egg yolks; combine with milk.
Add egg mixture to sugar mixture, stirring
constantly. Cook over medium heat, stirring
constantly, till mixture boils and thickens.
Remove from heat.
Add peanut butter, butter and vanilla. Stir till
thoroughly blended. Pour into baked pie
shell. (If using 10-inch pan, filling will be
quite thick. Eight-inch pie shells will result in
a filling about 1-inch thick.)
Top with meringue and crushed peanuts, if
desired. Bake in a preheated 350-degree
oven 10 to 15 minutes or until golden. Cool
before serving.
To make meringue: Whip egg whites until
frothy. Add cream of tartar and whip until
stiff, but not dry. Beat sugar in 1 tablespoon

at a time. Do not over beat. Spread over top of pie. Bake in a preheated 350-degree oven for 10 to 15 minutes or until golden.

Black Buggy Restaurant's famous peanut butter pie©

Makes 8 servings.

1	9-inch graham cracker pie crust
¾	cup confectioners' sugar
½	cup creamy peanut butter
3	cups milk
¾	cup sugar
¼	cup cornstarch
3	tablespoons all-purpose flour
3	egg yolks
¾	teaspoon vanilla
	Pinch salt
1½	tablespoons butter or margarine
	Cool Whip

Combine confectioners' sugar and peanut butter until crumbly. Set aside.
Heat 2 cups milk until warm.
Combine sugar, cornstarch, flour, egg yolks, vanilla and salt. While stirring, slowly add remaining cup of milk. Mix until well-blended. Add to warm milk, stirring constantly. Cook over medium-high heat until mixture thickens, about 15 minutes. Add butter. Stir until butter melts. Set aside to cool.
Sprinkle a third of the peanut butter crumbs onto bottom of prepared pie shell. Pour half the pudding mixture over the peanut butter crumbs. Sprinkle with another third of the peanut butter crumbs. Add remaining pudding mixture. When pie has cooled completely, top with Cool Whip and remaining third of peanut butter crumbs. Refrigerate until ready to serve.

Grayson's City Café's pecan pie©

Makes 8 servings.

1	9-inch unbaked deep-dish pastry shell
1	teaspoon vanilla
3	eggs, slightly beaten
1	cup corn syrup, light or dark
½	teaspoon salt
½	cup white sugar
½	cup brown sugar
2	cups coarsely chopped pecans

Make your favorite pasty shell or use the recipe for plain pastry at the beginning of this section.
Blend together vanilla, eggs, corn syrup, salt and sugars. Stir in pecans. Pour into unbaked pastry shell. Bake in a preheated 350-degree oven for about 50 minutes or until a knife inserted near the center comes out clean.

Maryland white potato pie©

1   unbaked 9-inch pastry shell
2¼   cups hot cooked, mashed potatoes
⅔   cup butter or margarine
1   cup sugar
½   teaspoon baking powder
½   teaspoon salt
¼   teaspoon ground nutmeg
4   eggs, beaten
2   teaspoons grated lemon rind
2   tablespoons lemon juice
½   cup milk
½   cup whipping cream
1   teaspoon vanilla extract

Makes 8 servings.
Preheat oven to 425 degrees.
Combine potatoes and butter. Stir until butter melts. Add sugar, baking powder, salt, nutmeg, eggs, lemon rind and juice, milk, whipping cream and vanilla. Beat just until smooth.
Pour filling into pastry shell. Bake in preheated oven for 5 minutes. Reduce heat to 350 degrees and bake an additional 40 minutes or until a knife inserted in center comes out clean. Cool pie before serving.

No-crust pumpkin pie©

2   cups pumpkin
½   cup brown sugar
1   teaspoon vanilla
2   teaspoons cinnamon
½   cup white sugar
½   cup Bisquick
2   eggs

Makes 8 servings.
Preheat oven to 350 degrees.
Place all ingredients in the large bowl of an electric mixer. Beat to combine. Pour into a 9-inch pie pan that has been sprayed with a non-stick vegetable spray. Bake in a preheated, 350-degree oven 35 to 40 minutes or until a knife inserted near center comes out clean.

My Thanksgiving pumpkin pie

2   9-inch deep-dish pastry shells
1   29-ounce can pumpkin
2   14-ounce cans Eagle Brand Sweetened Condensed Milk
1   teaspoon cloves
2   teaspoons cinnamon
2   teaspoons ginger

Makes 2 9-inch pies.
Prepare pastry shells according to recipe for double-crust pie shells. Divide dough into 2 equal portions. Roll each out and place one in each pie pan. Bake 8 minutes in a preheated 425-degree oven. Remove from oven and set aside.
To make pie filling: While pastry is baking, combine pumpkin, condensed milk, cloves,

1   teaspoon salt
¾   cup brown sugar
6   eggs, beaten

cinnamon, ginger, salt, brown sugar and eggs. Stir to combine thoroughly. Pour into prepared baked pastry shells, dividing equally. Bake in preheated 425-degree oven for 15 minutes. Reduce oven temperature to 350 degrees. Bake 40 to 50 minutes or until a knife inserted near center comes out clean.

Glazed strawberry pie©

1   9-inch pastry shell
2   tablespoons melted butter
2   tablespoons sugar
1   quart fresh strawberries
Glaze:
2   cups crushed strawberries
½   cup water
1   cup sugar
2½ tablespoons cornstarch
¼   teaspoon red food coloring
    (optional)
1   tablespoon butter
1   pint whipping cream
    (optional)

Makes 8 servings.
To make pastry shell: Bake pie shell. While hot, sprinkle bottom of crust with melted butter and sugar. Set aside to cool. Rinse and hull berries. Fill pie shell with a layer of fresh berries, stem side down. (There should be enough remaining berries for glaze.)
Glaze: In a saucepan combine all ingredients. Cook and stir over medium heat until clear, about 5 minutes. Pour over berries. Cool.
Top each serving with a dollop of whipped cream, if desired.

Strawberry-rhubarb pie

    Pastry for double-crust, 9-
    inch pie
2   cups rhubarb cut into ½-inch
    pieces
2   cups sliced strawberries
1¼ cups sugar
3   tablespoons quick-cooking
    tapioca
¼   teaspoon salt
¼   teaspoon freshly grated
    nutmeg

Makes 8 to 10 servings.
In a large bowl combine rhubarb, strawberries, sugar, tapioca, salt and nutmeg. Stir to combine. Let stand 20 minutes.
Prepare pastry according to recipe for double-crust pie shell or your favorite recipe. Divide pastry into two portions. Roll each portion into a circle – one to fit into a 9-inch pie pan and the other to make strips for a lattice top.
Line a 9-inch pie pan with 1 of the pastry

2   tablespoons butter
Cream or milk for brushing
crust
2   tablespoons sugar

rounds. Pour in the rhubarb/strawberry mixture. Dot with butter.
Make the lattice strips and crisscross them over the fruit. Seal the edges. Brush the pastry strips with cream or milk and sprinkle with sugar.
Bake in a preheated 400 degree oven 45 to 50 minutes.

The Golden Lamb's Sister Lizzie's Shaker sugar pie©

Makes 8 servings.

1   9-inch unbaked pastry shell
⅓ cup all-purpose flour
1   cup brown sugar
2   cups light cream
1   teaspoon vanilla
2   tablespoons butter
Nutmeg

Heat oven to 350 degrees. Thoroughly mix flour and brown sugar. Spread evenly in bottom of pie shell. Combine cream and vanilla. Pour over sugar mixture. Slice butter into pieces and distribute evenly over top of pie. Sprinkle with nutmeg. Bake for 40 to 45 minutes or until firm.

Cheesecakes

Basic graham cracker crust

Makes 1 9-inch crust.

1½ cups graham cracker crumbs
6   tablespoons butter, melted
¼ cup granulated sugar

Heat oven to 350 degrees.
Place crumbs in mixing bowl. Add butter and sugar. Blend well.
Press crumb mixture onto bottom and partly up sides of a greased 9-inch springform pan. Smooth crumb mixture along the bottom to an even thickness.
Bake for 10 minutes. Cool before filling.

Ricotta cheesecake

Makes 16 servings

Vanilla wafer crust:

To make crust: Place vanilla wafers in bowl

1½ cups (about 50) vanilla
wafers, crushed
6 tablespoons butter, melted
Cheesecake filling:
2 pounds homemade ricotta
cheese (see recipe in Dairy)
1⅓ cups sugar
4 extra-large eggs
2 teaspoons pure vanilla
extract
Sour cream topping:
1 cup sour cream
2 tablespoons sugar
½ teaspoon vanilla

of a food processor (or in a plastic zip bag).
Process or crush until wafers become
crumbs. Melt butter and add to crumbs. Mix
to thoroughly combine. Press onto bottom
and half way up the sides of a 9-inch lightly
greased springform pan. Set aside.
To make filling: Cream sugar with cheese
until well blended. Add eggs one at a time,
beating after each addition. Add vanilla and
blend. Pour into prepared springform pan.
Preheat oven to 325 degrees. Place a pan
of water on lower shelf under the
cheesecake (this helps prevent a cracked
top). Bake 50 to 60 minutes or until
cheesecake becomes dull on top (center will
still be shiny). Remove from oven.
Combine sour cream, sugar and vanilla.
Spread over top of cheesecake. Return to
oven to bake an additional 10 minutes.
Remove from oven to cool. When cool,
refrigerate at least 6 hours or overnight. Cut
with a wet knife.

Easy but good cheesecake©
This is a nice, small, tasty cheesecake that can be made in just a few minutes.

1 8-ounce package cream
cheese, room temperature
3 eggs, room temperature
⅔ cup sugar
¼ teaspoon almond extract or
vanilla
Topping:
1 cup sour cream
3 tablespoons sugar
1 teaspoon vanilla

Makes 6 to 8 small servings.
With an electric mixer, beat cream cheese
and 1 egg together thoroughly. Add
remaining 2 eggs, sugar and extract. Beat
until thoroughly blended. Pour mixture into a
greased 9-inch pie plate. Bake in a
preheated 350-degree oven for 25 minutes.
Remove from oven. Add topping and return
to oven for 10 minutes. Chill completely
before serving.
Topping: In a small bowl, combine sour
cream, sugar and vanilla. Stir to blend
thoroughly. Pour over top of partially baked
cheesecake. This cheesecake has no crust.

Sweet Surrender's praline cheesecake©

Praline:
- 1 cup sugar
- ¼ cup water
- ½ cup plus 2 tablespoons light corn syrup
- ½ cup butter
- ¾ cup chopped almonds

Graham-cracker crust:
- 1½ cups graham-cracker crumbs
- ⅓ cup sugar
- ⅓ cup melted butter

Cheesecake filling:
- 1⅔ cups sugar
- 2½ pounds cream cheese
- 5 extra-large eggs
- 1¼ teaspoons vanilla

Makes 16 servings.

To make praline: Butter an 8-by-8-by-2-inch square pan. In a heavy saucepan combine sugar, water, corn syrup and butter. Over medium heat bring to the hard crack stage (295 degrees on a candy thermometer), stirring occasionally. Remove from heat immediately and stir in almonds.

Pour into prepared pan. Allow to cool. Break into small pieces.

To make crust: Combine graham-cracker crumbs, sugar and butter. Mix well. Press onto bottom of a lightly greased 10-inch springform pan.

To make filling: Cream sugar and cheese until smooth. Add eggs and vanilla. Mix well.

Pour into prepared springform pan. Fold the praline pieces into the cheesecake batter. Bake in a 350-degree oven for 45 minutes. Turn oven down to 300 degrees and bake 30 to 45 minutes or until firm to the touch. The lower temperature helps prevent a cracked top and spillage.

Blue River Café's cheesecake©

Crust:
- 1¾ cups graham cracker crumbs
- ½ cup sugar
- ½ cup butter, melted

Filling:
- 2 pounds cream cheese, room temperature
- ½ teaspoon vanilla
- 1½ cups sugar
- ¼ cup all-purpose flour

Makes 12 servings.

To make the crust: Mix graham-cracker crumbs, ½ cup sugar and melted butter together. Press onto the bottom and sides of a 10-inch springform pan.

To make the filling: Heat oven to 450 degrees. Whip cream cheese until soft. Add vanilla, sugar, flour, salt and eggs, blending well after each addition. Blend in sour cream. Beat 1 minute. Pour into crust. Bake at 450 degrees for 10 minutes.

½   teaspoon salt
4   eggs
½   cup sour cream

Topping:
1   cup sour cream
2   tablespoons sugar
½   teaspoon vanilla
    Pinch salt

Reduce heat and bake at 300 degrees for 50 minutes. Remove from oven.
To make the topping: Combine sour cream, sugar, vanilla and salt. Spread over top of cheesecake (pan will be full). Bake in a 350 degree oven for 10 to 15 minutes. Remove from oven. Cool. Store in refrigerator.

Almond joy cheesecake©

Makes 16 servings.

Crust:
8   tablespoons lightly salted butter
1½ cups very finely ground crumbs from chocolate wafer cookies
½   cup toasted coconut
¼   cup sugar

Filling:
2   pounds (4 8-ounce packages) cream cheese
1½ cups sugar
1   8.5-ounce can cream of coconut
½   teaspoon almond extract
1   teaspoon coconut extract
    Pinch of salt
½   cup finely chopped almonds
4   large eggs

Topping:
1½ cups sour cream
¼   cup sugar
1   teaspoon coconut extract
½   cup cream of coconut
2   tablespoons blanched, sliced

Heat oven to 350 degrees.
To make crust: Melt butter over low heat. In a blender combine butter with crumbs, coconut and sugar. (Or combine in a plastic container with a fork.) Press mixture over bottom and up sides of an ungreased, 10-inch springform pan. There should be enough to coat the entire pan.
To make filling: In a large mixing bowl, combine cream cheese and sugar. Beat for 2 minutes, or until soft. Add ½ cup cream of coconut (reserve remainder for topping), almond extract, coconut extract, salt and almonds. Blend thoroughly.
The eggs need not be at room temperature either. Add them one at a time, keeping the mixer on the lowest speed. Mix until blended.
Pour filling into crust and bake for 40 minutes.
If ingredients are not at room temperature, add 5 minutes to baking time. Remove from oven and let stand for 10 minutes while you prepare the topping. This is an essential step.

almonds, toasted
½ cup coconut, toasted

To make topping: Combine sour cream, sugar, coconut extract and cream of coconut. Spread evenly over cheesecake. Sprinkle with almonds and coconut and return to 350-degree oven for 10 minutes. Remove from oven and immediately place in refrigerator to cool. This prevents cracks from forming.

George Warburton's lemon-glazed cheesecake©

(from Bon Appetit)

Makes 16 to 20 servings.

Crust:
2 cups graham cracker crumbs
6 tablespoons melted butter
2 tablespoons sugar

Filling:
3 8-ounce packages cream cheese
¾ cup sugar
3 eggs
¼ cup lemon juice
2 teaspoons grated lemon zest (yellow part of rind)
2 teaspoons vanilla

Topping:
2 cups sour cream
3 tablespoons sugar
1 teaspoon vanilla

Garnish:
Lemon glaze (recipe follows)
Curled lemon strip, large strawberry and mint leaves (garnish)

Lemon glaze:
½ cup sugar
1½ tablespoons cornstarch
¼ teaspoon salt

To make crust: Heat oven to 350 degrees. Combine graham cracker crumbs, melted butter and sugar. Press mixture evenly onto bottom and sides of buttered 9-by-3-inch springform pan. Bake 5 minutes. Cool.

To make filling: Beat cream cheese until soft. Add sugar, blending thoroughly. Add eggs one at a time, beating well after each addition. Mix in lemon juice, zest and vanilla. Blend well. Turn into baked crust in springform pan. Bake 35 minutes.

To make topping: While cake is baking, blend sour cream, sugar and vanilla. Remove cake from oven. Gently spread sour-cream mixture over top. Return to oven and bake 12 minutes. Cool on rack 30 minutes.

Spread with lemon glaze (recipe follows). Chill several hours or overnight before removing sides of pan. Garnish with curled strip of lemon zest, strawberry and mint leaves.

To make glaze: In heavy 1-quart saucepan mix sugar, cornstarch and salt. Combine water, lemon juice and egg yolk and add to sugar mixture. Cook over low

¾ cup water
⅓ cup lemon juice
1 egg yolk
1 tablespoon butter
1 teaspoon grated lemon zest

heat, stirring constantly, until the mixture comes to a slow boil and is thickened. Add butter and lemon rind. Allow to cool slightly, but spread on cheesecake before glaze sets.

Lynn's Paradise Café's chocolate cheesecake©

Makes 12 servings.

3 8-ounce packages cream cheese
1 cup granulated sugar
2 ounces white or bittersweet dark chocolate
2 eggs
5 tablespoons all-purpose flour
1 tablespoon vanilla
1 cup heavy whipping cream
Nuts and chocolate curls, for garnish

Preheat oven to 325 degrees.
In a large mixer bowl, beat cream cheese with an electric mixer on medium speed until smooth. Add sugar and beat on medium speed for 2 minutes.
Melt chocolate over double boiler just until melted, stirring occasionally; do not overheat. With mixer on low speed, add the following to cream cheese mixture, scraping bowl after each addition; eggs, flour, vanilla, cream and melted chocolate. Beat just until incorporated, taking care not to over mix.
Pour batter into a greased 9- or 10-inch springform pan. Place pan inside shallow baking pan partly filled with hot water. This will prevent cake from cracking.
Bake for 40 to 50 minutes or until set. Cool before removing sides of pan. Garnish with chopped nuts around bottom edge and chocolate shavings on top, if desired. Chill at least 1 hour before serving.
 Note: This cheesecake does not have a crust.

Cumberland House Italian cream cheesecake©

Makes 12 servings.

Crust:
1 cup graham cracker crumbs
3 tablespoons sugar
3 tablespoons soft butter or

To make crust: Mix graham cracker crumbs with sugar and butter or margarine and press in bottom of a 9- or 10-inch springform pan.
To make filling: Mix cream cheese and

margarine

Filling:

1½ **pounds cream cheese, softened**
1 **cup sugar**
½ **cup shredded or flaked coconut**
½ **cup pecan pieces**
3 **tablespoons all-purpose flour**
2 **tablespoons milk**
2 **tablespoons pure vanilla extract**
3 **well-beaten eggs**

Topping:

6 **ounces cream cheese, softened**
½ **cup sour cream**
¼ **cup confectioners' sugar**
1 **teaspoon pure vanilla extract**
¼ **cup shredded or flaked coconut**
¼ **cup pecan halves or pieces**

sugar until well-blended. Stir in coconut and pecan pieces, along with flour, milk, vanilla extract and well-beaten eggs. Mix until blended. Pour into prepared crust.

Bake in a 350-degree oven for about 1 hour and 10 minutes or until a knife inserted near the center comes out clean.

To make topping: Mix together softened cream cheese, sour cream, confectioners' sugar and vanilla. Spread over cooled cake. Sprinkle top with coconut and pecans.

Vincenzo's amaretto cheesecake©

3 **pounds cream cheese, room temperature**
2 **cups sugar**
7 **eggs**
¼ **cup cornstarch**
4 **tablespoons good quality amaretto**

Makes 12 to 16 servings.

Spray a round 10-by-4-inch baking pan with a non-stick spray. Line bottom of pan with parchment or wax paper. If using a springform pan, wrap outside of pan in foil to prevent water seeping into cheesecake.

Cream together the cream cheese and the sugar, scraping bowl often. Do not overbeat. Add eggs one at a time. Beat only until blended. Combine cornstarch with amaretto. Making a slurry of the mixture; blend it into cheese mixture.

Pour into prepared pan. Set pan in larger pan, add water halfway up side of baking pan and bake in a 340-degree oven on center rack for about 1½ hours, or until center is semi-firm to the touch.

Allow to cool at room temperature. Turn out on wire rack. Invert so top is up. Refrigerate overnight or until ready to serve.

This recipe is adaptable to a number of flavorings, including framboise, Kahlua and Grand Marnier.

Raspberry cheesecake©

Crumb crust:
- 10 graham crackers, crushed
- 4 tablespoons butter, melted

Filling:
- 1 cup fresh raspberries
- 1 tablespoon fresh lemon juice
- 1½ cups sugar
- 1 teaspoon cornstarch dissolved in ¼ cup water
- 2 pounds cream cheese
- 6 eggs
- 1 teaspoon vanilla or almond extract
- 2 tablespoons framboise (raspberry liqueur)

Raspberry sauce:
- 2 cups fresh raspberries
- ¼ to ½ cup sugar
- Juice of ½ lemon
- 2 tablespoons framboise (raspberry liqueur), optional

Makes 12 servings.

To make crust: With your fingers, mix the crackers and butter until the crumbs are evenly coated with butter. Press onto the bottom and partially up the sides of a 9-inch springform pan.

Bake at 350 degrees for 10 minutes. Remove and cool.

To make filling: In a small saucepan, heat the raspberries and lemon juice with ½ cup of the sugar. Bring to a boil. Add cornstarch mixture. Cook and stir until thickened, about a minute. Set aside to cool.

Beat the cream cheese until light. Gradually add the remaining 1 cup of sugar. One by one, add the eggs, beating on low speed just until each is blended. Stir in vanilla.

Fold the cooled raspberry mixture into the batter. Fold in the liqueur. Pour into prepared crust. Bake at 450 degrees for 10 minutes. Reduce heat to 300 degrees and bake for 1 hour, or until cake's center is firm and top is medium brown. Let cool in pan until sides of cake pull away. Remove from pan. Chill and serve in wedges with raspberry sauce.

To make raspberry sauce: Puree the raspberries in a blender or food processor with the sugar and lemon juice. If using framboise, stir into sauce. Chill. Serve over cheesecake.

Makes 1¼ cups.

Cheeseless cheesecake©

Makes 12 to 16 servings.

Crust:
- 1¼ cups graham cracker crumbs
- 2 tablespoons melted butter
- 2 tablespoons sugar

Filling:
- 4 eggs, separated
- 1 14-ounce can sweetened condensed milk
- ⅓ cup lemon juice
- 1 teaspoon lemon zest
- 1 teaspoon vanilla
- ½ teaspoon nutmeg
- 1 8-ounce can crushed pineapple, drained

Topping:
- 1 cup commercial sour cream
- 2 tablespoons sugar
- 1 teaspoon vanilla

To make crust: Combine graham cracker crumbs, melted butter and sugar. Stir until well-blended. Reserve 2 tablespoons for garnish. Press remainder onto bottom of a 8-inch springform pan.

To make filling: Beat egg yolks. Add sweetened condensed milk and mix well. Add lemon juice, lemon zest, vanilla, nutmeg and well-drained pineapple. Blend well. Beat egg whites until stiff but not dry. Fold into milk mixture. Slowly pour into crust. Bake in a preheated 325-degree oven for 30 minutes.

To make topping: Combine sour cream with sugar and vanilla. Spread over top of cheesecake. Sprinkle with reserved graham cracker crumbs. Return to oven for 10 minutes. Turn off oven. Cool cheesecake in oven with the door closed for 1 hour. Refrigerate 8 hours or overnight before serving.

Cookies and Brownies

White chocolate and cranberry cookies

Makes about 36 cookies.

Combine all ingredients. Mix until smooth.

- 1½ cups oats

1 cup all-purpose flour
½ cup white chocolate chips
½ cup dried cranberries
½ cup brown sugar
¾ cup granulated sugar
1 egg, room temperature, slightly beaten
½ cup butter, room temperature
1 teaspoon vanilla

Shape into 1-inch balls and place 2 inches apart on greased baking sheet. Bake in a preheated 375-degree oven for 10 to 12 minutes

Beau catchers from "Perfect Endings" by Nestle's©

Cookie mixture:
2 cups sifted all-purpose flour
½ teaspoon baking soda
½ teaspoon salt
1 cup semisweet chocolate pieces
1 tablespoon water
1 teaspoon vanilla extract
½ cup soft shortening
½ cup firmly packed brown sugar
1 egg

Chocolate-date filling:
1 cup semisweet chocolate pieces
¾ cup marshmallow cream
¼ cup sifted confectioners' sugar
2 teaspoons water
⅛ teaspoon salt
1 cup finely chopped dates
⅓ cup chopped nuts
1 tablespoon grated orange zest (orange part of rind)

Macaroon filling:
1 egg white

Makes 2 dozen.

To make cookie dough: Sift together flour, baking soda and salt. Set aside.

Combine chocolate pieces, water and vanilla extract and place over hot (not boiling) water. Stir until smooth. Remove from heat.

Combine shortening, brown sugar and egg. Beat until light and creamy. Gradually stir in flour mixture. Add the chocolate mixture. Blend well.

Shape one rounded tablespoon of dough around each chilled ball of filling (see recipes). Seal well.

Place on ungreased cookie sheet. Chill about 30 minutes.

Heat oven to 400 degrees. Bake cookies 6 minutes. Cool thoroughly before removing from cookie sheet.

To make chocolate-date filling: Melt chocolate pieces in a bowl placed over hot (not boiling) water. Remove from heat. Add marshmallow cream, confectioners' sugar, water and salt. Stir until blended. Add dates, nuts and orange zest. Stir until blended. Cool.

Shape into 1¼-inch balls, using 1 well-rounded teaspoon for each. Chill.

1 tablespoon vanilla extract
⅛ teaspoon salt
¼ cup sugar
2 cups grated coconut
Butterscotch crispy filling:
½ cup butterscotch chips
1 cup marshmallow cream
½ teaspoon vanilla extract
1½ cups oven-toasted rice cereal
Coffee filling:
1 tablespoon instant coffee granules
1 tablespoon water
1 cup finely chopped nuts
1 cup vanilla-wafer crumbs
½ cup marshmallow cream
¼ cup brown sugar
¼ teaspoon salt

Prepare cookie mixture and bake as above.
To make macaroon filling: Combine egg white, vanilla extract and salt. Beat until soft peaks form. Gradually add sugar. Beat until stiff and glossy. Stir in coconut. Shape into 1-inch balls, using 1 well-rounded teaspoon for each. Chill.
To make butterscotch crispy filling: Melt butterscotch chips over hot (not boiling) water. Stir in marshmallow cream and vanilla extract.
Place rice cereal in a large bowl. Add butterscotch mixture. Stir until well-blended. Shape into 1-inch balls, using 1 well-rounded teaspoon for each. Chill.
Prepare cookie mixture and bake, as above.
To make coffee filling: Combine instant coffee granules and water. Mix well. Add chopped nuts, vanilla-wafer crumbs, marshmallow cream, brown sugar and salt. Stir until well-blended.
Shape into 1¼-inch balls, using 1 well-rounded teaspoon for each. Chill.
Prepare cookie mixture and bake, as above.

Chocolate-filled cookies

1¼ cups all-purpose flour
½ teaspoon baking soda
⅔ cup packed brown sugar
5 tablespoons butter, room temperature
1 tablespoon water
1 cup (6 ounces) chocolate chips
1 egg, room temperature
1 teaspoon vanilla
Rolos, mints, peanut butter

Makes about 30 cookies.
Sift together flour and soda. Set aside.
In a saucepan combine brown sugar, butter and water. Cook over low heat until butter melts. Remove from heat. Add chocolate chips. Stir until melted. Add beaten egg and vanilla. Stir into chocolate mixture. Add flour mixture. Mix well. Chill dough for 30 minutes. When ready to bake, wrap a small amount of dough around a Rolo, peanut butter cup, part of a mint or a chocolate covered cherry.
Place on ungreased baking sheet. Bake in a

cups or chocolate covered
cherries

preheated 350-degree oven for 8 to 10
minutes.

Create-a-shape cookies©

These cookies are fun to make. Using cookie cutters I do signature cookies for each holiday. For Christmas, it's trees, Santas, wreaths, etc. Easter is bunnies, Easter bonnets, baskets, eggs. Derby I do hats and jockey silks. And in the fall, its autumn leaves—painting them with vodka or lemon extract and food coloring. You can make the cookies look exactly like leaves. Be creative.

¼ cup shortening
½ cup unsalted butter, room
temperature
1 cup sugar
2 eggs, room temperature
1 teaspoon pure vanilla extract
or ¼ teaspoon pure almond
extract
2½ cups all-purpose flour
1 teaspoon baking powder
1 teaspoon salt
Icing:
2 cups confectioners' sugar
3 tablespoons water
2 tablespoons light corn syrup
Royal icing:
1 large egg white
¼ teaspoon cream of tartar
1 teaspoon water
2 cups confectioners' sugar

Makes 18 to 20 3-inch cookies.
To make cookie dough: In a large bowl combine shortening, butter, sugar, eggs and flavoring. Sift together flour, baking powder and salt. Blend into creamed mixture. Chill at least 1 hour before baking. Heat oven to 350 degrees. On a lightly floured surface, roll dough to ¼ inch thickness. Dip cutter into flour, then cut dough into desired shapes. Bake on ungreased baking sheet 6 to 10 minutes or until golden on bottom. Remove to cooling rack. Cool completely before decorating.
To make icing: Place confectioner's sugar in a large bowl. Add water and corn syrup. Stir until smooth. If too thick, add water a drop at a time. Frosting should smooth out and hold its shape.
Makes about 1½ cups.
To make royal icing: Combine all ingredients in a bowl and beat at slow speed with an electric mixer until the icing forms very stiff peaks and turns pure white. Add more sugar if the icing is not stiff enough, or a few drops of water if it is too stiff.
Use immediately or cover bowl with a damp cloth to prevent drying when not in use. Allow royal-icing decorations to set at room temperature until dry..

Create-a-shape shortbread cookies©

½ cup confectioners' sugar
1 cup unsalted butter, room temperature
¾ teaspoon salt
1 teaspoon pure vanilla extract
2 tablespoons milk
2 cups all-purpose flour

Makes 14 to 16 3-inch cookies.
In a bowl combine the sugar, butter, salt, vanilla and milk. Gradually stir in flour to make soft dough. Roll to ¼-inch thickness. Cut into desired shapes and place on an ungreased baking sheet. Bake in a preheated 350-degree oven for 12 to 15 minutes or until golden on bottom. Cool completely before decorating.

Fat-free oatmeal cookies©

1 cup all-purpose flour
1 cup quick-cooking oatmeal
½ cup sugar
½ teaspoon salt
½ teaspoon baking powder
½ teaspoon baking soda
½ teaspoon cinnamon
2 eggs whites, lightly beaten with a fork
⅓ cup corn syrup (light or dark)
1 teaspoon vanilla
½ cup raisins

Makes 30 cookies.
Heat oven to 375 degrees. Spray baking sheet with non-stick cooking spray.
In a large bowl combine flour, oatmeal, sugar, salt, baking powder, baking soda and cinnamon. Stir in egg whites, corn syrup and vanilla. Mix until well-blended. Add raisins. Stir to combine (batter will be stiff). Drop by teaspoonfuls onto greased baking sheet. Bake 10 minutes or until firm. Do not over bake. Remove from baking sheet and cool on wire rack.

Monster oatmeal cookies©

¾ cup vegetable shortening
1 cup firmly packed brown sugar
½ cup granulated sugar
2 eggs
2 teaspoons vanilla
1 cup all-purpose flour
3½ cups uncooked oats

Makes about 18 cookies.
Grease 2 baking sheets. Heat the oven to 350 degrees.
Beat the shortening, sugars, eggs and vanilla until creamy and smooth. Add flour and oats, then remaining ingredients. Drop batter onto baking sheets 4 tablespoons per cookie. Bake 15 to 18 minutes. Diameter of cookies should be about 3 to 3½ inches. May also add raisins

1   cup milk
1   teaspoon salt
½   teaspoon baking soda
½   teaspoon cinnamon
1   cup flaked coconut
1½ cups (1 6-ounce package)
    mixed, dried fruit
1½ cups chopped dates
1   cup chopped nuts

or chocolate chips.

Heath Bar brittle oatmeal cookies

½   cup butter
1¼ cups peanut butter
1   cup light brown sugar
1   cup granulated sugar
1   teaspoon vanilla
3   eggs, slightly beaten
2   teaspoons baking soda
1   cup all-purpose flour
1   12-ounce package semisweet
    chocolate chips
3   cups oats
¾ to 1 cup Heath Bar brittle

Makes about 5 dozen cookies.
Cream butter and peanut butter together until fluffy and well-blended. Add sugars and beat well. Add vanilla and eggs and beat well to combine.
Sift flour and baking soda together. Stir into batter until evenly blended. Add chips, oats and Heath Bar brittle. Stir to combine evenly. Drop by teaspoons onto ungreased baking sheets. Bake 10 minutes in a preheated 350-degree oven. Remove from baking sheet and cool on rack.

I have four recipes for angel cookies – each very different and each very good. I couldn't decide which to include in the book so, I am sharing all.

Angel cookies 1©

½   cup firmly packed brown
    sugar
½   cup granulated sugar
1   cup butter or vegetable
    shortening
1   egg
1   teaspoon coconut flavoring
1   teaspoon baking soda

Makes 3 dozen cookies.
Cream together the sugars and shortening. Add egg and mix well. Add coconut flavoring.
Sift together the dry ingredients and add to first mixture, about ¼ at a time. Chill the dough for an hour, then shape into balls about the size of a walnut.
Dip each ball about halfway in water, then in

1   teaspoon cream of tartar
½   teaspoon salt
2   cups all-purpose flour

additional granulated sugar. Place sugar-side up on a greased cookie shoot. Bake at 350 degrees for 12 to 15 minutes. The balls will flatten during baking and will be light brown when done.
Let them sit for a few minutes before removing from cookie sheet.

Angel cookies 2©

3   egg whites
     Pinch salt
¼   teaspoon cream of tartar
1   cup sugar
¼   teaspoon almond extract
1   tablespoon all-purpose flour
1   cup chopped pecans

Makes 3 dozen cookies.
Place egg whites in bowl of electric mixer. Add salt and cream of tartar. Beat until foamy. While beating, slowly add sugar. Beat until stiff but not dry. Stir in almond extract.
Mix flour with pecans. Add to egg-white mixture. Drop by teaspoonfuls onto lightly greased baking sheet. Bake in a 300-degree oven for 30 minutes.

Angel cookies 3©

1   cup butter
1   cup white sugar
1   cup dark brown sugar
2   eggs, beaten
1   pound chopped dates
1   cup coconut
2   cups chopped pecans
1   teaspoon vanilla
4   cups Rice Krispies
     Confectioners' sugar

Makes 3 to 4 cozen.
Place butter, sugars, eggs and dates in a saucepan. Cook over low heat, stirring constantly. Bring to a boil and cook until thickened. Add coconut, pecans, and vanilla. Mix thoroughly. Pour over Rice Krispies, stirring to mix thoroughly.
Butter hands so you don't burn yourself. Pinch all small amounts of the mixture and roll into balls about 1 inch in diameter. Roll balls in confectioners' sugar. Work mixture while still warm. Place on a cookie sheet until dry. Store in airtight container.

Angels' tears
(Uses egg whites only)

Makes about 6 dozen.

4	egg whites
¼	teaspoon cream of tartar
	Few grains salt
1¼	cups confectioners' sugar
½	teaspoon vanilla

Combine unbeaten egg whites, cream of tartar and salt. Beat until stiff. Add confectioners' sugar very gradually, about 1 tablespoon at a time. When half the sugar has been added, add the vanilla. Continue adding remaining sugar. Beat until stiff and sugar is incorporated.

Shape cookies, using a teaspoon or cake decorator, onto heavy paper or foil placed on a baking sheet. Bake in a 250-degree oven for 45 minutes.

Gold cookies©
(Uses egg yolks only)

Makes about 5 dozen.

½	cup butter
1½	cups granulated sugar
4	egg yolks
1½	teaspoons vanilla
2	tablespoons half-and-half or milk
1½	cups all-purpose flour
½	teaspoon baking powder
¼	teaspoon salt
½	teaspoon nutmeg
2½	teaspoons cinnamon, divided
1	cup chopped nuts

Cream butter and sugar together. Mix in egg yolks, vanilla and half-and-half. Blend well. Sift flour and measure. Sift again with baking powder, salt, nutmeg and ½ teaspoon of the cinnamon. Add to creamed mixture and mix thoroughly. Chill dough 3 to 4 hours.

Combine remaining 2 teaspoons cinnamon with the chopped nuts. Shape dough into small balls and roll in nut mixture. Place balls about 2 inches apart on greased baking sheet.

Bake in a preheated 375-degree oven for 12 minutes or until golden brown. Cool on wire rack.

Almond cookies

½ cup butter
6 tablespoons granulated sugar
6 tablespoons brown sugar
1 teaspoon almond extract
1 egg
1 cup all-purpose flour
½ teaspoon baking soda
½ teaspoon salt
½ cup chopped almonds, optional

Makes 40 to 50 cookies.
Preheat oven to 375 degrees.
In the large bowl of an electric mixer, combine butter, granulated sugar, brown sugar and almond extract. Beat until creamy. Add egg and beat until blended.
In a small bowl, combine flour, baking soda and salt. Add to butter mixture. Blend thoroughly. Stir in chopped almonds.
Drop by rounded teaspoon onto ungreased baking sheet. Bake 10 to 12 minutes or until golden. Cool on baking sheet for a minute or two. Remove to wire rack to cool completely.

Pennsylvania Dutch funnel cakes©

2 beaten eggs
1½ cups milk
2 cups all-purpose flour
1 teaspoon baking powder
½ teaspoon salt
2 cups cooking oil
Confectioners' sugar or berries and whipped cream

Makes 5 to 6 large cakes.
Mix the eggs and milk. Sift together the flour, baking powder and salt. Add the flour mixture to the egg mixture and beat until smooth. If it's too thick to flow through a funnel, add a bit of milk.
Heat the cooking oil to 360 degrees in a heavy skillet. Cover the bottom of the funnel with a finger and pour a generous ½ cup of the batter into the top of the funnel. Holding funnel over hot oil remove finger and rotate funnel in a spiral motion, releasing batter. Fry cake until golden. Turn carefully (cakes are hard to turn and tend to break up somewhat), cook till done. Drain on paper towels, sprinkle with confectioners' sugar and serve hot or serve with berries and whipped cream.

Fairy cakes©

- ⅔ cup all-purpose flour
- 1   teaspoon baking powder
- 3   eggs
- ⅔ cup granulated sugar
- 2   tablespoons melted butter
- 1   tablespoon hot water

Whipped cream:
- 1   cup whipping cream
- ¼ cup granulated sugar
- ½ teaspoon vanilla

Makes 24 small cakes.
Preheat oven to 425 degrees. Sift flour with baking powder and set aside.
Place eggs and sugar in a bowl and whisk until thick. Fold in flour mixture with a metal spoon. Add melted butter and hot water. Blend thoroughly.
Divide mixture into 1½-inch muffin tins that have been well greased and floured. Bake 8 to 10 minutes. Remove from oven and allow to cool 10 minutes. Remove cakes from pans and allow to cool completely.
Prepare whipped cream. While beating whipping cream, gradually add sugar and vanilla. Beat until stiff, being careful not to over beat, thus forming butter. Use as filling for fairy cakes.
With a sharp, pointed knife, cut away risen area from top of cake and set aside. Fill hole with whipped cream. Cut cut-away section in half to form wings. Place "wings" on top of cream and you have fairy cakes.

Fortune cookies©

This recipe is from "The Great Big Cookie Book" by Barbara Grunes and Virginia Van Vynckt (Prima Publishing, 1997)

- 2   egg whites
- ¼ cup vegetable oil
- ½ teaspoon coconut flavoring or extract
- ½ cup all-purpose flour
- ¼ cup sugar
- 1   tablespoon cornstarch
- ⅛ teaspoon salt

Makes 30 cookies.
With electric mixer, beat egg whites until they begin to foam. Mix in oil, coconut flavoring, flour, sugar, cornstarch and salt. Add 2 tablespoons of water. Cover bowl and refrigerate for 30 minutes.
To prepare the cookies, use a non-stick griddle (it might be necessary to grease it just lightly). Heat pan over medium-high

2 to 4 tablespoons water

30 fortunes, typed or written on ½-by-2½-inch strips of paper

heat.

Stir batter to a medium consistency (if necessary, add water by the tablespoon). Spoon the batter by heaping teaspoonfuls onto the hot griddle, making about 3 cookies at a time. Using the back of the spoon, smooth batter into circles 2½ to 3 inches in diameter. When the cookies are golden brown on the underside – this will take only about 10 seconds or so – turn them over and brown the other side.

Moving quickly, remove 1 cookie at a time. Set a fortune in the center. Fold cookie in half and set it on the edge of a glass, pulling down the sides to make a fortune-cookie shape. Continue until all the cookies have been formed. They'll be soft, so let them cool on a wire rack overnight. To store, cover loosely, at room temperature.

Fortune tips: For extra silliness, make your fortunes very specific to the people who will be eating these, and "code" the cookies so you know which one to give to each person. Examples: "You will enjoy dinner in the company of good friends," for anyone at the table. "Happy Birthday," for the guest of honor. "Blue becomes you," for the friend who just bought a new dress in that color.

Butter pretzels from Cissy Gregg©

(December 8, 1948)

1 cup butter
½ cup sugar
1 tablespoon grated lemon zest
1 egg
3¾ cups sifted all-purpose flour
½ teaspoon salt

Makes about 7 dozen.
Thoroughly cream butter. Gradually add ½ cup sugar, creaming thoroughly. Add grated lemon zest and egg. Blend thoroughly.
Sift flour 3 times with the salt. Add this well-sifted mixture to the sugar-butter mixture alternately with the water. Wrap and place in

5   tablespoons water
     Granulated sugar

the refrigerator overnight.

Cut dough into quarters and leave all but what you are working with in the refrigerator until you are ready for it.

Cut off a small portion of the dough you are working with. Roll on a flat surface with the palms of your hands until you have a piece about 8 inches long and ¼ inch in diameter (a very small amount of flour on the surface or hands makes rolling easier). Swirl around to try to make it into a pretzel shape. Dip each "pretzel" in granulated sugar and place on a baking sheet. Bake in a preheated 375-degree oven for about 10 minutes.

Lemon drop cookies©

1   cup unsalted butter
1½   cups sugar
1   egg
1   tablespoon lemon zest
½   cup lemon juice
1   teaspoon salt
2¼   cups all-purpose flour

Lemon curd:

4   tablespoons unsalted butter
½   cup sugar
½   cup freshly squeezed lemon
     juice
4   egg yolks
1   tablespoon grated lemon zest
     (yellow part of peel only)

Makes 4 dozen cookies.

To make cookies: Cream butter and sugar. Add egg, lemon zest and juice. Stir to combine. Add salt and flour. Stir until well-blended. Chill dough for at least 30 minutes before baking. To bake, drop by teaspoonful onto greased cookie sheet. Make an indention in center of each cookie. Fill with lemon curd.

Bake in a preheated, 375-degree oven about 10 minutes or until edges turn a golden brown.

To make lemon curd: In a heavy, non-aluminum saucepan (or the top of a non-aluminum double boiler), combine butter, sugar, lemon juice and egg yolks. Cook over lowest heat (or simmering water), stirring constantly, until mixture thickens enough to heavily coat the back of a spoon. Do not let mixture boil or it will curdle.

Pour lemon curd into a small bowl and stir in the lemon zest. Makes 1 cup.

Lemon pectines©

Makes 4 dozen small cakes or up to 7 dozen if you have the tiny "gem" pans.

1¼ cups sugar, separated
2 cups cake flour
2 teaspoons baking powder
1 3-ounce package lemon-flavored gelatin
¾ cup milk
⅔ cup oil
2 tablespoons lemon extract
4 eggs, separated, at room temperature

Glaze:

Juice of 3 lemons
1 16-ounce box confectioners' sugar, sifted

To make pectines: Combine 1 cup of the sugar with the flour, baking powder and gelatin. Mix in large bowl of electric mixer. Combine milk, oil and lemon extract. Add to the dry ingredients, beating until quite smooth. Beat in egg yolks, one at a time. In separate bowl, beat egg whites stiff. Gradually beat in the remaining ¼ cup sugar. Stir in large spoonful of the beaten whites into the batter; carefully fold in the remainder of the whites.

Grease and dust your smallest muffin tins with flour (you can also use a madeleine pan). Fill half full with batter. Bake at 375 degrees 12 to 15 minutes. Turn out on wire racks. Dip in glaze and let dry on racks.

Note: 2 tablespoons lemon extract is the correct amount.

To make glaze: Combine juice and sugar. Heat in top of double boiler until hot. If you have a microwave, you can combine glaze ingredients in a glass, quart-size measuring cup. Put in microwave oven for a minute. Dip tops of cakes In hot glaze and allow to dry on racks.

Variation: Batter can be baked in a 9-inch aluminum tube pan, well-greased and floured, but do not use bundt pan; it will almost surely stick. Bake an hour or more, until it tests done. Pour glaze over cooled cake

Brownie chip cookies

1   18.9 ounce package brownie
    mix
2   eggs
¼   vegetable oil
1   cup semisweet chocolate
    chips
1   cup nuts, optional

Makes 4 to 5 dozen cookies.
Preheat oven to 350 degrees. Lightly grease a cookie sheet.
In a large bowl, combine brownie mix, eggs and oil. Beat with a spoon about 50 strokes. Stir in chocolate chips and nuts. Stir to blend. Drop by rounded teaspoon, 2-inches apart, onto cookie sheet. Bake in preheated oven 8 to 10 minutes. Cookies are soft to the touch. Cool slightly before removing from cookie sheet.

Irene Riley's persimmon cookies©

Cookies:
1   cup persimmon pulp
1   teaspoon baking soda
1   cup sugar
½   cup butter or margarine
1   egg, beaten
2   cups all-purpose flour
¼   teaspoon salt
½   teaspoon cinnamon
½   teaspoon ground cloves
¼   teaspoon nutmeg
½   cup dates
½   cup raisins
1   cup nuts
Frosting:
1   teaspoon butter or margarine
2   tablespoons orange juice
1½ cups confectioners' sugar

Makes about 4 dozen.
To make cookies: Combine persimmon pulp and baking soda. Mix and set aside. Cream sugar with butter or margarine. Add egg and persimmon pulp mixture. Mix thoroughly.
Sift flour and salt together. Add cinnamon, cloves and nutmeg. Add to creamed sugar. Stir in dates, raisins and nuts. Heat oven to 350 degrees. Drop by spoonful onto lightly greased cookie sheet. Bake 10 to 12 minutes.
To make frosting: Combine all ingredients. Mix well. Frost cookies while warm.
  Note: Store cookies in plastic or glass containers. Metal containers cause cookies to darken.

The Seelbach's chocolate chip cookie©

1	cup plus 3 tablespoons butter, room temperature
1	cup granulated sugar
¾	cup light brown sugar
3	eggs
1	teaspoon vanilla
½	teaspoon lemon juice
1	teaspoon baking soda
½	teaspoon cinnamon
½	cup oatmeal
1½	cups cake flour
1½	cups bread flour
16	ounces mini chocolate chips
2½	cups chopped pecans

Makes approximately 2 dozen (see note).

Heat oven to 350 degrees.

Cream butter. Add granulated and brown sugars. Beat until light and fluffy. Add eggs one at a time, beating after each addition. Add vanilla and lemon juice. Stir to blend. Mix baking soda, cinnamon, oatmeal and both flours together and incorporate into sugar mixture. Add chocolate chips and pecans. Mix just enough to incorporate evenly.

Bake until outside layer is slightly firm and inside is soft, about 10 to 12 minutes.

Note: Use a ¼ cup measure for dropping these cookies onto the baking sheet. The result is a cookie about 2 to 3 inches in diameter and ¾-inch thick.

When I tested the recipe, I made the regular-size cookie, not realizing how large the Seelbach version is. I had approximately 5 dozen cookies. No matter; both versions are excellent.

The Hedges at Neiman-Marcus cookie©

2½	cups blended oatmeal (see note)
1	cup butter (no substitutes)
1	cup firmly packed brown sugar
1	cup sugar
2	eggs
1	teaspoon vanilla
2	cups all-purpose flour

Makes 5 to 6 dozen.

Note: For blended oatmeal, measure oatmeal then process in blender or food processor with steel blade until fine. Set aside.

Heat oven to 375 degrees. Cream butter with both sugars. Add eggs one at a time and vanilla. Mix well.

Combine flour, blended oatmeal, salt, baking soda and baking powder. Stir into butter

½ teaspoon salt
1 teaspoon baking soda
1 teaspoon baking powder
1 4-ounce (or equivalent) Hershey candy bar, grated
1 12-ounce package semisweet chocolate chips

mixture. Add grated candy bar and chocolate chips. Stir until just blended. Refrigerate for ½ hour. Roll into balls and place 2 inches apart on a lightly greased cookie sheet. Bake for 6 minutes. Do not over bake. Cool on rack.

Cranberry-orange biscotti

1 pound almonds
1 cup granulated sugar
2 cups all-purpose flour
1 cup brown sugar
1 teaspoon cinnamon
1 teaspoon baking powder
3 tablespoons butter, room temperature
⅔ cup dried cranberries
Zest of 1 orange
2 large eggs, slightly beaten

Egg wash:
Make by beating 1 egg with 2 tablespoons water

Makes about 30 biscotti
Heat oven to 375 degrees. Spread almonds on a baking sheet or jellyroll pan and toast for 10 minutes. Set aside to cool.
When cool, coarsely chop almonds. To do this, I use the flat side of a metal meat tenderizing mallet
Grease and flour a baking sheet (this recipe makes two 15-by-4-inch logs – the first time you do this, you may want to prepare 2 baking sheets and use 1 for each log).
In a blender or food processor, combine ¼ of the almonds and ¼ cup of the sugar. Grind until fine. Transfer the ground mixture to a large bowl. Stir in the flour, the remaining ¾ cup sugar, brown sugar, cinnamon and baking powder. Stir everything until well-blended; add the butter and blend again until the mixture looks like fine crumbs.
Add the remaining almonds, cranberries and orange zest to the mixture. Stir. Add the lightly beaten eggs. Stir the dough in the bowl until everything is combined. The dough will still look like a crumbly mess. Don't worry, it's supposed to look that way. Turn the oven temperature to 350 degrees.
Divide the dough in half and, with floured hands, form each half into a 15-by-4-inch rectangle on the prepared baking sheet.

Press each log so that it's no more than 1-inch thick. Brush both logs with egg wash. (I know, this is messy but after I brush the logs with egg wash, I place one hand on top of the log and, using a spatula, press the loose crumbs into the side of the log. The egg wash holds everything together and gives a shine to the baked biscotti.)

Bake in a preheated 350-degree oven for 25 to 30 minutes, or until the logs are golden brown and a skewer comes out clean. Cool the logs on pans for 10 minutes. Cut the rectangles crosswise into ¾-inch thick slices and turn the slices so they rest on their side. Return to a turned-off but still warm oven. Allow the logs to continue cooking and cooling for at least 1 hour.

Store in an airtight container. May be placed in a freezer bag, in an airtight container and frozen.

Note: For chocolate-orange biscotti, replace the cranberries with ½ cup mini chocolate chips plus the orange zest. If you are giving them as a gift or for a special treat, you may want to dip one end of each cookie in melted chocolate.

For plain biscotti, omit the dried cranberries and orange zest. I make all three versions and give some of each as Christmas gifts and at Easter.

Crostoli©

Crostoli are cookies that are often served at Italian weddings. After we married here in Louisville, my mother-in-law wanted to introduce me to her friends in Rockford, Illinois so she had a reception for us in Rockford. She had large baskets full of these sitting around – the reception was over when we ran out of crostoli. They're like eating potato chips – you can't stop eating them.

Makes about 150 cookies

4	cups all-purpose flour
4½	teaspoons baking powder

Combine flour, baking powder and salt.
Using a pastry blender or 2 knives, cut in

1¼ teaspoons salt
2 tablespoons butter
¾ cups sugar
2 eggs, beaten
1 tablespoon vanilla
¼ cup bourbon
½ cup milk
Vegetable oil for frying
Confectioners' sugar, or
granulated sugar and
cinnamon (see note)

butter. Add sugar and stir. Make a hole in the center of flour mixture. Add beaten eggs, vanilla, bourbon and milk. Stir; knead to form a stiff dough. You will think all the flour will not work in – keep kneading a few more times until it does. Form into a ball. Cover bowl with a damp cloth. Let rest for 30 minutes.

While the dough is resting, prepare for the frying. Pour oil to about a depth of 2 inches in a deep pan (a deep fryer is great for this because you can control the heat). Heat oil to 375 degrees.

Divide dough into 4 pieces. Roll 1 piece at a time paper thin on a lightly floured surface. Cut into 1-by-3-inch cookies. Slip cookies, a few at a time, into hot oil (do not crowd). Fry until edges turn golden. Flip to cook back side. This takes only a few seconds so watch carefully. Remove and drain on paper toweling.

Place 1 cup of confectioners' sugar – or ½ cup granulated sugar mixed with ½ teaspoon cinnamon – in a paper bag. As the cookies are removed from the oil, put them in the bag with the sugar and shake. Replenish sugar as needed.

Makes about 150 cookies; the number depends on how thin the dough is rolled and the size of the cookies. I know, this seems like a lot of cookies but you can't stop eating them.

Note: When I make these cookies, I roll a few out at a time and fry as I go along. You have to work pretty fast but if you don't cut and fry as you go along, you would end up with cookies everywhere and they would dry before you could fry them. They are definitely worth the effort.

My mother's soft springerle©

Springerle is the beautiful embossed anise-flavored cookie that originated centuries ago in the German duchy of Swabia. Being of German descent, my mother always made them for Christmas and as gifts for her relatives and friends. My sister and I have continued the tradition – we each have our own list of relatives and friends who receive a dozen or two of these special treats.

4   eggs, room temperature
1   pound (4 cups) confectioners' sugar
1   tablespoon plus 1 teaspoon melted butter
1   tablespoon white corn syrup
1 ⅓   teaspoons baking powder
1   teaspoon anise oil (not flavoring or seed)
1   pound all-purpose flour (3 ½ cups)

Makes about 60 cookies.

In a large bowl beat eggs until lemon in color. Continue beating, gradually adding the sugar and then the melted butter. Still beating, add the syrup, baking powder and anise oil (use oil, not flavoring). Begin adding the flour a little at a time. When the dough becomes too stiff to work with the electric mixer, continue to work the flour in with a wooden spoon or your hands (I never have trouble working the flour in with the mixer—I have a KitchenAid). When the flour has been taken into the dough, cover with a cloth and allow to rest 15 to 20 minutes. Divide the dough into three sections. On a floured surface, roll out one section at a time to ¼ inch thickness. Keep remainder of dough covered with the cloth. Press rolled dough with springerle mold and cut at markings. Cut away dough can be kneaded together, rolled out, pressed and cut into cookies. Lay cookies on a cloth to dry at least 8 hours or overnight (room should be cool). Do not cover cookies while drying. Repeat with remaining two sections of dough.

To bake, heat oven to 325 degrees. Place cookies on a lightly greased baking sheet and bake 10 to 15 minutes. Bottom of cookie will brown slightly but top should not brown. After the cookies cool, store in tightly covered plastic or glass container. May be frozen.

Oatmeal chocolate chip cookies

½ cup rolled oats, regular or quick cooking
2¼ cups all-purpose flour
1½ teaspoons baking soda
½ teaspoon salt
¼ teaspoon cinnamon
1 cup (2 sticks) butter, room temperature
¾ cup firmly packed brown sugar
¾ cup granulated sugar
2 teaspoons vanilla extract
2 eggs
3 cups semisweet chocolate chips
1½ cups chopped nuts, optional

Makes 2 dozen.
Preheat oven to 350 degrees. Lightly grease two baking sheets.
In a large mixing bowl, combine oats, flour, baking soda, salt and cinnamon. Set aside. In large bowl of electric mixer, cream together butter, sugars and vanilla. Add eggs and beat until fluffy.
Stir the oat mixture into egg mixture, blending well. Add chocolate chips and nuts (if using) to the dough and mix well. Using ¼ cup dough for each cookie, scoop round balls with an ice-cream scoop and place 2½-inches apart on prepared baking sheets. Bake until cookies are lightly browned, 16 to 18 minutes. Transfer to a wire rack to cool completely. Store in a sealed container to keep soft and chewy.

Several years ago, I developed this recipe for a Derby party. It quickly became a favorite at our house. It's very rich so cut into small serving pieces.

Brownies for Derby

8 ounces unsweetened chocolate
1 cup butter (2 sticks)
2 large eggs
3 egg whites (reserve yolks)
3¾ cups sugar
¼ teaspoon salt
1½ cups all-purpose flour
2 tablespoons bourbon
2 cups chopped pecans or walnuts

These are very rich – cut into small servings.
Preheat oven to 350 degrees. Line a 9-by-13-by-2-inch pan with aluminum foil. This can be done by inverting the pan and pressing aluminum foil down around the sides and corners to shape like the pan. Remove the foil. Turn the pan right side up. Place the foil in the pan, pressing it against the sides of the pan. Grease the foil. **(See note)**. Set pan aside
To make the brownies: Place the chocolate and butter in a heavy saucepan

322

Frosting:
- 1   **5-ounce can evaporated milk**
- 1   **cup sugar**
- 3   **reserved eggs yolks, beaten**
- 1   **cup unsalted butter (2 sticks)**
- 2   **tablespoons bourbon or 2 teaspoons vanilla**
- 1   **cup chopped pecans or walnuts**

and, over very low heat, stir until chocolate and butter have melted. Remove from heat and set aside.

In the large bowl of an electric mixer, beat two whole eggs and the whites of three (save the three yolks for the frosting), sugar and salt at high speed for 10 minutes. On low speed, add the chocolate mixture and beat only until mixed. Add flour. Stir with a wooden spoon just until blended. Stir in the bourbon and nuts.

Pour into prepared pan and bake 45 minutes. The brownies will have a crisp crust on top but will be wet in the center. DO NOT BAKE ANY LONGER.

Remove brownies from oven and let stand at room temperature until cool. When cool, invert onto a rack or cutting board. Remove foil. Invert second time onto serving platter so top is up. Cover with frosting.

To make frosting: In a saucepan, combine milk, sugar, egg yolks and butter. Cook over medium heat, stirring constantly, for about 12 minutes or until mixture thickens. Remove from heat.

Stir in bourbon and nuts. Set pan in a bowl of ice. Beat until cool and of spreading consistency. Spread over top of brownies.

Note: Because chocolate burns easily, before baking the brownies I wrap a moistened cake pan strip around the outside of the pan. These strips can be purchased at cake supply stores or you can cut a terry towel into strips long enough to go around the outside of the pan plus a lap of about 1½ inches. The strips should be about 1½ inches wide. Moisten with water before wrapping around the outside of the pan. Pin in place. The wet band keeps the outside edge of the brownie batter cool, allowing time for the center batter to warm and begin cooking at about the same time as the outer edge begins to bake. The result is a nice even layer with outer edges that are tender and not over baked. I use the bands when baking any cake - this eliminates domed layers that crack when stacking.

Caramel brownies©

1½	cups unsalted butter, melted
1½	pounds brown sugar
3	eggs
3	cups all-purpose flour
⅓	cup warm water
¾	teaspoon salt
2	teaspoons pure vanilla extract
1½	cups chopped nuts (optional)

Makes 48 small servings

Heat oven to 350 degrees. Lightly butter a 9-by-13-by-2-inch baking pan.
In a medium bowl, mix the butter and sugar until smooth. Mix in the eggs. Add the flour, a little at a time, stirring constantly. Stir in the water. Mix in the salt, vanilla and nuts, if using. Pour into prepared pan. Bake about 40 minutes or until golden brown and firm. Cool before cutting. These brownies are very rich – make servings small.

Raspberry brownies©

2	ounces unsweetened chocolate
4	ounces (1 stick) unsalted butter
¼	teaspoon salt
1	teaspoon vanilla extract
1	cup sugar
2	large eggs
¼	cup all-purpose flour
1	cup pecans or walnut pieces
⅓	cup seedless red raspberry preserves

Makes 16 brownies.

Do not preheat the oven now. Prepare an 8-by-8-by-2-inch square cake pan as follows: Turn the pan over. Center a 12-inch square of aluminum foil over the pan. Fold down the sides and corners to shape the foil. Then remove it. Turn the pan over again, place the foil in the pan and press it gently into place.
Brush the foil with melted butter. Set pan aside.
Place the chocolate and butter in a heavy saucepan over low heat. Stir frequently until melted. Remove the pan from the heat, stir in the salt, vanilla, sugar and then eggs one

at a time, stirring until incorporated after each addition. Add the flour and stir until smooth. Stir in the nuts.

Pour half the batter into prepared pan. Spread over bottom of pan.

Place pan in freezer for about 30 minutes or until mixture is just firm enough for you to spread a thin layer of preserves on top.

Spread the preserves over the top. It will be a very thin layer, barely enough to cover the brownie mixture.

Pour or spoon small amounts at a time of the remaining brownie mixture over the preserves. Smooth with the back of a spoon. Let stand at room temperature at least 30 minutes or until frozen layer has thawed. Meanwhile, adjust a rack one-third up from the bottom of the oven. Preheat oven to 325 degrees.

Bake for 40 minutes until a toothpick inserted in the middle comes out clean.

Let stand in the pan until the cake reaches room temperature. Place the pan in the freezer until the cake is firm. To remove from pan cover with a small cutting board or a cookie sheet, turn the pan and board or sheet over, remove the pan, peel off the foil. Turn the cake right side up.

With a long, thin, sharp knife, cut the brownies into 16 squares or 32 small, finger-shaped pieces.

Therese Powers chocolate syrup brownies©

Makes 12 to 15 servings.

1	cup sugar
½	cup butter

Lightly grease and flour a 10½-by-15½-by-1-inch jelly roll pan. Preheat oven to 350

1   cup all-purpose flour
4   eggs
1   16-ounce can chocolate
    syrup

degrees.
Beat sugar and butter until blended. Add
remaining ingredients and stir until blended.
Pour into prepared pan. Bake 25 to 30
minutes.

Waffle iron brownies©

½   cup butter or margarine
¼   cup unsweetened cocoa
    powder
¾   cup granulated sugar
2   eggs, well-beaten
1   tablespoon water
1¼ cups all-purpose flour
¼   teaspoon salt
⅔   cup chopped walnuts
    Confectioners' sugar
    (optional)

Makes about 2½ dozen brownies.
Preheat waffle iron to medium setting.
Indicator light will go out when proper
temperature is reached.
Melt butter in a saucepan over low heat.
Remove from heat. Blend cocoa into butter
with a wooden spoon. Stir in sugar, beaten
eggs and water. Add flour and salt; beat
well. Add nuts; mix thoroughly.
Into each section of the preheated waffle
iron, drop 1 well-rounded teaspoon of batter.
You will have a cookie about 2-inches in
diameter, not something shaped like a waffle.
Close lid and bake about 1½ minutes. The
brownies are done if they do not stick to the
top of the waffle iron. Use the tip of a
wooden skewer to remove brownies easily.
Let cool on racks. Sprinkle with
confectioners' sugar, if desired.

Brownie mix ©

4   cups all-purpose flour
1½ teaspoons baking powder
3   teaspoons salt
8   cups sugar
2½ cups cocoa
2   cups vegetable shortening

For one batch of brownies:

**Makes enough mix for 5 batches of
brownies.**
Stir together the flour, baking powder, salt,
sugar and cocoa. Cut in shortening until
mixture resembles coarse meal. Divide into
plastic bags 3 cups at a time. Can be
refrigerated up to six weeks. Can be frozen
up to a year.
To make one batch of brownies:
Grease and flour an 8-by-8-by-2-inch baking

3	cups mix, see recipe above
3	eggs, beaten
1½	teaspoons vanilla extract
½	cup chopped pecans, optional

pan. Heat oven to 350 degrees.
Combine all ingredients until well-blended.
Spoon into prepared pan. Bake 35 to 40 minutes. Cut into squares.
Makes 16 brownies.

Desserts and Puddings

Mill Race Inn's Swedish cream©

1	16-ounce carton sour cream
1	pint half-and-half
1	teaspoon vanilla
½	cup sugar
1	¼ ounce package unflavored gelatin
1	package frozen raspberries or fruit of choice

Makes 6 to 8 servings.
In a large mixing bowl, beat the sour cream, one cup half-and-half and vanilla until thick. In a saucepan, combine sugar and gelatin. Slowly add remaining cup half-and-half. Heat mixture until sugar and gelatin have completely dissolved. Add to sour cream mixture and beat until thick and creamy. Pour into champagne glasses. Refrigerate 4 to 6 hours or until set. When ready to serve, top with raspberries or fruit of choice

Luckett's Swedish sour cream with raspberry sauce©

1	¼ ounce package gelatin
¼	cup cold water
¾	cup sugar
2	cups heavy cream
½	cup milk
2	cups sour cream
1	teaspoon vanilla

Raspberry sauce:

1	cup raspberry preserves
½	cup raspberries, fresh or frozen
2	tablespoons orange liqueur
	Water to thin

Makes 10 servings.
To make cream: Dissolve gelatin in cold water.
In a saucepan combine the gelatin mixture, sugar, heavy cream and milk. Heat and stir until sugar is completely dissolved. Cool. When it's completely cool, slowly stir gelatin mixture into the sour cream. Add vanilla. Chill until set or overnight.
Serve with raspberry sauce.
To make sauce: Combine all ingredients. Add water as needed.
Makes about 1½ cups.

No-fat Swedish crème and blueberries©

2 cups no-fat sour cream
2 cups liquid fat-free French vanilla non-dairy creamer
1 tablespoon unflavored gelatin
2 cups fresh blueberries
6 sprigs of mint for garnish
6 blueberries for garnish

Makes 6 servings.
In a large bowl, beat the sour cream and 1 cup fat-free non-dairy creamer until smooth. In a saucepan, combine remaining 1 cup of fat-free non-dairy creamer and gelatin. Heat just until gelatin dissolves. Add to sour cream mixture and beat until thoroughly combined. Layer crème and fresh blueberries in champagne or parfait glasses. Refrigerate 4 to 6 hours or until set. When ready to serve, top with a sprig of mint and a fresh blueberry. (About 260 calories per serving.)

Hasenour's crème brûlée©

⅓ vanilla bean
2 cups whipping cream
6 egg yolks
⅓ cup sugar
4 tablespoons brown sugar
4 strawberries, for garnish

Makes 4 servings.
Split vanilla bean lengthwise. Scrape out seeds and place them and bean in saucepan with cream. Heat to 160 degrees; **do not boil**. In a bowl, combine egg yolks and sugar.
When cream reaches desired temperature, slowly pour hot cream into egg-yolk mixture, stirring continuously until all is combined. Remove vanilla bean and ladle sauce into oven-proof serving cups, being sure to fill to top. Place the cups in a flat oven-proof dish (a 9-by-13-by-2-inch dish is excellent). Pour enough water into dish to come ¾ up the side of serving cups.
Bake in a preheated 300-degree oven for 1 hour or until a knife inserted near the edge of the cup comes out clean. The stored heat in the cups will finish the cooking process. Remove from pan and cool on a rack. Chill completely before caramelizing.

Before serving, top each evenly with 1 tablespoon brown sugar. Place under broiler until sugar caramelizes. Garnish with a fanned strawberry.

Ermin's Restaurant and Café's tiramisu©

Makes 10 to 12 servings.

6	egg yolks, beaten
½	cup confectioners' sugar
2	ounces Kahlua
2	ounces Grand Marnier
1	pound mascarpone cheese
	Zest (colored part of rind only) of 3 to 4 lemons or oranges
1	quart heavy cream
8	ounces espresso or strong coffee
40 to 60	ladyfingers
	Chocolate crumbs or miniature chocolate chips

In the top pan of a double-boiler combine beaten egg yolks and confectioners' sugar. Cook over simmering water, stirring constantly, until mixture reaches 160 degrees (10 to 15 minutes). Remove from heat and pour into another container. Refrigerate until completely chilled. Combine chilled egg yolk mixture with Kahlua, Grand Marnier, mascarpone cheese and zest. Beat until smooth. Set aside. Beat cream until stiff peaks form. Combine with egg yolk mixture. Stir to blend.

Dip one side of each ladyfinger into coffee and layer on the bottom of serving dish. Spread ½ of the cream mixture over ladyfingers. Repeat process twice more or until ladyfingers and cream mixture have been used.

Sprinkle top with chocolate crumbs or miniature chocolate chips. Refrigerate a couple of hours before serving.

Helen Friedman's Charlotte russe with strawberries©

Makes 16 servings.

Ladyfingers:

1	cup sugar
6	egg yolks
2	teaspoons vanilla
6	egg whites
⅛	teaspoon salt
2	tablespoons sugar

Ladyfingers: Heat oven to 300 degrees. Butter and flour a large baking sheet and two 9-inch round cake pans. Trace shape of pan onto parchment paper. Cut out to line both pans

Beat sugar into yolks. Add vanilla and beat until mixture is thick, pale yellow and

1⅓   cups cake flour
      Custard filling, recipe follows
2   **cups cream, sweetened and
      whipped**
1   **pint fresh strawberries,
      washed and hulled**
Custard filling:
2   **¼-ounce packages plain
      gelatin**
1   **quart milk**
2   **cups sugar**
6   **egg yolks**
2   **cups heavy cream**
2   **teaspoons vanilla**

"ribbons" when dropped from a spoon. In another bowl, beat egg whites and salt to soft peaks. Sprinkle with sugar and beat until stiff. Fold the whites into the yolk mixture, adding flour. Do not attempt to blend the mixture too thoroughly or it will deflate the batter. It must remain light and puffy.

Scoop batter into a pastry bag outfitted with a wide nozzle rather than a decorative tip. Squeeze into about 20 ladyfingers 4 inches long and 1½ inches wide, spaced 1 inch apart. Spread remaining batter evenly in baking pans.

Bake ladyfingers 20 minutes; the cakes, 25 to 30 minutes, or until pale brown. Cool. Then remove ladyfingers and cakes from pans. Peel off paper.

To assemble, line a 9-inch springform pan with plastic wrap. Place a sponge cake in the bottom. Arrange ladyfingers vertically around sides, touching. Pour in custard filling and top with second sponge cake. Trim ladyfingers even with second sponge cake and refrigerate overnight. Turn out, flip onto serving plate. Peel off plastic and decorate with piped rows of whipped cream and strawberries.

To make custard: Dissolve gelatin in ¼ cup cold milk. Heat remaining milk with sugar and gelatin mixture, stirring until gelatin dissolves. Beat yolks and add a small portion of hot milk to them, then stir yolks in their entirety into the milk and cook until a custard forms that coats a spoon, 10 minutes. Do not boil. Custard will not be thick. Set aside to cool. Refrigerate until custard begins to jell. Whip the cream with the vanilla until stiff. Fold into custard.

Debbie Keller's fudge ganache roulade©

Cake:
- 1 cup all-purpose flour
- 1 cup cocoa
- 4 teaspoons baking powder
- 4 egg whites
- ½ cup (1 stick) butter
- 2 cups sugar
- 2 cups milk
- 2 teaspoons vanilla
- 4 egg yolks

Ganache filling:
- 8 ounces semisweet chocolate
- 1 cup heavy cream
- 2 ounces Grand Marnier or good flavored liqueur

Makes about 60 bite-size servings or 16 dessert servings.

To make cake: Grease and flour a 10½ -by-15½–by-1-inch jellyroll pan. Heat oven to 350 degrees.

Sift together the flour, cocoa and baking powder.

In a mixing bowl, whip egg whites until firm but not dry. Set aside in a draft-free area. Cream the butter and sugar until light and fluffy. Add vanilla to milk. Alternately incorporate the dry ingredients and the milk into the butter mixture. Add the egg yolks and beat for another 2 minutes.

By hand or with a spatula gently fold the egg whites into the mixture. Do not use an electric mixer to do this. It is important to be gentle so as not to lose the volume of the egg whites.

Pour into the prepared pan and bake for 25 to 30 minutes. The edges will pull away from the sides of the pan. Do not over bake. Cake will have the appearance of a soft brownie.

Cool the cake for about 20 minutes. Turn the pan over onto wax or parchment paper and tap gently to remove the cake. Trim any crusty edges and roll into the shape of a jellyroll, along with wax or parchment paper, before the cake cools. When cool, unroll cake, remove paper, and fill.

To make filling: Place chocolate in a heat-proof bowl over hot, not boiling water. Be careful not to get any water in the chocolate. Heat the cream until warm. Mix the cream into the melted chocolate. Add liqueur and mix to a smooth consistency.

This mixture is now ready to use inside the cake roll or as a glaze for your favorite dessert or for topping on ice cream.

To assemble cake: Unroll cake and spread the filling to cover two-thirds of the top surface of cake. (If you are cutting into bite-size servings, cut cake in half to make 2 rolls. Cover two-thirds of the top of each half with filling.) Roll the cake tight like a jellyroll, starting with the filled end. Wrap in parchment or wax paper. Let sit in refrigerator or freezer at least 6 hours before serving.

After chilling cake, slice into thickness you desire. Serve as is or with fresh whipped cream, sauce anglaise (a thin custard) or fresh raspberry sauce.

Uptown Café's gateau ganache©

Meringue:
- 6 egg whites, room temperature
- 2 cups sugar
- 6 ounces (1¼ cups) ground walnuts
- 1½ teaspoons white wine vinegar
- ½ teaspoon vanilla extract

Filling and icing:
- 3 ounces semisweet chocolate
- 1½ cups heavy whipping cream
- ¼ cup confectioners' sugar

Makes 6 to 8 servings.

Heat oven to 350 degrees. Cut 2 rounds of parchment paper to fit the bottoms of 2 8-inch cake pans. Butter and flour the parchment paper, then butter and flour the cake pans. Line pans with buttered paper.

Meringue: Place egg whites in a large bowl. Beat until stiff. Add sugar and nuts all at once. Fold in gently. Add vinegar and vanilla. Stir to blend. Spoon mixture equally into the 2 prepared pans.

Bake meringue for 40 to 45 minutes or until crusty to the touch. Remove from oven, run a knife around edges and quickly turn upside down on cooling racks. Remove pans and peel off paper. Let cool.

Filling and icing: Break chocolate into very small pieces. Heat ½ cup of the whipping cream until warm. Add chocolate and stir until smooth. Set aside.

Whip remaining cup of whipping cream with confectioners' sugar until stiff.

Assembly: Place 1 meringue round on a serving platter. Cover with half of whipped cream. Drizzle top with half the melted chocolate. Top with remaining meringue and repeat with whipped cream and melted chocolate.

Refrigerate until ready to serve.

Hobnob Corner's apple crisp©

Makes 6 servings.

5 cups peeled and sliced Jonathan apples (or enough to fill a 1½ quart baking dish)
¾ cup all-purpose flour
1 cup firmly packed brown sugar
½ teaspoon freshly grated nutmeg
¼ teaspoon salt
½ cup butter, cut into small pieces

Heat oven to 350 degrees. Butter a 1½-quart baking dish. Spread the apples in the dish, having them about level with the top or slightly higher than the top of the dish. Combine the flour, sugar, nutmeg and salt. Stir to combine. Cut in butter using 2 knives or a pastry blender until mixture is coarse and crumbly. Scatter over apples, pressing very gently with hands to shape the mixture over the apples. Bake for 30 minutes or until the crust is brown.

George Bush's apple crisp©

Makes 6 to 8 servings.

4 cups peeled and sliced Granny Smith apples
¼ cup orange juice
1 cup sugar
¾ cup all-purpose flour, sifted
½ teaspoon cinnamon
¼ teaspoon nutmeg
Pinch salt
¼ cup butter, cut up
Heavy or whipping cream, optional

Preheat oven to 375 degrees. Butter a 9-inch glass pie plate. Arrange apples in pie plate, mounding them in center. Pour orange juice over apples.

In a bowl combine sugar, flour, cinnamon, nutmeg and salt. Cut in butter until mixture resembles coarse crumbs.

Sprinkle over apples. Bake 45 to 55 minutes or until light brown and apples are tender.

Pour a little cream over each serving or whip cream and add a dollop just before serving.

Adele's lemon dacquoise©

Dacquoise:
- 10 large egg whites
- ¼ teaspoon salt
- 2 cups granulated sugar
- 1 cup ground almonds
- 2 tablespoons flour

Lemon buttercream:
- 6 large egg yolks
- 2½ cup granulated sugar
- 3 tablespoons cornstarch
- 1½ cups milk, heated
- 1½ pounds butter, room temperature
- Grated zest of one lemon (yellow part of peel)
- Juice of 3 to 4 lemons (let your taste be your guide)

Garnish:
- 1 cup slivered almonds, toasted
- Raspberries

Makes 12 servings.

To make dacquoise: Heat oven to 250 degrees. Line a baking sheet with parchment paper. Using an 8-inch cake pan as a guide, draw 3 circles on the paper. (I used 2 baking sheets, tracing 2 circles on one and 1 circle on the other.) Set aside.

In a large, oil-free mixing bowl, beat the egg whites with the salt until soft peaks form. Start adding 1 cup of the sugar, about 1 tablespoon at a time, beating until egg whites form stiff peaks.

Combine remaining one cup sugar, ground almonds and flour. Fold this mixture into the beaten egg whites.

Fit a pastry bag with a No. 5 plain tip. Fill bag with meringue. Pipe meringue on top of the parchment circles, beginning in the center and spiraling outward, like a snail. Use all the meringue. Bake 1 hour or until slightly crisp on the outside. Set aside to cool.

To make buttercream: In a heavy, stainless-steel pan (don't use aluminum utensils – they will discolor the custard), mix the egg yolks with the sugar. Whisk in the cornstarch. Add hot milk, pouring in a slow and steady stream while stirring constantly. Place pan over low heat and cook, stirring constantly, until custard thickens (coats a spoon). Strain into a bowl. Beat until custard is at room temperature. Beat in butter, about 3 tablespoons at a time. After all butter is incorporated, add the lemon zest and juice. Place bowl in ice water and beat until buttercream reaches spreading consistency.

(If the buttercream breaks or curdles, place bowl over simmering water and heat gently until the buttercream begins to melt on the side of the bowl. Remove from heat and beat until smooth and fluffy.)

To assemble: Place 1 meringue layer on cake platter. If necessary, trim sides to form an even circle. Spread on a layer of lemon buttercream the same thickness as the meringue layer. Place another meringue layer on top of the buttercream. Spread on another layer of buttercream. Top with remaining meringue layer and spread with remaining buttercream, covering sides as well as top.

Garnish sides with toasted almonds. Refrigerate to set. Garnish top with raspberries before serving if desired.

Café Metro's dacquoise©

Meringue:
- 1 cup egg whites (about 8) at room temperature
- ¼ teaspoon cream of tartar
- 1 cup sugar
- 1 teaspoon vanilla extract
- 1 cup ground almonds

Buttercream:
- 1 cup semisweet chocolate chips
- ½ cup whipping cream
- 2 cups sugar
- ⅔ cup water
- ¼ teaspoon cream of tartar
- 10 egg yolks, at room temperature
- 2 cups (4 sticks) unsalted

Makes 16 servings.

To make meringues: Heat oven to 300 degrees.

Butter and flour 2 large baking sheets or line with parchment paper. Trace a 10-inch circle on each.

Beat egg whites with cream of tartar in a large bowl until soft peaks form. Gradually add sugar, beating until stiff peaks form. Blend in vanilla extract. Fold in ground almonds. Divide mixture between baking sheets, spreading gently and evenly into 2 10-inch circles. Bake until firm and light golden, about 1 to 1¼ hours. Cool briefly; transfer meringues to wire racks to cool completely.

To make buttercream: Combine chocolate chips and cream in a small heat-proof bowl

butter
Crème Chantilly:
1½ **cups whipping cream**
½ **cup confectioners' sugar (plus more for topping)**
2 **tablespoons dark rum**

or double boiler. Set over a pan of simmering water until chocolate melts. Stir occasionally. Let mixture cool completely. Combine sugar, water and cream of tartar in a medium saucepan over low heat. Cook until sugar dissolves, swirling pan occasionally, then increase heat to high and cook without stirring until syrup registers 250 degrees on a candy thermometer (hardball stage).

Meanwhile, beat yolks in a large bowl, with electric mixer at high speed, until thick and lemon-colored. Reduce mixer speed to medium. Add hot syrup in a thin stream, beating until mixture is completely cool. Add butter and beat until thick and smooth, about 10 minutes. Blend in cooled chocolate mixture. Refrigerate buttercream until firm enough to pipe through a pastry bag.

To make crème Chantilly: When ready to assemble dacquoise, beat cream with sugar and rum until stiff.

To assemble: Spoon buttercream into a pastry bag with a medium star tip. Pipe a ring of 1-inch-high rosettes around the edge of the first meringue round. Pipe more into the middle to get buttercream into every bite, but don't cover the bottom. Refrigerate meringue.

Coat second meringue with confectioners' sugar, leaving ½-inch margin at edge. Pipe ring of buttercream rosettes around edge and 1 rosette in center.

Fill center of first meringue with cream Chantilly, spreading evenly to the same height as rosettes. Top with second round. Refrigerate dacquoise until ready to use.

Le Relais' lemon macaroon dessert©

Lemon mousse:
- 2 cups heavy cream
- 12 tablespoons fresh lemon juice, divided
- 1 cup sugar
- 1 ¼ ounce package unflavored gelatin

Lemon cookie:
- 5 ounces almond flour or almonds, crushed
- 4 egg whites
- Grated zest (yellow part of rind) of 1 lemon
- 1⅔ cups confectioners' sugar

Raspberry sauce:
- ½ pint fresh raspberries
- ½ cup sugar
- ½ cup water

Makes 5 servings.

To make mousse: Whip heavy cream on high speed of electric mixer, adding 6 tablespoons of the lemon juice and the sugar halfway through the beating. Whip to soft-peak stage. Set aside.

Dissolve gelatin in remaining 6 tablespoons lemon juice over heat until gelatin is completely dissolved. Remove from heat. Continue to stir while cooling.

Using a rubber spatula, gently fold gelatin mixture into whipped cream. Refrigerate at least 1 hour.

To make cookies: If using almonds, place in food processor and process just long enough to crush the almonds. (If allowed to process too long, they will become almond paste.) Set aside.

Prepare cookie sheet by placing parchment paper over surface. Draw 10 4-inch circles onto paper. Butter paper.

Whip egg whites to stiff-peak stage. Fold in crushed almonds, lemon zest and confectioners' sugar. Gently fill circles on parchment paper with cookie mixture. Mixture will spread slightly. Bake in preheated 325-degree oven for 17 to 20 minutes or until lightly brown. Cool completely before assembling dessert.

To make sauce: In a saucepan, combine raspberries, sugar and water. Bring to a boil. Cook for 5 minutes. Puree. Add a touch of brandy, if desired. Chill.

To assemble: Just before serving, spread lemon mousse onto 5 cookies. Top with remaining 5 cookies. Float in raspberry sauce.

Raspberries Denise©

Raspberry coulis:
- 2 pints raspberries
- 1 cup confectioners' sugar
- ½ cup water

Tulip cups:
- 1 cup granulated sugar
- 1 egg
- 2 egg whites
- ⅓ cup canola oil
- 2 teaspoons vanilla
- ¾ cup all-purpose flour
- ¼ cup almonds, ground

Filling:
- 4 tablespoons sour cream
- 2 tablespoons heavy cream
- 24 ounces your favorite ice cream
- 1 pint raspberries
- 1 pint blueberries
- 4 sprigs mint

Makes 4 servings.

To make coulis: Prepare raspberry sauce by pureeing raspberries, confectioners' sugar and water in blender. After blending, pour mixture into saucepan and bring to a slow boil for 10 minutes over medium heat. Remove from heat and pass through a fine sieve. Add additional water if coulis is too thick. Chill.

To make cups: Preheat oven to 350 degrees. Combine sugar, egg, egg whites, canola oil, vanilla, flour, and almonds. Ladle ¼ cup mixture into center of a greased cookie sheet. Form into a 7-inch circle. Place in oven and bake till the center looks firm and edges are brown, about 10 minutes. Remove shell from cookie sheet, using a metal spatula. Transfer shell to an inverted glass tumbler and gently mold shell around base of glass to form a tulip shape. (The cookie should be warm and pliable; if it's too hot, it will pull apart.) Allow to cool completely before removing it from the glass. Repeat until you've made four tulip cups.

Note: Never bake more than two at a time, and wash spatula and cookie sheet after each use. This technique is a little tricky, but it's well worth the effort.

To prepare filling and assemble: When ready to serve, place the raspberry coulis on the base of 4 platters. Combine the cream and sour cream in a squeeze bottle and decorate the coulis by squeezing lines of the cream mixture across the coulis at 1-inch intervals. Drag a toothpick in the opposite direction across the lines of cream to make a design.

Place a scoop of ice cream (about 6 ounces) in each tulip cup. Place raspberries and blueberries on top. Garnish with mint leaves. Set each filled tulip cup atop sauce. Serve immediately.

Vanilla ice cream©

4	large eggs
1½	cups sugar
2	cups milk
1	cup half-and-half
⅛	teaspoon salt
1½	tablespoons vanilla extract
2	cups whipping cream

Makes about 2 quarts.

Place eggs in a large saucepan. Beat. Add sugar and stir to combine. Slowly add milk, stirring to combine thoroughly. Place over low heat and cook, stirring constantly, 25 to 30 minutes or until mixture thickens and will coat a spoon. Pour into a bowl. Cover and chill.

Stir half-and-half, salt, vanilla and whipping cream into chilled egg mixture. Pour into freezer container of a 4-quart freezer. Freeze according to manufacturer's instructions.

Serve immediately or spoon into an airtight container and freeze until ready to use.

Jack Fry's key lime pie ice cream©

1½	cups heavy whipping cream
6	large egg yolks
1	15-ounce can sweetened condensed milk
½	cup bottled key lime juice
1	7-ounce jar marshmallow cream
4	crumbled graham crackers

Makes 8 good-size servings.

In a heavy saucepan bring cream to a simmer. Place the egg yolks in a bowl. Slowly beat the hot cream into the egg yolks. Pour the mixture back into the pan and place over low heat. Stir constantly with a wooden spoon until the custard thickens slightly. Be careful not to let the mixture boil or eggs will scramble. Remove from heat. Pour hot custard through a strainer into a large, clean bowl. Allow the custard to cool slightly. Then stir in the sweetened condensed milk and key lime juice. Cover and refrigerate until cold or overnight. Stir the cold custard well; freeze in your ice-cream freezer according to manufacturer's instructions. Fold the marshmallow cream and crumbled graham crackers into the ice cream when it is finished.

Jean Willis' peppermint ice cream©

I like the fact that you don't need an ice cream freezer to make this ice cream.

8	sticks of 5-inch peppermint candy or 20 to 25 Starlight mints
1½	cups milk
⅓	cup sugar
1	tablespoon flour
⅛	teaspoon salt
1	egg, separated
1	cup whipping cream

Makes 6 servings.

Break candy into several pieces. Soak in milk overnight in the refrigerator. In the morning, stir well to dissolve candy completely.

In the top of a double boiler mix together sugar, flour and salt. Slowly add milk mixture. Stir and cook until smooth. Beat the egg yolk. Add several spoonfuls of hot milk mixture to the yolk. Stir. Return to the double boiler and cook until mixture reaches 160 degrees on an instant-read thermometer. Cool.

When cool, pour into freezer tray or similar pan. Freeze 2 hours. Stir well.

Whip cream until stiff. Add to partially frozen mixture. Whip egg white until stiff. Add to mixture. Continue freezing, stirring frequently until firm and smooth.

Peach ice cream©

1	cup half-and-half
1½	cups milk
1⅔	cups sugar
4	egg yolks
9	ripe peaches
	Juice of half lemon
¼	teaspoon salt
2	cups heavy cream

Makes 1 gallon.

In top of double boiler, combine half-and-half and milk. Heat to just below boiling. Have bottom of double boiler ready with hot water. Place top of double boiler over hot water. Return to heat.

Combine ⅔ cup sugar with egg yolks. Slowly add some hot milk mixture to egg mixture to temper it before adding it to the hot milk mixture. Cook over simmering water until the custard lightly coats a wooden spoon.

Remove from heat and pour into a clean bowl, cover with plastic wrap and refrigerate until custard is cold.

While the custard is cooling, peel peaches. Coarsely mash – you should have 4 to 5 cups. Add remaining sugar, lemon juice and salt. Stir. Cover and refrigerate for about an hour

When you are ready to make the ice cream, add the cream to the custard mixture and mix thoroughly. Freeze in an ice-cream freezer following manufacturer's directions until the custard has turned to a soft ice cream. Stop turning, remove the cover of the container and add the peaches. Mix them in with a long-handled spoon and continue to freeze.

Cannoli shells©

1¾   cups all-purpose flour
½   teaspoon salt
2   tablespoons sugar
1   egg, slightly beaten
2   tablespoons firm butter, cut into small pieces
4   tablespoons dry white wine
1   egg white, slightly beaten
  Shortening or vegetable oil for frying

Makes 25 shells.

In a large mixing bowl, blend flour with salt and sugar. Make a well in the center. Add butter. Using a pastry blender or fork, cut butter into flour mixture. Add beaten egg and 2 tablespoons of wine. Working from center out, moisten flour mixture. Add wine until flour mixture forms into a ball. Cover with a damp cloth and let stand for at least 15 minutes.

Divide dough into 4 portions. Roll out 1 portion at a time on a floured surface until about 1/16th of an inch thick. Cut into circles measuring about 3½ inches in diameter. Wrap each circle around aluminum cannoli tube; seal edge with beaten egg white. (Be careful not to get any egg white on the aluminum tube because the shell will stick and have to be broken off.)

In a deep fryer, heat 3 inches of oil to 350 degrees. Fry the shells, 2 or 3 at a time, for about 1 minute or until lightly golden. When the shells float to the top, remove and place on paper towels to drain.

Let shells cool about 5 seconds and then gently slip off the tube, being careful not to burn your fingers on the hot metal. Allow the tube to cool before wrapping another round of dough on it. Cool shells completely.

Shells can be stored in an airtight container for up to 1 month. They also can be frozen and will keep 4 to 6 months.

To fill, use a dinner knife or a pastry bag fitted with a plain large tip to force filling into the shells. If you use a dinner knife, fill half the shell, then turn and fill the opposite end. Fill only the number of shells you plan to serve at once, because the pastry will become soggy if left to sit. The shell should be crisp and crunchy when eaten.

Sift confectioners' sugar over filled cannoli. Ends of ricotta-filled cannoli can be garnished with chopped chocolate or chopped pistachios.

Colombo's cannoli filling (an Italian dessert)

Fills 6 to 8 cannolis.

3 cups ricotta cheese (homemade, if possible)
¼ cup chopped candied fruit cherries, pineapple, orange peel, citron and lemon peel)
Confectioners' sugar to taste
½ teaspoon vanilla
1 cup whipping cream (optional)

In a bowl, combine all ingredients. Chill until ready to fill shells.

To fill, place filling in a pastry bag that has been fitted with a large plain pastry tube. (You can use a butter knife.)

If using whipping cream, whip until peaks form. Fold into ricotta filling.

Baklava© (Greek dessert)

Syrup:
2	cups water
1¾	cups sugar
1	tablespoon bourbon
1	teaspoon lemon juice

Pastry:
1	pound fillo dough
1½	cups (3 sticks) butter

Filling:
2	cups chopped pecans, walnuts or pistachios or a combination
⅔	cup sugar
2	teaspoons cinnamon

Makes 24 to 36 servings.

To make syrup: Syrup should be made first. In a saucepan combine water, sugar, bourbon and lemon juice. Bring to a boil and cook for 30 minutes. Chill.

To make pastry: If dough is frozen, allow to thaw according to package directions. After it thaws, carefully unfold and place on a damp cloth that has been covered with a piece of wax paper. Cover dough with another damp cloth because it dries rapidly and becomes brittle. Keep it covered until you use it.

In a saucepan, over low heat, melt butter. While butter is melting, cut dough to fit a 9-by-13-by-2-inch baking dish. Coat dish with melted butter. Place one fillo sheet in dish and coat entire sheet with butter. A 2-inch pastry brush works well. Repeat this until you have used half of the fillo sheets.

To make filling: Mix nuts, sugar and cinnamon together. Spread evenly over the pastry-lined dish. Cover with the remaining sheets of dough, brushing each with butter as before. Brush the top surface with melted butter. With a sharp-pointed knife, cut through dough and filling making into strips about 1½ to 2 inches wide, then cut diagonally to form diamond-shaped servings. Bake in a preheated 325-degree oven for one hour. Immediately on removing baklava from the oven, pour chilled syrup over it. (The syrup should be the consistency of pancake syrup. If it is too thick, add a small amount of water and blend thoroughly to thin.) Cool.

Note: To make ahead, prepare and cut as

if you plan to finish the dish. Wrap and freeze. When ready to use, prepare the syrup and allow the baklava to thaw at room temperature. Bake as above and add cooled syrup.

Pavlova© (an Australian dessert)

6 egg whites at room temperature
Pinch of salt
2 cups sugar
1½ teaspoons cornstarch
1½ teaspoons vinegar
1½ teaspoons vanilla
Whipped cream for filling
Fresh fruit

Makes 8 to 10 servings.
Heat a gas oven to 450 degrees; an electric oven should be set at 300 degrees.
Beat egg whites with salt until soft peaks form. Add sugar, 1 tablespoon at a time, beating thoroughly after each addition. Sift cornstarch over the top of the egg whites and fold it in. Add vinegar and vanilla and fold in. Pile meringue into a greased 9-inch pie plate or springform pan (or trace a 9-inch circle on a lightly greased cookie sheet and spread the meringue in the circle).
If using a gas oven, turn the oven temperatue down to 275 degrees and bake the meringue 1½ hours. It should be crisp on top and straw-colored. If baking in an electric oven, bake for 45 minutes at 300 degrees. The meringue should puff up and crack slightly.
In either case, turn the oven off and leave the door shut for an hour after the meringue is finished baking.
When the meringue is fully cooled, it will sink a little. If you baked it in a springform pan, remove the sides of the pan.
Fill the depression with stiffly beaten whipped cream and top it with fresh fruit such as strawberries, ripe peaches or a combination of summer berries.

Pumpkin roll©

Makes 12 to 15 servings.

Cake:

3	eggs
1	cup sugar
¾	cup pumpkin
1	tablespoon lemon juice
¾	cup all-purpose flour
1	teaspoon baking powder
2	teaspoons cinnamon
½	teaspoon ground ginger
½	teaspoon salt
	Confectioners' sugar

Cream cheese filling:

1	8-ounce package cream cheese, room temperature
½	teaspoon vanilla
1	tablespoon butter, softened
1	cup confectioners' sugar

To make cake: Grease and flour a 10-by-15-by-1-inch jellyroll pan. Heat oven to 375 degrees. Beat eggs until thick and lemon-colored. While beating, slowly add sugar. Combine lemon juice and pumpkin. Add to egg mixture.

Sift together the flour, baking powder, cinnamon, ginger and salt. Add to egg mixture. Stir to combine thoroughly. Pour into prepared pan. Bake in preheated oven for 15 minutes.

While cake is baking, sprinkle a tea towel with confectioners' sugar. Upon removing cake from oven, turn out onto prepared towel. Remove pan and roll cake from long end like a jelly roll. Cool completely while rolled in towel.

To make filling and assemble: Combine cream cheese, vanilla, butter and confectioners' sugar. Combine thoroughly. When cool, unroll cake. Cover with filling and roll again. Wrap tightly in foil and refrigerate until ready to serve. Dust with confectioners' sugar before serving.

Peppercorn Duck Club's brownie pudding©

Makes 8 servings.

1¼	cups sugar
1	cup all-purpose flour
2	teaspoons baking powder
¼	teaspoon salt
½	cup butter
1	ounce unsweetened chocolate
½	cup milk

To make pudding: In a medium bowl combine ¾ cup of the sugar with flour, baking powder and salt. Set aside.

In a small pan placed over low heat melt the butter with the chocolate. Add to dry ingredients along with milk and vanilla. Beat until smooth. Add nuts. Pour into an 8-by-8-by-2-inch pan.

1   teaspoon vanilla
1   cup chopped walnuts
½   cup light brown sugar, packed
¼   cup cocoa
1   cup hot strong coffee or water

Crème Anglaise
2   cups half-and-half
6   egg yolks
¼   cup sugar
1   teaspoon vanilla

Combine remaining ½ cup sugar with the brown sugar and cocoa. Stir. Sprinkle over batter. DO NOT STIR. Pour coffee or water over top. DO NOT STIR. Bake in a 350-degree oven for 40 minutes.

To make Crème Anglaise: In a small saucepan, heat half-and-half. Do not boil. In a mixing bowl beat egg yolks and sugar until light in color. Slowly add scalded half-and-half in a stream, beating at low speed until combined. .Transfer to saucepan. Cook over low heat, stirring constantly until thickened. DO NOT BOIL. Remove from heat. Stir in vanilla. Strain sauce. Cover and chill. Serve over brownie pudding. Makes 3 cups.

Cottage Café's strawberry cream roll©

Flour for dusting pan, plus 1 cup sifted all-purpose flour for cake
1   teaspoon baking powder
¼   teaspoon salt
3   large eggs
1   cup granulated sugar
⅓   cup water
1   teaspoon vanilla
½   teaspoon freshly grated or minced lemon zest (yellow part of rind)
2   cups heavy whipping cream
Confectioners' sugar for dusting towel, plus ½ to ¾ cup sifted confectioners' sugar for cream
2   cups sliced sweetened strawberries

Makes 8 to 10 servings.
Preheat oven to 350 degrees. Grease a 15½-by-10½-by-1-inch jellyroll pan. Line with wax paper and grease and flour pan. Tap out excess flour. Set aside.
Sift together sifted flour, baking powder and salt. Set aside.
In the large bowl of an electric mixer beat eggs until thick and lemon-colored. With mixer running, gradually add sugar.
Turn mixer to low speed and add water, vanilla and lemon zest. Remove from mixer. Gradually stir in dry ingredients just until blended – do not over mix. Pour into prepared jellyroll pan.
Bake in preheated oven for 10 to 12 minutes or until cake springs back when lightly touched. Turn out onto a clean towel that has been generously dusted with sifted confectioners' sugar. Carefully remove wax

paper. Using a sharp knife, trim ¼-inch from all 4 sides of cake. Roll cake and towel together from narrow end. Cool on wire rack with seam side down.

Place whipping cream in large bowl of electric mixer. While beating, slowly add confectioners' sugar. Beat until stiff. Drain strawberries. Set aside.

When cake is completely cool, unroll and remove towel. Spread with sweetened, stiffly beaten whipped cream to ½-inch of edges. Place drained strawberries over cream to within 2 inches of bottom end of cake roll. Reroll. Dust top with more confectioners' sugar. Serve immediately or chill in refrigerator.

When serving, cut into thick slices.

Note: For a tipsy strawberry roll, add 2 teaspoons of Grand Marnier or Chambord liqueur to the whipping cream and about 1 tablespoon of either liqueur to the sweetened sliced strawberries.

Vincenzo's white chocolate mousse torte©

Makes 1 10-inch torte.

2	cups Oreo cookie crumbs (about 25 cookies)
6	tablespoons butter, melted
10	ounces semisweet chocolate
4¼	cups heavy whipping cream, divided
12	ounces white chocolate
2	egg yolks
1	¼ - ounce package clear gelatin
⅓	cup cold water

Puree cookies in a food processor or blender. Mix crumbs with melted butter. Pack into bottom of a 10-inch springform pan. Set aside.

In the top of a double boiler, melt semisweet chocolate with 1 cup whipping cream. Mix well. Pour over cookie crumbs. Set aside.

In the top of a double boiler, melt white chocolate with ¾ cup whipping cream. Beat egg yolks. Slowly add some of the white chocolate mixture to yolks. Blend thoroughly. Return to white chocolate mixture, stirring until yolks are blended.

Soften gelatin in cold water.
Add softened gelatin to remaining 2½ cups whipping cream. Beat to soft-peak stage. Add white-chocolate mixture to whipped cream. Combine well. Pour over semisweet chocolate mixture. Set in freezer until solid.

Kurtz Restaurant's biscuit pudding with bourbon sauce©

This is a favorite of mine.

1	cup raisins
3	tablespoons Jim Beam bourbon (or bourbon of choice)
12	1½-inch biscuits
1	quart milk
6	eggs
2	cups sugar
2	tablespoons vanilla
2	tablespoons melted butter

Jim Beam bourbon sauce:
8	tablespoons butter
1	cup sugar
¼	cup water
1	egg
⅓	cup Jim Beam bourbon or more, if desired

Makes 10 to 12 servings.

To make pudding: Soak raisins in bourbon overnight. The next morning, break biscuits into small pieces and put in a large bowl. Add milk and allow to soak for 5 minutes. Beat the eggs with sugar and vanilla. Add to biscuit mixture along with the bourbon-soaked raisins. Stir to blend.
Pour melted butter into a 2-quart baking dish. Add biscuit mixture. Bake in a preheated 350-degree oven for 1 hour or until set. Serve warm with Jim Beam bourbon sauce.

To make sauce: In a heavy saucepan, melt butter. Add sugar and water and cook over medium heat for 5 minutes, stirring occasionally. In a separate bowl, beat the egg. Remove butter mixture from heat. Gradually add this mixture to the egg, whisking constantly. Add bourbon and serve.
Makes 1½ cups.

The Seelbach's bourbon-laced bread pudding©

7	eggs
2	cups milk
2	cups heavy whipping cream

Makes 12 to 15 servings.

To make pudding: Heat oven to 350 degrees. Butter a 9-by-13-by-2-inch baking dish.

1	pound granulated sugar
6	each day-old muffins, Danish and croissants

Topping:

¾ to 1	quart heavy whipping cream
12	ounces granulated sugar
	Bourbon, to taste
2 to 3	tablespoons cornstarch
½	cup water
	Cinnamon

Whisk together eggs, milk and cream. Then whisk in sugar.

Crumble all pastries into buttered baking dish. Pour egg mixture over pastries. Stir to blend. Bake 20 to 30 minutes or until no visible liquid remains when poked down in the center.

To make topping: Heat whipping cream, sugar and bourbon. Combine cornstarch with water. Stir. Add to whipping cream. Cook to thicken until whisk leaves marks in sauce. Makes 6 cups.

Pour topping over bread pudding and sprinkle with cinnamon.

Baked peach pudding©

2	cups peeled and sliced raw peaches

Batter:

¾	cup sugar
4	tablespoons butter
1	cup all-purpose flour
½	teaspoon salt
1	teaspoon baking powder
½	cup milk

Topping:

1	cup sugar
1	tablespoon cornstarch
¼	teaspoon salt
1	cup boiling water

Makes 6 to 8 servings.

To make pudding: Preheat oven to 325 degrees. Arrange peach slices in the bottom of an 8-by-8-by-2-inch pan.

To make batter: Cream together sugar and butter. Sift together dry ingredients and add to creamed mixture alternately with milk. Spread over fruit.

To make topping: Mix sugar with cornstarch and salt and sift over the top of the batter. Pour the boiling water over all. Bake at 325 degrees for 50 minutes. Serve warm, with cream, if desired.

Gambino's bread pudding©

2¾	cups milk
4	eggs
1⅓	cups sugar
¾	teaspoon ground cinnamon

Makes 12 to 15 servings.

To make pudding: Combine milk eggs, sugar, cinnamon and vanilla in a large bowl. Stir well with wire whisk. Add bread cubes, raisins and pecans.

1   tablespoon vanilla extract
12   cups white bread, cut into
     cubes
1   cup seedless raisins
⅓   cup chopped pecans
Bourbon sauce topping:
1   pound butter
1   pound confectioners'
     sugar
4   eggs
1½ to 2   ounces bourbon

Pour into a greased 9-by-13-by-2 inch oven-proof dish. Bake in a preheated 350-degree oven for 35 to 40 minutes or until a knife inserted in center comes out clean. Serve warm with bourbon sauce topping.

To make topping: Combine ingredients in a heavy saucepan. Cook over medium heat stirring constantly, until mixture comes to a boil. Cook and stir for 1 minute more ,or until thickened.
Makes 2 cups.

Fitzpatrick persimmon pudding©

2   cups persimmon pulp
1½   cups sugar
2   eggs, beaten
1   teaspoon baking soda
1   cup buttermilk
1   cup evaporated milk
2   cups all-purpose flour
2   teaspoons baking powder
½   teaspoon cinnamon
     Pinch salt
1   teaspoon vanilla
¼   cup cooking oil

Makes 12 to 15 servings.
Combine pulp, sugar and eggs. Stir baking soda into buttermilk. Add both milks to batter; add the dry ingredients. Add the vanilla and oil. Transfer batter to an oiled 9-by-13-by-2-inch baking dish. Bake in a preheated 325-degree oven for 1 hour. Pudding will rise high and, when cool, fall some. It breaks away from the pan.

Vensel date pudding©

1   cup dates (6½-ounce
     package), finely chopped
1   cup boiling water
1½   cups all-purpose flour
1   teaspoon baking soda
1   cup sugar
½   cup butter or margarine

Makes 12 to 15 servings.
To make pudding: Lightly grease a 9-by-13-by-2-inch pan. Preheat oven to 375 degrees.
Pour boiling water over dates. Set aside to cool.
Sift flour and measure. Sift flour a second time, adding baking soda and sugar.

1   egg, slightly beaten
1   cup nuts (black walnuts
    preferred, or pecans)
1   teaspoon vanilla
Orange sauce:
2   tablespoons cornstarch
1   cup sugar
1   cup fresh orange juice
½   cup water
1   tablespoon butter or
    margarine
½   teaspoon vanilla
1   egg, beaten

When dates and water are almost cool, add butter or margarine. (This is the simplest way to get the butter or margarine evenly distributed.)

When date mixture is cool, combine with dry ingredients.

Add beaten egg, nuts and vanilla. Stir until all ingredients are mixed. Pour into prepared pan. While baking, mixture will double in size, so leave room for it to rise.

Bake 45 minutes or until firm in the center. Cool completely before attempting to remove from pan.

Serve topped with orange sauce.

To make sauce: Sift cornstarch with sugar, making sure cornstarch is well-mixed with sugar. Add orange juice, water, butter and vanilla to dry ingredients in saucepan. Cook over low heat, stirring constantly until thickened.

While stirring, slowly add about ½ cup hot sauce to the well-beaten egg. Add egg mixture to the rest of the sauce, stirring constantly until well-heated. The sauce can be served warm or well-chilled. To vary the thickness of the sauce to suit your own taste, vary the amount of cornstarch used.

The Oyster Bar chocolate gateau©

1   pound semisweet chocolate
½   cup heavy cream
2   tablespoons dark rum
1   teaspoon vanilla
¼   pound unsalted butter
8   eggs, separated
1   cup sugar
Crème anglaise:

Makes 12 servings.

To make gateau: Lightly grease and collar a 9-inch springform pan. To collar a springform pan, fold a strip of foil into thirds lengthwise. The foil should be long enough to go completely around the pan. Lightly grease before placing around pan. Tie In place with a piece of string.

In the top of a double boiler combine

2 cups half-and-half
4 egg yolks
½ cup sugar
1 teaspoon vanilla

Raspberry sauce:
10 ounces frozen raspberries or 1 pint fresh raspberries
½ cup orange juice or Grand Marnier liqueur
¾ cup water, divided
¼ cup sugar (or to taste)
1 well-rounded tablespoon cornstarch

chocolate, cream, rum, vanilla and butter. Place over hot (not boiling) water until melted.

Beat egg yolks and sugar until mixture forms pale yellow ribbons when beaters are lifted. Fold mixture gently into chocolate. Beat egg whites to soft peaks. Add to chocolate and gently fold until whites are well-incorporated. Pour mixture into prepared pan. Bake in a 300-degree oven for 2 hours and 30 minutes. Serve very thin wedges topped with crème anglaise and raspberry sauce.

To make anglaise: Warm the half-and-half for 10 to 15 minutes in a heavy non-aluminum saucepan then bring to a boil. Beat egg yolks, sugar and vanilla in a medium bowl. Continue beating egg yolks as you add hot half-and-half, first gradually, then more rapidly, until it is all combined. Put the mixture back in the saucepan and cook over medium-low heat, stirring nearly constantly, until the mixture coats a spoon. Pour it into a clean bowl or jar, cool briefly and chill.

Makes 2 cups.

To make raspberry sauce: Combine berries with orange juice or liqueur, ½ cup of the water, and sugar. (The amount of sugar depends on whether you started with fresh, unsweetened berries or frozen, sweetened berries – use less if they were sweetened.) Bring to a rolling boil.

Combine cornstarch with remaining ¼ cup water and mix well. Add to raspberry puree, beating constantly. Heat until it clears and thickens. Strain through a fine sieve and cool.

Makes about 2 cups.

Candies

I have always liked the challenge of making hand-dipped chocolates. I know it's challenging, it can be frustrating and it can be expensive BUT there is nothing like the taste of a great piece of candy made with the best ingredients.

When you start working and playing with chocolate - and it is like playing - start with confectionery coating (also called compound coating, summer coating, chocolate-flavored coating or pastel coating). They come in a variety of shapes, colors and flavors and can be purchased at candy and cake supply shops and in craft stores. They do not contain cocoa butter or significant amounts of chocolate liquor so they cannot be called chocolate and they do not have to be tempered.

Because of the sugar content, coatings melt at a higher temperature than chocolate and can scorch quickly. I think placing them in a container over hot water is much safer than using a microwave.

When you feel comfortable working with coatings, try your hand with the real thing - **CHOCOLATE**. There are four categories of chocolate.

Unsweetened chocolate is the purest of chocolate – made only from ground roasted cocoa beans – no additives. You may find it labeled as bitter, baking or cooking chocolate. It is sold in 8-ounce packages individually wrapped in 1-ounce pieces. Some popular brands are Baker's Unsweetened Baking Chocolate Squares, Hershey's Premium Unsweetened Baking Chocolate and Nestlé Toll House Unsweetened Baking Bar.

Semisweet chocolate is the one most used for baking and candy making. It contains at least 35 percent chocolate liquor and not more than 12 percent milk solids. You will find this in the baking section of your grocery store. Popular brands are Baker's Semi-Sweet Baking Chocolate Squares, Hershey's Premium Semi-Sweet Baking Bar, Hershey's Special Dark Sweet Chocolate and Nestlé Toll House Semi-Sweet Baking Bar.

Milk chocolate contains at least 10 percent chocolate liquor, more sugar and at least 3.39 percent butterfat and 12 percent milk solids. Because of more sugar and milk solids, this is a poor choice for baking but an excellent choice for candy making. Hershey's Milk Chocolate Bar, Nestlé Milk Chocolate Bar, Dove Milk Chocolate and Cadbury Dairy Milk are just a few of the brands available.

And, now, we come to **white chocolate** – which isn't a chocolate at all. White chocolate contains a minimum of 20 percent cocoa butter, 14 percent milk solids and a maximum 55 percent sucrose (sugar) but no chocolate liquor. Again, you can find it in supermarkets under the brand name of Baker's Premium White Chocolate Baking Squares, Ghirardelli Classic White Baking Confection and numerous other names. Always look for the words "cocoa butter" on the wrapper.

When chocolate leaves the manufacturer it is always in temper and, with proper storage and handling, remains in temper. Chocolate in temper is glossy and has a smooth texture. To see if chocolate is in temper, melt dark chocolate to 115 degrees (milk and white to 110 degrees). Smear a thin sample of melted chocolate on a piece of wax paper. Refrigerate 3 to 5 minutes. If the sample is dry to the touch and evenly glossy, the chocolate is in temper. Out-of-temper melted chocolate sets slowly and has a dull finish when it solidifies. It can have blemishes such as gray streaks and blotches - this is called "bloom".

Before you attempt to temper chocolate, you must have a chocolate thermometer or glass laboratory thermometer, rubber spatula and a double-boiler or nested bowls that can be used like a double boiler.

Following these few simple suggestions may help you conquer the art of melting chocolate. Chop the chocolate into small pieces. Place part of the chocolate in the top of a double boiler or use a stainless steel bowl placed over a shallow pan. The bottom pan should have enough hot water (130 to 140 degrees) to touch the bottom of the top vessel but not so much that the top vessel floats.

Place part of the chocolate in the top vessel. When the chocolate starts to melt, stir with a rubber spatula. Add the remaining chocolate gradually. Stir. Follow the procedure for tempering that fits the chocolate you are working with.

To temper chocolate, heat dark chocolate to 115 degrees F and milk and white chocolates to 110 degrees F. Remove from heat and, stirring, cool to 84 degrees F for dark chocolate and 82 degrees F for milk and white chocolate. Rewarm dark chocolate to less than 90 degrees F and milk and white to 88 degrees F. The chocolate should be in temper and ready to be tested and used.

If you have some chocolate that is not in temper and some that is, you can temper all by melting the untempered chocolate - dark to 115 degrees F (milk and white 110 degrees F). Add chunks of solid tempered chocolate to the melted untempered. Stir to lower the temperature to just less than 90 degrees F (88 degrees F for milk and white). Remove any chunks that have not melted (if all the chunks have melted and the temperature hasn't reached 90 degrees (88 degrees), add more tempered chunks and stir until chocolate reaches the correct temperature – less than 90 degrees. Remove chunks that have not melted. The chocolate is ready to test and use.

When chocolate is in temper, it can be used for dipping by just starting the melt. Remove it from the heat before it reaches 90 degrees for dark (88 degrees for milk or white). Stir the chocolate until it has melted completely. The chocolate is ready to be tested and used.

Keeping the temper in chocolate while using it is a bit tricky. The preferred method of doing this is to add small amounts of lukewarm, melted chocolate (95-100 degrees) from your reserved supply to the chocolate being used. This replenishes your supply and will help maintain its proper temperature.

You can place the bowl of tempered chocolate over a bowl of warm water (water temperature should not exceed the maximum temperature range allowed for tempered chocolate by more than 2 degrees).

The following recipe for cream fondant is my favorite filling for chocolates. It can be used as is for vanilla centers or it can be flavored with fruit paste, flavoring oils for food, bourbon or liqueurs, nuts, coconut, etc.

Cream fondant©

2 cups sugar
Dash salt
1 tablespoon light corn syrup
¾ cup heavy cream
½ teaspoon vanilla

Makes 1½ pounds.
Combine sugar, salt, syrup, and cream in a heavy 4-quart saucepan. Stir over medium heat until sugar is dissolved. Cover and cook for 3 minutes without stirring. This washes down any sugar crystals that may form on the sides of the saucepan.
Reduce heat and boil slowly without stirring until candy reaches the firm ball stage, or 240 degrees on a candy thermometer.
Pour candy on buttered marble slab or other cold surface. Cool to lukewarm. Work with a broad spatula or wooden paddle until white and creamy. Knead with hands until smooth. Add vanilla and knead until well-blended. Wrap in wax paper or plastic film and ripen in refrigerator for 24 hours. Fondant will keep several weeks. If it becomes dry, cover with a damp cloth before kneading. When ready to use, knead fondant until soft. Add flavoring and form into desired shapes.

   Note: Fondant can be used for centers of dipped chocolates, mints, filling for dried fruits and for candy pudding.
Candy pudding:
Chop nuts, coconut, candied cherries and any other candied fruit of your choice. Work the fondant until soft. Work in the fruit, nuts, cherries and coconut.
Shape into a log with tapered ends. Cover with chocolate. Store in a cool place.
Cut into thin slices for serving.
Bourbon balls: Soak 1 cup chopped pecans

in bourbon to cover overnight. If the nuts have not absorbed all the bourbon, drain. Work the nuts into the soft fondant. Roll into balls the size you prefer. Allow to dry about an hour. Dip in melted 86 to 90 degree tempered chocolate.

Flavored centers: Add flavoring of choice to kneaded fondant. Knead to infuse flavor into fondant (you be the judge as to the amount of flavoring used). If flavoring with oils, they are very strong so be lenient when using. Roll into ½-inch balls, air dry and dip.

Chocolate covered cherries: Drain maraschino cherries. Wrap fondant around each cherry. Dip into tempered chocolate. Allow cherries to sit a couple of days so the fondant can draw the juice from the cherry to liquefy the fondant. Delicious.

Helen Friedman's chocolate truffles©

Makes 100 to 125 pieces.

2	cups heavy cream
¼	pound butter
2	pounds good quality chocolate
½	cup liqueur
2	pounds chocolate coating or chocolate

In a saucepan combine cream and butter. Cook over low heat until butter has melted. Do not boil.

While butter is melting, shave chocolate or cut into very small pieces. Add to cream. Stir until smooth. Add liqueur. Stir. Refrigerate mixture until firm.

Melt chocolate coating or chocolate. Coat the inside of paper candy cup or plastic cup forms with chocolate coating. (These can be purchased at candy or specialty shops.) Place truffle mixture in a pastry bag fitted with a large star tip. Squeeze mixture into coated cup. If you are using plastic forms, place in the freezer. When solid, flip out so form may be used again.

To store, place in layers in a plastic or metal

container. Place crumbled foil around edge to keep next layer from crushing truffles. Place waxed cardboard over first layer. Continue to layer. Seal with cover. Freeze until ready to use.

   Note: Truffle mixture can be shaped into balls. Place in freezer. When solid, dip in melted chocolate, then into chocolate sprinkles, cocoa, coconut or splatter with white chocolate.

Georgia pecan candy©

1   cup light brown sugar
½   cup white sugar
½   cup heavy cream
2   tablespoons white corn syrup
⅛   teaspoon salt
3   tablespoons butter
1   teaspoon pure vanilla extract
2   cups pecan halves

Makes about 2 dozen candies, depending on size.

In a bowl, combine sugars, cream, corn syrup, salt and 2 tablespoons butter. Mix until sugars are saturated with the cream. (This is done to keep the ingredients from splattering on the sides of the pan and causing the sugar to crystalize, making a grainy candy.) Place mixture in a heavy pan over medium heat. Stir occasionally and wipe down crystals from the sides of the pan using a small brush that has been dipped in water, or put a lid on the pan and allow the steam to evaporate the crystals.

Cook syrup until it registers 236 degrees on a candy thermometer or a teaspoon of the syrup dropped in cold water forms a soft ball. Remove from heat and add remaining butter and vanilla. When the candy has cooled to 110 degrees, beat until it begins to lose its transparency.

Add nuts. Drop by tablespoonfuls on a buttered marble or pastry sheet in the form of clusters. Let cool and store in a container with a tight fitting lid.

Variation: This can be poured and made into fudge squares. In this case, use only 1 cup pecans.

Hard candy©

    Confectioners' sugar
3¾ cups sugar
1½ cups light corn syrup
1 cup water
1 teaspoon flavoring oil such as peppermint, spearmint, clove, cinnamon, orange, lemon, etc.
    Food coloring, optional

Makes 2¼ pounds.

Sprinkle an 18-by-14-inch strip of heavy-duty aluminum foil with confectioners' sugar. In a large, heavy saucepan, combine sugar, corn syrup and water. Place over medium heat and stir until sugar dissolves. Boil, without stirring, until temperature reaches 310 degrees on a candy thermometer or until drops of syrup form hard and brittle threads in cold water.

Remove from heat. Stir in flavoring oil and coloring, if desired. Pour onto foil. When cool, break into pieces. Store in an airtight container.

  Note: I color-code the candy – red is cinnamon, orange is orange, yellow is lemon, brown is clove, etc.

Butter mints

½ cup butter (1 stick)
    Few drops oil of peppermint
2 or 3 tablespoons evaporated milk
1 pound sifted confectioners' sugar

Number of mints depends on size.

In a bowl, combine butter, oil of peppermint and milk. Mix until smooth. Add confectioners' sugar until mixture reaches the consistency of pie dough (you may not need a pound or you may need a bit more). Press into molds or roll into small balls. Place in a container with a tight-fitting lid. Store in a cool place or in the freezer.

  Note: Oil of peppermint can be very intense so add it sparingly until you know the intensity you prefer. Add more if needed.

Cream cheese mints

1   **8-ounce package cream cheese, room temperature**
¼   **teaspoon oil of peppermint**
6⅔ **cups confectioners' sugar**
    Food coloring of choice

In a large bowl, combine cream cheese with oil of peppermint. Blend thoroughly. Add confectioners' sugar and a drop or two of food coloring while mixing. Enough confectioners' sugar has been added when the mixture is the consistency of pie dough. If the color isn't deep enough, add a bit more food coloring and knead until color is blended thoroughly. Chill several hours then roll into small balls, dip in granulated sugar. If desired, the balls can be pressed into a mold.. Molds can be purchased at craft stores or cake and candy decorating shops.

Caramels using evaporated milk©

2   **cups sugar**
2   **cups light corn syrup**
    Dash salt
½   **cup butter**
2   **cups evaporated milk**
1   **teaspoon pure vanilla extract**

In a heavy saucepan, combine sugar, light corn syrup and salt. Stir over medium heat until sugar is dissolved. Cover and cook 3 minutes without stirring. This washes down any sugar crystals that may form on the sides of the saucepan. Boil, stirring occasionally, until syrup is very thick and reaches 245 degrees on a candy thermometer. Add butter a bit at a time. Gradually add the evaporated milk. It is important the syrup doesn't stop boiling at any time. Stir constantly and cook rapidly to 242 degrees on a candy thermometer or until a few drops form a firm ball in a cup of cold water. The mixture will be very thick toward the end and will burn easily – watch and stir carefully. Remove from heat and add vanilla. Stir to blend. Pour into a greased 8-inch square pan without scrapping sides or bottom of pan (crystals on the side or bottom of the pan are likely to cause the sugar to crystalize, causing a grainy candy). Cool. When cool, cut into small squares and wrap each piece in wax paper..

Caramels using cream©

2	**cups sugar**
1	**cup light corn syrup**
2	**cups heavy cream, warm**
½	**teaspoon salt**
½	**teaspoon pure vanilla extract**

In a heavy-bottomed 3-quart saucepan, mix together the sugar, syrup and 1 cup of cream. Cook about 10 minutes, stirring thoroughly to dissolve the sugar before mixture comes to a strong boil. Insert thermometer. Thereafter, stir only if it seems necessary to prevent scorching. Add the other cup of cream very slowly, so as not to stop the cooking. When the thermometer reaches 240 degrees, cook more slowly to 244 degrees. Remove pan from heat and add salt and vanilla. Stir only enough to incorporate.

Your basic caramel is cooked, ready to use in any way you've planned. If it's nut caramels you want, add a cup of broken nuts and turn the candy into an oiled pan 8-inches square and place on cooling rack. When cold, turn out on a cutting board and cut into squares with a heavy knife. Wrap each piece in wax paper

Bourbon balls©

36	**pecan halves**
4	**tablespoons bourbon**
6	**tablespoons butter, room temperature**
4	**cups confectioners' sugar**
	Bourbon
½	**pound imported bittersweet or semisweet chocolate**

Makes 36 pieces.

Soak pecan halves in 4 tablespoons bourbon for 2 hours or overnight. Drain and reserve bourbon.

Combine softened butter with confectioners' sugar. Add bourbon just until mixture is soft enough to roll into balls. Place a pecan in the center of each ball. Refrigerate until ready to coat.

Remove bourbon balls from refrigerator. Grate chocolate. Melt over lukewarm water. Using a dipping tong or fork, dip each ball into chocolate to coat. Place in an airtight container and store in refrigerator.

Oklahoma brown candy©

6 cups sugar
2 cups half-and-half cream
¼ teaspoon baking soda
½ cup butter
1 teaspoon vanilla
4 cups pecans

Over low heat, caramelize 2 cups sugar in a heavy saucepan (I use an iron skillet). Place remaining 4 cups sugar and half-and-half in a large saucepan over low heat. Cook until sugar dissolves and half-and-half has warmed.

When the sugar in the skillet has caramelized (becomes a clear syrup ranging in color from golden to dark brown – 320 to 350 degrees on a candy thermometer), add, stirring constantly, to the liquid in the saucepan (this takes some time). With heat on low, cook to 244 to 248 degrees on a candy thermometer or until a soft ball forms when a small amount of liquid is dropped into a cup of cold water.

Remove from heat and stir in the baking soda to aerate the liquid (mixture will bubble up so continue to stir until mixture settles). Add butter and stir until melted. Set aside for 20 minutes. Add vanilla and beat until the gloss turns dull. Add pecan pieces. Stir to combine. Turn into a buttered 9-by-13-by-2-inch pan. Cut into 1-inch pieces. Store candy in a cool place in an airtight container. It gets better as it ages.

Here is a tip for making the type of fudge you prefer. Beating the cooked syrup while still hot will produce grainy fudge. If you let the syrup cool to 122 degrees before you beat it, it will become viscous and produce smooth fudge. Grainy or smooth, there is nothing like the taste of fudge.

Chocolate fudge (grainy fudge)©

Makes 1½ pounds.

2	cups sugar
½	cup milk
2	tablespoons butter
6	ounces semisweet chocolate, grated or chopped
1	teaspoon vanilla
1	cup nuts, optional

Place sugar into a saucepan and mix with the milk to form a thick paste. Add the butter and stir in the grated or chopped chocolate. Place pan over low heat and cook, stirring constantly. Do not let the contents of the saucepan come to a boil until the sugar has dissolved and the chocolate has melted. Increase heat slightly and let the mixture boil for about 5 minutes, or until it reaches the soft-ball stage (234 degrees on a candy thermometer).

Take the fudge off the heat and add vanilla and nuts. Beat until thick. Pour into a buttered 8-inch square pan. Cut the fudge into 1-inch squares before it has time to get cold.

Milk fudge (smooth fudge)©

Makes 2 pounds

1¼	cups milk
3½	cups sugar
	Pinch salt
½	cup butter
2	teaspoons vanilla extract

Place milk in a heavy saucepan. While stirring, add sugar, salt and butter. Heat mixture slowly until sugar dissolves and butter melts. Bring mixture to a boil and cover. Boil for 2 to 3 minutes. Remove cover and, without stirring, boil mixture for 10 to 15 minutes, or until mixture reaches the soft-ball stage (234 degrees on a candy thermometer).

Remove mixture from heat, dip the base of the pan briefly in cold water, stir in vanilla extract and let the fudge cool until lukewarm (122 degrees). Beat the fudge until it loses its glossy appearance and is thick and creamy. Pour into a greased 8-inch square pan.

Let the fudge cool completely before cutting into 1-inch squares.

Chocolate fudge©

4 cups sugar
1 12-ounce can evaporated milk
1 cup butter
1 10.5-ounce package miniature marshmallows
1 12-ounce package chocolate chips
1 tablespoon vanilla
1 cup chopped nuts, optional

Makes 3 to 4 pounds.

In a heavy saucepan combine sugar, evaporated milk and butter. Bring to a boil and cook covered 2 to 3 minutes until the steam washes down any crystals that may have formed on the sides of the pan. Remove cover, lower heat and cook slowly without stirring to the soft-ball stage – 234 degrees on a candy thermometer (or until a small amount of mixture forms a soft ball when dropped into cold water.)

Place the marshmallows and chocolate chips in a large bowl. Pour in the cooked mixture and vanilla. Stir until marshmallows and chips have melted. Add nuts and stir.

Pour into a buttered 9-by-13-by-2-inch pan. Cool before cutting.

Note: For bourbon fudge, add 4 to 5 tablespoons bourbon. Fudge can be frozen.

Uncle Vincent's peanut butter fudge

½ cup butter
1 pound light brown sugar

Makes 3½ pounds.

Lightly butter a 9-by-9-by-2-inch pan. Set aside.

½ cup milk
¾ cup peanut butter
1 teaspoon vanilla
1 pound confectioners' sugar

In a medium saucepan, melt butter. Stir in the brown sugar and milk. Stir until sugar melts and mixture begins to boil. Boil 2 minutes. Remove from heat. Stir in peanut butter and vanilla. Mix in confectioners' sugar. Beat until smooth. Spread into prepared pan. Chill until firm. Cut into 1-inch squares. Fudge can be frozen.

Toffee pecan crunch©

2 cups pecans
2 12-ounce packages semisweet chocolate chips
1 pound unsalted butter
2 cups sugar

Coat the bottom and sides of a 9-by-13-by-2-inch pan with butter.
Evenly sprinkle one cup nuts and one 12-ounce package chocolate chips over the bottom of the prepared dish.
Combine butter and sugar in a heavy pan. Cook over low heat until sugar dissolves. Cover pan and cook 3 minutes to wash down any sugar crystals that may have formed on side of pan. Remove cover and increase heat to medium. Cook until mixture reaches 300 degrees on a candy thermometer (this takes some time so be patient). Pour immediately over nuts and chocolate chips. Spread toffee with the back of a wooden spoon. Immediately sprinkle remaining 12-ounce package of chocolate chips over hot toffee and spread. Sprinkle remaining cup of nuts over chips. When completely cool, break into pieces.

Restaurants and Their Recipes

Uptown Café

Fusilli with sea scallops	195
Gateau ganache	331
Honey pecan chicken	170
Oyster-artichoke soup with Havarti cheese	49
Portobello mushroom sandwich	143
Wilted spinach salad with grilled chicken breast	66

Ursula's Bavarian Inn – Frankenmuth, MI

Cream of onion soup	46

Vincenzo's

Amaretto cheesecake	300
Caesar salad	61
Fettuccine Alfredo	210
Salmon with apple butter cream sauce	192
Vegetable torta	109
White chocolate mousse torte	346

Mrs. Wilkes – Savannah, GA

Sweet potato soufflé	124

Windward Inn – Virginia Beach, VA

Cabbage soup	33

Wonton Express

Sweet and sour chicken	231

Yen Ching's

Double-cooked pork	177
Moo goo gai pan	232

Zephyr Cove

Basil Alfredo	211

Index

A

B

C

F

P